PUBLIC AND PRIVATE IN SOCIAL LIFE

Public and Private in Social Life

Edited by
S.I. BENN and G.F. Gaus

CROOM HELM
London & Canberra
ST. MARTIN'S PRESS
New York

© 1983 S.I. Benn and G.F. Gaus
Croom Helm Ltd, Provident House, Burrell Row,
Beckenham, Kent BR3 1AT
Croom Helm Australia, P.O. Box 391, Manuka,
ACT 2603, Australia

British Library Cataloguing in Publication Data

Public and private in social life.
  1. Social institutions
  I. Benn, S.I.   II. Gaus, G.F.
  306   HM131
  ISBN 0-7099-0668-4

All rights reserved. For information write:
St. Martins Press, Inc., 175 Fifth Avenue, New York, N.Y. 10010
First Published in the United States of America in 1983

Library of Congress Cataloging in Publication Data
Main entry under title:

Public and Private in social life.

    Includes bibliographical references and index.
    1. Social role--Addresses, essays, lectures. 2. Individualism--Addresses, essays, lectures. 3. Self-perception--Addresses, essays, lectures. 4. Personality and culture--Addresses, essays, lectures. I. Benn, S.I. (Stanley I.) II. Gaus, Gerald F.
HM291.P84   1983   302.5   83-9539
ISBN 0-312-65357-3 (St. Martin's Press)

Printed and bound in Great Britain

CONTENTS

Preface · vii

INTRODUCTORY

1. The Public and the Private: Concepts and Action · 3
   Stanley I. Benn and Gerald F. Gaus

PART ONE   PUBLIC AND PRIVATE IN WESTERN CULTURES

2. The Liberal Conception of the Public and the Private · 31
   Stanley I. Benn and Gerald F. Gaus
3. Public Law – Private Law · 67
   Alice Erh-Soon Tay and Eugene Kamenka
4. Public Function – Private Action: A Common Law Dilemma · 93
   Paul Finn
5. Information Control: Availability and Exclusion · 113
   Ruth Gavison
6. Private Selves and Public Parts · 135
   Alan Ryan
7. Private and Public Morality: Clean Living and Dirty Hands · 155
   Stanley I. Benn
8. Public and Private Interests in Liberal Political Economy, Old and New · 183
   Gerald F. Gaus
9. Public and Private Property · 223
   Alan Ryan

PART TWO   CRITIQUES OF THE LIBERAL CONCEPTION OF PUBLIC AND PRIVATE

10. Public and Private Interests: Hegel on Civil Society and the State · 249
    Anthony S. Walton
11. Public/Private in Marxist Theory and Marxist Practice · 267
    Eugene Kamenka
12. Feminist Critiques of the Public/Private Dichotomy · 281
    Carole Pateman

PART THREE PUBLIC AND PRIVATE IN NON-LIBERAL CULTURES

13	Publicness, Privateness and 'Primitive Law' Martin Krygier	307
14	Privacy in a Mexican Indian Village Leslie K. Haviland and John B. Haviland	341
15	Classical Greek Conceptions of Public and Private Arlene Saxonhouse	363

Notes on Contributors   385

Index of Persons   387

Index of Subjects   392

PREFACE

In 1979 the Research School of Social Sciences of the Australian National University launched an interdisciplinary project on 'Conceptions of the Public and Private in Social Life'. While much of the School's research related to the public and private, it was realised that very little had been done that focused specifically on the nature of the concepts. The first stage of the project centred on the pilot conference held in September 1979, a conference that convinced us of the importance of our topic and the intense interest it aroused. Our plans for the project were greatly affected by the debates at the conference; and while we may still not have satisfied some of our more radical critics, we are nevertheless very grateful for their useful and challenging contributions to the discussions from which this book eventually emerged.

Several of the papers presented at the conference evolved into chapters of this book; all of the other chapters were written expressly for the book. For throughout our aim has been a truly collaborative work rather than a mere anthology. The book, we believe, forms a coherent whole, with a developing theme and structure. After an introductory essay in which we try to explain both the concerns underlying the study and map the general conceptual terrain, we proceed in Chapter 2 to present our own account of 'The Liberal Conception of the Public and the Private'. Contributors were furnished with early drafts of these chapters, and were invited to treat them, as far as they found useful, as focal points of their own analyses. We should like to thank all our contributors for their patience and co-operation; they have been wonderfully ready to give serious consideration to editorial suggestions which less tolerant authors might have seen as outrageous interferences with their original ideas.

Our special thanks go out to Harriet Halliday, whose work as research assistant, copy-editor, and production manager has been quite invaluable. She has lavished time, care and energy on the project far exceeding the calls of duty. Ms Halliday has been ably assisted by Ruth Booth and Ruth Wilson, who helped with bibliographical tasks and proof-reading, and by Jean Norman, who helped to prepare the Index. In the early stages of the project we benefited from the research assistance of David Dumaresq, Brian Embury and Jenny Kerr. We are also grateful to Caroline McAlpin, Hazel Gittins, Lois Newman and Mitzi Parkins, who have helped with typing and photocopying manuscripts. Louise Hogden, of Belconnen Typesetting, has done a fine job in preparing photo-ready copy for the printer, working to a very strict schedule.

Lastly, we would like to extend our deep thanks to the Research School of Social Sciences of the ANU. Not only has the School been generous in its financial support, but it has provided the opportunity for the editors to work together from 1979 to 1982, something for which we are both grateful.

STANLEY I. BENN	GERALD F. GAUS
AUSTRALIAN NATIONAL UNIVERSITY	WAKE FOREST UNIVERSITY
CANBERRA	WINSTON-SALEM
AUSTRALIA	NORTH CAROLINA
	U.S.A.

PUBLIC AND PRIVATE IN SOCIAL LIFE

INTRODUCTORY

1 THE PUBLIC AND THE PRIVATE: CONCEPTS AND ACTION

Stanley I. Benn and Gerald F. Gaus

I. Publicness and Privateness

This book is about the conceptions of publicness and privateness in social life. We use these awkward and unusual words rather than 'privacy' and 'publicity' because those are concerned mainly with access to, and dissemination of, information, which is but one of the topics that will be examined.[1] Nor, though we use it in our title, do we feel altogether satisfied with the phrase 'the public and the private'. Certainly that is one way of indicating an abstract topic for discussion, but in this instance only at the cost of making it look deceptively concrete. Worse, it suggests that privateness and publicness are homogeneous properties, which, given their range, is highly unlikely. Publicness, for instance, ranges over public places, public officials, public opinion and the public interest, while privateness is found to range over things as diverse as private property, private enterprise, and private parts. So our first task must be to determine how concepts such as these can range so widely over such disparate aspects of social life. But that is only one of our concerns. For this book deals not simply with the concepts of publicness and privateness but with their functions in social life. In what way, then, can concepts be said to affect action? And just what features of social life are structured by distinctions between publicness and privateness? Our aim in this introductory chapter is thus to lay a foundation not only for the extended treatment in Part One of the familiar liberal conception of privateness and publicness, but also for the critiques of that conception, and for the accounts of alternative conceptions, which are treated in Parts Two and Three.

II. Complex-structured Concepts

Let us begin by considering 'public' alone for the moment. Just because 'public' is ascribed to things with such different ontological statuses as property, interests, officials, opinions, places etc., it seems most unlikely that any property or set of properties will be common to all. One could hardly expect that anything predicated of officials could be predicated in the same way of opinions or places. It would be like expecting false lovers to be false in the same way as teeth or propositions. To be sure, common ground exists; anything public has to do, for instance, with persons in social relations, and thus the domain within which 'public' can have reference is circumscribed. But if nothing more interesting could be inferred from something's being public than that it had to do with social relations, 'publicness' would be a pretty blunt instrument with which to examine our environment.

Yet we do seem to use 'public' to say quite interesting and varied, albeit sometimes confused, things. Perhaps then we do not have a single concept here at all, but a case of mere homonymy, i.e. where the same vocable just happens to be used to evoke or symbolise distinct and unrelated concepts. 'Tense' is like this. One of its meanings derives from *tendere* (to stretch) while the other stems from *tempus* (time). But not so with 'public': an etymologist would insist that all senses of 'public' are senses of the same word. Of course, as Mill reminds us, 'etymology is slight evidence of what the idea now signified is . . .'[2] Between 'nice' meaning agreeable and 'nice' meaning precise is a gulf so wide that even a competent speaker of the language might be surprised to learn that they derive alike from *'nescius'* (ignorant), something that can be comprehended only by tracing their divergence throughout the history of 'nice'. But 'public' is not like that either. Diverse as they are, the present meanings of 'public' exhibit a semantic, not just a historical, continuity. Though the gap between 'public house' and 'public servant' may seem just as wide as that between 'a nice house' and 'a nice shade of meaning', a contemporary speaker of English will be familiar with many other senses of 'public' which, when appropriately interposed, ensure a continuity or chain of present meaning.[3] We need thus never make arbitrary leaps from one sense to a very different one.

This idea of a chain of meanings calls to mind Wittgenstein's notion of 'family resemblances'. The strength of a thread, he wrote in using yet another analogy, 'does not reside in the fact that some one fibre runs through its whole length, but in the overlapping of many fibres'.[4] But though such analogies correctly emphasise the continuity underlying the diversity, they miss the possibility that the relations obtaining among the many senses of 'public' may be systematic. It is not merely that a public library just happens to be public in two distinct senses (i.e. public *qua* open to all and public *qua* financed and controlled by the community), as a son may happen to have his mother's eyes and his father's ears. Rather, there is a strong presumption that facilities financed by the community at large should be open to all – since everyone pays for them through his taxes. Moreover, as Gerald Gaus points out in Chapter 8, liberal theory has long acknowledged the existence of a class of 'public goods' which, if supplied at all, must necessarily be supplied to all members of the public; and, as the liberal sees it, this provides a rationale for the provision of such goods by the public *qua* the state.

That something is or is not public in one sense, then, is often seen as a reason why it should or should not be public in another sense. In place of the idea of a family resemblance we thus want to suggest that the many senses of 'public' – or the many kinds of publicness – are systematically related to form a *complex-structured concept*. Embedded in a culture and its language are principles or presuppositions that account for the continuity of the various senses of 'public'. Tracing these relations – one might call them the internal semantic relations of publicness – will not be a simple task, for some connections may be very indirect. Moreover the connections are likely to be ideological rather than purely logical. That is, the principles of transition bridging the gaps between neighbouring senses will depend on certain beliefs about the natures of societies and of individuals, of collective agents and collective actions etc. rather than on purely logical entailments. Because in a plural culture like our own, such beliefs and principles are contested, the concepts of publicness and privateness are also contested. And, as we shall see in Part Three of this book, other cultures have radically different conceptions; indeed, one might reasonably question whether some others have any such conceptions at all (see §VIII, below).

III. Concepts and Social Life

An account of the internal relations of publicness, and correspondingly of privateness, and of the way (or ways) in which they are distinguished, will amount to a semantic theory of publicness and privateness in that culture. The theory will be about the ways in which the categories of public and private regulate a people's institutions, practices, activities and aspirations. For the distinction between publicness and privateness is a practical one, part of a conceptual framework that organises action in a social environment.

This framework is part, of course, of our social endowment. Although that endowment is not fixed, as shown by the fact that we can construct new concepts, any such creation or innovation occurs within a surrounding framework of concepts, and the new ones will be intelligible to the extent that they can be coherently related to the greater part — though not necessarily to all — of this pre-existing conceptual framework. This is one of the fundamental senses in which we are social beings: our ontological status as intentional agents depends on the conceptual equipment that we bring to experiencing the world, and we acquire and learn the use of that equipment in learning our language. And because, in western culture at any rate, we apprehend a great deal of our social world by distinguishing things that are public and things that are private, how those concepts are structured necessarily informs not only what we ourselves say and do but also what responses to our actions we expect from others, how we assess their actions, and so on. To say 'There is a private letter for Smith' is immediately to suggest a complex of expectations and requirements for action and forbearance — for oneself, for Smith, and for the world at large — that would be unintelligible and untranslatable to a person whose language and culture possessed no concept corresponding to *privacy*. Teaching him would involve providing him not with a word substitution table or lexicon, but with an induction into the culture in which access to information is regulated precisely under the conditions of privacy and publicity and not, for instance, under the conditions of the esoteric and the exoteric, the sacred and the profane, or the classified and the unclassified.

Because human beings are agents and not simply behaving subjects, any description of their actions as such (as distinct, for instance, from a description of the corresponding biochemical events in their bodies) must take account of this conceptual context. An adequate account of action must include the agent's own understanding of what he is doing, and that requires reference to the conceptual universe within which he acts. In forming or recognising an intention an agent must conceptualise his world; he must see it under some description and must see the possibility that the action he is contemplating will make the world something else, under another description. He need not articulate any such intention, but he must perceive the situation in which he acts as being thus and not so, and he must also be able to conceive of some action as fitting or appropriate, whether normatively or instrumentally, to the situation so perceived. But such things cannot be done without concepts, within or through which we grasp and intelligibly experience our world *as* something.[5]

IV. The Dimensions of Publicness and Privateness

We have called publicness and privateness complex-structured concepts, and the distinction between them, which plays so great a part in frameworks of social action, is necessarily complex too. Given the broad domain of activities and practices over which the distinction ranges, it could hardly be simple. But a further reason for its complexity is that the features of those activities and practices in terms of which it categorises them as public or private are themselves diverse, ranging from the public availability of books in a library to the public authority possessed by a government. Nevertheless it is possible to discern in this variety of features — availability, authority and the like — three broad types, constituting what we shall call the dimensions of publicness and privateness. These are features relating to access, agency and interest, three dimensions of social organisation which, as we shall suggest later, are probably universal categories, though not necessarily in the form of a public/private distinction. For even a culture without that distinction would still require *some* way of so ordering its relations and activities that it could recognise, discuss, explain or justify the allocation of *access* to information, resources etc., the capacities in which *agents* enjoyed that access, and in whose *interest* it was used.

A. Access

The access dimension can be further divided into four subdimensions: *physical* access to spaces, access to *activities and intercourse*, access to *information* and access to *resources*.

Physical Access. Places and spaces, like gardens, beaches, rooms and theatres are public when anyone is entitled to be physically present in them; they are private when someone, or some group, having the right of access, can choose whether to deny or allow access to others.

Access to Activities and Intercourse. Often we are concerned with access to a space because we are interested in access to what is going on there. A public meeting is one to which anyone has access; a public discussion is at least one to which anyone may listen, or more public still, one in which anyone may participate. Access to a private meeting, by contrast, is restricted to persons with specific rights to attend (invited guests, for instance, or club members).

Because, then, human activities commonly take up physical space, privacy of access to activities and intercourse requires privacy of access to space. Even in a public place a meeting between friends imposes upon others a kind of obligation of tact and good manners not to invade their 'conversational preserve' — that part of public space needed for the privacy of the activity.[6] For how otherwise could the activity remain restricted? It has been observed that in some communes where a good deal of ordinary living — including eating meals — is done collectively, certain activities such as entertaining friends are nonetheless recognised as private. Thus, for example, other members of the commune sitting at a table at which these activities are going on will avert their gaze and attention to produce a kind of private space in which the activity can proceed. By contrast, an activity like a Salvation Army prayer meeting taking place in a public place is recognised as open to all; not only do casual passers-by stop and watch, but some join the hymn-singing too. Access to both space and activity is public.

Access to Information. As Ruth Gavison points out in Chapter 5, information access is a central focus of most analyses of privacy. A concern for one's privacy is typically a concern to be able to control the dissemination of information about oneself: to insist that a certain piece of information is private is not necessarily to assert that no one but oneself should have access to it, but rather that the access should be under one's own control. Contemporary worry about data banks stems, in part at least, from this threat of loss of control of information about oneself. According to Alan Ryan, however (Ch. 6, below), this is only one aspect of our more general concern to manage the appearance we make upon the public stage. We have an interest in presenting certain faces to the public, in rehearsing these roles in private places, and in deciding in advance what to reveal of ourselves, and to whom. According to both Ryan and Gavison, such information control is fundamental to both personality and social life.

Information that is made public is available to the public at large or to any interested member of the public. Our 'public face' is thus that which we allow anyone to see, our 'private side' is that to which we restrict access. But although we often contrast 'publicity' and 'privacy' in this way, the former is at least as often opposed to 'secrecy'. Like privacy, the notion of secrecy regulates — by restricting — access to information. But significant differences separate these two concepts. Some secrets, for example, are culpable — criminal, even — and so need not be kept by someone who penetrates them; by contrast, if something is deemed a private matter, it is almost always deemed appropriate, too, that it be kept private. As we shall see a little later, this difference points to a fundamental difference in the natures of the two concepts.

Access to Resources. Someone has access to resources if he is able to manipulate some elements in his environment to bring about new and intended states of affairs. Of course, to have physical access to a particular space is at least in some small degree to have a capacity to affect intentionally what goes on there. Similarly, to have access to activities and intercourse is to have an opportunity to change them. And the concern that is often felt by individuals whose privacy is threatened by listening devices and data banks, and, correspondingly, the importance they attach to publicity as a shield against government abuse and malpractice, make it clear that access to information is access to a formidable resource. But these are special cases of a more general notion of access to resources, such as motorcars, lawnmowers, blast furnaces, coal mines and finance capital — all of which one enjoys or uses to change states of affairs.

Access to lawnmowers is generally private; access to a well or a drinking fountain can be public in the sense that anyone may use it. Access to a sewing machine in a clothing factory is hardly ever public in that sense, but neither is it private in the way that access to the seamstress's own machine is private. What seems more important — certainly more important in political discourse — is whether the *control* of access is public or private. And that generally means whether the power to give the seamstress access to the machine belongs to a public agent, such as an official of the Ministry of Textile Production or to the manager of one of its workshops, or to a private agent, like a firm of clothing manufacturers. Who controls access is a question of agency.

B. *Agency*

This second dimension is concerned, then, with the status of agents. The basic distinction is between an agent acting privately, i.e. on his own account, or publicly, i.e. as an officer of the city, community, commonwealth, state etc. The public/private distinction is thus important in answering the questions: What is your standing as agent? What significance do your actions and decisions have for the status of other people? If someone is entitled to use a stock of resources, to invest it, to sell it or give it away, to grant or withhold access to it, and if the warrant or title derives from no public office that he holds, the resources are private. A public official may be able to do precisely equivalent things, but only by virtue of a warrant or authorisation deriving from his office. Perhaps even more importantly, as Paul Finn points out in Chapter 4, a public officer may be warranted in performing actions which, if done by a private citizen, would be illegal. On the other hand, a public official has special duties — often enforceable through law — which greatly circumscribe his freedom of action in comparison with a private citizen. He can be held accountable in ways in which a private citizen cannot. He can properly be asked to justify actions done under warrant, or intended, or in performance of his special obligations, and for the most part an adequate justification must relate to his capacity as an officer of the public and to the powers and duties of that office.[7] But because public agents are not only officers of the public but private persons, too, with consciences of their own, what they perceive as the duties of their office may conflict with the demands of their private morality, creating for them dilemmas such as the ones Stanley Benn discusses in Chapter 7.

C. Interest

The antithesis between public and private interest is, of course, salient in political rhetoric. For something to affect someone's interest is for it to be to his advantage or disadvantage. So the interest dimension of the public/private distinction is concerned with the status of the people who will be better or worse off for whatever is in question.

A private business is private in this dimension in respect of the standing of its beneficiaries (the proprietors or shareholders, or perhaps its directors) whose advantage or profit is supposed to be the ultimately regulative end of its operations. By contrast, the supposed end of a public enterprise is to serve the public interest (providing either a service to any or every member of the community or to the state considered as a *res publica*). To be sure, classical liberal economists held that in a properly structured market, the outcome of the pursuit by each private agent of his private interest would be to the public advantage, even though no individual in the market had either motive or duty to pursue it directly (see Ch. 8, below). Nevertheless, the classical liberals did not attempt to blur the distinction between private and public interests; rather, they believed that the former could be used to promote the latter.

The notion of multi-dimensionality helps one to understand some of the conceptual confusions that abound in discussions of property. This is a concept that spans all three of our dimensions. Although the distinction between public and private property is most obviously applicable to access to spaces, places and resources, it is also applicable to questions of agency (e.g. does one have a right of access to a building by virtue of an office?) and of interest, too (who benefits?). And just because property is multi-dimensional, it may be difficult to determine whether a particular piece of property is public or private, the more because 'property' ranges over a diverse cluster of rights of ownership, enjoyment and control, which, as Ryan points out in Chapter 9, can be split between public and private agencies in innumerable ways.

V. The Normative Character of Publicness and Privateness

Given, then, that the distinction between publicness and privateness helps to structure social life regarding access, agency and interest, it remains to ask how it does it. Perhaps the most basic way in which concepts help us organise our environment is by providing us with the means to pick out certain of its features and so to describe them. Describing a letter as 'secret', for instance, points to a *de facto* restriction of access as well as to the desire of someone to keep it restricted. But publicness and privateness are not essentially descriptive in this way: they necessarily presuppose norms, and any application of them will be contextually related to some particular norms. In contrast, secrets may or may not be related to norms. To be sure, military and intelligence organisations have complex norms regulating access to their secrets; but this is not to say that the notion of a secret presupposes a norm, but rather that secrecy requirements can be enshrined in norms. By contrast, norms seem much more fundamental to publicness and privateness. Reading a letter without the permission of the recipient or the sender is a breach of privacy if and only if it contravenes a social norm. In a culture which had no norm restraining that sort of action but allowed anyone to read whatever material came his way or put constraints only on the reading of, say, arcane religious material, a letter could never be described as 'private' because, if the concept of privateness could be formulated at all, it would have to be in a way that excluded its application to letters.

Admittedly, in some contexts 'public' and 'private' do not seem to function normatively at all. As Ruth Gavison claims in Chapter 5, 'public' and 'private' are often used in ways that seem entirely descriptive. Though a 'private beach' is generally one to which access is restricted under an existing system of norms, to 'enjoy the privacy' of a secluded beach one need only be pleased that no one else is there. It is plausible, however, to regard such purely descriptive usages as derivative or secondary instances of publicness and privateness. Precisely because a privacy right is a standard way of securing the interest in being secluded, having seclusion secured *de facto* (e.g. by physical isolation) is enough like having it secured *de jure* for the notion of privacy to be extended to it, albeit without its normative associations. So when one loses one's seclusion, even when no normative change occurs, one describes it as a loss of privacy.

However, it does not follow from a concept's being normative in the sense specified that it cannot also function descriptively. On the contrary: precisely because 'private' relates to social norms, to describe an object as private implies that it satisfies some, at least, of a bounded set of conditions specified in the norms, without which the normative implications would not hold. A private letter bears the marks of privateness, either in its mode of address (not, for instance, 'To whomsoever it may concern') or in its subject matter. Though to call it 'private' does not specify which of the marks in particular the letter bears, it does imply that it satisfies one or more of the conditions necessary for privateness; and that constitutes a description of sorts.

In addition to the normative and descriptive uses, Gavison points to a third function,[8] to what might be called the *prescriptive* use of publicness and privateness. The prescriptive function is tightly tied, of course, to the normative use: 'Smith's letter is private (so don't read it)' invokes norms of privacy regarding letters and also prescribes a consequent forbearance. 'Private' can have this prescriptive force just because the normative 'private' is lurking in the background as a reason for the prescription. 'Don't tell anyone; it's a secret' can sometimes mean something similar, when there is a norm that such secrets should be kept. But the reason for maintaining secrecy need not be normative at all: maybe we just have a common interest in keeping the secret, and the implied reason invokes no norm whatsoever.

But whereas the prescriptive uses of publicness and privateness seem to invoke the normative sense, the converse does not necessarily hold: normative uses do not always issue in prescriptions. 'Private enterprise', for example, is certainly normative; no one totally ignorant of the norms which distinguish the responsibilities of the directors of British Steel from those of Marks and Spencer could grasp what it meant to call M & S a private firm. Nevertheless, economic historians could certainly employ this concept to trace changes over a given period in the proportion of Britain's gross national product attributable to organisations like BS as opposed to those like M & S. And this may be a matter of collecting and tabulating statistics — a pretty non-prescriptive kind of activity. It can be done because the norms governing the activities are institutional and can function, therefore, simply as descriptions of how things are done in that society; accordingly, they provide the conditions for assigning instances to one column of the table rather than another.

VI. The Liberal Tendency to a Dichotomous Distinction

A. *Dichotomous vs. Continuous*

The difference between the descriptive and prescriptive uses of 'public' and 'private' bears directly on whether we treat the relation between them as dichotomous or continuous. Sometimes it seems perfectly adequate to assume that publicness and privateness constitute a continuum, along which particular instances can be ordered, ranging from the more public to the more private. So though one's favourite out-of-the-way beach may become less private when some other people finally discover it, it does not become 'altogether public' until one day a freeway extension is built to give easy access to hordes of swimmers. It would seem, then, that privacy can certainly be regarded as a matter of degree. And that may account for some of the uncertainty we sometimes have in deciding whether something is really public or really private. Lukewarm water is not exactly hot or cold.

Where finding something to be public (or private) calls for or permits one sort of action rather than another, however, a continuous conception will not do. In Chapter 4, for example, Finn stresses the 'dramatic' consequences of finding an office to be public rather than private: different remedies will be available to injured parties depending on whether they are injured by private persons or public officials. If, therefore, one wants to know whether a criminal action can be brought against a common carrier (a ferryman, for instance) for malfeasance, it is of no help to be told that a common carrier is rather less of a public official than is a sanitary inspector, but rather more of one than is a schoolteacher. To take a more homely example: if one asks 'Is this a private letter?', would one be satisfied with the reply, 'More private than the one on file, but not so private as the one I wrote yesterday'? Well, one might be, if 'private' can be taken as a description of its subject matter. For instance, the letter written yesterday may have been a love letter, the one on the file an application for a dog licence, and this one a confirmation of a dinner appointment with a friend. But if the point of the question is to know whether anyone — including the inquirer — is at liberty to read this letter, only a yes-or-no answer will do. In the matter of beaches, 'private' and 'public' can be strictly descriptive; in the case of the letter, the main force is prescriptive.

Distinctions of the yes-or-no kind are dichotomous; that is to say, the domain to which they apply is divided sharply so that, in principle, every case can be allocated to one or the other category. Nevertheless, doubt may arise in a particular instance. Even when the concepts are defined sharply enough to make every case determinable in principle, we may lack sufficient knowledge to make the determination in practice. The biological criteria for male and female may be sharp enough but the relevant data not always available, and we have to go on indicators such as voice, length of hair and so on, that are not always reliable. The concepts themselves would then be consistent with dichotomy, but the ascriptions would sometimes be doubtful.

Uncertainty of ascription can come about not only from lack of information but from a fuzziness in the criteria themselves. We might divide economic institutions into state agencies, which are public, and the rest, which are private. Among the class of public institutions would fall, unambiguously, Telecom Australia, most central banks, and British Rail. But what should we say of a corporation in which a government holds 51 percent (or 49 percent) of the shares? Or of an organisation like the National Trust which is not answerable in general to Parliament, but which disburses public monies? Or of a social welfare society which acts through voluntary workers but is financed partly by government and which agrees to implement government welfare policies? The concept of a state agency, while sharp enough to pick out a number of paradigm instances, is not sharp enough to determine every case. That is not a reason for saying that there is a continuum, but only that the criteria are not fully determining in all cases.

This kind of indeterminacy arises from the multi-dimensionality of the criteria themselves. One of the reasons that 'state agency' does not yield an unambiguous determination is that there are multiple criteria for deciding that something is a state agency. But we do not have to look at the multi-dimensionality of the idea of a state to account for the uncertainties of publicness. For, as we have seen, publicness – like privateness – is itself a multi-dimensional concept. A city's transport system may be public in so far as it is accessible to any member of the public, but the agency that runs it may yet be a private firm, acting in the interest of its shareholders. Whether we refer to it as public or private may well depend on which dimension of its social field is salient, given the particular interest we have in it.

B. Bi-polarity vs. Multi-polarity

We have not so far raised the question whether whatever is not public must therefore be private, and whether whatever is public necessarily cannot be private. We have recognised that the distinction may sometimes be continuous rather than dichotomous, but we have taken it for granted that even then the continuum would be bi-polar. Certainly, the polar opposition of the public and the private is familiar as a rhetorical device, and the *Oxford English Dictionary* assures us that public is 'in general, and in most senses, the opposite of PRIVATE' and that private is 'in general the opposite of PUBLIC'.

Yet this bi-polarity often breaks down. We noted above that if access to a sewing machine in a factory was restricted to the regular operator, access to it was not public; yet, unlike her access to the machine she has at home, it would not be private either. A Certificate of Registration of a Motor Lorry in New South Wales distinguishes 'private use' and 'business use'. Use of the Wilbur Cross Parkway in Connecticut, however, has been restricted to private cars and public cars, the barred residual category being commercial vehicles. Again, as we have seen, information that is not public may not be private – it may be simply secret.

In fact, not only does the bi-polarity of publicness and privateness often break down, but the way in which it does so is systematically related to our three dimensions – access, agency and interest. Consider *access*. If access to a piece of land is quite unrestricted, it is public. But access to aboriginal sacred sites, to defence installations or to the tabernacle in a Catholic church, closed to all but initiates, is neither public nor private. Nor are the activities that normally go on in these places. Some records of information not accessible to the public are private (like personal diaries), but others are official secrets, or records of arcane and esoteric mysteries, guarded from the public by the initiate.

In all these cases, what is open to anyone and everyone in the absence of a special restriction is therefore public. To call something private in respect of access is to give a ground of a particular sort for withdrawing it from the range of the publicly accessible. But privateness is only one of a number of grounds that might defeat the presumption of publicness. And in most cases, at any rate, when the ground is not private, it relates to some particular and institutionalised form of life, such as religion, government, defence or business, for the sake of which the restriction is imposed. But because, in the absence of such conditions, access is public, publicness may be termed the residual category. However, within a context that from a particular standpoint is itself private, there can be further distinctions between what is private and what is not, and then the residual category will not be public but will relate to that particular context. Within a family, for instance, which for many purposes counts as paradigmatically private, rooms which are private to particular persons are distinguished from others which are family rooms, not public rooms. Again, 'public areas' in private business premises will be those accessible to the general public; but within the area restricted to personnel employed in the business, only senior executives may have private rooms, the remainder working, perhaps, in a 'general office'. If the distinction between the restricted and the unrestricted is itself encapsulated in a restricted, i.e. non-public, field, what is restricted may be private, but the unrestricted is not public.

In the dimensions of *agency* the presumption is generally the other way about from that of access. A person will be taken to 'own his action' simply as a private agent, unless there is a reason for looking at it differently. If Smith rents a house in Spain for a holiday, he will be taken as doing so simply as Smith, even though he also happens to be Minister of the Interior. But other actions that are not private acts might not count as public either (at least, not in the dimension of agency); for instance, reading the lesson in church, or presiding over the Royal Society. Ecclesiastical, commercial, or professional activities can all sustain non-public roles distinguishing some of Smith's actions from those he does in the residual private capacity — simply as Smith. But as with access, the conditions that rebut the presumption — in this case of privateness — usually relate to structured activities in which people act in special roles which create for them special capacities.

It is a feature of private agency that as long as a person does not step over into the generally impermissible, he does not require a warrant to act, nor does he need to account for his actions to anyone. It is special institutional capacity which calls for authorisation and creates special accountability. Possessed of it, an agent may be empowered to do things that would overstep the permissible limits of private action; and even when they do not, they may yet have very different normative implications. Generally speaking, anyone can enter into contractual commitments, but only those signed by public officials create a charge on general revenue. While private persons are agents in nature, the public has no natural manner of acting. To be sure, 'opinion' and 'reaction' are often attributed to it; but it can act only through a mediating institution, i.e. through persons acting in official roles. That is why private agency is the presumptive and residual category, public agency the one that has to be established.

The distinction between what is public and what is private is, of course, very much an ideological issue. Should an artist's work be treated as private, or is art a political activity, and an artist willy-nilly a participant in profound social conflicts with a quasi-official role of apologist or revolutionary activist? The ideological importance of the distinction is particularly apparent in the dimension of *interest*. In liberal thinking, private interest is residual, in the sense that it is taken to provide the most general explanatory motive for action, and, in the absence of overriding reasons, to be a legitimate motive, too. The public interest may override it, but how it functions as a motive and how it relates to private interests of individuals is problematic for liberalism. This tension between individual interests and collective interests is a recurrent theme of this book. We return to it in Chapter 2; Paul Finn looks at particular cases in the development of the common law in Chapter 4; Anthony Walton considers Hegel's attempt at reconciliation in Chapter 10; and Eugene Kamenka shows, in Chapter 11, how Marx rejected it as one aspect of human alienation that would be overcome in a communist society.

Liberalism exhibits strong theoretical pressures towards a bi-polar view of social life, tending as it does to assimilate the deviant cases noted above to one or the other of the two poles. From the perspective of a liberal secular individualist, churches and business firms are private associations. Reading a lesson in church is something Smith does in his private capacity. From the standpoint of the rest of the society, this is, and ought to be, treated as something peculiar to Smith. Public life tends to be equated with political life, because the idea of political organisation exhausts the understanding of the social whole. What is often called civil society, as distinct from the polity, is then firmly privatised; it is an area in which, whatever one's role, it is not like that of a state official, so one ought not to be held accountable for it to society at large. But, as we shall see, liberalism also exhibits countertendencies towards assimilating a great deal of non-personal, non-domestic activity to the public realm, and towards a rather broader conception of 'public life'.

At least for the liberal, the distinction between publicness and privateness applies to the life of every member of the society. This is the strength of the bi-polar structure. We noticed earlier that in many contexts the opposite of public may be something other than private, and of private something other than public. But whatever these other opposites may be, and no matter how important some of them may be for the lives of particular sections of the community, there is no antithesis except this one that the liberal employs universally, structuring his conception of *anyone's* social life. Admittedly, Carole Pateman's feminist critique of liberalism (Ch. 12, below) makes a good deal of the connection between the public/private antithesis and a number of others that she attributes to liberalism, notably political/personal, justice/love, power/morality, and freedom/subjection. But the point of her case is that these are aspects of the single comprehensive duality male/female: in claiming, she says, that the public/private split applies to everyone's life, the liberal simply overlooks, in a kind of false consciousness, the female half of the society whose life is wholly private, within the family. Pateman denies not the bi-polarity of liberal conceptions, but that this bi-polar distinction applies, as liberals believe that it does, to everyone's life. Instead, she claims that the distinction splits society itself, between the males who have a place in public life, and the females who do not.

Some writers have held, however, that the liberal conception of society is not bi-polar but tripartite, the favoured candidate for the third category being the 'social'. Hannah Arendt, for example, has used the term 'social' for the economic and commercial activities that, once private, have now moved increasingly into the public realm, eroding the original sense of the public/private distinction and forcing a re-definition of what the public realm constitutes.[9] This may be a useful and illuminating way of looking afresh at the world we know. But the culture in question does not use the categories practically in this way; rather, the contents of the basic two categories change over time, and this means that the basic bi-polarity is being redefined, not that it is being abandoned in favour of a tripartite perspective. Moreover, it does not seem that a term such as 'social' can be adequately contrasted with 'public' and 'private'. Whereas either the public or the private can stand alongside a number of possible counterclaims, like the religious or the professional, it is not clear that such concepts can usefully be lumped into a third realm – the social – to stand alongside the other two. It would certainly be odd to try to structure a social realm in terms of the dimensions of access, interest and agency, analogous to the structuring of the private and the public. One reason may be that, as we observed earlier, the categories that provide the alternatives to publicness and privateness all relate to structured activities, each setting up, as it were, its own institutional realm, with agency roles, rules of access, and characteristic interests. By contrast, no sort of access, agency or interest is *social* in any very clear sense that can be set alongside public and private. Society is not itself a form of activity or an institution, nor does it constitute a perspicuous residual category when these others are negated.

VII. Intersecting Distinctions – Public/Private, Temporal/Spiritual

The liberal claim that no antithesis besides the public/private is part of the structure of everyone's social life would certainly not have been acceptable – even, perhaps, intelligible – to Christians in the Middle Ages. Besides their life in the polity, and their private lives in their families, all men and women were thought to participate in a universal religious or spiritual community, the Church. In Augustinian terms, the distinction was made between the worldly city and the City of God. The fifth century Pope Gelasius made it into a politically crucial distinction between the temporal authority of the Emperor and the spiritual authority of the Pope, each with its own legitimacy directly from God, each presiding over a universal domain of human life, each, ultimately, with its own legal system and courts, of civil and canon law, with jurisdictions affecting everyone's life. The relation between these authorities was a subject of dispute throughout the Middle Ages, popes claiming supremacy, emperors and kings claiming an equal and autonomous legitimacy, if not supremacy, over the Church, each within his own realm. But whatever the stance on that question, none but a few isolated radical thinkers such as Marsilius and Wyclif challenged, before the Reformation, the universality of the temporal/spiritual duality, or thought that religious life could be assimilated either to public or to private life. Things changed with the Reformation. In England and parts of Germany religion became almost wholly public for a time. On the Erastian principle that it was the monarch's responsibility to reform the Church, the English parliament declared in the 1534 Act of Supremacy that the king was 'Supreme Head in earth of the Church of England', and in the 1559 Act of Uniformity made *The Book of Common Prayer* the only legal form of worship. By contrast, in Calvin's Geneva and in Massachusetts the public world became the secular instrument of the spiritual. But in England, in the course of Elizabeth's reign, one begins to glimpse a different way of looking at things: while public conformity to the state religion is a matter of political allegiance, what one does discreetly in the privacy of one's home is something the state need not concern itself with. The steps from there to religious toleration, though halting and taken without much consciousness of their general direction, led to the privatisation of religion. By the early twentieth century it became nearly as unacceptable for a gentleman to talk about religion in his club, as about what he did in bed with his wife. Religious education was barred from public schools in America and Australia, and survived in England only in a form so pallid and emasculated that it might be supposed inoffensive to any private conscience. It became possible, moreover, for secularists to insist that when the churches meddled in politics and the great social issues of the day, they trespassed beyond their proper bounds.

A society clearly needs to relate the religious life, which makes its own claims on individuals and communities in God's name, to its conceptions of public and private life, each with its own demands. The shifts in the Christian story show particularly well the varieties of accommodation possible even within a single tradition. By contrast with that tradition, however, religion in classical Greece and Rome never achieved the status of a third world, as it did in medieval Europe, but neither did it fall firmly on one side or the other of the public/private divide. Instead, relations between men and the gods mirrored the public/private structure of social life and its possible conflicts. In Greece, as Arlene Saxonhouse shows in Chapter 15 below, the ancestral gods presided over the private life of the family, and the gods of the city over public life. Conflicts between family and political obligations were also religious conflicts. In republican Rome, much the same was true: the public world was that of the civic pantheon, acknowledged in the performance of civic duties and one's attendance at public rites; the family, on the other hand, was the world of the household gods, the Lares, the Penates, and the Manes, whom the *pater familias* served as priest, his devotions reflecting his responsibility for the continuity of the family and for handing it on in trust, as it were, to future generations. The close correspondence between the temporal and divine worlds is illustrated by the high degree of specialisation attributed to the gods, both in the private and the public domains, every particular contingency having its own tutelary deity.

With the decay of the traditional religion in imperial Rome, public religious observance became little more than a token of good citizenship, and the duties owed to the household gods a kind of polite observance of the decencies. As befitted an imperial power, Rome made room hospitably in the city for the gods of the peoples it absorbed into the empire. Beyond these public and private formalities, however, there developed a variety of mystical cults – of Mithras, Dionysus, and Isis, for instance; and the philosophies of Stoicism and Epicureanism, which were already influential at the end of the republican period, continued to attract adherents. These doctrines and practices, however, were regarded as much more nearly private in a modern liberal sense – an individual's own affair, separated alike from the formal observance and role responsibilities of both Empire and family. This notion of a personal, inward life introduced something into late classical culture that may be seen as the first step in the ideological revolution that culminated in modern individualism.

Nevertheless, such personal beliefs did not postulate a third world, a dimension of social life that was a dimension of every individual's life, in the style of medieval Christianity. They had to do, rather, with an overriding conception of the way to manage one's life as a whole. In this respect, at least, they resembled Judaic and Islamic cultures. In each of these the religious life is neither a third world, nor a world divided, as in Greece and Rome, nor a political world, as in Geneva, nor a private world, as in modern liberal cultures. The basic religious conception is the person-to-God relationship which provides a spiritual framework embracing the whole of life, both personal and interpersonal. In both cases a divinely appointed code serves both for law and for morals. In each case, too, the people of the code — the chosen Jewish people on the one hand, the *ummat al-nabī*, the Community of the Prophet, on the other — constitute a single world in which individuals together strive in the way of righteousness to implement God's law on earth. Neither has an institutional *sacerdotium* to set against an *imperium*. In each, therefore, spiritual duties inform every aspect of life without the conceptual dislocations to which Christianity has been subject.

Judaism has been on the whole quietist and submissive towards political authorities, on Rabbi Chanina's principle: 'Pray for the welfare of the government, since but for the fear thereof men would swallow one another alive.'[10] But because Jews have enjoyed little good, on the whole, from their rulers over two thousand years, there is little sense, at least in pre-Enlightenment Jewish culture, of participating in a public, political world. The Jew's own public world has been that of his people, his community and his synagogue, embedded in an alien and usually hostile environment. Consequently, the *Halachah*, the traditional code, is strong on man's duty to God, and under God to his fellow-men in their interpersonal relations, in the family and in his community; it has sustained a juridical system administering essentially private law in the Beth Din. But it is generally lacking in a notion of the public, save as that might be applied to that ideal entity, the Jewish People. The absorption by Jewry of western cultural ideas over the last two centuries and the recent emergence of the State of Israel, the outcome of the grafting of western liberal nationalism on to the ancient tradition, has vastly complicated the picture. Jews now have a problem of living at once in many worlds, and the question, 'What is a Jew?' is for many a genuine crisis of identity, raising for them the questions, 'What is my public world? What is my private self?'[11]

Islam, by contrast, succeeeded in part in evolving and in part in superimposing itself upon political institutions, as far apart as the eastern Mediterranean and islands of Southeast Asia, in a way achieved by Judaism, in the modern State of Israel, only after a two thousand year political hiatus. Because Islamic social and political life was regulated by the Sharī'a, a term explained more adequately by a phrase such as 'the broad highway of life' than by a term such as 'code', it needed to develop an overriding conceptual structure within which it could function as a universal point of reference. This involved difficulties of a special kind. Since the Sharī'a is, by definition, both perfect and eternally self-sufficient, the notion of a legislative authority other than that of God is alien to Islam. Initially, therefore, everything depended on the ability of the judicial power, administered in the court of a learned qādī, according to the consensus of learned jurists of the community, to build up systems of application of the Sharī'a by analogy, precedent and interpretation. It began to be clear by the eleventh century, however, that 'while the Sharī'a doctrine embodies the ideal order of things for Islam, the overriding duty of the ruler is to protect the public interest; and in particular circumstances of time and place the public interest might necessitate deviations from the strict Sharī'a doctrine.'[12] Accordingly there emerged a second set of courts — the Mazālim jurisdiction — established by the ruler but sanctioned by the doctrine of *siyāsa shar'iyya* — 'government in accordance with the precepts of divine law' for the sake of public policy. 'During the latter part of the nineteenth century the dichotomy in Islamic legal practice became much more pronounced',[13] coming close to a dichotomy between secular and religious law, though always justified by a transcendent religious principle.[14] The emergence of Muslim integrism as a radical ideology, however, in Pakistan and Iran is reasserting the unity of the spiritual world of the Sharī'a against the creeping secularism of 'public policy'.

This movement tends also to override a widespread Islamic practice that has tacitly recognised a distinction between the public and private in the spiritual life. Though Islam maintains that law and ethics are continuous, not discrete, worlds, it has also made a distinction between the jurisdiction of the courts over acts done in public and acts done in private. Because, for instance, it is the function of the political authority to maintain a God-fearing community, it is the responsibility of the police to ensure that the fast of Ramadan is observed *in public*; but for what one does in the privacy of one's home one must answer to

God alone.[15] A corresponding distinction *in practice* has emerged in respect of the offence of fornication, proof of which requires 'four qualified, male, adult Muslim eyewitnesses of the carnal act itself'.[16] Fornication within the privacy of one's home, therefore, falls effectively outside the jurisdiction of the courts, despite the very severe penalties to which one would be liable were the offence proved according to law.

VIII. Alternative Conceptions of the Public and Private

Such cross-cultural comparisons, like social anthropology, create a problem for the methodological foundations of our project. Given the different ways in which issues of access, agency and interest have been organised — both within our western liberal culture and between it and other cultures — how can we distinguish (a) a conception of publicness and privateness that is different from the dominant liberal conception, and therefore an alternative to it from (b) a concept that is so different from the dominant liberal conception as not to be a conception of publicness and privateness at all? When studying the past of our own culture, historical continuity seems reason enough for holding, say, that the medieval world had conceptions of publicness and privateness, though ones that are distinct from our own. If we can trace how the later developed from the earlier we can grasp an identity and a difference. But how to go about deciding whether some culture very different from ours has *any* conception of publicness and privateness, or whether we should do well not to confuse ourselves by importing ethnocentric presuppositions into our study? Can a conception be a conception of publicness and privateness at all if it is different from our own, given that the only conception of publicness and privateness available to us when we ask whether another culture possesses such a conception, is the one embedded in our own culture?

We suggested earlier that the domain of the public and the private was the domain of social relations in so far as these are structured along the dimensions of access, agency, and interest. But these dimensions have a wider application. It is hard to imagine a culture, whether or not it employed the public/private distinction, that would not need some concepts in terms of which it organised its social life in these dimensions. To the extent that it regulated access to some places, some sorts of activities, some resources or some types of information, it would need a way of distinguishing not only what was restricted and what was not, but a kind of principle for identifying who had access. Similarly, no society that recognised that, in given situations, actions should be for the advantage of some person or group rather than another, could do without ways of categorising types of interest. Perhaps the utopias of some communitarians manage to abolish the interest dimension by immersing everybody so totally in the whole that no one would ever think of asking 'Who benefits?' But as long as members of a society can conceive of benefits accruing differentially, whether to individuals, families, clans or villages, some dimension of interest exists. The least likely of our three dimensions to apply universally might seem to be *agency*. As Martin Krygier shows in Chapter 13, some stateless societies have no notion of an agent acting on behalf of the whole group. But the claim that a society possesses no way of distinguishing types of agency would be much stronger than that: members of that society would have no idea of what it is to act according to a role or in a capacity. A culture which had the notion of a kind of action which was appropriate to fathers but not to non-fathers would already have a way of distinguishing practices in the dimension of agency. Only a society which was so simply organised that it had no norms of that kind at all would be devoid of an agency dimension.

However, while the dimensions of access, interest and agency may well be universal features of social life, a society might organise life on these dimensions in ways which cut right across those with which we are familiar. For instance, the Zinacanteco peasants in Mexico, discussed by Leslie and John Haviland in Chapter 14, are morbidly anxious (by our standards) to deny information about their household affairs to their neighbours and to keep them out of their houses; but they have no corresponding notion that it is inappropriate to pry, nor do individuals expect that some matters could be reserved within the household even from members of the family. And if, besides, they have only a very thin notion of an interest in which some group wider than the family shares, while yet acknowledging that such a group exists, shall we say that they have a conception of the public and the private?

There are no settled criteria for the cross-cultural identity of concepts; the fact that a concept functions a bit differently there from here because it is related to rather different beliefs and values allows us a good deal of latitude in choosing whether to treat it as the same concept or not. But to refuse absolutely to acknowledge that concepts embedded in another culture could have anything in common with ours is to make any understanding of another culture impossible. For we can only understand others' concepts in relation to our own. If we can begin with a rough notion of cross-cultural similarities, recognising, perhaps, that two concepts have common functions in regulating access, we might then discover where they diverged by recognising where expected extensions broke down. If, for instance, matters recognised as of *public* concern (i.e. affecting the well-being of everyone in the society) never seemed to be the business of any agent acting in a role characterised by some term systematically related to that notion of *public*, but were handled instead as affairs for priests to settle in holy conclave with the god, we should have to conclude that though there was a concept resembling our notion of the public in respect of interest, its agency dimension came closer to our notion of the sacred.

IX. Conclusion: Public and Private in Social Life

'Publicness' and 'privateness', then, are particular concepts by which our western liberal society organises such areas of social life as involve ascriptions of access, agency and interest. Though they are not universal or necessary concepts, they are profoundly important ones in western societies. They are also obviously and inherently ideological in the sense that they presuppose a secular society in which individuals confront each other in the context of a legal framework upheld by the state, the institutional embodiment of the public — everyone. The aim of Part One of this book is to explore the liberal conception of the public and private and the part it plays in structuring our social life. In Chapter 2 we shall attempt to provide a semantic theory of the liberal conception, while in Chapters 3 to 9 we examine the application of the liberal distinction to particular problems of access, agency and interest. Throughout these chapters we shall repeatedly encounter evidence of the normative and prescriptive character of publicness and privateness as well as tendencies to mutual exclusiveness and bi-polarity. The liberal social world, we shall discover, evinces a strong tendency to split itself into two distinct parts: what is public and what is private. And from this split it draws a multitude of consequences for actions.

But we shall also see throughout Part One that, despite its best efforts, the liberal world view cannot always sustain a consistent and clean cut between what is public and what is private. Civil society, for example, is sometimes seen as public, sometimes as private. Again: criminal law is sometimes seen as private, sometimes as public and sometimes as distinct from both. Such amgibuities and tensions — which provide one focus of Chapter 2 — reveal as much about liberalism as its more successful efforts to structure social life along the lines of the public and the private. And, as we will see in Part Two, they set the stage for some of the critiques of the liberal conception of the public and private in social life. Finally, we turn in Part Three to look at a few examples of alternative ways of structuring social life. Already, in this present chapter, we have sketched some of the many possible ways in which cultures employing some kind of public/private distinction might mesh this with a temporal/spiritual one. It is impossible, however, within the compass of this book, to deal specifically with the conceptual structures of complex cultures like those of Islam, China or Japan. Each has its own characteristic ways of conceptualising its practices in respect of access, agency, and interest; each would require a treatment as elaborate as the treatment we have given to western liberalism. However, by considering some aspects of social life in a few cultures less developed and less sophisticated than our own, we have raised the question: Have these cultures − so unlike our own that its complex-structured concepts of publicness and privateness would be quite out of place in them − found it necessary nevertheless to generate some corresponding distinctions to meet some recognisably similar cultural needs?

Notes

The authors acknowledge with thanks the helpful comments, suggestions and criticisms of friends and colleagues. They would like to thank, in particular, Fred D'Agostino, Keith Campbell, Philip Pettit, Miriam Benn, Beryl Rawson, Mohammad Nawawi and Tony Johns, all of whom gave generously of their time and knowledge.

1. The *Oxford English Dictionary* sanctions our choice, characterising 'privateness' as 'the quality of being private in various senses' (which it then proceeds to list), whereas the senses of 'privacy' are more restricted. 'Publicness' and 'publicity' are similarly related.

2. J.S. Mill, *Utilitarianism* in *Utilitarianism, Liberty, Representative Government* (Dent, London, 1954), p. 43.

3. One such chain, connecting 'public house' to 'public servant' might go like this: a 'public house', the *O.E.D.* tells us, is a 'house for the entertainment of any member of the community, in consideration of payment', adding that currently the entertainment is largely restricted to the consumption of 'alcoholic liquors'. A public house is thus public in the sense that it is open to all. But the *O.E.D.* also notes that many things that are public in this sense are also public in another sense, viz. that they are 'provided or supported at public expense, and under public control; as in *public elementary school*'. They are not only open to all, they are supported by all: the public *qua* state or civic government typically provides the funds and controls such public facilities. This sense of public also informs the *O.E.D.*'s definition of public offices, being 'a building or set of

buildings used for various departments of civic business' in which municipal officials are housed. And from the idea of municipal official to that of public servant is but a short step.

4. Ludwig Wittgenstein, *Philosophical Investigations*, 3rd edn, G.E.M. Anscombe (trans.) (Macmillan, New York, 1958), §67.

5. Such an account of action does not preclude the possibility, of course, that an agent may be doing things of which he is not aware. Nevertheless, if what the agent does is, properly speaking, an act and not just a kind of behaving, he must be able to give some answer to the question: 'What do you think you are doing?', even if the answer falls short of all the things he is doing, or is even mistaken in respect of some of them.

6. Erving Goffman, *Relations in Public* (Penguin, Harmondsworth, 1971), pp. 51-65. Alan Ryan discusses Goffman's work in Ch. 6, below.

7. Where it is *interference* with the actions of a private individual that stand in need of justification, it would thus seem that *action* by the public official requires justification. See S.I. Benn, 'Freedom, Autonomy and the Concept of a Person' in *Proceedings of the Aristotelian Society* (1976), pp. 109-30.

8. Our account differs somewhat from hers regarding this third function. See below Ch. 5, §1A.

9. See Hannah Arendt, *The Human Condition* (Doubleday, New York, 1959), Pt. II. See also Michael Oakeshott, *On Human Conduct* (Clarendon Press, Oxford, 1975).

10. *Ethics of the Fathers*, III, 3.

11. Isaac Bashevis Singer's novels *The Manor* and *The Estate* are largely concerned with the bewilderment of young Polish Jews in the second half of the 19th century, emerging from the ghetto world of the *stetl* into the sophisticated western world, trying to give a meaning to 'publicness' in their own lives, consonant with their residual Jewishness. Many of Singer's short stories show the same process at work in later generations confronted with nazism and communism.

12. N.J. Coulson, *Conflicts and Tensions in Islamic Jurisprudence* (University of Chicago Press, Chicago, 1969), p. 68.

13. Ibid., p. 71.

14. Louis Gardet provides an intriguing example of the possibilities: Strict enforcement of the fast of Ramadan disrupts economic life for a month. President Bourguiba proposed suppressing in Tunisia the *legal* obligation to observe the fast, basing his case on the concept of *jihād*, the holy struggle to progress along the way of God. The true *jihād* at the present time was the struggle against underdevelopment. Observing the fast entailed a setback in this *jihād*. So suspending the enforcement of the fast would be the course required by God's law. *L'Islam* (Desclée de Brouwer, Paris, 1967), p. 332.

15. Ibid., p. 127.

16. Coulson, *Conflicts and Tensions in Islamic Jurisprudence*, p. 65.

PART ONE

PUBLIC AND PRIVATE IN WESTERN CULTURES

2 THE LIBERAL CONCEPTION OF THE PUBLIC AND THE PRIVATE

Stanley I. Benn and Gerald F. Gaus

I. Introductory

The political agenda of liberal societies is permeated by issues of the bounds of the public and the private. What information should be private, and what information would it be wrong to keep from the public? Should the state regulate obscene materials to protect public morals? When is discrimination a private matter, and when does it become a public concern? To what extent is public policy to be constrained by private rights? What is to be in the public and what in the private sector?

Liberals' preoccupation with such issues reflects, we believe, their more general commitment to an equilibrium of the public and private spheres of life.[1] The aim of this chapter is to go behind this commitment by examining the conceptions of publicness and privateness embedded in such debates. Our general thesis is that the liberal conception draws, in both theory and practice, on two divergent models, each of which provides a systematic and internally consistent account of the complex structures of publicness and privateness. (See Ch. 1, sec. II, above, on complex-structured concepts.) They are based nevertheless on quite different, and perhaps incompatible, conceptions of individuals in society. In section II we develop an *individualist* model of publicness and privateness. This is the traditional and still, we believe, the dominant model of liberal theory and discourse. But readily recognisable features of liberalism do not fit this dominant model. So in section III we explore an *organic* model of the public and private. In section IV, we briefly consider how our two-model account relates to some of the tensions and ambivalences of liberal theory.

II. An Individualist Model

Consider Sir George Cornewall Lewis's definition of 'public', which Brian Barry claims 'is impossible to improve upon':

Public, as opposed to *private*, is that which has no immediate relation to any specified person or persons, but may directly concern any member or members of the community, without distinction. Thus the acts of a magistrate, or a member of a legislative assembly, done by them in those capacities, are called public; the acts done by the same persons towards their family or friends, or in their dealings with strangers for their own peculiar purposes, are called private. So a theatre, or a place of amusement, is said to be public not because it is actually visited by every member of the community, but because it is open to all indifferently; and any person may, if he desire, enter it. The same remark applies to public houses, public inns, public meetings, &c. The publication of a book is the exposing of it to sale in such a manner that it may be procured by any person who desires to purchase it: it would be equally published, if not a single copy was sold. In the language of our law, public appear to be distinguished from private acts of parliament, on the ground that the one class directly affects the whole community, the other some definite person or persons.[2]

To this Barry adjoins a passage from Bentham distinguishing the privateness and publicness of different classes of offence in law:

'1st. *Private Offences*. Those which are injurious to such or such assignable individuals. An *assignable* individual is such or such an individual in particular, to the exclusion of every other; as Peter, Paul or William other than the delinquent himself... 4th. *Public Offences*. Those which produce some common danger to all the members of the state, or to an indefinite number of non-assignable individuals, although it does not appear that any one in particular is more likely to suffer than any other.'[3]

We shall try to show that these passages point to four distinct levels on which the privateness/publicness distinction can be made. Neither Lewis nor Bentham (nor, for that matter, Barry) remarks upon this, and they all seem to slide happily enough from one to another. In our view, however, these transitions come so easily and unreflectively only because there is a systematic theoretical or ideological connection between the levels.

A. The First Level: The Privateness of the Specific Person and the Publicness of the Non-assignable

Bentham's 'assignable individual' is much the same, presumably, as Cornewall Lewis's 'specified person'. He can be identified by name, by pointing him out as *this* or *that* person, or by a description such as 'the person with red hair who was standing by me ten minutes ago'. This suggests a principle, which we shall term *the basic principle of differentiation* of this model, by which *private* is distinguished from *public*: whatever is private pertains to a specific person, and to that person exclusively, and not as he is a member of a general class. In contrast, whatever is public pertains to him simply as a member of the general class of persons and would equally pertain to anyone in that class. Subject to certain boundary restrictions to be considered later on, this corresponds to the publicness of Bentham's 'non-assignable' or, in Cornewall Lewis's phrase, to 'whatever may concern any member or members of the community without distinction'.

Within this model, then, this distinction is basic and, as we shall see, is manifested in one way or another at all its levels. It will not suffice on its own, however, as an analysis of the public/private distinction.

The domain of the distinction is the world of persons. Ants and eagles can be in swarms or solitary, but only persons have public and private lives. Admittedly, there have been nature films entitled 'The Private Life of the Fox', and so on; but this is to use an impoverished sense, equivalent to 'normally unobserved', and intelligible only by derivation from the richer sense, which is applicable only to persons. This is not simply a case of species chauvinism, but stems from our notion of a person as a self-aware project-maker. Indeed, if we came to believe that foxes were aware of themselves as makers of projects, we should have good reason for including them in the domain of the public/private distinction.

A self-aware project-maker is a distinct centre of self-consciousness, having the notion of himself as a distinct entity alongside other similar entities. If instead we were all telepathically and inescapably plugged in to the same common consciousness, it is hard to see how one could differentiate himself from others. He can do this only because he is conscious of experiences — thoughts and feelings — to which others can have no access unless he communicates them. To be sure, this can happen involuntarily, by signs, for instance, that betray one's feelings; but the idea that feelings can be 'betrayed' is itself evidence of the importance in our self-experience of this notion of privileged immediate access.[4] This privilege does not entail the claim, of course, that one's beliefs about oneself are necessarily true; we make mistakes in interpreting our own experience, and the observer sometimes understands better than the actor what is really going on. But the observer is then only making better use of what he has seen and heard than does the actor of what he experiences immediately.

Now a person so characterised will be aware not only that he can extend access to the restricted things by choice, but that he may also be able to exclude access, by concealment, to things that are in principle readily accessible to the observer. Such capacities are of very great importance to someone who is a person in the further sense of a project-maker – who conceives plans for shaping the future course of events, managing his environment, including his relations with other persons, assuming roles appropriate to his projects, and so on. For all these purposes, the possibility of choosing whether to be, or to act, in company or alone, observed or unobserved, is clearly important. (See below, Chs. 5 and 6, for arguments supporting the importance of such privacy.) It is not surprising, then, that persons with experiences so structured have conceived normative patterns that increase their control over these conditions, moving, conceptually, from being merely alone to being 'in private', and from being merely observed to 'acting publicly'. (See Ch. 1, sec. V, above, on the normative nature of publicness and privateness.)

We take the public/private distinction to depend, then, on the human capacity for self-differentiation and on the importance for personal action, at least in western culture, of the awareness that access to things about oneself can be extended or withheld, particularly when social rules evolve to regulate such access. For the individualist, self-consciousness and creative action of this kind can be attributed, without constructive elaboration or metaphor, only to individual persons. The 'assignable individual' who knows who he is, is thus the most basic, the logically most primitive, subject of privateness, and the public/private distinction is applicable to groups and institutions only by some logical or ideological process by which they can be built up from individuals. Even in the most intimate of private groups, it is still logically possible for an individual to withdraw something from the group as private to himself alone.

Correspondingly, the most basic publicness refers to the set of individual persons considered severally but indiscriminately, not specifically: to anybody, any person, anyone. A park that is open to the public can thus be said to be open to anyone. The notion of being 'out in public', so stressed by Sennett, is similar: when one is out in public one may meet anyone, and one does not know most of the people thus met as specific individuals, but, at best, as instances of types — a plumber, say, or a policeman.[5]

Just as the principle of differentiation in this model is the distinction between the specific or assignable and the non-specific or non-assignable, so the *methodological principle* which generates the model is precisely the logical primacy of the individual person. The other levels of the model are arrived at, as we shall see, by three *transition principles*, by which more complex notions of publicness and privateness are built up from these basic first-level ones. While the organic model (the subject of sec. III) will be found to have four stages roughly corresponding to the four levels of the individualist model, its methodological principle, principle of differentiation and principles of transition are all different.

B. *The Second Level: The Privateness of the Group of Specifiable Persons and the Publicness of 'Everyone'*

The transition in this model from the first to the second levels is effected by *aggregation*. The privateness of love affairs, of the home, of friendships, of private parties and private meetings all relate to aggregations of particular persons, known and specifiable one to another. So the boundaries of a private party are determined by specific invitation, or, like the boundary of a group of friends, by common consent.[6] Similarly, the 'anyones' of first-level *publicness* are aggregated into the 'everyone', the individualist's second-level publicness. The contrast between these two levels of publicness is nicely brought out in the passage from Bentham quoted earlier in which he defines a 'public offence' as one that produces a common danger either to 'an indefinite number of non-assignable individuals' or 'to all members of the state'. The first refers to a distributive, first-level publicness, the second to a level on which what is public pertains not just to anyone but aggregatively to everyone.[7] Something is public on this second level, then, if everyone, or at least everyone in some relevant set, has the same interest in it or is otherwise related to it in the same way. It might be said, for instance, that 'public curiosity has been awakened' or 'the public demands to know'; although it may not be literally true that absolutely everyone is curious or demanding, the general idea is that so many individuals are at one on the matter that the exceptions can be reasonably disregarded.

This idea of 'the public' as the overwhelming mass is central to liberal theory. Liberalism is committed to the protection of the individual's conscience and projects; and when his beliefs and plans are unpopular, this commitment translates into a defence of the individual from the pressures of public opinion. The tendency of liberals to applaud an independent minority who refuse to bow to the pressure of public opinion sometimes stems, as in de Tocqueville and J.S. Mill, from a disparagement of the masses as a 'collective mediocrity';[8] but liberals are also prepared to support the rights of a misguided minority who shun the true beliefs embedded in public opinion. Because the liberal places a value on independence and self-direction, he is always apt to be wary of public or mass opinion which might undermine these virtues by producing an unreflective conformity. This opposition between second-level publicness and first-level privateness seems at the heart of the liberal saga of the beleaguered minority struggling against the pressure to conform brought to bear by the overwhelming majority.

One sort of aggregate use of 'public', however, falls short of attributing something to everyone, or even to nearly everyone, in a community. Film stars and rock groups, for example, are sometimes said to have 'publics'. And we talk of the 'racing public' and the 'reading public'. In all these cases the boundary of each 'public' is some interest that, by implication, is not common to *all* members of the community. Nevertheless, even here the claim is implicit that what is predicated of the public is true of every member.

The need to define the boundary of a public is not, however, confined to second-level publicness. It can arise, too, in relation to the public as 'anyone'. Generally speaking, only residents may borrow from a public library — not just anyone, but only any member of the relevant public. A member of a relevant public is thus not a wholly unspecified 'anyone' but an unspecified member of that particular public. The specification of a particular public requires not only the notion of unspecified individuals (considered either severally or collectively according to level) but also a boundary condition. And not just anything will do. The set of persons each weighing ten stone five pounds would constitute a public only if having this weight gave them some common aim or interest. For only properties of persons that tend to action seem able to serve as defining features of a public.

Such 'publics' are distinct, on the one hand, from sectional or vested interest groups (see sec. II.E) and, on the other, from private groups, like a gathering of friends. This latter distinction, i.e. between a public and a private grouping, is central to the judgements in *Race Relations*

Board v. *Charter and Others* (1973) H.L.(E). The *Race Relations Act*, 1968, of the United Kingdom Parliament made it 'unlawful for any person concerned with the provision to the public or a section of the public . . . of any goods, facilities or services to discriminate' on the grounds of colour, race, ethnic or national origins 'against any person seeking to obtain or use those goods, facilities or services by refusing or deliberately omitting to provide him with any of them'. The East Ham South Conservative Club had refused membership, on the chairman's casting vote, to one Amarjit Singh Shah. It was alleged (and not contested) that the chairman was opposed to the application on the grounds of Mr Shah's colour. The question for settlement was whether those for whom the Club's facilities were provided constituted what we have called 'a public', for if not the Club would have been exempted from the requirements of the Act.

Counsel for the Club maintained, on appeal to the House of Lords, that 'the Act is not intended to interfere with the conduct of people's private lives. So, when they gather together in private groupings with a link of personal relationship among the members this is in the private and not the public domain.' It was not strictly necessary for the Court to determine whether, should the Club not count as public, it must necessarily count as private. It did hold, however (Lord Morris of Borth-y-Gest dissenting), that 'public' in the Act was indeed being used in contrast to 'private', and that no element of publicness entered into the case as long as a personally selected group of people met in private premises and the club they constituted did not provide facilities or services to the public or any section thereof. Consequently, as the East Ham South Conservative Club provided facilities exclusively for its members and their guests, and membership was 'by nomination and personal selection', the provisions of the Act were held not to apply.

Eligibility for membership in the Club was restricted to male conservatives. But that alone would not have exempted it from the Act, for that would have been consistent with provision of facilities to a section of the public of which Mr Shah was indisputably a member — the class of male conservatives. No matter how restrictive the qualifying boundary conditions, the Club would not have been exempt had the selection procedure not involved 'the personal selection of members with a view to their common acceptability' (Lord Simon of Glaisdale, 902). To be so recruited, members must be considered as specific individuals, not merely as instances of some general class such as male conservatives.

Argument in this case highlighted another feature of the individualist model. Counsel for the Race Relations Board argued that in the present instance the antithesis of 'public' was not 'private' but 'domestic'. (See Ch. 1, pp. 15-18, above, for a discussion of such non-standard antitheses.) Consequently, though family relations would admittedly fall outside the scope of the Act (a father providing facilities for his sons and daughters is not providing for a section of the public), associations of individuals not connected by family ties would be bound by it. Lord Morris alone accepted this interpretation, holding that a non-domestic group might be simultaneously private and a section of the public. In his view the Act exempted only provisions within a family or in contexts similar to those where one invites friends to dinner or to share a holiday. Apparently to Lord Morris any provision short of letting someone into one's domestic circle would count as a provision to the public. He took it as fatal to the appellant's case that the Club was open to application for membership instead of recruiting by special invitation only. For presumably only then would the crucial domestic analogy apply.

All parties in the case accepted the family circle as a paradigm of something set apart from the public arena.[9] In classical times — and this is still true of some cultures today — the family household was conceived as an extension of the personality of the *pater familias* (see Ch. 3, pp. 68-69, below). From the standpoint of outsiders, its interests and concerns were as much and exclusively his as anything that touched his personality. Intervening in a man's family affairs was an invasion of his personal private sphere, private at our *first* level of privateness, in essence no different from requiring him to take baths more often, eat less cheese or cut his toenails. In recognising the claims of other members of the family, however, in addition to, and often against, the *pater familias*, public authorities have increasingly crossed the domestic frontier. Correspondingly, the idea that the moral standing of the domestic tyrant's wife, children and servants is that of his own person — akin to his property — has been seriously undermined. The generally received conception of a family now comes closer to a group or association of mutually dependent persons having a special kind of involvement with one another, instead of a head with more or less personally integral appendages, like arms and legs. But precisely because this new kind of involvement includes knowledge of personal and intimate things, because the relations that evolve within a family cannot readily be captured in universal descriptions, and because those relations are commonly thought to be necessary for the satisfactory development of individual personality, the domestic scene remains the paradigmatic private *grouping*, in which members are intimately aware of each other as specific individualities.[10]

C. The Third Level: The Institutionalisation of Privateness and Publicness

At the second level of the individualist model, then, private things concern groups of specifiable individuals, and things that are public concern every member of some set, all members of which satisfy appropriate boundary conditions. The transition to the third level is made by *institutionalising* and treating the group as a corporate agent. Unlike a family or a group of friends, a private subject at the third level has a kind of corporate identity, a constitution, however informal, that enables one to ascribe to it actions, decisions and responsibility without, however, ascribing those actions etc. severally to every member. But it is also unlike the broad classes that we call 'publics' or 'sections of the public', though the interests that members of a public have in common may be the reason for the existence of the institutionalised agent (e.g. a motoring association like the Royal Automobile Club is a private corporation dedicated to the interests of the motoring public).

The privateness of the corporation, the firm and sectionally-based associations, however, is not only by analogy with individual persons as agents. According to liberal individualism, such agencies are vehicles through which individuals pursue their own private interests, whether as entrepreneurs, shareholders, trade unionists or members of voluntary organisations. Not that such institutionalised private interests need be wholly self-regarding, as private charitable organisations demonstrate. Nor are they immune to legal restraints, both to safeguard the legitimate interests and opportunities of others and, as in the case of a trust, to ensure that the interests served are those of the proper beneficiaries. But as private institutions they are under no obligation to conduct their affairs for the sake of the public interest. Like private individuals, private companies and associations are held to possess goals of their own, contributing to or reflecting the purposes of their members, but quite legitimately opposed to the aims of others in the society.

By contrast, to say that the policy pursued by a public agency is contrary to the interest of some set of individuals is *prima facie* to attack it as partisan, unless that interest is contrary to the public interest (see sec. II.E). For publicness at this third level institutionalises the 'everybody' — summed up paradigmatically in the Roman notion of the *res publica*, and its modern equivalent, the state. According to Hobbes, perhaps the father of the modern conception of the state,

> a commonwealth is said to be instituted, when a multitude of men do agree, and covenant, *every one* with *every one*, that to whatso-

ever man, or assembly of men, shall be given by the major part, the right to present the person of them *all* . . . *every one* . . . shall authorize all the actions and judgements of that man, or assembly of men . . .[11]

The liberal state thus purports to be the institutional embodiment of everyone, as opposed to the specific corporate person which is an individual writ large. To be sure, the state also is a specific authority structure with identifiable officers; but, at least according to the individualist liberal ideal, it is not the instrument of specific persons or devoted to promoting specific goals or purposes. This ideal, it seems, is not unlike Oakeshott's understanding of a *res publica* as a form of association not devoted to specific interests or goods, and thus quite unlike even the most mammoth private organisations.[12]

In recent years, however, students of administration have become increasingly preoccupied with institutions that seem to straddle the public/private divide. They have given particular attention on one hand to certain non-statutory bodies which are not part of the state authority structure and which therefore qualify *prima facie* as private, but which expend public funds in performing services for governments and thus are required to account for the expenditures to governments. On the other hand, there are statutory bodies such as Britain's 'public corporations' which are not government agencies in any straightforward sense and are actually required to operate by commercial success criteria; nevertheless, they are supposed to serve the public interest and are accountable to representatives of the state. And, unlike private corporations, their profits are not distributed to private shareholders. Acronyms like *QUAGO* (Quasi-Governmental Organisation) and *QUANGO* (Quasi-Autonomous-Non-Governmental Organisation) have been coined to cope with such administrative oddities. Such bodies cannot be categorised clearly as public or private because of the multi-dimensionality of the notion of the state that we noted in Chapter 1 (p. 14, above). Because at this level 'public' is defined with reference to the state, any institution that is in some ways a state institution and in other ways not will be correspondingly in some ways public and in other ways not.

Besides this difficulty in applying the individualist model, a further conceptual difficulty begins to emerge at this level. We observed earlier that the notion of the public requires a boundary condition within which it applies to 'anyone' or 'everyone'. How, then, are we to formulate the boundary conditions for the 'everyone' that the state is supposed to represent? For as yet, at any rate, the model has offered no set of unspecified persons such that one can say: Every person of the aggregation within this boundary is represented by the state, which exists to promote his interests and which can claim on that account to be the institutionalised public entity – the *res publica*. Cornewall Lewis's easy reference to 'the community' merely begs the question of what transforms an aggregation of unspecified individuals into a community capable of institutional personification as a public agency. What sort of an account can an individualist give of political community? We move to the fourth level of the model to resolve that problem.

D. *The Fourth Level: The Generalised Abstraction of the Private and the Public*

The notion of specifiable individuals, each going about his own business, and of the associations they form as they do so, leads naturally to a conception of a network of private relations developing among them. So from the very specificity of the private develop a number of abstract notions such as 'private enterprise', 'the private sector', 'the market economy' and, most generally, 'civil society'.

But what can the individualist put on the side of publicness to correspond to 'civil society'? Cornewall Lewis, as we have seen, invokes the notion of 'the whole community'; but it is not clear what he means, or what an individualist would be entitled to mean, by that phrase. Bentham, a rigorous methodological individualist, is quite explicit about *his* use of 'community':

> The community is a fictitious *body*, composed of the individual persons who are considered as constituting as it were its *members*. The interest of the community then is, what? – the sum of the interests of the several members who compose it.[13]

So when Bentham uses 'public' for what pertains to 'the whole community', he is still at the second level of publicness, that of simple aggregation. Even so, we still need a boundary condition, indicating who is to count among 'the several members who compose' the aggregation. We might fall back, perhaps, on the state's territoriality, defining its public by reference to its geographical boundaries. But why should spatial co-ordinates be more relevant to publicness than, say, possessing a body weight of ten stone five pounds?

Contract theory can offer a solution of sorts. One version – a sort of Lockean story – might go thus: private individuals, as they pursue their own interests in civil society, come to see the need for certain kinds of co-ordinated outcomes that cannot be achieved by contract but which require authoritative decisions, perhaps backed by coercion. The social contract, then, is put forward as a means to create such authoritative co-ordination out of a world of purely private, contractual operators: private individuals, as it were, contract to create a sphere of non-contractual co-ordination. The contractual theory of political obligation is thus a way of getting morally exacting publicness – public authority – out of an individualist model of social relations in which life is basically private. So out of civil society arises polity, the abstract notion of the political relations existing among the contracting individuals who constitute a civil society. But this merely transfers the boundary problem to civil society. What forms the boundary of a civil society and why is it significant for publicness?

If one could depict the humanity-wide nexus of social and economic intercourse as a network of lines linking the participants, resembling a map of the world's air routes, it would not be spread evenly over the world but would rather show clusters where the textures were particularly dense. We might well call these clusters civil societies. Because the members of such a civil society generally share many more interests with one another than with people in other clusters, a public authority to order and sustain their relations and further those interests will be uniquely appropriate to a civil society. And because political organisation itself tends to thicken the texture of social relations, both facilitating intercourse within the organised areas, and often impeding intercourse across their boundaries, the formation of civil societies and the growth of public authority are mutually reinforcing processes.

According to the individualist liberal conception of the social order, then, the polity exists for the sake of civil society; it provides the framework – and hence the constraint – that enables civil society to prosper. In the heyday of individualist liberalism what was private thus belonged to civil society, which included, indeed may have coincided with, the market economy. What was public pertained to the framework, to the polity, and therefore to the state as its active authority structure. In recent policy discussions, however, both distinctions, i.e. between state and civil society, economy and polity, have given way to the distinction between the public and private sectors (see Ch. 8, below). But sectors of what? Primarily of the economy. In liberal theory, the state stood largely aloof and separate, an authority structure generating decisions implicating in one way or another the whole polity, and imposing upon the economy the terms on which the constituent private individuals might operate. So what was public pertained to the political and the legal. But today any activity performed by agencies of the state — and a good many of them are economic — are included in the public sector, the rest in the private sector. Civil society, one might say, has been invaded by the state. Nationalisation of industries and increased socialisation of welfare services have drawn what were generally private activities into what is clearly the public realm.

Yet it is clearly a mistake to view the state as a leviathan progressively consuming civil society. Indeed, one school of political scientists, the exchange theorists, have virtually assimilated the polity to civil society by taking contractual exchange as the paradigm of political — and in some instance of all — social relations.[14] Overmighty subjects, e.g. trade unions and business corporations,[15] force the state into bargaining. Like the medieval king, it is one power centre among many. Rather than Hobbes's 'mortal god' created by contract among private men, states in the 1970s and 1980s, again like medieval kings, find themselves parties to 'social contracts', specifying compromises struck with their semi-sovereign subjects.[16] And because the state again finds itself a contracting operator among operators, understanding its role and influence may not be greatly assisted by stressing the publicness of its authority.

E. The Limitations of the Individualist Model

A model of the kind we have been examining might be faulted in two ways. First, it might be incoherent; that is, it might contain inconsistent postulates, or some concept essential to the model might be capable of explication only by drawing upon an idea that the model could not accept as meaningful. For instance, if the boundary requirement noted in our analysis of third and fourth level publicness could be met only by resorting to some notion of community inconsistent with the model's individualist methodological principle, the model would be incoherent. We have noted above that the individualist model does have some difficulties on this score, though they do not seem insuperable.

There is, however, another way in which a model of the liberal conception of publicness and privateness might be faulted. The function of such a model is to exhibit the structure of that conception, which in turn organises practices in a liberal society (see Ch. 1, above). If some of the society's practices and related modes of reasoning and advocacy cannot be integrated into the model, it can be faulted as insufficient rather than incoherent. And in some respects the individualist model does indeed seem defective in this way, particularly in regard to two important liberal sentiments, the moral claims of the public interest and the value of participation in public life.

The Public Interest. Consider the role of the notion of public interest in liberal theory and discourse. As Bentham noted, a social world in which all interests are those of individuals, be they specified or unspecified, does not leave much room for a public interest.

> The interest of individuals, it is said, ought to yield to the public interest. But what does that mean? Is not one individual as much a part of the public as another? This public interest, which you introduce as a person, is only an abstract term; it represents nothing but the mass of individual interests. It is necessary to take them all into account, instead of considering some as all, and the others as nothing ... In one word, the interest of everybody is sacred, or the interest of nobody.
> Individual interests are the only real interests.[17]

As Bentham says, political discourse often treats 'the public' as a sort of person. But this sort of reification of 'the public' — which usually seems to equate the public with some notion of 'community' — has an uncomfortable place in the individualist scheme of things. So it appears that all a methodological individualist like Bentham can mean by 'public interest' is the interest of everyone (level two publicness) as, for example, when it is claimed that clean air is in the public interest. But this sense of 'public interest' is of very limited use: used in this way, it is logically impossible that the interests of a significant number of individuals could be opposed to the public interest. Thus, while we can say that clean air is in the public's (that is, everyone's) interest, we cannot say that pollution controls are too, since they may well be against the interests of the small, but significant, class of industrialists.

But it might be argued that while the conception of the public interest as the *net interest* of everyone is not very useful for political discourse, we can construct a useful and thoroughly individualist notion of the public interest by defining it as *an* interest common to, or shared by, everyone; that is, it need be no more than one of the interests of everyone; it would be *a* public interest. Thus the clean air that would result from controls would be in the interest of everyone (as everyone breathes and, presumably, can get lung disease), but instituting controls may not be in the net interests of everyone. But this notion embraces too much: everyone, let us say, has an interest in clean clothes, yet it does not seem at all right to say that there is a public interest in clean clothes. It is more accurate, perhaps, to define a public interest as an interest shared by everyone but which either must be provided jointly or is such as to be enjoyed jointly.¹⁸ Such a conception would allow us to talk of a public interest in good roads, even if they oppose the net interests of owners of railways. But still we meet difficulties. First, this shared interests conception still requires that a public interest be an interest of everyone; thus, for example, to show that federal aid to decaying eastern and midwestern American cities is a public interest of Americans, it would have to be demonstrated that those in other regions, as well as the rural population within the east and midwest, have interests served by such aid. A more serious difficulty is that, a public interest being only a type of interest shared by everyone, it need not be important to anyone. This would seem to be the reason why, in liberal rhetoric, showing that something is '*a* public interest' is so much weaker a claim than asserting that it is '*the* public interest'. To show that a policy or measure is *a* public interest in the sense which we have been considering — i.e. *an* interest shared by everyone — is to provide an argument, but not a particularly strong one, in its favour.¹⁹ Other considerations, based on private rights or even private interests, seem able to override it. In contrast, to claim that some policy is in *the* public interest is, to borrow a phrase from Ronald Dworkin, to 'trump' other sorts of arguments.²⁰

Brian Barry has proposed an apparently individualist conception of the public interest that (unlike the net-interest conception) allows us to say that the public interest is opposed by a significant minority, while (in contrast to the 'one of the interests' conception) it seems to retain its strength as a moral claim.²¹ The key to Barry's proposal is the distinction between a person's net interests and his interests in various capacities or roles, e.g. as a plumber, a father, a sports fan. To say that something is in the public interest, says Barry, is to hold that it is in the interests of everyone in his capacity as a member of the public. Thus Barry might say that not only clean air but also pollution controls are in the public interest because they are in the interest of everyone in his capacity as a member of the public. Of course they may be against one's interests as an industrialist, and even when all his interests are tallied up it still may be in the industrialist's net interests to oppose them. But, on Barry's analysis, the important point is that *qua* member of the public, controls are in *everyone's* interest.²²

It is not clear, however, that one could elicit the idea of a capacity or role as member of the public from the aggregative notion of public. Say we have two groups of eleven strangers: the first is put into a room together, the second is formed into a soccer team. Clearly the members of the second group will have interests *qua* members of the team; they will presumably have an interest in winning and those things that are means to winning. But it is at best unclear what interests our eleven strangers in the room will have *qua* members of the aggregation. Of course they may have common interests as, for instance, in getting out of the room. They may even have an interest in agreeing on a common plan to escape. Still, their common interest is not *qua* members of the eleven, but simply as individuals wanting to escape. More broadly, being a member of a simple aggregation does not seem to be a role with attached interests. Only when the aggregation is transformed into a sort of association with functions or goals (a firm, a family, a soccer team) do roles with attendant interests arise.

Still, although our eleven strangers do not share a common interest *qua* members of the aggregation, they do have a common interest in escaping. Indeed, we can say that the *typical* member of the aggregation has an interest in escaping. Of course, each one may have his own especial interests — e.g. one of them may have the only tool box and so be in a position to extort money from the rest. This provides the reasoning for another liberal individualist conception of the public interest: the public interest as the interest of the typical or representative citizen who has no special interest at stake. In the pollution case, the public interest would be the interest in the clean air that results from the controls, since that is the interest of the modal person. The industrialist's interest is a special interest, and thus is not to be included in the public interest. And, furthermore, according to this account, this special interest is to be subordinated to the public interest.

But this raises a fundamental problem: how are we to distinguish special interests which are to be subordinated to the public interest from legitimate special interests? The obvious answer, of course, is that any special interests which are not in opposition to the public interest are legitimate and are to be upheld, while those which conflict with it are, at best, suspect. This analysis has the additional attraction that it seems to provide a basis for distinguishing what we have called 'public' or 'sections of the public' from vested or sectional interests (see sec. II.B). Special interests that characterise members of a section of the public would not oppose the interests of the typical member of the *general* public. By contrast, those persons and groups with special interests opposed to the interest of the general public are, as it were, removed from the public altogether.

Unfortunately for this analysis, however, not all interests opposed to that of the typical person are assumed illegitimate or suspect. Liberal arts students have a special interest in government aid to liberal arts education; but having to pay the resulting taxes is hardly in the interest of the representative or typical person. Yet even a liberal who was uncertain whether the average taxpayer gained from such aid would resist classing such students with industrialists opposing pollution controls. He may well feel that the student interest is a legitimate interest, worthy of being promoted, whatever its effect in lower taxes on the interest of the typical citizen; and if he cannot make the case in terms of the public interest, he will take care not to make it appear contrary to it. Perhaps he will talk of 'doing right by our children' or 'ensuring to our future citizens the free choice of educational programmes'. It seems that only if the special interest is one which is not to be advanced, does its opposition to the public interest enter into the question. As far as the individualist model is concerned, *the* public interest can only signal a conclusion, not an argument. Once the arguments have been weighed, the decision is confirmed by the rhetorical stamp of approval 'and this is the public interest'. This would seem to accord with Bentham's suspicion of the use of public interest in political discourse. Yet if the individualist dismisses the 'public interest' as mere rhetoric, he needs to explain why it is effective rhetoric in liberal societies. To be effective it must appeal to something that evokes a positive response within the liberal conception. Individualist theories find it hard to say what that something is.

Participation in Politics. We have examined at some length the notion of public interest so as to show just how difficult it is to formulate a consistently individualist conception that can do the sort of work often assigned to 'public interest' in liberal discourse. Another aspect of liberal theory that seems more than a little foreign to the individualist model is concern for participation in public life. Apart from a short spell in the 1950s when liberal writers were disposed to defend political apathy as a welcome respite from the excesses of ideology, liberalism has generally set considerable store by widespread participation in public affairs, not only through the political process but by involvement in community matters. As is so often the case, Mill supplies the representative liberal text:

> Still more salutary is the moral part of the instruction afforded by the participation of the private citizen, if even rarely, in public functions. He is called upon, while so engaged, to weigh interests not his own; to be guided, in case of conflicting claims, by another rule than his private partialities: to apply, at every turn, principles and maxims

which have for their reason of existence the common good ... He is made to feel himself one of the public, and whatever is for their benefit to be for his benefit. Where this school of public spirit does not exist, scarcely any sense is entertained that private persons, in no eminent social situation, owe any duties to society, except to obey the laws and submit to the government. There is no unselfish sentiment of identification with the public. Every thought or feeling, either of interest or duty, is absorbed in the individual and in the family.[23]

According to the individualist model, 'public life' is that sector of social activity associated with the polity, either with the performance of official functions, as officers of the state, or with forms of political activity aimed directly or indirectly at influencing the outcomes of state decision-making. But surely this fails to capture the crux of Mill's plea. In this passage Mill is insisting that we need to concern ourselves with the general affairs of the community if we are to think of ourselves as members of the public. We must, Mill insists, not only experience those aspects of life in which our particular private interests reign, but also engage in those activities which induce us to think of the general, that is public, interest. Now it is not clear why anyone accepting the individualist model would say any of this or just what he could mean by it if he did. What would it mean, for instance, for an individualist to value consciousness of his membership in an aggregation? Why would an individualist seek an 'unselfish sentiment of identification with the public'? And what does it mean for a person to consider public interests that, as Mill says, are 'not his own' and do not concern his 'private partialities'? The individualist model just does not seem able to bear the weight of this idea of the public. Not surprisingly, therefore, we find in the liberal tradition, alongside the dominant individualist model, a second, organic, model to which liberals turn when the resources of the first are too impoverished to express adequately their intuitions about the relations of individuals in society.

III. An Organic Model

Liberal theory has been shaped not only by Hobbes, Locke and Bentham but also by Rousseau and Hegel. These latter have infused into much liberal thinking the idea that societies or nations possess a characteristic unity that separates them from mere aggregations of individuals. Whether or not these two perspectives can be, or indeed need be, reconciled is of course an important issue for liberal theory, and we shall briefly address the question in section IV.[24] Now, however, our point is merely that liberal thought does indeed possess an 'organic' strain and that some things that liberalism wants to say about publicness and privateness cannot be explained without resort to it.

We have sought to make this second model comparable, as far as is consistent with its very different thrust, to our exposition of the first. Where we have distinguished four *levels* in the individualist model, here we identify — in a sort of Hegelian spirit — four *modes* of publicness and privateness. Some modes correspond to levels while others do not. And, perhaps most interestingly, this second model sometimes deems private what to the individualist is public. We hope to show later that these conflicts are reflected in liberal theory.

A. The First Mode: The Publicness of Wholes and the Privateness of Aggregations

Running throughout the writings of Rousseau, Hegel, Green, Bosanquet and others is the distinction between, on the one hand, a 'people', 'nation' or 'organism' and, on the other, a 'mass', 'aggregation' or, as Ritchie so nicely puts it, a 'heap' of individuals.[25] Consider, for example, the following passage from Rousseau's *Social Contract*:

> No matter how many separate individuals a single person might enslave, they would amount to nothing but a master and his slaves, not at all to a people and its ruler; it would be, perhaps, an aggregation but not an association; it has no public good and no body politic. Even if he should enslave half the world, he remains only a particular individual, his interest, always something apart from the interest of the others, is never anything except a private interest.[26]

To Bosanquet, Rousseau's doctrine rests on what he calls the 'fundamental contrast between a mere aggregate and an organic unity'.[27] Aggregations, according to such theorists — as well as the *Oxford English Dictionary* — are 'wholes composed of many particulars'. In contrast, the *O.E.D.* tells us that an 'organism' is an 'organised body, consisting of mutually connected and dependent parts constituted to share a common life'.

Both Rousseau and Bosanquet relate the public/private distinction to this contrast. Where an aggregation is a collection of private, particular persons, without what Bosanquet calls a 'public or truly general aspect',[28] an organic unity is marked precisely by such generality and commonality — hence, according to this model, by publicness. The *basic principle of differentiation* for this model is thus between the public as that which pertains to the whole, i.e. the general, and the private as that which concerns groups and individuals in their particularity. This principle of differentiation is quite different from the individualist model's distinction between the private as specified and the public as unspecified. 'Particular' as used here does not mean that which concerns a specific person but rather that which relates to any or every person apart from his character as a member of the whole. Similarly, the 'general' is not the unspecified, but rather that which pertains to the organised body as a whole. Publicness is not just what relates to everyone, for on this model something could concern each and every member of the social organism and yet not be public. An interest, for example, in personal luxury may mark each member of the community, but because it relates to each in his particularity it is not a truly general concern, comparable to the interest in the economic well-being of the society.

The method of this model, then, is to start by examining groups of people and characterise as public those things that pertain to the group as a whole; the private is that which applies to the members considered particularly, even to something that contingently applies to each one of them alike. Thus whereas the individualist model takes the individual person as logically the most primitive notion, in the organic model the most primitive notion is the social group. Fundamental to the organic view is Hegel's conviction that we cannot proceed atomistically and build on the basis of single individuals[29] if we are to understand the nature of social wholes. As L.T. Hobhouse put it, 'every association of men is legitimately regarded as an entity possessing certain characteristics of its own, characteristics which do not belong to the individuals apart from their membership of that association'. Consequently, 'in any human association it is true, in a sense, that the whole is something more than the sum of its parts'.[30] Not of course that organic theorists agree on that sense: some, such as Hobhouse and T.H. Green, stress the individuality of the parts much more than others.[31] Nevertheless, they do agree that publicness arises out of a certain bond between members of an organic group, and hence can never be explained by an account stressing aggregation.

B. The Second Mode: The Publicness of the State and the Privateness of Civil Society

Political association, and more particularly the state, provides the institutional structure that integrates and organises the whole. To

Ritchie the state was 'society organised',[32] to Ernest Barker it was 'a juridically organised nation',[33] while to Dewey it was 'a public articulated and acting through its representative officers'.[34] Accordingly, the transition in this model from the first to the second mode of publicness is effected by the idea of *an institutional realisation* of what exists in the first mode as an abstract notion of an organic whole. Similarly, in this model, civil society and the family provide the institutional framework within which individuals, socially aggregated by the necessities of competition and collaboration, pursue their particular, i.e. private, ends.

The state has usually been thought necessary for the realisation of the public for at least two reasons. First, it helps provide the boundaries of a 'people'. Although linguistic, religious or other shared cultural values may fairly well identify a people, the boundaries of the state are likely to be much sharper. And of course the state's boundaries may be especially important in delimiting the public if its population is not as homogeneous as the idea of a 'people' suggests.[35] But secondly, a state — or, perhaps more accurately, a government — is necessary to provide the public or community with the capacity for agency and for the pursuit of collective goals. As nineteenth-century liberal nationalists like Mazzini emphasised, a nation requires a state to give effect to its will.[36]

In contrast to the state, which is the institutional realisation of the group as a whole, civil society is a system composed of 'private persons whose end is their own interest'.[37] But this system of private ends is not ultimately self-regulating; as in the individualist model, the organic state provides through law for the 'effective adjustment of the claims of individuals'.[38] But here it is not the servant of individual (particular) interests, no matter how widely shared: 'particular interests which are common to everyone', Hegel maintained, 'fall within civil society and lie outside the absolutely universal interest of the state proper'.[39] So for Rousseau one of the chief dangers is that overly strong private interests may capture the state, turn it into an instrument of the private, and so destroy it.[40]

Without doubt, liberal political attitudes draw on such conceptual resources, even if the particular theorists we have cited are not always to be found in the liberal pantheon. J.S. Mill and, more recently, John Rawls, have argued that although in economic activity the individual can properly be guided by his own interests, it is wrong to be so guided in civic affairs, where the public, not his private, good ought to be before his mind.[41] Now if, as the individualist model postulates, the state is essentially a framework for the satisfaction of private interests, it is difficult to see why one should not vote according to his private interests. After all, if one can vote according to one's interests at a shareholders' meeting, why can't one do likewise on election day — the shareholders' meeting of the biggest joint-stock company of all, the state? Yet, as Ritchie said of himself and many fellow liberals, 'some of us believe, with Burke, that the State is not simply a joint-stock company or a private club. Some of us really do believe that, in some respects, society is an organism...'[42] And thus we find in the liberal tradition the conviction that '[p]arty government, like every other, if selfishly worked, is bad...'[43]

C. *The Third Mode: Public and Private Life*

We cited earlier, as an instance of a liberal attitude that assorted ill with the individualist model, the importance attached by J.S. Mill to participation by the 'private citizen' (i.e. by a member of the polity holding no public office) in 'public functions', decrying the total absorption of individuals in personal or family affairs. This distinction between the *domains of public and private life*, understood as two kinds of activity, is captured by the transition to the third mode of the organic model, the *practical realisation*, as against the institutional realisation, of publicness and privateness.

Someone who takes part in public life or public affairs is actively concerned with the general affairs of the community, but not necessarily involved with government. While politicians are essentially concerned with them, not all bureaucrats are. 'Public officials', as agents of the state, are public in the second mode, but their actual activities may be narrowly administrative — not at all what we mean by being 'in public life'. Conversely, many who have no formal tie to the state, or only the minimal one of citizenship, are involved in public affairs or are participants in public life. To be sure, as the state is considered the guardian of the public interest, public life and public affairs often do relate somehow to state activity. But they need not, and even when they do, the relation is often tenuous.

Bosanquet — often accused of being something of a state worshipper — was quite clear that political action was but a subset of public activity. According to him, we ought to use 'public' 'in order to indicate those functions and interests which are more than private, and demand in some way the best attention of the community, and then to distinguish within the class so indicated the functions which are strictly political from those which might rather be described as social or as public without being political'.[44] Not only Bosanquet, but such 'solid liberals' as Mill and F.A. Hayek are committed to the idea that a large part of public activity ought to take place in non-political, voluntary associations. Like Mill,[45] Hayek stresses that 'in a truly free society, public affairs are not confined to the affairs of government (least of all central government) and public spirit should not exhaust itself in an interest in government'.[46] In this mode, then, private activity is contrasted with public, not in the sense of political, but of civic.

Now on the face of it, the Hegelian categories of civil society and the family fall squarely within the private rather than the civic realm, just as they do in the individualist model. Yet it is not clear, at least of civil society, that liberalism sees it wholly in that way. Classical liberalism relied largely on an economic theory that supposed that, subject to certain qualifications, public good would be maximised through free contractual relations between individuals, each attending rationally and legitimately to his private interest. With the emergence of large-scale corporate enterprises, sectional associations of producers, and trade unions, many liberals have lost confidence in this spontaneous harmony, even as a possibility, under the actual conditions of civil society in developed nations. In the theory of the competitive market, a decision by a single participant – consumer or producer – would have no significant effect on the public interest. But according to many liberals, such as J.K. Galbraith and Charles Lindblom, this is true nowadays only in a few relatively unimportant parts of the economy. A great automobile corporation is capable of rocking, if not wrecking, an entire nation's economy by its policy choices, and its policy-makers are perfectly well aware that this is so. 'Businessmen thus become a kind of public official and exercise what, in a broad view of their role, are public functions. The significant logical consequence of this for polyarchy', which is Lindblom's term for liberal democracy, 'is that a broad area of public decision making is removed from polyarchal control.'[47]

From anti-trust legislation to nationalisation, liberals have sought ways to bring these economic giants under either the impersonal control of the market order or the public control of the state. (See, however, Ch. 8, below, for the distinction between public control aimed at securing the public interest and public control as an ultimate value and for a discussion of other issues raised in these paragraphs.) For only thus could the traditional liberal distinction between the privateness of civil society and the publicness of the state remain intact. But nowadays even liberals very devoted to the ideals of private enterprise can be found looking, albeit sometimes in vain, to these economic titans for signs of 'social responsibility', to subordinate private to the public interest in which, indeed, the corporation's own interest is thought to be embedded. Liberal rhetoric and liberal theory alike to that extent admit a corporate interplay with government. They recognise the importance of economic *policy* in modern industrial states, and that policies emerge not from a spontaneous harmony of economic agents, nor from a disinterested umpire-state enjoying a godlike detachment, but from just that interplay of state and civil society. Industrialists and businessmen come to be seen as guardians or trustees of the public interest, in a way that fits not at all with the individualist conception of the public and the private,[48] but accords well enough with the organic conception that even partial corporations can have a general mode of being as they participate in the greater whole, in public life.[49]

Where the components of civil society in the mode of public and private life are seen to have a general as well as a particular aspect, domestic life seems paradigmatically private, in this model as in the individualist one. Family life has been singled out in the modern world as that realm in which the particular concerns, interests and needs of individuals are dominant and from which political and other public matters are largely excluded. The family has often been conceived as a private refuge from the exacting demands of civil society[50] and the *res publica*.[51] The United States Supreme Court judgement in *Griswold* amply illustrates the way in which the internal relations of marriage and the family are withdrawn both from politics and from other social or public concerns. In upholding in marriage 'a right to privacy older than the Bill of Rights — older than our political parties, older than our school system', the Court called it 'an association that promotes a way of life, not causes; a harmony of living, not political faiths; a bilateral loyalty, not commercial or social projects'.[52]

It might be thought, nevertheless, that the family is a strange paradigm of privateness for a model in which the principle of differentiation is between particularity and generality, between aggregation and wholeness. For there is no difficulty in giving an organic account of the *internal* relations of a family. 'The family . . . is something other than one person, plus another. It is an enduring form of association in which members of the group stand from the beginning in relation to one another, and in which each member gets direction for his conduct by thinking of the whole group and his place in it.'[53] How, then, can the organic model consistently characterise any organic whole as private?

The answer lies in the relativity of the general and particular. Recall Rousseau's worry in *The Social Contract* that if 'sectional associations are formed at the expense of the larger association, the will of each of these associations will become general in relation to its members and particular in relation to the state'.[54] This suggests, then, that each group will form a 'micro-general will' and hence be a small organic association; taken severally, however, these groups will not form an organic whole but rather will present themselves as an aggregation of particular private wills. Now much the same can be said of a family: although each family forms a small organic association, in relation to the community they are particularistic and private. And taken together, all the families would simply constitute an aggregation of particulars, not an organic whole. Just as an aggregation of individual wills can yield only a 'will of all' and not a 'general will', an aggregation of family wills would be also a mere will of all. Consequently, in so far as individuals act as family members or representatives of families rather than as citizens, they do not realise their character as members of the wider organic association, thus, even if the constituents are themselves organic groups, they must grasp their membership in the wider whole if they are to form a community. So when we say that privateness is a characteristic of aggregations of particulars, we must not be taken to imply that the particular units are isolated individuals or aggregations of individuals: the particular units may well be organic wholes themselves. The crucial point is that the particular units of an aggregation are not organised into an organic whole, and thus do not share a common life.

A particular family, however, may well be a perfect organic whole in respect to its own members, and in its organic aspect it has a sort of public life. Family life as a sharing of experiences and concerns is not unlike the common life of the community stressed by organic theorists.[55] Yet, as we suggested in Chapter 1 (pp. 15-16, above) members of the family have their own particular concerns, too, that, in respect to other members of the family, are 'private'; not only the colour of one's room but what one does in it may be claimed as 'private' matters.[56] For the liberal organicist, then, the family is not the ultimately private category, as it was perhaps, for the ancient Athenian who would not have envisaged the possibility that an individual's interests could be private, in opposition to his family's (see Arlene Saxonhouse's account in Ch. 15). Of course in practice the liberal does not contrast such private matters with 'public matters' but rather with 'family matters'. Nevertheless, the family in these contexts is indeed a sort of small public.[57]

This conception accords well with the importance attributed to the family by organic theorists, as a learning ground for participation in the organic life of the community where one first experiences a common life and devotion to a common good. Admittedly, while the family is a first lesson in organic life, it must be transcended if individuals are to take up their positions as members of the larger community. Families that fail to encourage this capacity for a more inclusive common life are thus, for the organicist, perversions of the ideal, being merely schools in particularistic loyalties. 'The family', as Bosanquet said, 'may be the nursery of manhood (including womanhood) and citizenship, or their grave.'[58]

D. *The Fourth Mode: The Public and Private Aspects of Individuals*

The division of social life into public and private spheres implies that every individual who participates in both domains will have a public and a private aspect. As a participant in civil society, the economy, the family etc., he will pursue his own particular goals and interests. But as a member of the organic whole he will have a public character; he will share a common life with his fellow citizens, giving rise to common concerns, interests etc. In Hegelian language, 'he is at one and the same time both a private person and also a thinking consciousness, a will which wills the universal'.[59] This suggests a fourth mode of publicness and privateness: we call this the *individualised realisation* of the public and private.

This notion of (to use Dewey's term) the 'dual capacity' of citizens is fundamental to a great deal of liberal-democratic theory. From Rousseau to the present we encounter the idea that 'each citizen is . . . a private person free within the common limits to pursue his own ends. But each is also an agent of the body politic . . .'[60] And when engaged in politics, such theorists insist that citizens must act in their capacity as public agents. Of course, as Dewey admitted, 'they still have their private interests to serve and interests of special groups, those of family, clique or class to which they belong'. Thus Dewey acknowledged that '[r]arely can a person sink himself in his political function; the best which most men can attain to is the domination by the public weal of their other desires'.[61]

Needless to say, the idea that all citizens have such a dual capacity has not always been realised in practice. Women, for example, have had historically little or no public aspect. Until the twentieth century, not only were most women barred from voting, but, as Susan B. Anthony had discovered earlier, it was often thought improper for women to even speak on public affairs.[62] They were to that extent restricted to the domestic realm – the sphere of private, particular interests. Indeed, to the extent that families have not been organic wholes but rather aggregations dominated by a particular will — which was Rousseau's paradigm of a private group — women have been deprived of even domestic common life. In a significant sense, then, women have been private persons *par excellence*. (Liberalism's attitudes towards the family and, in particular, towards women is the focus of Carole Pateman's analysis in Ch. 12, below.)

E. Liberalism's Difficulties with the Organic Model

The organic model can account for some aspects of liberal theory and practice that pose difficulties for the individualist model. Certainly it has no problems with valuing participation in public life and identification with the public. And neither does it have the individualist model's problems with public interest. Whereas the individualist model has to search and strain for a useful and morally compelling conception of the public interest, the organic model's notion of the public readily lends itself to the idea of a public interest as the general interest of the social whole. And, on the organic model, such an interest may well be opposed to the particular interests of a good many.

Liberals, however, are generally uncomfortable with the organic analysis on at least two related counts. Most obviously, few liberals are entirely at ease with the methodological principle of the model, according to which the social grouping is logically most primitive. To many, undermining the ontological priority of the individual over the group inevitably leads to a parallel undermining of his ethical priority. The charge that Hegelian philosophy is willing to sacrifice the individual for the good of society, because the latter is in some sense more basic or real, is common in liberal writings. But even if we reject any notion of a slide from ontological to ethical priority, the liberal is still apt to be unhappy with an organic account. Because the organic model does not begin with the central experience of an individual aware of himself as a distinct centre of consciousness, it does not seem to capture the importance of private life and privacy in liberalism. The individualist model coheres so well with these commitments because it takes the self-conscious individual with a private mental life as its logical and ideological point of departure: the private is thus obviously essential and valuable. In contrast, to the organicist, participation in social groups is the primary phenomenological fact. Private life is first and foremost participation in particularistic associations and activities. And when this sort of participation is compared to public life, in which each takes part in the common life of the organic whole, the idea of privateness comes much closer to the notion of 'privation' than is typical of liberalism. More fundamentally, the idea of private life and personality implied by the organic analysis seems to depart from the traditional liberal position. Although an individual is certainly a member of a family, clubs, corporations etc., it is not his experience as a member of these groups that is central to the liberal conception of privateness. Indeed the point is rather the opposite. In private we can put aside our many roles and concentrate on the life of the underlying self. In a world without individual privacy we could still be members of various particularistic groups and associations. The liberal's worry is whether such a world has any room for personality. For, most assuredly, the liberal ideal of personality cannot be explained in terms of group memberships, no matter how complex the accounts. (On the relation of roles and personality, see Alan Ryan's analysis in Ch. 6, below.)

IV. Liberalism and the Two Models

Our thesis, then, is that liberalism draws on two very different models of the public and private: a dominant individualist one and a secondary organic one. No single model of public and private can provide a coherent account of all aspects of the public and private in liberal theory and practice. Of course such a single all-embracing model might exist; it would certainly be more elegant than ours. Yet there still might be a reason for preferring our two-model theory, namely, that it deepens our understanding of some of the enduring tensions in liberal thought. The following four instances illustrate the point.

(1) Liberalism provides an ambiguous account of the role of sectional interests. Mill, as usual, nicely illustrates the liberal's ambivalence. On the one hand, Mill argued that 'a great number of the electors will have two sets of preferences — those on private and those on public grounds'; and, included in the former, he tells us, are 'the interests or prejudices of class or sect'.[63] Yet, though Mill was adamant in maintaining that the public good ought to be the voters' sole guide, he nevertheless endorsed election procedures designed to ensure that the views and *legitimate* interests of each class or major group would be represented in the legislature.[64] We have already seen that the individualist model appears unable to provide an adequate account of this distinction between vested interests and the legitimate interests of sections of the public. Ultimately, a thoroughgoing individualist would

have to agree with Bentham that all interests must be taken into account; 'considering some as all, and others as nothing', because the latter conflict with a greater, public interest, and are therefore illegitimate, must be simply a rhetorical flourish. Yet the individualist would still be at a loss to explain the power of such rhetoric. That power stems, in our view, from the belief of many liberals that some sort of class and sect interests do indeed — as the organicist would claim — pose a threat to the public character of the state and its pursuit of the common will. In the end, the attitude of most liberals towards such interests is far more deeply ambiguous than either model would suggest: they believe both that all interests ought to be represented and that some are dangerous and suspect and so ought to be discounted.

(2) A central liberal thesis is that all individuals have, or at least ought to possess, rights. Traditionally, rights have been divided into civil, or 'rights of private action', and political, or 'rights of public action'.[65] As Rawls notes, 'One of the tenets of classical liberalism is that political liberties are of less intrinsic importance than liberty of conscience and freedom of the person.'[66] For the classical liberal, the real value of political rights is in securing the all-important private rights. Others, however, are not nearly so ready to assign such a clear priority to private rights. Green, for example, believed that although the maintenance of private rights can create 'loyal subjects', political participation is necessary to make 'intelligent patriots'.[67] Thus Rawls makes room in his theory for 'different opinions' as to the relative weights of civil and political rights.[68]

Pretty clearly these 'different opinions' about the relative importance of private and public rights relate to our two models. The classical liberal favours private rights because his is a world of private individuals: the state, and thus political rights, are merely elaborate devices enabling individuals to efficiently pursue their private ends. For the organicist, of course, public rights and the political participation they secure encourage the individual 'to regard the work of the state as a whole, and to transfer to the whole the interest which otherwise his particular experience would lead him to feel only in that part of its work that goes to the maintenance of his own and his neighbour's [private] rights'.[69]

(3) We observed earlier (pp. 44-47), when looking at the possible shortcomings of the individualist model, that a theory of liberalism that relied exclusively on that model to account for liberal values and judgements would find it hard to explain the rhetorical effectiveness of

the claim that a course of action is 'in the public interest'. We were able to suggest ways in which an individualist might invoke particular public interests as substantial reasons for decisions, but none of these interpretations seemed strong enough to explain why describing a course as 'in the public interest' should appear to clinch a case for overriding private rights. And this is a move that is made repeatedly, both in judicial pronouncements and in political controversy. That claim, we suggested, is really much more like a stamp of final approval on a decision arrived at on different, substantial grounds; the invoking of the public interest does not add another ground to them.

That is not to say that public interests are never substantial grounds; it is rather that *a* public interest (as distinct from '*the* public interest') need not be conclusive, sometimes because it is opposed by a countervailing public interest, sometimes because it is overridden by a private right. An individualist, we suggested, might fairly comfortably claim a public interest in, for instance, a document's being kept secret for the sake of, perhaps, efficient administration. But it might still be countered by a claim in terms of the rights of a private person to see what information a government department has on file about him, rights recognised by a number of countries in freedom of information or privacy legislation. To be sure, if the outcome of such a confrontation favours official secrecy, it may well be said that *the* public interest overrides the private right in this matter, or even that there can be no private right against the common good, a characteristic organicist formulation.[70] What is more remarkable, however, is that even if the verdict should go the other way, the judgement may very likely wrap up the victorious private right of access in the cloak of a wider public interest in, say, open government, or in sustaining justice, or even in individuals being assured of their rights. While recognising that a public interest is involved may not necessarily require, then, the surrendering of private rights, it does seem to commit the liberal to making his bid for them in terms of some principle that the public allegedly has an interest in safeguarding. And it is not at all clear that a purely individualist rhetoric with an acknowledged concern for private rights would put that onus on him.

An invocation of public interest is not necessarily rhetorically preeminent, then, if the appeal is to a specific public interest. While there is indeed a tendency in liberal rhetoric to express a private right, such as the right to access to information about oneself on public files, in the guise of a public interest – the interest of *any* citizen – that tendency could be seen as evidence of the strength of the individualist model. Such an appeal is always defeasible by a counter-appeal. By contrast, the rhetorical pre-eminence of the appeal to *the* public interest is evidence of the persuasive power of the organic model. The fact that 'public interest' and 'private right' are capable of these transformations goes to show, however, not that these terms are harmoniously functioning elements within a single decision-making model, but rather that such terms, while capable of employment as reasons, can also be emptied of substance and made to function rhetorically to support decisions arising out of quite genuine clashes of public interest and private right which can go either way. It is this clash in liberalism, rather than the spurious harmony, that our double model captures.

(4) This manifestation of liberalism's reliance upon both models points to a wider issue. It is often heard that one of the basic issues of liberal theory is the relation of the individual to society.[71] Now within its own terms each model tells a perfectly consistent story of this relation, and thus again it is difficult to see how a problem could arise. To the individualist, society is an aggregation of individuals; whatever is said of society could be translated into talk about individuals. Similarly, the organicist has a consistent and fairly clear picture of society as a single whole of which individual persons are merely constituents, each being nothing more than terms in various social relations. But try to combine the models, and the individual's relation to society certainly will be a puzzle. He will be seen both as an independent agent standing apart from others and a member intimately tied to a social whole and sharing a common life. And it does not seem at all misleading to say that these are the two pictures of man upon which liberalism draws.

Notes

The authors note with thanks their indebtedness to J. Roland Pennock, Chris Provis, Thomas Scanlon and Fred Whalen, who made helpful comments and suggestions on earlier drafts of this chapter.

1. See Edward Shils, *The Torment of Secrecy* (Free Press, Glencoe, Ill., 1956), pp. 26-27, 154, 235.
2. George Cornewall Lewis, *Remarks on the Use and Abuse of Some Political Terms* (London, 1832), pp. 22-24, as quoted by Brian Barry, *Political Argument* (Routledge and Kegan Paul, London, 1965), pp. 190-91.
3. Jeremy Bentham, *Theory of Legislation*, 2nd edn (Trübner, London, 1871), p. 240, quoted by Barry, ibid., pp. 191-92.
4. This has a reverse side; certain things about us can be known by others but we cannot — logically cannot — know about them ourselves (e.g. that we are under a delusion). This has been called 'counterprivacy'. See André Gombay, 'What You Don't Know Doesn't Hurt You', *Proceedings of the Aristotelian Society* (1979), pp. 239-49.

5. Richard Sennett, *The Fall of Public Man* (Cambridge University Press, Cambridge, 1976), see esp. Ch. 4.

6. See Alexis de Tocqueville, *Democracy in America* (Alfred A. Knopf, New York, 1953), vol. II, Ch. XIII.

7. The debate on how services should be provided to the public provides an example of the importance of recognising the difference between the first and second levels of publicness. The market can be said to provide services to the public in the first level sense that anyone willing and able to pay the market price can obtain them. Those unwilling or unable to pay are, of course, excluded. But such exclusion is impossible for some goods (e.g. defence); to provide them for anyone is to provide them for everyone. Because the market can neither provide such goods efficiently nor allocate their cost fairly, the state may 'purchase' them for everyone, and everyone pays for them in his taxes. But the state also provides some goods from which such exclusion is possible (e.g. transport, medical care, museums). Such goods are public in the first level distributive sense with respect to access and, in the second level aggregative sense too when provided by the state without charge to the user. Anyone can use them (though some may not want to), but everyone pays. See Ch. 8, below.

8. J.S. Mill, *On Liberty* in *Utilitarianism, Liberty and Representative Government* (J.M. Dent, London, 1910), Ch. III, p. 124. See also de Tocqueville, *Democracy in America*, vol. II, p. 10.

9. A passage from Lord Cross's judgement reinforces the view that, whether or not it entails privateness, the specificity implied by a description tied to particular, identifiable persons is not consistent with publicness. 'No group united by a tie of personal relationship such as descent from a common ancestor or of employment by a common employer or of common membership of an association could be a section of the public for the purpose of the law of charity' and could not, therefore, be beneficiaries of a charitable trust, which has to be 'for the benefit of the public or a "section of the public".' (907) The descendants of John Doe, or his employees, or the members of the East Ham Conservative Club could not be, as such, sections of the public. (Lord Cross did not regard this support as conclusive for Charter's case, however, since it arose in a quite different branch of the law.)

10. It is significant that in western cultures a family name has come to form a part of the name by which a person is generally identified, replacing, for the most part, patronymic identification. A symptom of the tension between the traditional view of the nuclear family and the aims of the women's movement, however, is that the relation between family and personal identity – and therefore personal names – is becoming increasingly uncertain; indeed, it is being questioned whether families need be named at all.

11. Thomas Hobbes, *Leviathan* in Michael Oakeshott (ed.) (Basil Blackwell, Oxford, 1947 [n.d.]), p. 113. Emphasis added; author's italics romanised.

12. Michael Oakeshott, *On Human Conduct* (Clarendon Press, Oxford, 1975), pp. 147ff. For a consideration of the type of relations existing among members of a *res publica*, see also Sennett, *The Fall of Public Man*, pp. 3-4.

13. Jeremy Bentham, *Introduction to the Principles of Morals and Legislation*, J.H. Burns and H.L.A. Hart (eds.) (Athlone Press, London, 1970), Ch. I, §4.

14. See Peter M. Blau, *Exchange and Power in Social Life* (J. Wiley, New York, 1964); also W.J.M. Mackenzie's discussion of E.C. Banfield, *Political Influence* (Free Press, Glencoe, Ill., 1961) in *Politics and Social Science* (Penguin Books, Harmondsworth, 1967). Mackenzie, describing exchange analyses of metropolitan politics, uses the phrase 'a market in influence' (p. 238).

15. Especially significant are the multinational corporations which possess resources beyond the control of any particular state. According to one study of

these corporations, 'There is increasing concern around the world that global corporations are in a position to dominate governments, dislocate national economies, and upset world currency flows. Corporate managers have such power to shift capital, develop (or suppress) technology, and mold public moods and appetites that even the most powerful governments worry about their ability to control them.' Richard J. Barnet and Ronald E. Müller, *Global Reach: The Power of the Multinational Corporations* (Simon and Schuster, New York, 1974), p. 23.

16. The term 'social contract' has of course actually been used to describe the agreement between Britain's former Labour government and the trade unions. For the contrast between the two types of social contracts, i.e. those among the people and those between the people and the government, see J.W. Gough, *The Social Contract*, 2nd edn (Clarendon Press, Oxford, 1957), pp. 2-3.

17. Bentham, *Theory of Legislation*, p. 144.

18. This formulation is imprecise in at least two ways: (i) Some sorts of 'shared' interests are competing while others are complementary. In a race, for example, all share an interest in winning, but clearly the interests are competing; in contrast, members of the same baseball team have a shared, and complementary, interest in winning. (ii) Neither is it unproblematic as to what constitutes 'joint' enjoyment. It may mean merely that we all use it, though it is used by each individually (e.g. a footpath). Or it might mean that we use it together as a collectivity (e.g. a town meeting hall). However, this general formulation suffices for our purposes. See Barry, *Political Argument*, pp. 229-33.

19. See Barry, ibid., pp. 229-36, for arguments aimed at strengthening this conception of public interest.

20. *Taking Rights Seriously* (Harvard University Press, Cambridge, Mass., 1978), p. xi. Dworkin, however, uses the term in reference to rights which, he says, trump policy considerations.

21. 'The Public Interest', *Proceedings of the Aristotelian Society* (1964), supp. vol. 38, pp. 1-18, at §v.

22. Alternatively, we could say that they were in the interest of any member of the public; this conception of public interest could thus be stated on either level one or two.

23. *Considerations on Representative Government* in *Utilitarianism, Liberty, and Representative Government*, Ch. III, p. 217.

24. Hobhouse considers the question in some detail. See *The Metaphysical Theory of the State* (Allen and Unwin, London, 1926), Lecture 1.

25. D.G. Ritchie, *The Principles of State Interference: Four Essays on the Political Philosophy of Mr Herbert Spencer, J.S. Mill and T.H. Green* (George Allen and Co., London, 1902), p. 13.

26. Rousseau, *The Social Contract*, Bk. I, Ch. 5 (our translation).

27. B. Bosanquet, *The Philosophical Theory of the State* (Macmillan, London, 1951), p. 105.

28. Ibid.

29. G.W.F. Hegel, *The Philosophy of Right*, T.M. Knox (trans.) (Clarendon Press, Oxford, 1945), supp. to §156, p. 261.

30. Hobhouse, *The Metaphysical Theory of the State*, p. 27.

31. Cf. T.H. Green, *Prologomena to Ethics*, A.C. Bradley (ed.) (Clarendon Press, Oxford, 1980), p. 193:

The saying that "a nation is merely an aggregate of individuals" is indeed fallacious, but mainly on account of the introduction of the emphatic "merely". The fallacy lies in the implication that the individuals could be what they are, could have their moral and spiritual qualities, independently of their existence in a nation ... But it is none the less true that the life of a national has no real existence except as the life of the individuals composing the nation ...

32. Ritchie, *The Principles of State Interference*, p. 23n.

33. Ernest Barker, *Reflections on Government* (Oxford University Press, London, 1942), p. xiv.
34. John Dewey, *The Public and Its Problems* (Swallow Press, Chicago, 1954), p. 67.
35. Political organisation certainly assisted in developing a 'public life' in the United States. The Austro-Hungarian Empire, however, never achieved one. The organic model's condition for being a state is not necessarily satisfied by every polity. Though political organisation helps to create a common life, it does not necessarily bring it about where cultural divisions go deep.
36. See Giuseppe Mazzini, *Selected Writings*, N. Gangulee (ed.) (L. Drummond, London, 1945), Pts. II & IV.
37. Hegel, *The Philosophy of Right*, §187, p. 124.
38. Bosanquet, *The Philosophical Theory of the State*, pp. 172-73.
39. Hegel, *The Philosophy of Right*, §288, p. 189.
40. Rousseau, *The Social Contract*, Bk. II, Ch. 3. Bosanquet says of Rousseau's theory that it 'presupposes that the whole always acts according to its idea as a whole, and neither is "captured" by individual interests nor transgresses the limits set to its action by restriction to true public concerns'. *The Philosophical Theory of the State*, p. 88.
41. For Mill see: *Principles of Political Economy*, Sir William Ashley (ed.) (Augustus M. Kelley, Fairfield, N.J., 1976), Bk. II, Ch. i and ii; Bk. IV, Ch. vi, §2; *Considerations on Representative Government*, Ch. X, pp. 298-300. For John Rawls see *A Theory of Justice* (The Belknap Press of Harvard University Press, Cambridge, Mass., 1971), pp. 234, 360.
42. Ritchie, *Principles of State Interference*, pp. 72-73.
43. E.F. Carritt, *Ethical and Political Thinking* (Clarendon Press, Oxford, 1947), p. 153.
44. Bosanquet, *Social and International Ideals* (Macmillan, London, 1917), p. 123.
45. 'Centralisation' in J.M. Robson (ed.), *Essays on Politics and Society* (University of Toronto Press, Toronto, 1977), pp. 603-4.
46. F.A. Hayek, *Law, Legislation and Liberty*, vol. 2: *The Mirage of Social Justice* (University of Chicago Press, Chicago, 1976), p. 151.
47. Charles E. Lindblom, *Politics and Markets* (Basic Books, New York, 1977), p. 172.
48. 'In place of a doctrine of laissez-faire, founded on the claim that private profit-making promotes the general happiness, business spokesmen began to speak of service to the community, of the social responsibilities of industry. Managers were represented as professionals, whose authority derived from their expertise, and whose responsibilities were social in nature: they served the community rather than owners of capital.' David Miller, *Social Justice* (Clarendon Press, Oxford, 1976), p. 307.
49. Bosanquet, *The Philosophical Theory of the State*, pp. 259-60.
50. According to Sennett, the idea that the 'stable bourgeois' family is 'the antithesis of public life and its discontents' took root in the mid-nineteenth century. *The Fall of Public Man*, pp. 177ff.
51. See Hannah Arendt, *The Human Condition* (University of Chicago Press, Chicago, 1958), p. 38.
52. *Griswold* v. *Connecticut*, 381 U.S. 479 (1965).
53. John Dewey and James H. Tufts, *Ethics*, rev. edn (Henry Holt, New York, 1932), p. 332.
54. *The Social Contract* (our translation), Bk. II, Ch. 3. Our principle of differentiation for this model seems assumed in Maurice Cranston's translation of *The Social Contract*; rather than wills that are 'particular (*particulière*) in relation

to the State', Cranston's translation reads 'private in relation to the State'. (Penguin Books, Harmondsworth, 1968).

55. See e.g. T.H. Green, *Lectures on the Principles of Political Obligation* in *Works of Thomas Hill Green* (Longman's, London, 1889), vol. II, para 238.

56. See S.I. Benn, 'The Protection of Privacy', *Australian Law Journal*, 52 (Nov.-Dec., 1978), pp. 601-12 and 686-92, at p. 603.

57. This relativity of the general and particular applies to the community and the state too; as Bosanquet suggested, in some ways 'your family is to your country as your country [is] to mankind'. *Social and International Ideals* (Macmillan, London, 1917), p. 4, but see also pp. 291-95. The state, like the family, is general and public in respect to its members but particularistic in regard to the rest of mankind. Hegel's reluctance to say so notwithstanding, it does not seem wrong to say, with Hobbes, that states confront each other as 'private persons'.

58. Bosanquet, *Social and International Ideals*, p. 5.

59. Hegel, *The Philosophy of Right*, para. 308, p. 200.

60. Joseph Tussman, 'The Citizen as Public Agent' in Henry S. Kariel (ed.), *Frontiers of Democratic Theory* (Random House, New York, 1970), pp. 17-29, at p. 26.

61. Dewey, *The Public and Its Problems*, p. 76.

62. *Dictionary of American Biography* (Charles Scribner's Sons, New York, 1928), vol. I, p. 319.

63. *Considerations on Representative Government* in *Utilitarianism, Liberty, and Representative Government*, Ch. X, p. 306.

64. See Dennis F. Thompson, *John Stuart Mill and Representative Government* (Princeton University Press, Princeton, 1976), p. 19.

65. Barker, *Reflections on Government*, p. 30.

66. Rawls, *A Theory of Justice*, p. 229.

67. Lack of which, Green thought, was the chief reason for Rome's fall. *Lectures on the Principles of Political Obligation*, para. 122.

68. Rawls, *A Theory of Justice*, p. 230.

69. Green, *Lectures on the Principles of Political Obligation*, para. 122.

70. See e.g. A.J.M. Milne, *Freedom and Rights: A Philosophical Synthesis* (Humanities Press, New York, 1968), p. 333.

71. See Hobhouse, *Liberalism* (Oxford University Press, Oxford, 1964), Ch. VII.

3 PUBLIC LAW — PRIVATE LAW

Alice Erh-Soon Tay and Eugene Kamenka

I. Roman Law and Western Development

A conceptual distinction between public and private law has long been central to the Western legal tradition and therefore to much Western social, legal and political thought. In the formulation attributed to Ulpian, it was enshrined, in identical words, in the opening chapter of each of the two great classics of Roman law, the *Digest* and the *Institutes*, issued in the name of the (Eastern) Roman Emperor Justinian in 533/4 A.D.: 'Public law is that which pertains to the Roman State, private that which concerns the well-being of the individual.' For the 6th century Roman Imperial lawyer the distinction was one concerning the parties involved, or perhaps of the end in view, of the interest served and protected; it was not a distinction of origin or of the greater universality of public law. The state regulated and laid or confirmed the foundations of private law as much as it regulated and laid or confirmed the foundations of public law. In a sense, indeed, private law was the more universal institution, even if in cases of conflict it gave way to public law. The demands, concerns and advantages of the Roman State, or of any other historical state, though overriding, were a matter of time and geography, of specific traditions and enactments, of positive law. Private law, on the other hand, the *Institutes* tell us (under the influence of Stoicism), 'is threefold, for it consists of natural precepts, of those observed generally by nations and of those of a given State' — i.e. of precepts drawn from natural law, of precepts drawn from the *ius gentium* or the legal customs common to civilised nations and of precepts drawn from the positive law of the specific community in question. Classical Roman legal writers, indeed, had no great interest in public law except for the purpose of distinguishing it from private law and that purpose was primarily in the context of university instruction, not of practice. (The *Institutes*, after all, were written for teaching purposes.) Only private law came to be considered of genuine intellectual interest, in the potential richness of its conceptual structure and the fundamental universal character of its moral and legal principles. Classical Roman lawyers wrote almost nothing on public law and the legacy they have left us, with its overwhelming influence on Western legal thought, is entirely a legacy of private law. No doubt, this attitude of theirs itself helped to shape subsequent events and opinions, but they were not wrong in seeing Roman public law, or perhaps any public law, indeed, as far more time-bound and particular. Roman public law, indeed, is dead and gone, while Roman private law, through subsequent receptions, continues to stand at the centre of the Western legal tradition. It even came to inform the medieval and post-medieval conceptions of proper legal relations between states, i.e. our present public international law. *Pacta sunt servanda* is a conception stemming from Roman private law, not from Roman public law; so, too, is the public international law conception of the legal personality and equality of sovereign states.

Within the Western legal tradition, it has often been argued, there is an important set of distinctions between Roman law and the initially independent legal traditions of the Germanic peoples that shaped much of the common law, for instance. Early Roman law was based on a central concept of authority, or of two authorities, from which all power and legitimacy derived. There was, first, the authority of the Roman State, the People and the Senate of Rome, over the legally competent citizen. It was a strong authority, also exercised by the magistrates as representatives of the People of Rome and therefore of the community as a whole. This was originally the source of the *ius publicum*. We have no specific text which connects such a *ius publicum* in Rome with the immunity of magistrates and with the exemption of the state from the rules of conveyancing, though the term *publicum* initially referred to the *property* of the state. Some authorities, such as J.A.C. Thomas, believe that in Roman law 'the very fact of public participation — through magistrate or functionary — in a transaction made it one of public law and thus quite distinct from a private transaction, identical in economic function'.[1] It is not clear to us now how, if at all, the didactic division between public and private law operated technically in Roman practice; Ulpian does elaborate slightly in the *Digest* to say that public law concerns religion, the priesthood and the magistracies. Certainly, Ulpian's definition of public law, quoted above, as 'pertaining to the Roman State' — does not make it absolutely clear whether he is defining in terms of the status of the parties involved or of the interest served, whereas his definition of private focuses on the well-being of the individual. There are two competing views of the basis of the public/private distinction in law here to which we return. What the Romans themselves thought at Ulpian's period or earlier is not clear.

The strength of Roman public authority was equalled and reinforced by a second authority — authority of the *pater familias* or male head of household. He had *patria potestas*, legally recognised power, over all others in his household and they had no independent legal capacity. Initially, this was a matter of custom and tradition, with the *ius privatum* developing to regulate relations between formally equal heads of households acting in a private capacity. Gradually, even more importantly, the *ius privatum* was extended through the creative work of the judicial official designated to deal with legal relations between Romans and foreigners, the *praetor peregrinus*, to regulate relations that stood outside pater-familial custom. There were relations between strangers and between Romans and strangers, increasingly significant as commerce developed and as more foreigners flocked to Rome. There is, from the beginning, a connection between private law, equality and universality absent from public law, which is concerned with elevating and exempting — i.e. not with arbitrating between equals, but with treating the parties to a relationship differently, according to their standing and authority.

The ascendancy of Roman private law over Roman public law was, of course, greatly facilitated by the collapse of the single Roman Imperial State and the decline of centralised public authority in the West that followed it. Equally important was the intrusion of Germanic (Frankish) tradition into the new feudal compact on the basis of which medieval society came to be organised. The feudal compact, in keeping with Germanic tradition, was not an act of authority but a voluntary agreement between independent legal persons — one agreeing to serve, the other to provide and protect. It was an enforceable contract which bound the king or lord as much as it bound the subject or liegeman. In a very important sense, it brought the whole basis of political authority and obedience into the area of private law, of relations between individuals capable, for the purposes of law, of abstract equality and of rationally and freely seeking their individual well-being and subordinating themselves voluntarily. Those not capable of such freedom, e.g. serfs, were not fully legal persons.

Such an account of feudalism, admittedly, emphasises certain primary conceptual presuppositions of the feudal contract often obscured for people in established medieval society and for the modern mind by the much more striking *Gemeinschaft* character of feudalism to be discussed below, which gave all private relationships a public character. Nevertheless, one cannot understand European feudalism without recognising that, despite countervailing trends, the feudalisation of Europe meant, to a significant extent, the privatisation of law in Europe. Medieval theory and practice distinguished weakly and confusedly, if at all, between dominion over property and sovereignty. The very administration of justice, or the right to administer it, was seen as belonging to the domain, i.e., as part of the legal powers that went with holding land in a certain way. It could be transferred, sold, exchanged, divided and entailed, much as in England the right to present a parson to the Church — the advowson — could be. Medieval society was a fragmented society; its law was 'open' in the sense of being also fragmented, unsystematic, often uncertain, not a coherent whole or deriving from a single sovereign source. At the basis of the self-perception of medieval *Gemeinschaft* stood not the individual but relationships, those of occupying and acting in a certain status or of belonging to a certain group, at least for the purpose in question. Laws varied from locality to locality, from estate to estate; each legally competent man could in principle be part of many corporations, owe allegiance to many masters. There was territorial law, feudal law, manorial and service law, town law and the law of religious institutions and corporations. Man was subject not to one law but to many laws, he was governed by overlapping or complementary authorities. In this sense, all law was private, particular, not in principle overriding or expressing a universal social or state interest. In another sense, the very distinction between private and public law had no intellectual force or material reality in these conditions — all feudal relationships were both private and public. Feudal society, though rooted in an individual act of fealty, was largely seen not as a collection of individuals but as a system of special or partial — rather than individual — interests and estates, represented by *parlements*, corporations and other bodies. The affair of state was another such interest, the *chose publique*, which was the special affair of the king and in that sense as private and particular as the demands of *parlements* and corporations. The evolution of the state as truly public and comprehensive in its claims to authority, the gradual development of public function from a fief through an office to a public and revocable *commission* was a slow affair, not consummated fully until the French Revolution of 1789-99.

In England, the special position of the King and his success, from Henry II onward, in creating a non-feudal and eventually exclusive, royal system of justice led to a somewhat different situation. Justice became public (accessible to all, independent of status) earlier than in most of Continental Europe, but it was not tied to a distinction between public and private law. A single system of royal courts dealt and largely still deals with both. Yet the English state, in legal theory, is more firmly subordinated to a legal system until recently seen as overwhelmingly private in Ulpian's sense; it has not been allowed, since the fall of the Stuarts, to create a separate system of public law treating the state and its officers differently from the way that citizens are treated. Constitutional law, in England, has been seen as consisting of voluntary compacts, undertakings, customs and traditions. The French *droit administratif*, for instance, recognises, indeed exists to protect and regulate, the power of the state to amend or breach contracts with individuals, even unilaterally, because the state occupies a different *status* as a contracting party. *Droit administratif* exists to ensure that the individual shall be justly compensated for any loss caused by such arbitrary acts of authority. Public law (the *droit administratif*) applies wherever an official acting as agent of the public, the state, is involved, and the state is liable on his behalf. The English administrative law, in contrast, developed in the attempt to prevent arbitrary acts of authority by public officers or their failure to act when they had a duty to do so. It rests on the assumption that when an official acts wrongly in his official capacity he ceases to be an official to be obeyed and becomes a private person, putting himself in reach — admittedly through special remedies — of the principles and procedures of a dominantly private law. [See Ch. 4 for a more detailed treatment of the liability of public officials in common law — Eds.] The now much-weakened doctrine that the King can do no wrong put him, and for a time his officers, outside the reach of much of the law, not into a special category of law. Once the state is before the court it appears simply as another party, assuming a private capacity, as it were, through such fictions as the 'nominal defendant' standing in for the Crown, which is thereby, for the purpose of the proceedings, bereft of its majesty, and of its *public* character and authority.

The total story of the development of law in Europe is a complex story in which Germanic and other local customs and laws, direct Roman influences, Christian conceptions in Roman dress, Roman conceptions in Christian dress and subsequent receptions and revivals of classical Roman legal learning intermingle. The contrast between Germanic custom and Roman law, for instance, has long been a *casus belli*, in German legal history at least. The struggle between Germanists and Romanists over the 19th-century German civil codification is well known; the story is told in every subsequent German textbook and history of private law. The contrast was dear to the Nazis; their legal philosopher Carl Schmitt saw deep and fundamental constitutional significance in Point 19 of the 1920 National Socialist Party Programme, with its demand for 'replacing the Roman law, serving a materialistic world-order, with a German common or communal law (*Gemeinrecht*)'.

Not the respect for authority of Roman law, but its private character, its recognition of the abstract individual and the importance of his individual interests, was under attack here, as it has often been by socialists and fascists since.

In fact, of course, there is no pure, or unbroken, Germanic legal tradition. The barbarian conquests of Rome and the legal arrangements of the increasingly self-regulating Western Roman provinces produced in late antiquity and the early Middle Ages a vulgar, simplified Roman law for the use of barbarians and a series of codexes in which Roman and Germanic law became inextricably intermingled. In Italy, itself, knowledge of the *Codex* and the *Institutes* was never lost. With Christianisation, Roman concepts and principles were further strengthened through the growing influence and authority of the representatives and followers of the Bishop of Rome. The Merovingian and Carolingian kings forged a state that came to see itself as the new Holy Roman Empire of the German nation, though it became much too feudalised to restore in any genuine and complete sense the Roman concept of *imperium*. The 12th and 13th centuries, which saw a remarkable early flowering of European nationalisms, saw also a remarkable development of national legal literatures and written laws: Fleta, Glanvill, Bracton and the *Leges Henrici Primi* in England, the *Sachsenspiegel*, the *Schwabenspiegel* and the *Mühlhäuser Rechtsbuch* in Germany, the *Skanske Lov* in Denmark, the *Västgötalagen* and the *Ostgötalag* in Sweden, the work of Beaumanoir in France, the *Fueros* of Léon, Castile, Navarre and Aragón, and the *Siete Partidas*, issued by King Alfonso X in Castile.

Some of these texts begin to show the influence of the equally remarkable revival and reception of classical Roman legal learning that spread from the University of Bologna in the 12th century, both through Gratian's work on canon law and through the renewed study, in the second half of the 11th century, of the Roman private law of the *Digests*, which, with the *Codex* and the *Institutes*, were to be known, from 1583 onward, as the *Corpus Juris Civilis* of Justinian. Glossators, post-Glossators, commentators and conciliar theorists reworked and gave a theoretical structure to the classical Roman legal learning and worked from it toward a theory of statutes and a theory of conflict of laws. But while a formal distinction between private and public law, taken over from Ulpian, lay at the base of this legal learning and was reaffirmed by it, the distinction did not play any central conceptual or even significant part in the actual legislation and legal compilation of the late medieval and early modern period.

There was no practical separation of European law into public and private law until the French Revolution of 1789-99 and the creation of the *Code Napoléon*. The rise of absolutism, however, did lay the foundations for that development, creating the conceptions of public commissions, public service and of a public power and interest independent of and above estates and corporations. Bodin and Hobbes developed the new theory of exclusive and undivided sovereignty. Montesquieu in his *De l'Esprit des Lois* drew a distinction between 'political law' and 'civil law' on the basis of distinguishing between disputes that involve the state and those that involve individuals. He thought it ridiculous to use the same maxims to determine the rights of kingdoms as are used to determine rights of individuals.

The (royalist) Lord Chancellor Francis Bacon at the beginning of the 17th century declared in his *A Preparation Towards the Union of Laws*: 'I consider . . . that it is a true and received division of law into *jus publicum* and *privatum*.'[2] To the Parliamentarians who followed him, however, the division seemed to set the King above the law. Since their victory in the Civil War and the overthrow of the prerogative courts of Star Chamber and High Commission which in the early 17th century threatened to rival the Courts of Common Law in the interest of royal authority, the denial of a practical distinction between private and public law and the rejection of two parallel legal systems has been traditional English legal doctrine, only recently brought into question. The strictly legal doctrine that the King can do no wrong continues to survive, though in ever-more limited form — a survival easily understood if we consider the difficulty of both vesting the symbol of sovereignty in a person and treating that person as one that can be hailed before his or her own courts, i.e., treated as not sovereign. Even English lawyers have not been willing to see such immunity spread rather than contract. Medieval pluralism, the concept of authority spread throughout the society, has shaped English law far more than the concept of sovereignty elevated by Hobbes and Bodin and Bacon.

The medieval *Gemeinschaft* in theory, and medieval and early modern law in practice, saw all social and legal relationships as both private and public. The clear separation of public from private power, interest and activity, as Marx argued, develops with modern, commercial-individualistic society, with the 'bourgeois' (or modern) *Gesellschaft*, though it has a pre-history in the rise of centralised national states, and, to an extent that most Marxists are uncomfortable with, in the conceptual implications of Roman private law and of commercial activity even in pre-medieval urban centres. In social and political theory, it is associated, above all, with the growth of individualism and the social contract theory of the state, with the development of a dichotomy between individualistic, atomised civil society and the public organisation and purpose of the state. The thought of Locke and Rousseau came to be incorporated in the theory and practice of the French Revolution and of the American Revolution before it, where 'magistrates', in the sense of public officers, were proclaimed, on the one hand accountable and on the other hand guardians and representatives of a general or public interest sharply distinguished from and seen as capable of colliding with specific individual interest. Together with these developments went the theory of the separation of powers — the belief that in a constitutional state legislative, judicial and administrative functions must be kept distinct. The French Revolution, accordingly, in its law of 16 August 1790 and 16 Fructidor of the Year III (1795), forbade judges to intervene in matters of administration or to bring members of the administration before them for acts done as part of their office. Instead, by a decree of 6-11 September 1790, administrative controversies were to come before administrative bodies. The Jacobins, after their victory in May 1793, saw matters differently and, exercising undifferentiated powers in their Committee of Public Safety, rejected the separation of powers, as the Soviet Constitution and the Soviet Communist Party do today. But in France, the Jacobins were in turn defeated and in the Constitution of the Year VIII (1800) a Supreme Administrative Tribunal, the *Conseil d'Etat*, was established as the apex of a separate system of administrative law, i.e. of law which is public in the sense of being separated out because it involves the work of the state and its officers.

In Germany, where there was no revolution but also a marked 18th-century growth of state power and of a formalised professional civil service, the development was slower and less clear-cut. In the early modern period, the idea of the unity and indivisibility of law was not yet firmly rooted. Here the Imperial power had not been strong enough to establish an effective centralised power, while the territorial princes in societies organised on the principle of patrimonial estates held a bundle of acquired rights i.e., rights which were derived not simply from their position as princes but from various legal titles and which were confronted by acquired rights of equal force held by their subjects and other bodies. Charles Szladits sketches the situation and subsequent developments well:

> The princes could only exercise their acquired rights of official authority against these acquired rights on the basis of their *ius*

eminens, that is, in the interest of the public good (*ius disponendi de rebus propriis civium salutis publicae causa*). Protection of these acquired rights was granted by the jurisdiction of the imperial courts (*Reichskammergericht* of 1495 and *Reichshofrat* of 1501) where territorial prince and subject could litigate on an equal footing, no difference being made between public and private rights. Consequently, any subject who felt injured in his right by the exercise of official authority (*Hoheitsrecht*) by the prince could sue him before the *Reichskammergericht*.[3]

As Szladits points out, however, this formal equality between subject and prince was eroded by the successful efforts of the latter to gain independence from Imperial power. Their upshot was an all-powerful state the interests of which were held to take precedence over private individual interests. The power of this new 'police-state' (*Polizeistaat*) was justified and extended through the theory of police power (*ius politiae*), whereby the prince had an obligation to protect the welfare and security of his subjects; accordingly, he might rightfully order anything which he deemed to be pursuant to those interests.[4] This conception of the prince as the guardian of the welfare of all entailed that he might legitimately be concerned with even the smallest details of his subjects' private lives, even down to the number of guests that might attend family feasts, and the amount of beer that might be drunk, both subjects of regulation at this time. As Szladits puts it, 'there may be said to have been a "publicization" of private rights'.

Such authoritative police regulations (administration, *Regierung*) as distinct from justice (*Justiz*) were not subject to direct control by law. Police power was an essentially discretionary power exercised through civil servants (as well as special collegiate bodies). Because such power was discretionary, publication even of the rules instructing officials in the administration of their duties (issued under names such as *Mandat, Ordre, Statut*, etc.) was equally at the prince's discretion. By contrast, the administration of justice had to proceed through published, and hence generally known, enactments (*Edikt, Reskripten*, etc.). Moreover, so long as a subject might sue his prince on an equal footing in the imperial courts, these rules of justice could in some way be brought to bear on the prince even in his administrative actions, whereas the prince's own courts had good grounds for dismissing 'police' powers as lying outside their jurisdiction. However, after the Peace of Westphalia (1648), an increasing number of princely territories were freed from this sort of control. The privilege of exemption (*privile-*

gium de non appellando), granted by the Empire, gave the princes supreme legal control over their lands. Because a sovereign could not be sued in his own court, the subject was thus left with no remedy against him. But some remedy against administrative acts was clearly necessary, and was found by distinguishing between, on the one hand, the prince or sovereign state and, on the other, the public patrimony. According to the theory of the fisc (*fiscus*, treasury), the public patrimony belonged to a distinct legal entity, the *Fiskus*, a legal personality held distinct from the prince and subject to the usual laws of property; and, as property law belonged to private law, the fisc was viewed as a private person and so subject to civil jurisdiction. In reality this meant that the subject could now sue the sovereign in the latter's own courts, provided that the subject cast his claim in terms of a property claim. Thus, for example, instead of directly suing the sovereign for expropriation, the fisc could be sued for a forced sale. Indeed, public offices themselves were viewed as contracts for services. Szladits explains how the theory of the fisc was developed to protect citizens against the prince's use of his police power:

> though the civil courts could not abrogate decisions based on the police power of the authorities, they could indirectly hold the *Fiskus* liable for compensation if an 'acquired private right' was injured by the administrative act. Vested [or inherent] private rights (*wohlerworbene Privatrechte*) formed the basis for this enhanced legal protection of the individual against the public administration. Thus it was the development of the theory of the *Fiskus* which subjected the public administration in many fields to private law and to civil jurisdiction. This development coincided with a view prevalent in the early nineteenth century (especially espoused by *Otto Bähr*) that the protectors of justice are the civil courts, in contrast to the French reliance upon administrative jurisdiction.[5]

Only with the development of the constitutional state in the 19th century, when the judicial power became independent of the monarch and both justice and administration, though kept distinct, became subject to the legislature, was the *fiscus* no longer considered an entity apart from the state, but simply the property side of the state. The growth of a measure of democracy, however, also led to growing demands that all disputes between citizens and the public administration should be decided by a judicial authority independent of the administration. Baden, always receptive to French influence, established a formal system of administrative courts in 1863 and Prussia followed in 1872 and 1875. From then on, the Germans, like the French and unlike the English, have had parallel systems of private and public law, though fiscal matters remain in the jurisdiction of the civil courts. At the same time, the general 19th-century movement toward codification, in the wake of the great model provided by Napoleon, also enshrined a more complex and less clear-cut division between private and public law, with codes being assigned, by theoreticians at least, to one or the other. Tables 3.1 and 3.2 summarise the French and German classifications which, according to Szladits, are archetypal, other European legal systems following one or the other.

Table 3.1: Public and Private in French Law

Public Law (*droit publique*)	Private Law (*droit privé*)
constitutional law (*droit constitutionnel*)	private law proper (*droit civil*)
administrative law (*droit administratif*)	commercial law (*droit commercial*)
financial law (*législation financière*)	— including maritime law (*droit maritime*)
public international law (*droit international publique*)	civil procedure (*procédure civile*)
	penal law (*droit pénal*)

	certain special branches of law (in which public law and private law rules are actually intermingled) including:
	— labour law
	  (*droit du travail*)
	— agricultural law
	  (*droit rural*)
	— industrial property law; copyright law
	  (*droit de propriété industrielle; droit d'auteur*)
	— air law
	  (*droit aérien*)
	— forestry law
	  (*droit forestier*)
	— mining law
	  (*droit minier*)
	— insurance law
	  (*droit des assurances*)
	— transport law
	  (*droit des transports*)

	private international law (*droit international privé*)

Based on Charles Szladits, 'The Civil Law System' in Konrad Zweigert *et al.* (eds.), *The International Encyclopedia of Comparative Law*, vol. II, Ch. 2, pp. 21-22.

Clearly there are a number of ambiguous cases. Private international law, for example, in dealing with matters such as the nationality of aliens, includes subjects that seem inherently part of public law. Some authors, indeed, suggest a third category, 'mixed laws', in which they place some types of law normally included in private law (for example, air law, labour law, commercial law). Again, civil procedures and penal law are sometimes distinguished (as *droits sanctionnateurs*) from private law on the grounds that their aim is the enforcement of private law, some authors maintaining that the former is more closely bound to public law than to private. Indeed, as Table 3.2 shows, penal law and civil procedures are included under public law in the German didactic classification; and even in common law, where the distinction between private and public law is theoretical rather than practical, theorists have never been happy with treating criminal law as falling unambiguously in either camp.

Table 3.2: Public and Private in German Law

Public Law (öffentliches Recht)	Private Law (Privatrecht)
constitutional law (Verfassungsrecht)	civil law proper* (bürgerliches Recht)
administrative law (Verwaltungsrecht)	the special part of the private law (Sonderprivatrecht) which includes:
tax law (Steuerrecht)	— commercial law (Handelsrecht)
penal law (Strafrecht)	— law of companies (Gesellschaftsrecht)
criminal procedure (Strafprozessrecht)	— law of negotiable instruments (Wertpapierrecht)
civil procedure (Zivilprozessrecht) including: — the law of execution (Zwangsvollstreckungsrecht) — bankruptcy (Konkursrecht)	— copyright (Urheberrecht) — law of competition (Wettbewerbsrecht) including: • patents (Patentrecht) • trademarks (Warenzeichenrecht) • designs (Geschmackmuster)
law of non-contentious litigation (freiwillige Gerichtsbarkeit)	— private international law (internationales Privatrecht)
church law (Kirchenrecht)	
public international law (Völkerrecht)	

*Contained in the Civil Code (BGB) and its supplementary laws.

Within the German classification, public law (*offentliches Recht*) broadly speaking covers the legal relations between states, the organisation of the state and of other public bodies, the relation between such public bodies, and between them and individuals. As with French law, not all types of law can be fitted into one or the other category: although labour law (*Arbeitsrecht*) is sometimes included in private law, it is typically viewed as a field *sui generis* which is neither part of public nor private law.

In all the states that follow these models, the classification of laws into private and public law is based on the division of laws into various codes. Private law (civil law), civil procedure, commercial law, penal law and criminal procedure have in general been codified. Public law, by contrast, if we exclude criminal law and procedure and civil procedure, seen as public law only by some systems and theories, exists largely in the form of special enactments, with no codified statement of its general roles and principles.

Common lawyers, in the absence of substantial codification or of an imposed legislative division between private and public law, have thought primarily in terms of the grand traditional divisions of contract, torts, criminal law, real property, succession, equity and trust, constitutional law and such newer branches as administrative law, labour law, landlord and tenant, etc. There has been no inbuilt tendency to categorise these branches as belonging to realms of private or public law; and theoretical attempts to do so have been under continental influence or part of a modern tendency to see public law, in a conceptual sense, as increasingly overwhelming private law. English law, and English judges in particular, have focused their attention rather on a conception of the public interest as the specific interest of the state or the community to which private interests may sometimes have to give way. In the 15th and 16th centuries, the requirements of the 'common weal' were seen by lawyers as quite overriding; in the 18th and 19th centuries, the emphasis came to be placed on a concept of striking the balance in specific areas of conflict, e.g. the restraint of trade, between public interests and private or social interests, none of them seen as in principle always subordinate or superior. Public interest was here seen quite specifically as a particular interest in each case; only in the 20th century has there been a tendency to interpret the public interest more widely by linking it with a concept of broad public and social policies intended to guide both law and life in various social areas. [For the shifting senses of 'public interest' and its relation to private rights in the development of the common law, see Paul Finn in Ch. 4, below – Eds.]

Marxist-socialist countries, after an initial radical rejection of bourgeois legalism in the USSR in the 1920s and in Maoist China in 1957-77, have all adopted the general structure and formal division of codes and legal areas of the continental civil law systems, though public law in the sense of administrative law is always called 'State law', and, quite recently, 'Constitutional law'. Private or 'civil' law in the strict sense is defined as based on the relation of debtor and creditor, which will continue as long as money exists, though contracts between state enterprises are adjudicated through a special system of state arbitration, itself formally legalistic in practice, if not in theory. In the 1920s, E.B. Pashukanis, soon to become a member of the Communist Academy and Head of the Soviet Institute of Law and Socialist Construction, had argued that socialism meant the disappearance of the juridical category from human affairs, since law was based on the abstract and alienated individualism of a bourgeois commodity-producing society and not on conceptions of social production and social use. The essentially private, individualist concepts of 'bourgeois' law — e.g. 'fault' and 'guilt' — would give way to the working out of social policies and the administrative application of socio-technical norms through plan; liability and punishment, in a transitional stage, would be tied to the non-individualist concepts of 'social harm' and 'social danger'. Mao, in keeping with a strain in Chinese tradition and aspects of Marxist theory, proclaimed that disputes among the people should be resolved informally (and politically) by mediation and conciliation; only disputes between the people and its enemies required law and then a harsh, coercive law that destroyed and reeducated. Both Pashukanis and Mao have fallen from grace. The importance of written, formal law, in part based on general legal conceptions and the past legal experience of mankind, adapted to socialist purposes, is now emphasised in the Soviet bloc and China as necessary for stability, predictability, rationality and fairness, and for the protection of the individual from arbitrary exercise of power (the latter point being much emphasised by Khrushchev and Deng Xiaoping, but not by the present rulers of the USSR or Poland). But while much of the civil law of Marxist-socialist countries is orthodoxly continental in form, legislators there — let alone political leaders, party bureaucrats and secret policemen — do insist, through the Constitutions and other provisions, on the subordinate character of private law and individual rights, making the latter conditional on support of the socialist system and the performance of social duties. The general view, held more strongly now than some years ago, emphasises the basically administrative function of all law — law as a means of steering society.

The struggle between those Soviet and Chinese lawyers who want to introduce an economic code, with its essentially administrative character, and those who think that economic enterprises can also be governed effectively and sufficiently by the general civil code is a struggle between more administrative and more individualistic views of (private) law. But it is recognised and indeed emphasised that such steering requires the promulgation and observance of formal, systematic and complex legal norms which must protect both individuals and social requirements.

II. The Conceptual Distinction

The distinction between public and private law, we have seen, begins in Roman times with a distinction between disputes which involve the state or its functionaries and disputes that involve individuals only. Behind this lurks an even older distinction which Aristotle made between two kinds of justice: commutative or corrective justice and distributive justice. Commutative justice, suitable for the settling of disputes between citizens, proceeded on the principle that parties to a suit, citizens before a judge or jury, must be treated equally. Distributive justice gave to each according to his merit or desert and according to Aristotle was used by the state in allocating offices, prizes and rewards. The *Institutes* brought the two together in the single definition of justice as 'the set and constant purpose to give every man his due', but the Aristotelian distinction has survived in most important legal philosophy and has provided content for much theoretical discussion of the distinction between the principles of private and the principles of public law. Thus Aquinas thought that commutative or corrective justice should govern the economic affairs of individuals while distributive justice should inform the policy of the state. Many, perhaps most, socialists in the 19th and 20th centuries have seen themselves as upholders of distributive as opposed to commutative or corrective justice, and therefore of public law as opposed to private law.

The actual development of Western legal systems and legal classifications, as we have seen, is more complex and ambiguous than the categories of the theorists. The distinction between public and private law has in fact raised three different, if partly related or relatable, issues: (1) Are there or should there be separate systems of justice, of courts and judicial administration for private and public law? (2) Can all law be classified as being either public or private and, if so, on what basis?

(3) Are there general principles or presuppositions of private law and can these be distinguished from the principles and presuppositions of public law?

It is convenient to take the second issue, the basis and scope of the classification into public and private law, first. One reason for this is that there is an obvious sense in which all law is social and public, preceding any given individual and confronting him as something outside himself, backed by the state or the community. The classification of law into public and private is a classification *within* this general feature of law, distinguishing some bodies of law from others within a single system. Various theories have been propounded, all of them bedevilled by the fact that an exhaustive arrangement of laws or even of areas of law into private and public is not part of any Western legal system as opposed to legal theory. (The French approach such an arrangement most closely.) One obvious but not very satisfactory move has been the attempt to define public law as the law regulating relationships in which the state or another public authority participates on at least one side. This theory is popular in France, where it corresponds reasonably well with the basis for separating out the *droit administratif*. But the state takes part in numerous relationships which in other countries or apart from the provisions of the *droit administratif* would be considered private law relations. More German versions of the theory emphasise function and form, rather than mere status of the parties, e.g. the view 'that in public law the dominion (*Herrschaft*) of the state over the individual manifests itself through command (*Befehl*) and constraint (*Zwang*), whereas in private law the relations between equals is characterized by claim (*Forderung*) and action (*Klage*)'.[6] The Swiss lawyer Burckhardt argued[7] that public law is by its nature coercive, mandatory on the individual, whereas private law is permissive or facilitatory law — its norms are applicable only if the parties do not stipulate otherwise and are enforced only on demand, whereas public law is enforced *ex officio*. The social democratic German legal philosopher Gustav Radbruch[8] distinguished between private law as 'coordinating law' which secures interests by reparation and the like, treating all individuals as equals, and public law as 'subordinating law' which prefers some interests to others according to a measure of values built into that law. For Radbruch the distinction between private and public law reflected quite specifically the distinction between corrective and distributive justice. Theorists like Hans Kelsen,[9] on the other hand, insisting that law is always a command and derivable from a basic norm, were consistent, within their argument, in rejecting the dichotomy between private and public altogether and treating all law as part of an administrative order imposed by the state. For those who see all law as a command of the sovereign — as in an unworked-out way the Romans did, too — the distinction between private and public law cannot be absolutely fundamental for the nature of law in general. A worked-out theory of private law might well involve the rejection not only of Kelsen's analysis but of command theories of law in general, at least in so far as they make historical and sociological claims or pretend to describe judicial reasoning. Can the state be the sole source of law if it is itself a legal category? Solidarist theorists like Duguit[10] also denied the distinction between public and private law in any fundamental sense — the individual must be subordinate to the requirements of the collectivity, what is called private law must be shaped and determined by public law and ultimately seen as part of it. All law, he and Durkheim[11] insisted, is social — strictly, there is no such thing as 'private' law; even in the supervision of action by government bodies there is only a difference of degree.

Basically, however, the significance of distinctions between public and private law is not well brought out by semantic analysis or by a classificatory approach. Both of these, in the case of law, tend to smack of circularity or to run into considerable conflict between the theoretical interest in consistency and the enormous impact of historical accident and peculiarity on the actual development of legal systems. Classificatory approaches are forced to recognise the existence of mixed forms and though they can do so without overt contradiction, such recognition does not help to illuminate the reasons for the mixture, the nature of the conflict or the character of legal trends. A far better approach is to think of private and public law in terms of conflicting paradigms or ideal types, representing internally coherent and externally conflicting logical trends or 'moments' within the law. The jurisprudence of interests, deriving from Ihering's classic *Der Geist des römischen Rechts*, laid one foundation for this by tying the distinction between public and private law, as Ulpian half does, to the nature of the interests served — public or social interests as distinguished from private or individual interests, the collectivity as distinguished from the citizen. These two will be in conflict and law is public or private according to the extent that it aims principally to promote one or the other. Roscoe Pound enables us to see such a distinction in an historical context.[12] Law, he argued, moves through a series of stages, each of which elevates one particular interest or requirement. The first or 'primitive' stage is the establishment of the supremacy of law, of a peaceful ordering of the community — the concept, in common law, of the King's Peace. The second stage is that of certainty and uniformity in that ordering, the stage of strict law, written in form. The third stage introduces a notion of equity and of natural law, of good faith and of moral conduct based on reason as requirements in the law. The fourth stage elevates the interests of the individual, the concept of individual rights, while the fifth — current — stage gives primacy to the requirements of society as a whole and to social interests. The attempt to order these steps into an evolutionary schema is forced, even mistaken, though Pound was not wrong in seeing that specific interests or requirements are given special attention at the expense of other interests and requirements in particular historical periods and that all those he mentioned are a necessary part of the conception of a fully developed system of law. It is better to treat the interests he referred to as 'moments' or impulses in the life of the law, each generating its own principles and procedures and standing in some conflict with other 'moments'. Neither law generally, nor specific sections such as private or public law, or criminal or commercial law, serve just one function or interest. They do not display a single coherent 'essence'. At best, we can look for guiding threads and structural tendencies shaping or seeking to shape diverse legal inputs.

The most illuminating account of private law — or, as he would have then put it, of the essentially private character of all law — is that given by the Soviet theorist E.B. Pashukanis in his *General Theory of Law and Marxism*.[13] Pashukanis argued that law is distinguished from administration by its presupposition of and insistence upon the equality and equivalence of the parties, its rejection of any order of subordination between them, its belief in their essential individuality and capacity for free will and rational determination, its emphasis upon the recognition of rights as opposed to the imposition of duties, which in law are only the obverse of rights. The essence of law, for Pashukanis, lies in the freedom of choice, reciprocity and interchangeability of parties who enter into a contract. The legal assumptions that underlie this contractual model reflect the assumptions of the market, of the exchange of commodities. Law is thus a commercial phenomenon reaching its apogee in bourgeois society which establishes the Republic of the Market in all walks of social life, privatises all social and legal relations. Criminal law is organised on the basis of the *quid pro quo*, the *post factum* 'payment' for a crime according to a fixed scale of penalties. The state, in the theory of the social contract and the constitutions based on it, becomes another party having rights and duties *vis-a-vis* the citizen just as the citizen has rights and duties *vis-à-vis* it. Family law dissolves the *Gemeinschaft* of the family into a network of reciprocal rights and duties, gradually rejecting all questions of status. Labour law is organised on the basis of the contract of employment, international law on the basis of contractual and reciprocal rights of sovereign states. Everything, to become part of law, has to be reduced to the individuality (legal personality), equality and interchangeability of a party *to the action*.

Public law, for Pashukanis, was not law at all, but administration, based on a hierarchy of norms and values and on vertical as opposed to horizontal relations between legal (or rather administrative) subjects. Socialism would mean the dissolution of (private) law and its replacement by a comprehensive system of policies and administrative arrangements, the application of socio-economic norms.

In capitalist societies, he argued, the Republic of the Market, which law reflects, concealed the Despotism of the Factory, for which the state was needed. The state, for Pashukanis, was not strictly a legal category at all. It represented domination, an extra-legal relationship. The judicialising of modern society was the work of the bourgeoisie and could not be carried out coherently: the bourgeoisie tended to privatise all law while yet needing public law to safeguard its position as a ruling class. The distinction between public and private was one of the (ideological) contradictions of capitalism:

> For us [the Soviets] there cannot even be a discussion of the limitation of state intervention in any sphere of economic activity — but this is the very first thing that follows from the division of law into two spheres.
>
> ... The roots of the division of law into public and private must be sought in the distinction between property and the social totality, the separation of civil society and political organization, and in the enhancement of the individuality of man and the citizen ... The contrast between private and public law is most typical for bourgeois society, and impossible to eliminate. The monopoly of private property in the hands of individual members of the capitalist class, the separation of the state from society as a special organization of the ruling class for the purpose of supporting the relations of capitalist exploitation — this is the basis for the division of law into private and public. The bourgeois (as owner) concludes commodity transactions of purchase and sale, including purchase and sale of labour power — this is private law. The bourgeois as a member

of the ruling class exercises authority and punishes the violators of capitalist principles – this is public law.

. . . Legal theory cannot equate 'the rights of parliament', 'the rights of executive authority' etc., for example, with the creditor's right to repayment of a debt. This would be to place a distinct private interest where bourgeois ideology presumes the authority of a general impersonal state interest . . . Public law can exist only as the reflection of the form of private law in the sphere of political organization, or else it ceases to be law.[14]

III. Centrality of Private Law

Neither the definition nor the classification of law is an activity usefully carried out *in vacuo*. Definitions and classifications, if they are sound, bring out real features of the material, but they do so for specific intellectual purposes, as part of the study and explanation of specific issues or phenomena. Distinctions that are interesting or central for one purpose are irrelevant or misleading for another. The defining characteristics of law, and what we count as law, vary according to our intellectual enterprise, what it is that we want to study or bring out, what it is that we need to contrast law with. The same is true of conceptions of the private and public in general and of private and public law in particular. Law serves no single function and has no single coherent character. Neither does any branch of it.

Sociologists have distinguished three major functions of law – that of a peaceful ordering of the community, that of resolving disputes and that of allocating resources. Pound, who recognises these, reminds us of others – of providing certainty and uniformity, of linking law with received morality, of creating and protecting individual rights. The legal positivist tends to see law simply as the total system of state-sanctioned norms, though such a system may contain legitimating rules (rules of recognition) and procedures for applying, extending and interpreting the law justly. For him, the distinction between public and private law will not be central or fundamental – all law is in a sense state law, to be distinguished, rather, from custom, tradition and fireside equity. For those, like us and Pashukanis, who see law as a social institution embodying its own tradition or traditions, the situation is more complex and the distinction between public and private law points to a problem of central importance – which cannot, however, simply be solved by abstract definition or conceptual analysis of the terms 'public' and 'private'.

Elsewhere,[15] we have distinguished three paradigms of law and social organisation and considered the conflicts and affinities between them. These are the *Gemeinschaft*, the *Gesellschaft* and the bureaucratic-administrative paradigms. The first two of these paradigms are close cousins of the organic and individualist modes used by Benn and Gaus in their analysis in Chapter 2, above, of the liberal conception of the private and the public. But they have nothing corresponding to our bureaucratic-administrative paradigm. And this is not surprising, since liberalism has always been uncomfortable with it.

The *Gemeinschaft* paradigm emphasises an organic conception of a society held together by custom, tradition, a common religion or ideology which sees every member of the society as a member of a social family. The emphasis is on face-to-face relations, substantive fireside equity, mediation and reconciliation. The basic components of the society are not atomic and abstract individuals but relationships. Law, politics and administration are not sharply distinguished; there is no distinction, as a matter of principle, between the private and the public; the distinction between commutative and distributive justice is merged in the overriding conception of the *ius communis*. The *Gesellschaft* paradigm, strengthened by the growth of individualism, commerce, cities, social and geographical mobility and protest against the status society, assumes a society made up of atomic individuals and private interests, each in principle equivalent to the other, capable of agreeing on common means to diverse ends. The *Gesellschaft* emphasises formal procedure, impartiality, adjudicative justice, precise legal provisions and definitions, and the rationality and predictability of legal administration. It is oriented to the precise definition of the rights and duties of the individual through an intellectual sharpening of the point at issue and not to the day-to-day *ad hoc* and emotive maintenance of social harmony, community tradition and organic solidarity; it reduces the public interest to another, only *sometimes* overriding, private interest. It distinguishes sharply between law and administration, between the public and the private, the legal and the moral, between commutative or corrective and distributive justice and between the civil obligation and the criminal offence. Its model for all law is contract and the *quid pro quo* associated with commercial exchange, which also demands rationality and predictability. It has difficulty in dealing with the state and state instrumentalities, with corporations, social interests and the administrative requirements of social planning or a process of production, unless it reduces them to the interests of a 'party' to the proceedings, confronting another 'party' on the basis of formal equivalence and legal interchangeability. Its tendency is to 'privatise' criminal law; to make the malefactor confront his prosecutor as an equal with equal rights. Pashukanis's 1920s theory of the essentially private character of all law as based on the abstract individual juridical subject confronting all other juridical subjects on the basis of equality and equivalence is a particularly penetrating exposition of the *Gesellschaft* paradigm, even if his attempt to reduce all law to that paradigm is forced and unconvincing.

Where the *Gemeinschaft* paradigm elevates an organic community and the relationships within it, where the *Gesellschaft* elevates the abstract legal subject and its rights, the bureaucratic-administrative paradigm elevates 'rational' planning and the socio-technical norms associated with such planning. It is structured around the conception of a hierarchy of interests, not of an equality of subjects; it tends to see all law as public, subordinating; it elevates vertical over horizontal relationships and tends to merge law with administration and to emphasise distributive over corrective justice.

The overwhelming significance of private law in the Western legal tradition and more recently in the history of Western social thought lies in the extent to which the practical and theoretical development of a Roman-based private law has acted as the systematic foundation and carrier of the *Gesellschaft* paradigm and of the liberal democratic view of society associated with it. It has been and is a remarkably rich and subtle tradition, with a strong bias toward fairness, justice, equality and social and political independence, capable of principled confrontation with kings, prelates, dictators and mobs. To a degree absent from both the *Gemeinschaft* and the bureaucratic-administrative paradigms, it has had a specific theory of law and a fundamental belief that law *counts*, that it is not only an outstanding feature of social organisation, but that its rules, procedures and techniques are capable of dealing, justly and under the framework of general precepts and conceptions, with all important human activities.

The three great, original characteristics of Roman private law as a living system up to the time of Justinian were firstly, a complexity which enabled it to cover the main social relationships of human life; secondly, a degree of abstraction enabling many of its principles to apply to a wide range of social relationships and over long periods of time without major change; thirdly, an autonomy of structure and development which gave law an independent role in the development of society as a whole. It became strongly linked with a systematic and worked-out set of moral precepts, also capable of modification and change, and with a conception of justice as an intellectual activity, as the intellectual consideration and resolution of conflict by an impartial and disinterested third party whose judgement the parties or their social *niveau* in principle accept. As an intellectual activity, the activity and judgement of justice in the private law have carried with them the ethic of discourse and enquiry (often counterposed to strident claims of public urgency and public policy); the careful, impartial, disinterested examination of claims and of the nature of the matter; the consideration of consequences, in the situation, for the parties and for the society around them and the rules by which it lives; the assessment of the strength and authenticity of competing interests and demands, of public interest, moral sentiment and customary expectations; and the relation of all this to a systematic, coherent and comparatively predictable set of social rules capable of accommodating the existing complexity of interests and the likelihood of significant social change.

Once we recognise these central characteristics of the development of the concept of private law in the Western legal tradition we recognise the absurdity of suggesting that the private law remains or is forced to remain within the ambit of abstract and abstracted individualism, as distinct from recognising individuals as subjects and not objects. Private law is not private in that sense: it deals with people forming social relationships, acting on the basis of or in defiance of social expectations, benefiting from and harming others. It recognises that not all interests are individual and that some interests may be more central or far-reaching than others. But it does not begin *a priori* with a hierarchy of (usually unexamined) interests as public law tends to; it has no sacred cows except the welfare, relative autonomy and actual empirical interests of people to be derived from actual existing situations. It is capable of accommodating and has accommodated changes in social attitudes, arrangements and expectations to a much greater extent than is commonly realised, especially, perhaps, in common law jurisdictions.

No law, however, is ever of the pure *Gemeinschaft, Gesellschaft* or bureaucratic-administrative type; all complex legal systems and even many simple ones have seen incipient or open conflict between these paradigms, each having advantages in dealing with some situations or satisfying some interests as opposed to others: the *Gemeinschaft* in combating depersonalisation and seeking the justice of the individual case; the bureaucratic-administrative in regulating activities and social provinces rather than individual actions. The demands made on law today elevate these various paradigms in various areas, often inconsistently, against the general background of a feeling that *Gesellschaft* principles do not deal well with major inequalities of power or the rational control of future activities and interests. This is certainly so, and many of the changes of the mix of *Gemeinschaft, Gesellschaft* and bureaucratic-administrative principles and procedures are to be welcomed. But only the *Gesellschaft* tradition of private law, we would argue, systematically subordinates interests themselves to scrutiny with a degree of care and rationality, and concern for people, conspicuously absent in politics; only the *Gesellschaft* tradition of law systematically elevates a bias toward freedom, fairness and equality, together with a concern for consequences. It is the only suitable matrix for a theory of social as well as legal justice, though it must be and can be supplemented with *Gemeinschaft* and bureaucratic-administrative arrangements. But the lack of a worked-out theory of public law not derived from private law principles is, as the Marxists say, no accident. Public law is law in so far as it incorporates principles, traditions and procedures drawn from private law; it is distinguished from private law by subordinating the legal to something else, by not exposing to critical scrutiny the very concept of 'a' or even 'the' social or public interest, or of the moral primacy of the state.

We are now in a position to return to the three separate but related questions we posed at the beginning of Section II. The classification of law into public or private cannot be given a systematic and coherent foundation independently of an appreciation of the tradition, of the general principles and presuppositions, of private law. The belief that the state or its agencies should *in principle* be subject to a different system of law has formed one basis of the distinction between public and private law, but seems to us in principle and in practice vicious, though we do recognise the possible practical convenience of having distinct courts or tribunals dealing with some aspects of state activity, but on principles that will not see the state as by its very nature outside private law. In the end, in a democratic society, all law is both public and private in all the many senses of those terms, but the private law tradition lies and continues to lie at the root of democracy. 'Steering society' is not a democratic concept, nor is that of the Great Helmsman. Public law has not, and cannot have, a coherent, systematic conception of justice (as distinct from policy) that is not logically and historically parasitic on private law.

Nevertheless, a host of modern developments are seriously weakening the role of the *Gesellschaft* paradigm in legal systems of advanced post-industrial, post-bourgeois societies. The ever-increasing role of the state in directly regulating more and more social activities brings ever-increasing public elements even into the central areas of private law — more and more contracts, for instance, have more and more of their contractual terms 'dictated from above' by legislative requirements independent of the will of the parties. The sheer multiplication of laws destroys the plausibility of seeing private law as the Romans did — a conceptually subtle but basically simple and coherent set of rules governing most important aspects of human relationships effectively and impartially. We legislate less and less for people in general and more and more for classes of people occupying a particular status or carrying out a particular economic function. We are aware of social realities — concentration of power, inequalities of income and knowledge, lack of access or sheer incompetence — which make a legal system holding fast to the principle of the equality and interchangeability of legal parties work badly in practice in protecting the poor, the incompetent, the irrational. As population increases enormously, we are aware of the sheer social cost of doing justice in detail, case by case, in the common law tradition and in that of private law generally. As human interdependence increases, as our neighbours' actions (or those of the nuclear power station, the dam constructor, the industrial complex) come to affect us on an ever-greater and often-irreversible scale, we demand that law regulate harm before it occurs and that it regulate types of activities rather than individual actions. Socially important property is no longer, for most people, the garden they cultivate, the house they built with their own hands, the tools they use themselves. It is no longer plausibly seen as the product of private effort and private will, as the expression and content of individual personality. The petrol company, the shopping complex, the airlines cannot be distinguished from each other by ordinary people by reference to whether they are privately or publicly owned — property on that scale *is public* in its ramifications, its role in other people's lives, its scale and its relationship and power *vis-à-vis* state activity, or, alternatively, in its dependence upon it. All this erodes the strength of the *Gesellschaft* ideal, as does a renewed emphasis, in disillusionment with science and technology, on direct human relationships, emotional comfort and self-expression, participation and the need to be heard saying what one feels rather than what one thinks.

There are, in keeping with our insistence on the complex struggle of paradigms, countervailing trends, however. The great and ever-increasing concern with protecting citizens against state as well as private power has led to a certain increased privatisation of public law through the concept and protection of human rights, deeply rooted in *Gesellschaft* ideology and *Gesellschaft* procedures. As private law becomes more public, public law — constitutions, international and transnational law and administrative law — becomes more private, elevating to a degree not known before the individual and his or her rights.

Notes

We are indebted to Roger Wilkins, Research Assistant in the Department of Jurisprudence, University of Sydney, for much material and some illuminating suggestions and to the editors of this volume, S.I. Benn and G.F. Gaus, for detailed and helpful criticism of our first draft which, we think, has led to many improvements.

1. J.A.C. Thomas, *The Institutes of Justinian: Text, Translation and Commentary* (North Holland, Amsterdam, 1975), p. 4.
2. Francis Bacon, *Works* (London, 1859), vol. VII, pp. 731-32, cited in Tony Weir, 'The Common Law System', in Konrad Zweigert et al. (eds.), *The International Encyclopedia of Comparative Law* (J.C.G. Mohr, Tübingen, 1974), vol. II, Ch. 2, p. 94.
3. Charles Szladits, 'The Civil Law System', in *The International Encyclopedia of Comparative Law*, vol. II, Ch. 2, p. 18.
4. 'Police' here has not the modern sense but the sense it had in the works of Adam Smith: that which has to do with the organisation and administration of the polity as such.
5. Szladits, 'The Civil Law System', p. 20.
6. Ibid., p. 22.
7. Walther Burckhardt, *Methode und System des Rechts* (Polygraphischer Verlag, Zurich, 1936), and his *Einführung in die Rechtswissenschaft* (Polygraphischer Verlag, Zurich, 1939).
8. Gustav Radbruch, *Legal Philosophy*, 3rd edn, Kurt Wilk (trans.) in *The Legal Philosophies of Lask, Radbruch and Dabin* (Harvard University Press, Cambridge, Mass., 1950), pp. 152-55.
9. Hans Kelsen, *General Theory of Law and State*, Anders Wedberg (trans.) (Russell and Russell, New York, 1961), pp. 201-7. See also his *Pure Theory of Law*, Max Knight (trans.) (University of California Press, Berkeley and Los Angeles, 1967), pp. 280ff.
10. Leon Duguit, *Law in the Modern State*, F. and H. Laski (trans.) (Allen & Unwin, London, 1921).
11. Emile Durkheim, *The Division of Labor in Society* (1893), George Simpson (trans.) (Free Press of Glencoe, New York, 1964), pp. 127-29, 206-29.
12. Roscoe Pound, *Jurisprudence* (West Publishing Co., St. Paul, Minn., 1959), vol. II, Pt. III, Ch. 11, pp. 215-79.
13. E.B. Pashukanis, *General Theory of Law and Marxism* (Moscow, 1924).
14. E.B. Pashukanis, *Selected Writings on Marxism and Law*, Piers Beirne and Robert Sharlet (eds.) (Academic Press, New York, 1980), pp. 330, 327, 73 (the first two extracts being from Pashukanis's contribution to Pashukanis and L. Ya. Ginsburg, *A Course on Soviet Economic Law* (Moscow, 1935), and the last from his *General Theory of Law and Marxism*.
15. See esp. our 'Social Traditions, Legal Traditions' and our ' "Transforming" the Law, "Steering" Society', both in Kamenka and Tay (eds.), *Law and Social Control* (E. Arnold, London, 1980), pp. 3-26 and 105-16.

4 PUBLIC FUNCTION — PRIVATE ACTION: A COMMON LAW DILEMMA

Paul Finn

Our starting point is England at the turn of the eighteenth century. The Commonwealth gone, Parliament and not the monarch now occupies the centre of the governmental stage. With this new polity, changes are occurring in the constitutional vocabulary of lawyers and of legislators. But alongside these changes, old usages persist. 'The King' and its supposed synonym 'the Crown' remain. But they are acquiring a settled and distinctive constitutional meaning increasingly removed from the natural person of the monarch.[1] Among the new is 'the Publick', a term which quickly assumes a number of roles. In one role, for example, it is merely a substitute for the more ancient term 'common'; in this sense 'public' refers simply to the subjects of the kingdom, sometimes as individuals, sometimes as an aggregation. So 'common ways', 'common nuisances' become 'public ways', 'public nuisances'. This particular usage straddles the first and second levels of the individualist model sketched by Benn and Gaus in Chapter 1 — the 'publics' of 'anyone' and 'everyone'. In a more complex role 'the public' is used to signify the community at large, the body enjoying the benefits, carrying the burdens, of civil government and police, approximating to the fourth level of the model — what Benn and Gaus call 'the polity'. This 'public' is then institutionalised; the Public Debt is born. Governmental officers, be they the king's officers or those of local corporations, become public officers, the institutionalised representatives and servants of the collective public. And lands vested in the king can now be characterised as being held for the public benefit. However, none of the various 'publicks' which appear in the late seventeenth and early eighteenth centuries were to evolve in England or in Australia into a legal personification of the state. This would have been to compromise the constitutional position of the monarch.[2] Rather, lawyers were to set 'the public' and its satellites, 'public interest' and 'public policy', to work in lesser roles, and the concern of this chapter is with some of these.

Over the centuries the common law came in a very general way to regard the sphere of the public as embodying the criminal law, the sphere of the private as being that of the civil. For example, Sir Matthew Hale, the outstanding seventeenth-century judge and legal scholar, categorised legal wrongs into two classes: 'Such as are criminal or public, wherein the wrong-doer is proceeded against criminally ... Such as are civil or private, wherein at the suit ... of the party injured, he had reparation or right done.'[3] Breach of a public duty or violation of a public right would, thus, carry the primary sanctions of a fine or of imprisonment. Breach of a private duty or violation of a private right would result only in damages in civil proceedings. But this simple division has, for centuries, concealed a major problem for lawyers. A person may be subject to a public duty: a duty to keep the peace, a duty to repair a public facility, or a duty to issue licences. A failure to discharge that duty may well constitute a criminal offence. But can it also give rise to a private and civil action at the suit of someone injured as a result of that neglect? Here the lawyers have had an abiding fear. In the realm of public rights and duties a single act or omission may tend to the injury of a large and indeterminate number of persons: the unauthorised blocking of a public right of way has been a common example. The concern at the potentially ruinous consequences of a multiplicity of actions in respect of the same wrong early led the courts to the conclusion that, where many may have been injured, then, ordinarily, 'no one person injured shall be allowed to have an action, because the rest might have the same'.[4] The appropriate remedy in such a case was the public and criminal one. Nevertheless, many public duties have been characterised as ones owed to members of the public individually such that their breach gave rise to a private and actionable civil wrong and this over and above any possible criminal consequences. Indeed, as will be seen, the courts have, on occasion, imposed a public character upon the activities of private functionaries with the express purpose in mind of making their neglects, etc., civilly actionable at the suit of members of the public adversely affected.

The concern of this chapter, then, is with this problem: Where a person, whether a governmental official or otherwise, discharges a 'public function' — a function in the discharge of which the public is interested — should a citizen aggrieved by the non-performance or by the improper performance of that function be entitled in a civil (i.e. a private) action to claim pecuniary redress (i.e. damages) for any injury suffered thereby? In particular, this chapter examines three areas of the common law in which this problem arises. And, as we will see, all three areas exhibit in one way or another the conflict of three interests: the first is the interest of the community as beneficiaries of legal institutions and public services; the second is the interest of some individual member of the community adversely affected by the neglects or defaults of some person or corporation charged with the performance of a public service or function; the third is the private interest of that same person or corporation. The courts early perceived that there were certain forms of 'public' service, whether provided by officials or otherwise, that the citizen should be able to enjoy as of right and to secure by action. But equally they acknowledged that in permitting suit to members of the public they could be placing that very service — and the public interest it served — in jeopardy by allowing its providers to be drained by damages claims. Again, tender as the courts have been in their solicitude for private rights, they have acknowledged that these may well have to yield to wider public interests so that on occasion, 'it is better to suffer a private mischief, than a public inconvenience'.[5] In seeking to balance these interests, the courts have, over the years, been involved in a complex series of advances and retreats. The following pages, it is hoped, will provide some insight into the law's approaches to these tasks and to roles that conceptions of the public and the private have played therein.

I. Public Interest Regulation of 'Service' Enterprise

It has been the staple of the common law to regulate in civil proceedings the competing individual interests of members of the community. With less regularity, but still with some frequency, the common law has been prepared to proscribe the agreements and activities of individuals on the ground that the substance or object of an agreement or activity is offensive to some judicially perceived community or public interest or policy. The courts will not, for example, enforce contracts to commit crimes, will not enforce contracts in restraint of trade and will not enforce a duty of secrecy if the disclosure of the secret is held to be in the public interest. Here, although the courts identify specific public interests or policies to justify their denial of judicial remedies, they use them in a negative way. They use public interest or policy to deny efficacy to private rights, private duties — rights and duties arising in dealings between individual members of the community and which would be enforced but for that public interest or public policy. It has, however, been exceedingly rare for the courts to go beyond this negative and prohibitory usage and to employ the public interest positively as a vehicle justifying the imposition of enforceable obligations upon individuals and for the benefit of the members of the community. This section is concerned with one of these rare examples: the positive regulation of services provided to the public.

From at least the time of the Black Death both the common law and statute took to defining and to regulating the obligations and privileges of persons who followed callings in which labour or service was made available to or for the public generally — the 'common' callings as they were known.[6] A common labourer was obliged to serve whomsoever sought and retained him; common hostelers and common victuallers had to sell their food at market price; the common gaoler had definite duties in relation to the reception and care of prisoners. This complex pattern of regulation reflected the pervasive orderings of medieval life. And while no single set of rules was applied indiscriminately to all of the common callings, it does seem clear that the callings were regulated each in its own way, because they were common.

If the medieval system set the courts upon the path of regulation, the decay of that system and the rise of liberalism led to a contraction of the types of calling which they would regulate. By the eighteenth century those judicially controlled were rapidly becoming limited to the trio which survives to this day — the innkeeper, the common carrier and the ferryman — and this seemingly because of their continuing social and economic importance. The form of regulation imposed was becoming uniform. The common callings had a 'public duty' to serve all comers to the extent of their particular calling and failure to do so would render them both civilly liable to any person thus wronged and criminally liable for the public wrong. Equally they could only charge reasonable rates for their services.

Certain anachronisms were, however, now creeping into judicial thinking. The callings were being equated with public officials with whose civil and criminal liabilities there was a close approximation. Thus in an action for neglect of duty against a common carrier, it could be observed: 'This is an action against a person who, by ancient law, held as it were a public office, and was bound to the public.'[7] If the equation added emphasis to the public dimension of the callings it was, however, an imperfect one and one no longer made today. Many public officials, undoubtedly, were and are required to provide services directly to such members of the public as wished to avail themselves of those services. They were thus 'bound to the public'. But with other officials

Public Function – Private Action: A Common Law Dilemma   97

this was not so. An auditor in the Exchequer or a constable acting in his peace-keeping role acts unquestionably as a public official and this because of the 'public' – or 'state' – interest in his respective functions. What gives an office its public character is not coextensive with what affects a calling. It does, however, seem clear that, analogy or no analogy, the courts did not lose sight of what gave a calling its public character. Lord Holt in his judgement in *Lane* v. *Cotton* in 1701 was to reaffirm the simple medieval view of service to the public:

> wherever any Subject takes upon himself a Publick Trust for the Benefit of the rest of his fellow Subjects, he is *eo ipso* bound to serve the Subject in all the Things that are within the Reach and Comprehension of such an Office, under Pain of an Action against him . . . If on the Road a Shoe fall off my Horse, and I come to a Smith to have one put on, and the Smith refuse to do it, an Action will lie against him, because he has made Profession of a Trade which is for the Publick Good, and has thereby exposed and *vested an interest of himself in all the King's Subjects* that will employ him in the Way of his Trade . . . [O]ne that has made Profession of a public Employment, is bound to the utmost Extent of that Employment to serve the Publick.[8]

Holt's 'public' does not yet distinguish the collective interest of 'everyone' in the service being available, from the particular interest of some individual member of the public who has occasion to use it. As we shall see, these interests can, and do, diverge as public services expand.

As the regulation of the callings contracted to the narrow class noted above, a new and not dissimilar form of regulation emerged in another sphere of private enterprise. From at least the middle of the seventeenth century it is becoming clear that if an individual or corporation is given a charter or franchise by the Crown or by Parliament to provide some service to the public generally, and if the effect of that charter or franchise is to give that individual etc. a legal or de facto monopoly in that service, then the manner of provision of that service may be regulated in 'the public interest' – and may be regulated in a manner that closely parallels that of the common callings. Thus Lord Hale's observations on service charges:

> A man for his own private advantage may in a port town set up a wharf or crane, and may take what rates he and his customers may

agree for cranage etc.... for he doth no more than is lawful for any man to do, viz. make the most of his own. [But] if the subject have a publick wharf unto which all persons that come to that port must come ... because there is no other wharf ... there cannot be taken arbitrary and excessive duties for cranage etc.... but the duties must be reasonable and moderate ... For now the wharf and crane and other conveniences are affected with a publick interest, and they cease to be *juris privati* only.[9]

Lord Hale is still firmly rooted in the medieval tradition.

It seems reasonably clear that this *common law* public interest regulation could be invoked where the service monopoly was of official creation — where it required some legislative or executive authorisation for its being carried on at all or for its being carried on in a place to which the public had a right of access. It is less clear whether this regulation would be applied to privately created monopolies. If these were to be so regulated, it would have to be upon some dual analogy with both the 'official' monopoly and the common calling, that is, upon the basis that the undertaker enjoys a monopoly in a service meeting a significant social need and that he holds himself out as willing to serve the public without restriction or selection. As will be seen, in the United States in the late nineteenth century these analogies were adopted for the purpose of justifying *statutory* regulation in private monopolies.

By the turn of the eighteenth century, then, English courts were furnished with two guiding theories for the public interest regulation of service enterprises. But the medievalist theory was to give way to a liberal theory of sorts — slowly at first and then by total abdication. The advent of privately owned statutory corporations using new technologies in the provision of community services — the water, railway, gas, telegraphic and electricity corporations — led the courts to a complete reappraisal of public interest liabilities. Initially, in England, some lip service was to be paid to common-calling analogies, this most notably with railway companies.[10] Later, however, enthusiasm for such analogies was to evaporate. English courts would not, for example, treat telegraph companies as a species of common carrier.[11] Similarly the courts were becoming increasingly reluctant to hold that members of the community had enforceable rights to the provision of particular services,[12] or to services of a particular standard;[13] and this even where the service was provided by a publicly owned corporation. Water and sewerage were notable examples. If the activities of service corporations were to be regulated, i.e. if the citizen was to have rights in the provision of such services, it was, in the courts' view, for Parliament and Parliament alone to effect such regulation, to confer such rights. Furthermore from the nineteenth century the English judiciary, with rare exceptions,[14] was to adopt a positive policy of protectionism for statutory corporations and at the expense of the individual. Any liability rule which could jeopardise the viability of a privately owned statutory 'service' corporation or which could result in an increase in the burdens imposed on all rate-payers (as in the case of local authority services) was strenuously resisted. And in scrutinising the exercise of the statutory powers of such corporations and authorities, the courts committed themselves to the view that property damage sustained by any community member as a result of the authorised operations of a corporation etc. was not to give rise to any claim for compensation unless such was expressly granted by Parliament. That damage was the price an individual had to pay so that the community might have the benefit of the service or facility provided. The interests of particular members of the public were to be sacrificed to the public collectively. The Holts and Hales were turned on their heads, the public interest being used to deny the suit of the individual rather than to justify it. Collective public interest, and the interests of particular members of the public were now manifestly diverging.

In the United States the story of public interest regulation was a totally different one. From the middle of the nineteenth century, at least, the courts accepted that public monopolies were at common law to be subjected to actionable duties to serve the public at reasonable prices and without discrimination. Furthermore, and notwithstanding the protection afforded to private property by the Fourteenth Amendment to the Constitution, U.S. courts were to uphold the constitutionality of state regulation of the activities of monopolists — public and private — in services of community importance:

> When one devotes his property to a use in which the public has an interest, he, in effect, grants to the public an interest in that use, and must submit to be controlled by the public for the common good, to the extent of the interest he has thus created.[15]

Upon these foundations have been erected a complex of laws regulating public utility corporations. The reasoning of Holt and Hale — the vesting in the public of an interest in oneself — is honoured, but in another land.

Australian courts were, predictably, to follow English courts in the main for most of the last one hundred and fifty years. In the early 1960s, for example, they would assert, unlike in the United States, that no doctrine had been established in the common law that a public authority exercising an exclusive franchise was bound to provide the service covered by the franchise.[16] However, by the early 1970s, as the bonds of legal colonialism were progressively loosened, the courts were to move tentatively along the road followed in the United States, at least in relation to the provision of postal and telephonic services supplied by a publicly owned monopolist. It has now been acknowledged that the citizen may have a right to have such services provided, a right arising in part at least from the acknowledgement of the immediate community interest in having access to such services.[17] Public interest regulation is being cautiously reasserted in defence of the several claims of individual members of the public.

II. Civil Liability and the 'Public Duty' Rule

As one emerges from the Tudor period one finds that in a number of quite divergent fields the common law has made available both criminal *and* civil sanctions as means for enforcing particular duties, and for securing the enjoyment of certain rights. The wrongful obstruction of a common right of way could, for example, carry criminal and civil liabilities. A public official who neglected his duty risked prosecution and civil suit. But it was not until the eighteenth century that a coherent theory explained this conjunction of liabilities, and when they would be invoked. The principal instances of the dual liabilities involved the common callings, duties to repair roads and sea walls, common nuisance, public officials and breach of statutory duty. In each of these the courts were to perceive some public dimension or interest. To profess a common calling was to vest in the public an interest in one's self; duties to repair roads etc. could be classified as duties in the discharge of which the public had an interest;[18] a public official, as will be seen, came to be defined as an official who discharged duties in the discharge of which the public was interested; a common nuisance was 'an offence against the public';[19] and a statutory duty might on occasion be characterised as relating to a matter 'affecting the public'.[20] The publics here are various. And though they tend to fall primarily into the first three levels of the individualist model proposed by Benn and Gaus, one can detect elements in some of the judgements of the organic model, which supposes a public interest which is neither an interest of a state institution nor that of each and every member. This is most apparent in cases of criminal prosecutions of public officials.[21] By characterising rights, duties, and injuries as 'public', the courts, as indicated in the introduction to this chapter, brought their protection, enforcement and redress within the realm of the criminal law. For a brief time such a characterisation was to justify the invocation of the civil law too.

In 1786, with the decision of the Court of Exchequer in *Sutton* v. *Johnstone*,[22] one encounters one of the first major generalisations of civil liability for a public wrongdoing: 'every breach of a public duty, working wrong and loss to another, is an injury and is actionable'. The 'public duty' rule, a rule of immense potential, had been created. If it unified the disparate strands of civil liability noted above, it also gave the courts a vehicle for ensuring that individuals within the community could secure the enjoyment of duties and prohibitions which could be said to exist for their benefit. But the rule's flowering – if colourful – was brief.[23]

Within two years of *Sutton* v. *Johnstone*, the civil rule was seen in the famous highway-nonfeasance case, *Russell* v. *Men of Devon*, to be qualified.[24] It was held that no action would lie against the inhabitants of a county for injury sustained as a result of their failure to discharge their public duty to repair a bridge: to permit the claim would be to invite 'an infinity of actions'. But more importantly the courts were soon to perceive the serious economic and social implications of the public duty rule. First, from the turn of the nineteenth century it was apparent that a rigid application of the rule would pose special problems for trustees and commissioners charged with the construction and/or maintenance of highways, sewers, canals and ports. Resources were limited. Competing priorities could leave duties undischarged. The trustees and commissioners were usually unincorporated and unpaid, the possible claimants upon them numerous. Secondly, if the rule was formulated in a climate of leisurely law making, it soon found itself in a legislative explosion. Parliament, increasingly, was enacting regulatory legislation – legislation 'affecting the public'. An inflexible liability rule – and the 'public duty rule' was such – applied indiscriminately to such legislation could lead to damages actions being brought in situations where Parliament clearly would not have desired such a sanction to lie. Thirdly, the advent of local authorities and of statutory utility corporations providing services directly to householders *en masse* gave the rule a scope of alarming proportions. If water and gas companies in particular were not to be exposed to the possibility of widespread claims for neglect of statutory duty caused simply by deficiencies in the technologies employed, a new rule had to be found.

A change was forced upon the courts and it had its origins in the law governing privately owned statutory corporations. From the beginning of the nineteenth century, at least, the courts were to categorise the 'private Acts' creating such companies — for canals, railways, waterworks or whatever — as being in the nature of *contracts* between the statutory undertakers and the Parliament acting 'on behalf of every person interested in anything to be done under them'.[25] Initially the contract theory was used to protect 'persons interested' against excessive uses of statutory power. But in the latter half of the nineteenth century it provided the foundations for a direct onslaught upon the public duty rule. Faced with the prospect of an 'infinity of ruinous actions' against statutory corporations for breaches of their statutory duties, the courts were to hold that a civil action for such breaches would only lie where that consequence must have been intended by the 'contracting parties'. Rarely would they so intend. Thus where a person was unable to extinguish a house fire because a water company had failed in its duty to keep up water pressure, it was held that no civil action for that failure was contemplated in the legislation imposing the company's duties.[26]

It was then but a small step to apply this 'intention' approach to all statutory duties whether contained in private or in public Acts. A civil action only lay for breach of statutory duty where this was intended by Parliament.[27] And Parliament, of course, seldom adverts to the matter.

The practical consequences of this change in approach were various. First, until recent times, the sanctioning of breach of statutes fell almost exclusively into the province of the criminal law. Secondly, the public duty rule was rendered a spent force. With statute being the principal and ever-growing source of 'public duties' and with breach of statutes no longer being remedied by the damages action, the rule itself had lost all meaning. Thirdly, after their century or so of union under the same rubric, the civil liability rules for officials, the callings, duties to repair roads etc. again each went its own way. And, as will be seen in section III, this was to have profound consequences for the future shaping of the civil liabilities of public officials and of statutory authorities. Finally, the demise of the damages action as a means for enforcing statutes has been the catalyst for a search for an alternative civil remedy. Today one of the most contentious issues in the law lies in defining the circumstances in which an interested person will be given standing to enforce a statute through the medium of an injunction.

III. Public Officers

> Officers are distinguished into civil and military according to the nature of their several trusts; and every man is a publick officer who hath any duty concerning the publick; and he is not the less a publick officer where his authority is confined to narrow limits, because 'tis the duty of his office, and the nature of that duty, which makes him a publick officer, and not the extent of his authority.[28]

The medieval system imposed a stamp upon the law governing offices and officials which was to subsist into modern times. In a world dominated by concepts of property and of tenure, lawyers readily accepted that offices were, ordinarily, proprietary in character. Upon this (to us) peculiar notion a complex of laws developed, though much of it has now fallen into desuetude. The nineteenth-century English reforms in the civil service and in local government gave new directions to thinking about offices. Contract has progressively supplanted property in thinking about the relations between the Crown and its officials. But the status-related aspects of the older system have been of enduring significance.

As the quotation opening this section illustrates, it was — and is — the function performed in an office which gives it its public character. Are the official's duties ones in the discharge of which the public is interested?

Historically the courts seemed to have answered this question simply by a crude typification of the duty: irrespective of its source, the function performed is one in which the public could be said to have some concern even if some members of the public have a more immediate concern than the public at large. Today with the general demise of (1) offices remunerated by fees, (2) offices capable of being sold and inherited, and (3) private rights to appoint to public office, the typification process has ceased to be one of real difficulty. The sources of the office's power/duties (i.e. public act or private instrument) and of its remuneration (public funds/private funds) will ordinarily give rise to a presumption that the duties are public or private. In those cases where the duties stem from legislation, Crown prerogative etc., and the remuneration is from public funds, the office will invariably be designated a public one and its duties prima facie public. That prima facie conclusion will be displaced if it can positively be shown that the duties imposed are such as to bring about an alternative/additional legal relationship, distinct from that simply of an official and a member of the public affected by the exercise of the official's duties. Examples of such additional relations are lawyer-client (Public Defender's Officer), trustee-beneficiary (Public Curator), bailor-bailee (lost property officers), doctor-patient (public hospitals), vendor-purchaser (primary produce marketing officers), teacher-pupil (state school teachers). To the extent that the officer acts in that relationship he will not ordinarily be accountable for his actions as a public officer.

The consequences of finding an office to be public as opposed to private are dramatic. At common law the primary medium of accountability for the private officer was through the civil law and by civil action. Thus if a private agent, trustee etc. was bribed he was only civilly accountable therefor to the individual to whom he owed his duty. But 'if a man accepts an office of trust and confidence concerning the public, he is answerable to the King for his execution of that office ... and he can only answer to the King in a criminal prosecution'.[29] In the case of a bribe, for example, the public official was indictable at common law. Supplementing the criminal law are a variety of civil law remedies available to individual members of the public adversely affected by official action. The remaining part of this chapter is concerned with one such remedy: the damages action.

From at least the time of Edward I it was accepted both by the courts and by Parliaments that those officers of the King entrusted with the administration of civil justice and police, had, by virtue of their positions, a peculiar capacity to harm and to oppress individuals within their power. In the securing of redress for aggrieved subjects a system of judicial regulation was evolved which acquired the dual objectives of policing the agents of government and of protecting the individual's person and property from the irregular or erroneous exercise of official power. But the implementation of these through civil law sanctions came into conflict with governmental needs. With the dramatic growth in the powers of the central government from the late Tudor period there was concern that too stringent judicial supervision of official action could stifle efficient and effective administration. And this concern was reinforced by the consideration that the King had total immunity from liability for the wrongs of his officers. If the subject was to be compensated for an official's error etc. that compensation would have to come from out of that official's own pocket. The implications in this for recruitment to public office and for effective official action were obvious both to Parliaments — which from the seventeenth century were to grant many officials total or partial immunity from civil suit — and to the judges.

The problem is illustrated simply by an observation in an eighteenth-century American decision:

> it is mentioned, that the Lord Mayor of London, in 1666, when that city was on fire, would not give directions for, or consent to, the pulling down 40 wooden houses, or to the removing the furniture, &c. belonging to the Lawyers of Temple, then on the Circuit, for fear he should be answerable for a trespass; and in consequence of this conduct half that great city was burnt.[30]

The liability rules evolved in the courts had, then, to accommodate three potentially conflicting interests: those of the community as beneficiaries of the system of civil administration, those of the individual adversely affected in a particular instance by an official's action etc.; and those of that official. No immutable balance has been struck. And the balances at any time have tended to vary from common law country to common law country.

First, an official who exceeds his authority or jurisdiction. Under certain conditions many officials have authority to act, to take or implement decisions in ways which, if done by a mere member of the community, would be a civil law wrong, a tort. If however an official acts in the absence of the appropriate facts or conditions, then because authorisation for that action etc. is lacking in that instance, the official will be liable as if he or she were but a member of the community. This rule can be traced to the fourteenth century. In its application it has allowed the courts to balance the various interests mentioned above, as the following example illustrates. An official had authority to destroy animals infected with a specified disease. He had reasonable grounds for believing that certain animals were diseased. The animals were destroyed. It was subsequently ascertained that the animals were in fact disease free. Is the official to be held liable for his trespass or is his reasonable belief as to the existence of facts upon which his authority depends, a defence? Whose interests are to be preferred? In Anglo-Australian and until recently in U.S. jurisdictions the preference has been for the aggrieved citizen — and the official has been made an insurer of the correctness of his own actions and judgements.[31]

But now in the United States the balance has shifted: the official is protected from his error — and the citizen must seek his own insurance.[32]

Secondly the official's liability as an official and for conduct in office. By the Tudor period offices were being classified into two types, judicial and ministerial. As to judicial officers, it had been laid down — and is still the rule today — that they were not to be held liable in civil proceedings for any negligent or malicious decision given within jurisdiction. In modern times this immunity has been founded firmly upon public policy:

> This freedom from action and question at the suit of an individual is given by the law to the judges, not so much for their own sake as for the sake of the public, and for the advancement of justice, that being free from actions, they may be free in thought and independent in judgment, as all who are to administer justice ought to be.[33]

With the nonjudicial officer — the ministerial officer, for example, the sheriff, the constable, the registrar — it was otherwise. Increasingly he was being held strictly liable for injuries suffered as a result of his neglects and misfeasances. Indeed so much was this so that from the Stuart period onwards successive Parliaments pursued a piecemeal policy of protecting officials from civil litigation. In both cases, however, the liability and immunity rules were imposed because the defendant was a public officer and acting as such.

By the eighteenth century it was acknowledged that this two-fold classification of officers was inadequate. Many officials, though not judges, nonetheless exercised discretionary functions — functions in which they were obliged to make choices between competing courses of action. And if decision-making was not to be stifled, such officials had to be accorded the freedom to make mistakes. In the great constitutional cause of *Ashby* v. *White*,[34] it was held that officials exercising discretionary functions were to be liable only for malicious exercises of discretion but not for negligent or erroneous ones. The law now had three tiers of official liability and these depended upon the function performed by an official: a judicial function attracted absolute immunity, a discretionary function attracted partial immunity, and a ministerial function carried extensive and often strict liabilities.

With the rise and fall of the public duty rule discussed in section II much of this was to be thrown into confusion. And in any event the paths of the Anglo-Australian and U.S. courts were to diverge. In England and Australia the law on liability for discretionary and ministerial functions was to be all but forgotten in the late nineteenth century. The reasons for this are not capable of simple elaboration. Suffice it to say for present purposes that the law was coming increasingly to view public bodies and public officials as if they were private agencies, at least for tort liability purposes. This process coincided with the rise of the modern tort of negligence. In the twentieth century the 'privatisation' of public bodies and officials accelerated in Anglo-Australian law, and at the same time the tort of negligence came to dominate legal thinking wherever a person was injured as a result of the actions of another. Today, when courts are called upon to adjudicate upon the claim of an individual injured as a result of some exercise of official power or the discharge of an official function, their usual response is to characterise the parties not as public official/body and member of the public but as 'neighbours'. It has, however, been forced upon the courts that the public status and functions of one of the parties cannot be ignored, and this has led them into what is now one of the great unresolved issues of the law of negligence — the extent to which a liability rule, founded upon considerations apposite to the activities of private individuals, of neighbours, can be permitted to regulate the conduct of civil administration and government. As was observed by Lord Wilberforce in *Anns* v. *Merton London Borough* when commenting on the possible liability of a local authority for negligence when exercising its power of inspection of building foundations:

> I do not think that a description of the council's duty can be based upon the 'neighbourhood' principle alone ... So to base it would be to neglect an essential factor which is that the local authority is a public body discharging functions under statute: its powers and duties are definable in terms of public not private law. The problem which this type of action creates, is to define the circumstances in which the law should impose over and above, or perhaps alongside, these public law powers and duties, a duty in private law towards individuals such that they may sue for damages in a civil court.[35]

In the United States the story has been a very different one. In the nineteenth century the courts were to formulate a new and quite distinctive 'public duty' rule for public officials — a rule designed to produce precisely the opposite result to that arrived at by the English courts with their eighteenth-century 'public duty' rule, which is discussed above in section II. If a duty imposed upon an officer was a duty to the public, failure to perform it, or an erroneous performance of it, was a public injury to be redressed by a public prosecution, not a private injury to be redressed by civil action — and this even though an individual citizen may have suffered great personal injury. Civil actionability, however, began at the point where the official's duty was, in the circumstances, one owed, or owed as well, to the individual injured. So, for example, police failure to arrest a known law-breaker who then occasions foreseeable injury to someone else is not actionable by that other, the duty to apprehend being owed to the public alone.[36] But police failure to provide adequate protection to a person who had received and reported death threats as a result of assisting the police in apprehending a fugitive is civilly actionable — such a duty being owed in the circumstances by the police to a person who has so assisted them.[37]

Much of the controversy in U.S. law on official liability has turned upon differentiating the two different types of duty — the public and the personal — in individual cases. In very recent times in several states in the United States, however, the public duty rule has been circumvented by the court's treating the official agency as if it were a private litigant subject to the ordinary rules of negligence and of civil actionability,[38] thus bringing the law into line with the modern English law of negligence as applied to public bodies. Furthermore, even when the courts found a duty to be one owed to an individual, they have maintained the old discretionary/ministerial dichotomy.\ But, unlike in the earlier English cases, they were, as a rule, to accord an absolute immunity to discretionary functions.[39] Here the judges were to use the dichotomy as a vehicle for making policy decisions on whether particular official functions should be vulnerable to civil litigation. The practical anomaly of this approach has been that the less significant the official function, the more likely it would be for it to be classified as ministerial: and so liability is thrown upon those less likely to be able to pay. One can, nonetheless, conclude of the U.S. law that it has kept a concept of the public at the forefront of its litigation rules. Courts have acknowledged the peculiar requirements of government and have moulded their liability rules accordingly, even if this has meant that the individual interest has been made subservient to the public.

Conclusion

In addressing itself to the liability question in the areas considered in this chapter, the law has had the problem of reconciling, albeit in quite diverse fields of enterprise and activity, three potentially competing interests. These are, first, those of the individual member of the public adversely affected by the non-performance or by the erroneous performance of some public function; second, those of the community for whose ultimate benefit public services are provided, and functions discharged; and third, those of the agency which, in the particular instance, has been negligent etc. in discharging the public function imposed upon it. In the process of balancing the claims of these interests, one can divine, not indeed a guiding principle but a common approach, one which gives primacy to the 'public interest'.

Of the competing interests, only the second — those of the community — are always and for all purposes capable of categorisation as 'public interests'. The interests of the injured citizen, as also those of the injuring agency, are capable of being categorised either as private or as public. The injured citizen may be regarded either as a member of the public or as a private claimant; likewise the injuring agency may be regarded either as a public functionary or as a private individual (or at least as a neighbour).

But while the assignment of status in a given instance may thus determine whether the disputant's interest is to be labelled 'public' or 'private', the liability question is not necessarily and essentially related to the question: is the claimant suing or is the agency being sued as a public or private person? In a negligence action the relationship of the parties is treated as if it were private, as if it were one of neighbours. But in an action by an individual against a public official for neglect of duty, the protagonists are cast in the public roles of injured member of the public and defaulting public officer. Indeed the assignment of a status to a party will often turn simply upon the nature of the particular cause of action the citizen is attempting to mount: actions for negligence and for trespass are quintessentially actions between private actors; actions against public officials as such and actions against those professing a common calling attribute public characters to both parties.

The general formulation of a liability rule for a public wrongdoing turns, it seems, upon the question whether the interests of the citizen in being accorded relief or the interests of the agency in being accorded protection from suit clash or harmonise with the judicially perceived 'public interest', the interest of the community collectively. Where the citizen's and the public's interests harmonise, civil suit will be allowed. Where the agency's and the public's interests harmonise, it will be denied. While the case law does not always separate the various interests, the public interest on occasion being equated with or subsumed by the interests of one or other of the disputants, the question posed above does, it is suggested, reflect the essence of the court's approach to liability. We cannot formulate, however, a guiding principle but only describe a judicial approach, since judicial perceptions of *what* constitutes 'the public interest' vary. But this said, one can, nonetheless, identify the foci of the public interest. It is predominantly but not exclusively concerned to evaluate the possible detriment to the public — the community as a whole — which could be occasioned by making an agency liable when discharging a function of the type which has in fact occasioned injury; less commonly, it is concerned with whether it is in the interests of the public to promote or to hinder a type of claim asserted by a citizen-claimant.

There are many examples of the first concern. In varying degrees in U.S. and Anglo-Australian law the liability rules imposed upon public officials have been moulded so as not to prejudice the community's interest in the effective discharge of certain types of public function. Judges, as we have seen, have been granted total immunity from suit for acts and omissions within jurisdiction. Again the courts have been sensitive to the possibly ruinous consequences of allowing claims for neglect of duty against local authorities and certain public utilities. And the availability to the citizen of a negligence claim against a public agency turns in the first instance upon the court's being satisfied that the injury occasioning function can be the object of the 'neighbourhood' principle without prejudice to its proper discharge.

Examples where the focus is primarily upon the citizen are few but significant. A longstanding concern has been with whether the citizen's alleged injury is merely one which he suffers in common with the rest of the members of the public. If so, to prevent a possible multiplicity of actions, the court will assert that the appropriate remedy is a public, and not a private and civil, one. This approach is the commonplace, in Anglo-Australian law, in public nuisance and breach of statutory duty actions. By way of contrast, in the common callings cases and in those of a monopoly affected with a public interest, one is asking whether there is a public interest in the citizen's having a right to the provision of a particular service. That question will turn in part upon the nature and availability of the particular service itself.

The courts, then, will not, in formulating a liability rule, sacrifice what is perceived to be the public interest. At least in the area of the discharge of public functions it would indeed be odd if they acted otherwise. How the courts arrive at that perception, and whether they take adequate steps to inform themselves on all the issues relevant to it, is, however, a separate question.

Public Function – Private Action: A Common Law Dilemma 111

Notes

1. See Maitland, 'The Crown as Corporation' (1901) 17 L.Q.R. 131. But see *R* v. *Bembridge* (1783) 22 St. Tr. 1, at 155-56 for an atypical usage.
2. See Maitland, 'The Crown as Corporation', at 136-37.
3. Hale's Analysis of the Civil Part of the Law, 71.
4. *Ashby* v. *White* (1704) 14 St. Tr. 695, at 788.
5. *Respublica* v. *Sparhawk* (1788) 1 Dall. 357, at 362 (Pa. Sup. Ct. 1788).
6. See generally A.W.B. Simpson, *A History of the Common Law of Contract* (Clarendon Press, Oxford, 1975), at 229-33.
7. *Ansell* v. *Waterhouse* (1817) 2 Ch.R.1, at 4 per Holroyd J.
8. *Lane* v. *Cotton* (1701) 12 Mod. 472, at 484-85. (Author's emphasis.)
9. Lord Hale, *De Portibus Maris*, 77 (c. 1660).
10. Cf. *Johnson* v. *Midland Railway Co.* (1849) 4 Ex. 367.
11. E.g. *Dickson* v. *Reuter's Telegram Co.* (1877) 3 C.P.D.1.
12. E.g. *Glossop* v. *Heston & Isleworth Local Board* (1879) 12 Ch.D.102.
13. E.g. *Atkinson* v. *Newcastle & Gateshead Waterworks Co.* (1877) 2 Ex.D.441.
14. See e.g. Bramwell B. in *Vaughan* v. *Taff Vale Railway Co.* (1860) 5 H. & N. 679.
15. *Munn* v. *Illinois*, 94 U.S. 113, at 126 (1876); see also C.K. Burdick, 'The Origins of the Peculiar Duties of Public Service Corporations', 11 Colum. L. Rev. 515 (1911).
16. E.g. *Bennet & Fisher* v. *Electricity Trust (S.A.)* (1962) 106 C.L.R. 492.
17. See e.g. *John Fairfax Ltd* v. *Australian Postal Commission* (1977) 2 N.S.W.R. 124.
18. *Mayor of Lyme Regis* v. *Henley* (1834) 8 Bli. N.S. 690.
19. Bacon's Abridgement, vol. 6, 787.
20. *Chamberlaine* v. *The Chester & Birkenhead Railway Co.* (1848) 1 Ex. 870, at 876.
21. See e.g. *R* v. *Bembridge*, *supra* note 1.
22. (1786) 1 T.R. 493, at 509.
23. For two notable examples see *Mayor of Lyme Regis* v. *Henley*, *supra* note 18; *Ferguson* v. *Kinnoull* (1842) 9 Cl. & Fin. 251.
24. (1788) 2 T.R. 667.
25. *Blakemore* v. *Glamorganshire Canal Navigation* (1825) 1 My. & K154, at 162.
26. *Atkinson* v. *Newcastle Waterworks Co.* (1977) 2 Ex. D.441.
27. *Cutler* v. *Wandsworth Stadium* (1949) A.C. 398.
28. *R* v. *Dr. Burnell* (1698) Carth.478, at 479.
29. *R* v. *Bembridge* (1783) 22 St. Tr. 1, at 155.
30. *Respublica* v. *Sparhawk*, *supra* note 5.
31. See *Warne* v. *Varley* (1795) 6 T.R. 443; *Miller* v. *Horton* (1891) 26 N.E. 100.
32. *Gildea* v. *Ellershaw*, 298 N.E. 2d 847 (1973).
33. *Garnet* v. *Ferrand* (1827) 6 B. & C. 611, at 625.
34. (1703) 2 Ld. Raym. 938.
35. (1978) A.C. 728, at 754.
36. *Massengill* v. *Yuma County*, 456 P.2d 376 (1969).
37. Cf. *Schuster* v. *City of New York*, 180 N.Y.S.2d 265 (1958).
38. Cf. *Adams* v. *State of Alaska*, 555 P.2d 235 (1976).
39. Cf. *Gregoire* v. *Biddle*, 177 F.2d 579 (1949).

5 INFORMATION CONTROL: AVAILABILITY AND EXCLUSION

Ruth Gavison

Control of information is a subject of growing concern in modern societies, in part on account of the rapid development of technologies which facilitate the acquisition, storage, processing, linking, retrieval and dissemination of information. The main purpose of this chapter is to point to some of the general considerations which have to be taken into account in deciding the scope and form of legal controls over these processes. Whether or not a society conceptualised itself and its practices in terms of publicness and privateness, it would still need to deal with ways in which information is sought, gathered and used. But because publicness and privateness and the distinction between them do loom large, in fact, in discussions about information and its regulation, a chapter on this topic clearly has a place in a book like this. Demands that information of certain kinds should not be sought, or should not be disseminated, or that certain methods of information-seeking should be banned, are often justified as claims to 'privacy'. Conversely, many demands that information should be regulated, whether to increase or restrict its availability, are justified in terms of the public interest. Moreover, the privateness, or the publicness, of the content, subject, circumstances of acquisition, or the source of information is often deemed a relevant, if not a conclusive, consideration in deciding whether access to such information should be restricted or unrestricted.

The first part of the chapter analyses the relationships between the 'private'/'public' terminology and conflicts over information controls. The second part explains some of the difficulties inherent in attempting to resolve such conflicts. The third part suggests some general guidelines for such resolution.

I. Private and Public

The ambiguity inherent in current usages of the terms 'private' and 'public' illuminates some of the strategies employed in arguments about legal control of information, and explains both the usefulness of this terminology and its limits in helping to resolve conflicts over such control.

A. *Senses of 'Private' and 'Public'*

Two types of ambiguity may be distinguished. One type concerns what Benn and Gaus have called the dimensions of privateness and publicness (see above Ch. 1, sec. IV), and though the dimensions that I have identified for my own analytical purposes do not exactly match theirs (access, agency and interest), they are obviously related to them quite closely. The second type of ambiguity relates to the status of private/public ascriptions, as normative or descriptive (see above Ch. 1, sec. V).

Dimensions. In the present context, the obvious dimension of privateness/publicness is that of *being known*. The more widely known an item of information is, the more 'public' it seems and vice versa. A related dimension is that of *accessibility*, which is in turn related to that of *ownership* and *control*. One of the rights which often goes with ownership is the right to exclude others and limit their access to the thing owned. If I am the 'private owner' of a beach I may — but need not — keep it inaccessible to the public. The more accessible it is, the more likely it is that people will in fact frequent it, and the more likely it is that they will witness and thus know what happens on it. Nonetheless, it is clearly possible to know a lot about private (inaccessible) things, and to be totally ignorant of something which has happened in a place which is public, in the sense of accessible, or which has been published in a public place which is available to all.[1]

Another cluster of dimensions is that related to *accountability* and *effect*. Mill's self-regarding conduct is private in the sense that it does not affect the interests of others and consequently should not be regulated by society. Other-regarding conduct, on the other hand, is open to public regulation and control. A related dimension is that of *intimacy*. There is something private in sexual intercourse even when it takes place in a public park.

Some of these dimensions, like ownership and accountability, function mainly as all-or-nothing concepts. Others, such as being known or accessibility, admit of intermediate degrees of being more or less private/public.[2]

Normative-Descriptive Status. There are at least three different senses in which we may want to say that 'this is a private beach'. Taking the dimension of access, we may say (1) that people in fact do not come/

come very often to this beach. 'Private'/'public' is here used in a descriptive sense, saying something about what individuals in fact do. Accordingly, I shall refer to this as 'private$_d$/public$_d$'. We may also say (2) that under an existing system of norms, either social or legal, people have/do not have free access to this beach. 'Private'/'public' here is used to make a claim under the existing norm. I shall refer to this as 'private$_n$/public$_n$'. Finally, we may say (3) that, on the moral merits of the situation, the beach *should* be out of reach/accessible to all — 'private$_m$/public$_m$'. While a beach may be private/public in all three senses, being private/public in one of them does not entail that it is necessarily private/public in the others. A beach may be private$_d$ (in fact) although it is public$_n$ (accessible to all under existing norms), merely because people do not know of it, or because it is hard to get to. It may be public$_d$ although it is private$_n$ if the excluding norms are not obeyed and enforced. In addition there may be a disparity between positive and ideal norms, so that things which are private$_m$ (i.e. that should be excluded, all things considered) are regarded as public$_n$ by existing norms, and vice versa.

In some of its usages, 'private'/'public' does not have the purely descriptive meaning. Most notable is 'private property'. Since property rights are created and conferred by norms, to assert that something is a person's private property must be to invoke a norm.

The ambiguity of the normative-descriptive status cuts across most of the dimensions mentioned above. It also plagues concepts central to our discussion, such as 'public interest'. Saying that something is of public interest may mean that (1) the public is in fact interested in it; or (2) there is an existing norm under which the fact is of public concern; or (3) the public should have an interest in it, whether or not it is in fact interested, or required or permitted to be interested in it under an existing norm.

B. *Arguments about Information Control*

A decision to introduce legal controls over information is a decision to *make* some information private$_n$/public$_n$, through a legal, deliberate norm, so that it can be kept, as far as possible, private$_d$/public$_d$. The primary dimension of this decision is *being known*, or the availability vs. exclusion of the information. I shall use availability and being known as interchangeable, although they are distinct: One can know things although information about them is not available, and there is no way to force knowledge of even the most available of information. Still, the best way to facilitate knowledge is by ensuring that it is available, and in a discussion of controls, availability rather than knowledge is the relevant factor.

Within any single dimension of private/public, we can move along the normative-descriptive range. If we believe that information should be made $private_n/public_n$ in law, we must consider that this information is $private_m/public_m$ (that it should not/should, all things considered, be made available). The converse, however, does not necessarily hold: We may well believe that some information should be known/unknown, and yet think that the law cannot, should not or need not be used to attain this goal. It may, indeed, already be $private_n/public_n$ according to non-legal social norms, and these may be sufficient to ensure that it is $private_d/public_d$, so that there is no need for institutionalised legal norms. The prevalence of existing social norms may *increase* the need for legal controls, however; for information may be $private_n/public_n$ according to social norms, which we nevertheless consider $public_m/private_m$. In such situations, only explicit legal norms may counteract the practices which hinder the availability of information we think should be made known, or enhance the publication of information we believe should be kept secret. An example of the first is the duty to give evidence when called upon by a court. In the absence of a legal duty, conventional practices discouraging 'informing', combined with the reluctance to get involved, may make the detection of crime and the conviction of offenders much more difficult. Conversely, we may need a legal norm to prohibit the publication of books such as Irving Wallace et al., *The Intimate Sex Life of Famous People*,[3] if we think it is undesirable. The demand for them is clearly enough to provide financial incentive to publish, and social censure is not strong enough to discourage it.

Public Interest. It is common to find in information legislation the provision that publication should be privileged, or its suppression justified, if such actions are 'in the public interest'. Similarly, 'public interest' is typically invoked as the criterion by which to decide whether items of information might properly be published even though the item is of a kind that is $private_n$ or $private_m$.[4] For example, this criterion was adopted in the Israeli *Protection of Privacy Act*, 1981, §18(3), to warrant exemption from the privacy rule, and in the Israeli *Prohibition of Defamation Act*, 1965, §14, where truth is not an absolute defence but might be so if conjoined with public interest. Similar provisions occur in other jurisdictions. Such formulations make it appear as if the 'public interest' were the final determinant of the question whether information is legally private$_n$/public$_n$, thereby resolving the privacy/publicity conflict. But this formulation is misleadingly simple.

It is usually conceded that resolution of conflicts requires some balancing of the conflicting interests. The solution adopted is, then, the conclusion of this process, and its evaluation involves a critical study of how it is done. We may distinguish interests by their subjects: Public interests belong to the community at large, private interests to individuals, parties or groups. We may also distinguish interests by their information implications: we may have interests in privacy or in publicity. Usually the public's interest is in publicity, the individual's in privacy. But this is not necessarily so: An individual may have an interest in a public trial to prevent a miscarriage of justice; the public may have an interest in the suppression of some military or political information. In attempting to resolve a particular conflict, we identify all competing interests and balance them.

Invoking 'public interest' may be understood in either of the two following ways:

1. On the first interpretation, whenever the conflict is between private and public interests, the latter should always win. This is indeed a suggested resolution to this type of conflict. But it leaves indeterminate the resolution of the frequently occurring conflict between two public interests. In the English decision in *British Steel Corp.* v. *Granada Television*,[5] Granada published material based on documents of B.S.C., 'leaked' to it by an employee of the company. B.S.C. requested that Granada be ordered to disclose the name of this employee. Lord Denning said that the case involved the balancing of two public interests: that of protecting freedom of the press by permitting it not to disclose its sources, and that of helping B.S.C. in identifying the offending employee.[6] The primacy of public interest, then, decides nothing.

Nor, indeed, does the primacy of public interest necessarily reflect our actual resolutions of conflicts: When the interest of the public is public$_d$ or public$_n$ only, we are often reluctant to move from identification of an interest of the public to a resolution in its favour. The mere fact that the public is interested in some information, or that there exists a social norm justifying such an interest, cannot be a conclusive reason for frustrating the wish of an individual not to be harmed by embarrassing publication. The distinction is often made between that which is 'of interest to the public' and does not, in itself, justify publication, and that which is 'in the public interest'.[7] Even when the interest of the public is legitimate, as a result of balancing we may sometimes prefer the private interest. The interest of the public in knowing the state of health of an actual or proposed prime minister is a paradigmatic case of legitimate interest. Yet it is not always thought to justify regular detailed public bulletins.

2. According to the second interpretation, we should balance all the interests involved in a case, and whatever emerges as the desirable balance is the solution required by the public interest, and the one to be enforced. This may indeed be an accurate description of the balancing, but it does not help in identifying the interests to be balanced, nor does it tell us their relative weights. It does not even tell us in which sense of 'public', on the normative-descriptive range, we should take the term. It is possible, of course, to use 'public interest' as a portmanteau term in legislation, accompanying it with a list of more specific conditions which count as instances of it. But then the expression 'the public interest' adds nothing of itself to these conditions.[8]

There is some sense, however, in which legitimate interests of the public have priority over individuals' interests, and to identify an interest as both legitimate and public is helpful in resolving a conflict. Furthermore, in some cases even the identification of a $public_n$ or a $public_d$ interest may suggest a solution, on the grounds that it satisfies more wants than another. But this falls a long way short of the notion that some all-encompassing concept of public interest can infallibly supply an answer to problems of this kind. Because such a concept is never more than a synonym for 'the desirable solution', it cannot help in deciding what it is.

'Private' and 'Public'. It is sometimes argued that only publication of private information is an invasion of privacy, or that all information which is public should be made available to all. If 'private'/'public' is used here as $private_m$/$public_m$ in the dimension of being known, the statements are tautologies rather than arguments. They are significant, but not necessarily true, if the terms are used in the descriptive or normative senses, or in a dimension different from that of being known. Thus Dean Prosser claims that only the publication of facts that are private both in the sense of intimate and not already known would be *prima facie* an invasion of privacy.[9]

On the dimension of being known, the move from $private_d$/$public_d$ or $private_n$/$public_n$ to $private_m$/$public_m$ may be suggestive but not conclusive. In some cases it makes good moral sense to impose legal limits on the publication of information just because most people think this information is $private_m$, or, in other words, when the information is private$_n$ according to a social norm. In other contexts, it may make sense to impose such limits only if the information is *in fact* unknown. Again, there may be cases in which we would want to protect information which has already become available and known to some, at some time, from being repeated or further discussed. A central case is that of the revival of already published information which can be found in old newspapers. In the United States such revival is generally permitted, unless it conflicts with the interest to permit rehabilitation.[10] And as mentioned above, in other cases the purpose of the control may be to fight the prevalent social standards which permit exposure, where we think such exposure is undesirable. Conversely, as with the duty to give evidence, we may need a norm compelling disclosure precisely because existing norms permit the secrecy which is in fact maintained, in cases where such secrecy is deemed undesirable.

When 'private'/'public' is used, not of information but of a place, action or function, that ascription may be used as an argument for keeping some information unknown/available. To evaluate the argument, however, we must make it explicit rather than simply accept the slide of meanings. A number of such arguments are discussed below, and for purposes of illustration I shall sketch three typical strategies.

First is the move from freedom to privacy, from accountability to availability. It may seem tempting to argue that one is entitled to conceal all self-regarding conduct, but that one has no right to conceal facts for which one is accountable. A complex argument may indeed be made for both propositions in some circumstances. For instance, it might be argued that individuals should be free to do anything that is private$_m$ (properly private because self-regarding), but that they may well be under pressure from people who disapprove of what they want to do. Freedom may then require secrecy. On the other hand, accountability requires that a person stand by what he has done and bear the consequences, and it may be held that anyone offending against the norms of his society ought to be open about it. Because society has an interest in law enforcement, no one, it may be said, is entitled to keep such facts to himself. Nevertheless, this move is not inevitable or necessary, as shown by the fact that the law does recognise a right to remain silent, acknowledging that a witness or an accused person is not under an obligation to incriminate himself. Similarly, the right to keep information unknown and non-accountability are conceptually distinct. An obligation to report abortions may exist and be justified even in a legal system which views abortion as self-regarding and free from state interference.

The second strategy is to move from the content or nature of the information to its availability. It is said, for example, that intimate information should not be freely available, whereas information concerning the way an official performs his official duties should be.[11] In most cases there are good reasons for these judgements: Intimacy cannot thrive under the risk of publicity, and public officials cannot be called to account if information about their performance is not made available. But the connection between the nature of the information and its availability is not conceptual or necessary, and in some cases the judgement cannot be supported. We may impose on an intended spouse a duty to disclose his/her proven inability to have children, despite the intimate nature of the information. And we may exempt a public official, in certain cases, from disclosing how he arrives at a decision.

The third strategy is to move from accessibility to availability of information. It is often held that events occurring in a public (accessible) place, or information recorded on a 'public' record, may be reported against the wish of the individuals concerned;[12] but that information about what takes place in closed meetings or in private need not be freely available. As to the former, it may be argued that to appear in a public place is implicitly to consent to being reported on. But that presumption may be rebutted when it is clear that the individual did not intend, or could not control, the nature of his appearance in public. Thus a U.S. court prohibited the publication of a picture of the plaintiff with her dress billowing up in a 'fun house'.[13] The move need not be made, therefore, from the fact that information is accessible to its being made freely available. Another move may be to claim that what occurs in public is already $public_d$, so it may as well be $public_n$. But as we have seen, neither of the steps are inevitable. Conversely, the mere fact that a person chose to hide his activity does not entitle him to maintain information privacy about it. Clearly, a murder committed in private should be made public. Statements made in a private meeting, though, raise more complex questions. We may want to protect our privacy in order to ensure the reliability and effectiveness of the communication.[14]

C. *Privacy/Publicity vs. Availability/Exclusion*

Legal questions affecting the control of information range far more widely, of course, than those on which attention is focused by the privacy/publicity dichotomy, including questions such as accuracy and reliability. Even within the concern with availability, the privacy/publicity framework limits the field: Persons, both individual and corporate, have interests in controlling information about their financial dealings, patents, trade secrets and so on, and therefore in limiting availability. When, as in this chapter, publicity is taken in opposition to privacy, which is often defined as related only to concerns with liberty, individuality, self-image and autonomy — values peculiarly applicable to individual persons — concerns common to both individuals and corporations are excluded.[15] Equally, privacy is not always limited to questions of the availability of information, and other chapters in this book (e.g. Ch. 4) take up other, related issues. In this chapter, however, I shall confine myself to this narrower conception: privacy and publicity as they relate to information.[16]

The terminology of availability is more useful, perhaps, than the private/public terminology in that it does not seem to demand all-or-nothing distinctions. The description of information as private or public is rarely complete, in fact, without its being specified to whom it is available and who is excluded from it. The answer is rarely 'available to all' or 'excluded from all'. This feature of information states-of-affairs is important in discussing the resolution of conflicts.

II. Some Difficulties in Resolving Privacy/Publicity Conflicts

To have information can be a form of power and a source of control, and so too is the ability to deny information to others. Thus it is not surprising that people want information and want to exclude others from having it. In our terms, they typically want to protect the privacy of information they have (unless they think that it is in their interest to make it available), while claiming a right of access to the information they want. (This latter claim may be, but does not have to be, couched in terms of claims of publicity.) As with most other wants, satisfying one person very often frustrates someone else. Conflicts cannot be resolved and controls justified in terms of want-satisfaction alone;[17] justification calls for reasons which typically link certain information states-of-affairs with some value or goal we wish to promote or protect. The privacy/publicity conflict is then resolved by balancing these goals and by estimating how far the regulation of information will contribute to their promotion or protection.

A number of difficulties beset attempts to resolve privacy/publicity conflicts in this way. The causal connections between information states-of-affairs and the goals are often highly speculative. Moreover, in society and in individual life, the desirable solution of the privacy/

publicity conflict is rarely complete privacy or total publicity but some balance between the two which cannot be abstractly specified. Again, ranking competing goals and determining the optimal information regulation for each is never easy.

Formidable as such difficulties are, however, they are not peculiar to the privacy/publicity area of conflict. There is, however, one further difficulty which is peculiar to it, namely, that the very values that together form our ideal picture of individuals in society can themselves generate competing information requirements. Such conflicts are especially painful, since the tension sheds doubts on the coherence of our ideals and most basic values. Because this special difficulty explains, I believe, the special status and vehemence of some privacy/publicity controversies, it warrants extended discussion; I shall devote the rest of this chapter to it.

The 'ideal picture' to which I refer is one shared by most contemporary western democracies: A group of autonomous individuals, each striking a balance between pursuit of his own goals and involvement in the life of the community, each aware of himself as a moral agent and respecting himself and others as moral agents and choosers. Such individuals have meaningful relations with others and live in a pluralistic, tolerant and democratic society, where the rights and liberties of all are equally protected by law and in which the institutions and basic principles are just.

This ideal picture takes certain conditions for granted, either as necessary for the existence even of less-than-ideal societies, or as general goals, related in no special way to those that give this ideal its particular character. Efficiency, security, law enforcement, economic growth and profit are all important in this way but are not especially related to this ideal. They may come into conflict, nevertheless, with its special requirements. However, conflicts between privacy/publicity and such values will not be discussed in this chapter. My present purpose is limited to highlighting a cluster of tensions arising within the special requirements of the ideal itself.

A. *Tension Between Information Requirements of the Same Ideal*

Most of the ideals comprising the ideal picture may require exposure and availability on the one hand and privacy and exclusion on the other. Only intimacy and relaxation, which are part of the picture of the good life, are positively related to privacy only — there is nothing in availability or publicity to promote them, and fear of publicity may inhibit them.

The Personality Ideal. The claim has been made by Jourard that sanity itself requires a degree of privacy. Individuals, he argues, need to escape at times the social pressures to conform and 'to behave'.[18] Moreover, we need to be able to present different pictures of ourselves in different contexts, to assume different roles for different audiences (see Alan Ryan's 'theatrical' account in Ch. 6). Privacy protects us as we put on and take off the masks. On the other hand, we need contact with other individuals and information about the conditions in which we are called upon to make decisions, or we lose touch with the world, and, like Joseph K. in Kafka's *The Trial*, become inert, possibly insane, paralysed, oppressed by a sense of helplessness in the face of the incomprehensible.

Information is necessary, too, for personal autonomy, which is part of the personality ideal. Autonomy consists in the capacity to evaluate critically the norms, practices, and decisions that affect a person's life, and the capacity to reach independent judgements about them. Being autonomous does not mean that one is necessarily a nonconformist; one may make a critical evaluation and yet endorse the society's standards. But that cannot be guaranteed. Since it is impossible, in any case, to make an intelligent judgement of consequences and alternatives without information, denying a person reliable information is a sure way to inhibit autonomy. This is particularly relevant, of course, in making judgements and decisions that closely affect one's own private life. Paternalistic refusals by doctors to provide their patients with information about their prospects and prognoses, and about the possible side-effects of alternative treatments, amount, it is said, to a denial of the patients' rights to make autonomous, informed decisions about their own lives.

As regards more public concerns, autonomy requires that individuals have available to them, in addition to all relevant general facts, knowledge of the critical thinking that goes on in their society, and of other individuals who are inclined to make critical judgements similar to their own. The possibility that autonomous judgement may lead to nonconformity may not only be perceived as a possible threat to the society, but may also be perceived by the critical individual himself as a source of danger to himself. To have available the information that there are like-minded individuals in one's society (and to be free to contact them) may provide a much-needed support for holders of unpopular views. Conversely, however, the same possibility that non-conformity may provoke hostility can be adduced as an argument linking autonomy and privacy. It might be argued that privacy will work *against* autonomy by encouraging a person not to stand up for his commitments, which is a public act. Yet for the tentative stage of making and reaching a commitment, privacy is essential. The ability to conceal one's deviant opinions, if one chooses, protects the process of autonomous judgement by providing immunity from pressure just at the stage at which the individual is still making tentative moves and articulating possible positions, before formulating a final and mature judgement on which he would be willing to take an open stand. A similar case can be made quite generally for giving people immunity from public observation, criticism, and harassment while still learning and developing personal, technical and moral capacities in the exercise of which they have not yet achieved certain levels of self-confidence. Admittedly, learning may well require sympathetic guidance in the acquisition of standards and, therefore, some exposure to tutorial criticism; but it may require, too, that that exposure be appropriately restricted.

Just as personal development requires both that certain kinds of information be accessible to a person, and that he be in a position to exclude others from knowing certain things about himself, so the development of moral agency requires both. On the one hand, the respect due to a person as a moral agent is a reason against, for instance, surreptitious surveillance, which treats him as an object, taking no account of his own view of his situation and his actions, and his preferences for appearing one way or another – or not at all – on the public stage. On the other hand, as a moral agent a person is a chooser, and to choose effectively he must have access to reliable information relating to his options, including, for instance, information about the people with whom he does business, or mixes socially, or seeks intimacy. Interpersonal relations also require availability of information. Charles Fried has argued that relations of trust, love and friendship depend on there being information about a person that is not generally known, that that person can choose to disclose to his partner. Without privacy there could be no such information to entrust, and without the liberty not to disclose information, no confidentiality and no intimacy.[19] On the other hand, the growth of a relationship may also require its public acknowledgement. Marriage owes much of its symbolic importance to its public nature.

The Social and Political Ideal. All governments claim that to do their job they must seek, require, gather and process information. They claim, on the other hand, that they must conduct their business with some secrecy, prohibiting civil servants from disclosing information obtained through their employment and creating a category of 'state secrets'. Governments always claim the right to negotiate secretly, and at times to keep the resulting agreements secret too.

Democracies are unique, however, in the claims they make on behalf of their citizens: It is argued that if the freedom (or the civic duty) to participate in affairs of state is to be meaningful, individuals must be entitled to all the information relevant to making decisions. Furthermore, since in a democracy an elected official can be called to account, the record of his performance should be available to citizens. And between elections, citizens have the freedom to seek to influence political processes and decisions through their protests and to lobby for changes in the law. All these activities require that relevant information be available to them.[20] Finally, citizens of a democracy may claim that no opinions or attempts to disseminate information should be repressed, and they may even go further and argue that all points of view have rights to (equal?) access to the media.[21] Arguments *against* making information freely available rarely invoke the need to maintain the democratic nature of the state; but there have been exceptions, as when demands have been made that, in the defence of democracy itself, the views of anti-democratic groups, such as communist or neo-nazi groups, should be suppressed.

Yet some claims for privacy, or for limiting access (and the right to seek information), can be based on the democratic requirement that citizens shall be able, at the least, to cast their votes freely and to enjoy freedom of political opinion. In a society where one is sure to suffer painful consequences for casting the 'wrong' vote, or for holding the 'wrong' beliefs, or for belonging to the 'wrong' party or association, keeping these facts about individuals secret (in the sense of not requiring their public disclosure or not making their disclosure a condition of employment) may be the least institutional guarantee of that crucial freedom. On this ground – the right of free expression under the First Amendment of the U.S. Constitution – voluntary political groups were held to be under no obligation to disclose the names of their members.[22] Such institutionalised guarantees are especially needed in a society that is intolerant of unconventional views.

Freedoms, of course, are not restricted to those related to the democratic process, and privacy is relevant to those other freedoms too. It is clear that in many cases we cannot make the law tolerant (e.g. the failure to abolish, in some countries, the offence of 'unnatural' sexual conduct), and that even if on the institutional level tolerance is achieved, there remains much social censure of unconventional conduct. Privacy then serves as a shield against this censure, and it thus contributes to freedom of action.[23] In an ideal pluralist society, there would be less need for this function of privacy since there would be more acceptance of the right to be different. Nonetheless, there will always be some areas in which freedom will obtain only in privacy: The freedom to lower one's guard when one is doing nothing wrong; the freedom to be ridiculous at times; the freedom to be uninhibited; and the freedom to be vulnerable and weak without fear that one will be hurt.[24]

Alongside the democratic values, the rule of law and the administration of justice figure large in the picture of the ideal society. Both are invoked in favour of publicity and availability. The most general claim is that laws should be promulgated and made public so that individuals will know how to behave legally and avoid legal sanctions. The same principle of legality is invoked against retrospective legislation. In law enforcement contexts, 'due process', or 'natural justice', requires that court proceedings be public, as a guarantee against abuses; that defendants or, more generally, people harmed by a decision, should be given access to the evidence upon which it is based so that they can challenge the record and/or prepare a defence; this right will normally include the right to know the sources of the evidence, so that they can be personally cross-examined and challenged. Another availability requirement is the general duty to give evidence, so that fact-finding tribunals will have all relevant information.[25]

The tensions between information implications of the rule of law and the administration of justice are revealed when we study the many exceptions to these requirements. Individuals are allowed not to give evidence 'against themselves'.[26] Individuals in particular relationships with parties to law suits (e.g. in solicitor-client relationships) are permitted, sometimes obliged, not to give evidence concerning information passed or acquired within the relationship. Exceptions are sometimes, if rarely, allowed to the principle that identity of witnesses and evidence should be disclosed. In judicial proceedings, such exceptions are justified by reference to security or the needs of law enforcement. At times courts are permitted, or even obliged, to hold their sessions *in camera*, either at the instance of an accused person who would like to avoid the publicity of open court or of the prosecution, again for such reasons as security, and against the wishes of the accused.

Similar tensions exist between availability and privacy in less structured contexts, such as the giving of references and recommendations, where non-disclosure of sources is justified in various ways. It is worth noting, however, that in some jurisdictions where such non-disclosure was formerly permitted, freedom of information legislation has perceptibly narrowed the area covered by the cloak of confidentiality in the interest of permitting individuals to defend themselves against misleading and damaging reports.

B. Tensions Between Components of the Ideal Picture

Two major tensions within the ideal picture have information implications: the tension between freedom and accountability, and the tension between democracy (seen as a procedure of decision-making) and the end-states of democratic freedom, tolerance and justice.

Accountability, on the individual and the official level, is clearly a part of the ideal picture. There is no moral agency without some form of public accountability, and there is no sense to democratic elections if officials cannot be held accountable for their tenure of office. Yet there are many instances in which accountability is not desirable, and in these publicity, as we have seen, may lead to undesirable limitations of freedom. A partial solution of this tension is to permit areas of privacy in which accountability is in fact limited, freedom in fact increased, without admitting to the desirability of these private areas. The tension is one between accountability and freedom themselves, and the tension between the information implications of these values is just a reflection of the primary tension.

Democracy is an integral part of the ideal picture, since by recognising the right of individuals to participate in making the decisions affecting them, it presupposes and affirms the picture of the individual as autonomous and as a moral agent. Yet it is conceivable that democratic regulation might threaten both autonomy and independence, thus limiting both personal development and freedom of action.[27] The existence of laws prohibiting a certain type of conduct usually goes with police powers to investigate violations and detect crimes that may lead to losses of privacy. When such regulation itself is not consistent with the ideal of free individuals living in an open and tolerant society, we have a conflict between democracy and the rule of law and these other elements of the ideal picture. This conflict has obvious implications for information issues and for deciding what conduct is to be private, what public. This conflict was dramatically illustrated in the American case of *Griswold* v. *Connecticut*,[28] in which the Court held that the law prohibiting married couples from using contraceptives was an unconstitutional invasion of the privacy of marital relations, and thus invalid. Part of the reasoning of the Court was that the existence of the law inevitably justified investigating possible violations, and that such investigation would involve 'peeping' into the bedrooms of couples, which is an unacceptable invasion of privacy. The Court may have used the language of privacy and information to disguise its possibly non-democratic challenge to an undesirable liberty-limiting statute.

C. Exclusion as a Requirement for Availability

Finally, in addition to these tensions between the information requirements of the various values in our ideal picture, a tension exists in every instance in which it is desirable that information be made available. In some of these cases, a guarantee of exclusion, secrecy or confidentiality is necessary to ensure that the information is indeed available to the desired extent. In these cases, we pay for availability by limiting availability itself.

The contexts in which this may happen are many and diverse. As I suggested earlier, spontaneity and trust in personal relations require candour, but in order to promote candour we need the shield of confidentiality. The same holds, for other reasons, for the relationships between lawyers and their clients, doctors and their patients, ministers and their parishioners. For these latter relations, the law grants the recipients of information a privilege which is an exception to the general duty to give evidence when required to do so in court. The law here is willing to forgo the availability of relevant information in order not to undermine the availability of information within the relationship. A similar rationale is the basis of duties of confidentiality imposed by law on many official agencies, which are authorised to collect information about identifiable individuals. To encourage individuals to give reliable and truthful information to census-takers, tax inspectors and research workers, it is found necessary to promise limited access to it.[29]

III. Some Practical Guidelines

The previous section implies that there are no easily identified, right solutions to information conflicts, even within the limited domain I have considered. Frequently there are ways of at least limiting the area of conflict, so that the arrangements are not damaging in terms of the values inherent in the ideals of personality and society sketched above; or, should that be impossible, guidelines can be formulated to minimise such damage.

A. Limiting the Area of Conflict

All the arguments that I have given favouring limited access to information relate to information about identifiable individuals. Most claims that information be available relate to other types of information and are thus not touched by the claims of privacy here discussed. Information about philosophical arguments, scientific data, political developments, interpretations of history, predictions and consequences are all necessary for the development of personality, for learning, and the making of autonomous judgements; and nothing in my analysis of the good life would justify curbing the desire to seek, gather and disclose this kind of information. To the contrary, it may justify some positive aids in support of such efforts. There is conflict only where the same information required to satisfy a particular value in one respect would need to be excluded to serve the same value in another respect, or another value within the same ideal picture. A conflict of the first kind might occur if making available an official record to one individual to check the accuracy of personal details recorded about himself unavoidably put him in possession of similar information about someone else. A conflict of the second kind would be between the claims of privacy and availability in respect of a person's state of health, when that person is a candidate for high political office. Similarly, the values of autonomy, sanity, personal development and intimacy clearly require some freedom from observation, some freedom to withdraw and relax, some freedom to explore and experiment in a supportive environment or alone. Yet these freedoms are quite consistent with requiring openness and accountability in many other aspects of individuals' lives. Furthermore, some claims for privacy and secrecy are only temporary in nature. Accountability may be required for all mature exercises of freedom, but it might be consistent with allowing a protected time for learning, practising and experimenting.

Finally, some privacy claims relate only to special types of information. Only the most intimate kind of information is relevant to some of Fried's argument that privacy is necessary to trust, love and friendship, and it is only in respect of information of this kind that one would insist that it should be private even from one's closest partners, if one chose to keep it so. The privacy of other information, even when it relates to identifiable individuals, is not justified by this kind of argument.

B. The Limits of Legal Controls

There are some contexts in which legal, institutionalised controls are inadequate or inappropriate, and then there is no need to resolve conflicts in advance by stating general rules. One obvious example is that of information controls within intimate and family relations. Even if the information requirements of values related to such relations were crystal clear, legal duties either of disclosure or privacy are not the right way to implement them. The texture of these relations is usually too delicate to sustain crude interference by legal norms, with the possible litigation which their enforcement entails. The relationship might not survive a serious invasion of privacy or a substantial lack of candour, but in any event the matter lies outside the scope of the law. The law cannot revive love or effectively compensate a person for loss of self-respect or the capacity to trust. In most cases, these losses 'lie where they fall' as far as the law is concerned, and no legal controls can shift them.

Sometimes, of course, matters of this kind — such as custody and divorce settlement cases — must be settled in court. Because some people at least find the public airing of such cases inappropriate and unpleasant, there have been suggestions that such proceedings should be held *in camera* to avoid adding publicity to the inherent unpleasantness of the legal proceedings themselves. A related problem, where the courts cannot help intervening, arises when the law is used to prevent proposed publication of intimate information acquired during a relationship. Seeking a court order to prevent publication itself brings the matter into the public realm. In situations like this, the fabric of the relationship has been destroyed, but the hurt to the sensibilities of the applicant caused by publicity may still be severe.

C. *Natural Regulators*

When there are 'natural regulators' tending to sustain the desirable state of affairs with respect to information, legal controls may not be needed. Such regulators include social norms, limits on opportunities or curiosity, costs, human nature or the limits of the available technologies and possibilities. This list suggests that the need for legal controls may change with these natural regulators. It is not surprising, for instance, that the interest in privacy became more intense with the emergence of the mass media, which changed the range and breadth of dissemination, and with the development of technologies facilitating acquisition and processing of information. In general, however, a greater readiness has been shown, in many countries sharing such concerns, to respond by legal regulation to threats to privacy posed by techniques of the latter kind, than by threats posed by mass publication. Restraints on freedom of publication draw far more criticism and are in general more narrowly confined.[30] And, indeed, for most individuals most of the time, limits on curiosity and interest and considerations of cost, together with the growing anonymity of modern life and the growing ability to withdraw into a 'private' space, provide more opportunities than before to maintain the desirable level of privacy without relying on legal regulation.

Just as some natural regulators work for privacy, so there are some that work for publicity: Many individuals court publicity and fame, and do not object to information about themselves (including very intimate information) being known to the public at large. Some even actively seek to gain such publicity. In addition, there are many occupations in which making information public has become a way to attain respect and success. The entertainment industry is an obvious example. Moreover, people have needs to disclose information and to be frank, at least some of the time and in some contexts. And most people do not hesitate to gossip — to pass on information which they think their listener will find useful, intriguing or of interest.

D. Minimising the Losses

In the case, however, of legal control, the result is generally that someone's desire either for publicity or information privacy, as the case may be, will be frustrated, a desire that may nevertheless be justified in its turn by reference to one of the values forming a part of the ideal picture. Every frustration then counts as a cost to be set against the case for control. Many of these conflicts can be resolved easily. In some the harm due to loss of privacy will be large, while the gains in the values served by publicity will be minimal;[31] in others, the reverse will be true. And while no formula can be given for resolving harder cases in which the costs and benefits are more finely balanced, it is still possible to suggest certain procedural rules and guidelines, one set tending to safeguard interests in privacy, another protecting the interest in availability and information publicity.

The protection of privacy will benefit if attention is paid to the following guidelines:

1. Claims that information about individuals is needed should be checked for relevance and importance.

2. Such a need having been established, the information should be sought and acquired in the least intrusive way; often this would be to ask the person concerned. He would then know what information was being sought, could challenge its relevance, and provide only what was necessary, without the spill-over of irrelevant material obtained by surveillance.

3. Verification of information should be done under due process of law.

4. Confidentiality provisions should be strictly enforced. Access to information should be limited to the purposes for which it is gathered.

5. Where observation is deemed necessary, preference should be given to observation with the knowledge of the observed. When this is impractical, care should be taken to limit the duration of observation, and to allow as much as possible for unobserved intimacy and relaxation.

6. Publishers of information should always consider whether the story requires names or identification. If not, and the publication is likely to be harmful, naming should be avoided.

7. All irrelevant or obsolete information should periodically be deleted from files.

8. Agencies which have an interest in gathering, processing and seeking information should be under external supervision when making decisions to acquire or disseminate information without the subject's knowledge and consent.

Effective protection of interests in publicity and availability requires that:

1. The freedom to seek and disseminate information should not be curbed in general, and all exceptions should be narrowly conceived and drafted (including the exception to protect privacy).

2. Censorship or any other form of 'prior constraint' should be avoided as far as possible.

3. Accountable individuals and organisations should, in general, be under an obligation to provide open access to information about their activities.

4. Holders of information about individuals, or those who make decisions affecting individuals, should in general be under an obligation to disclose the information to the subjects of such records.

5. Legal norms and institutional practices should be made public and accessible to all those affected by them.

6. Professional workers (such as medical practitioners) should be under a general obligation to disclose to people affected by a decision all the information necessary for them to evaluate it independently.

7. Wherever 'informed consent' is required, the subject should be given access to all the information relevant to the decision. Paternalistic considerations against disclosure should be, if at all, rarely admitted.

8. Some form of immunity from legal sanction should be given to anyone who frustrates illegal and undesirable attempts to suppress information, the publication of which is in the public interest.

Notes

In these notes I freely use material from different legal systems to show that all legal systems grapple with these problems in their own way. The literature of these problems is huge, and no attempt at comprehensiveness can be made here. The legal sources are used for illustration only.

1. For a discussion of these relationships, see H. Gross, 'The Concept of Privacy', *New York University Law Review*, 42 (1967), p. 34.
2. For these dimensions, the concepts private and public are 'ideal types', which are neither actual nor desirable. The more useful concepts are *loss* of privacy or availability, rather than |*total* privacy or publicity. See my 'Privacy and Its Legal Protection', unpublished D. Phil. thesis, Oxford, 1975, pp. 23-24.
3. I. Wallace et al., *The Intimate Sex Life of Famous People* (Delacorte Press, New York, 1981).
4. See the seminal article by S. Warren and L. Brandeis, 'The Right to Privacy', *Harvard Law Review*, 4 (1890), pp. 193-220, at p. 218.
5. [1980] 3 *Weekly Law Reports* 774.
6. [1980] 3 *Weekly Law Reports* 803.
7. See e.g. U.K. Press Council, *Declaration on Privacy* (April 1976). Failure to note this distinction has sometimes caused confusion and is at least partly responsible for the erratic state of the law: Note, 'The Right to Privacy: Normative-Descriptive Confusion in the Defense of Newsworthiness', *University of Chicago Law Review*, 30 (1976), p. 722.
8. For such a usage, see e.g. Report No. 11 of the Australian Law Reform Commission, *Unfair Publication: Defamation and Privacy* (1979), para. 247, pp. 132-33. Note the variety of senses in which 'private' and 'public' are used in this elaboration.
9. W. Prosser, *The Law of Torts*, 4th edn (West Publishing Co., St. Paul, Minn., 1971), pp. 809-12.
10. *Melvin* v. *Reid*, 112 Cal. App. 285, 297 P. 91 (1931); *Briscoe* v. *Reader's Digest Ass'n* (1971), Cal. 3d 529, 483 P.2d 34.
11. See *Unfair Publication*, pp. 133, 124.
12. See ibid., p. 125; Prosser, *Torts*, p. 810.
13. *Daily Times Democrat* v. *Graham*, 276 Ala. 380, 162 So. 2d 474 (1964). The 'public record' cases are more complex, since the existence of a public record attests to a judgement that there are good reasons for availability. See the recent decision in *Cox Broadcasting Corp.* v. *Cohn*, 420 U.S. 469 (1975), for a refusal to prohibit the publication of a rape victim's name where it appeared on the record of her rapist murderer's trial.
14. See R. Posner, 'The Right to Privacy', *Georgia Law Review*, 12 (1978), pp. 401-3.
15. The legal position is not always clear. The Israeli *Protection of Privacy Act* 1981 explicitly limits the application of the law to individuals. In the United States, courts have ruled that only individuals could sue for invasion of privacy. (Prosser, *Torts*, pp. 814-15.) On the other hand, courts have granted individuals protection where the concern was clearly commercial: M.B. Nimmer, 'The Right of Publicity', *Law and Contemporary Problems*, 19 (1954), pp. 203-23. Some writers feel that the distinction between individuals and legal entities in this context is unfortunate: Posner, 'The Right to Privacy', p. 393.

16. Elsewhere I have used a broader analysis: see my 'Privacy and the Limits of Law', *Yale Law Journal*, 89, no. 3 (1980), pp. 421-71 at pp. 425-40.

17. For a detailed discussion of want-satisfaction arguments and their insufficiency in this context, see my 'Privacy and Its Legal Protection', pp. 62-73.

18. S.M. Jourard, 'Some Psychological Aspects of Privacy', *Law and Contemporary Problems*, 31 (1966), p. 307. See also S.I. Benn, 'Privacy, Freedom and Respect for Persons', in J.R. Pennock and J.W. Chapman (eds.), *NOMOS XIII: Privacy* (Atherton Press, New York, 1971), pp. 1-26, at pp. 24-25.

19. C. Fried, 'Privacy', *Yale Law Journal*, 77 (1968), p. 485. For one critical analysis, see Reiman, 'Privacy, Intimacy and Personhood', *Philosophy and Public Affairs*, 6 (1977), pp. 31-36. Yet Reiman, too, presents an argument linking intimacy and privacy. See also R. Gerstein, 'Privacy and Intimacy', *Ethics*, 89 (1978), p. 76.

20. For an argument for availability in these terms, see A. Meiklejohn, *Political Freedom* (Oxford University Press, New York, 1965).

21. Regulation of equal access to the media involves a deviation from the classical conception of the freedom of the press. For some of the problems, see J. Barron, 'Access to the Press – A New First Amendment Right', *Harvard Law Review*, 80 (1967), at p. 1641.

22. *NNACP* v. *Alabama*, 357 U.S. 449 (1958).

23. This condensed formulation cannot do justice to the complex relationships between privacy and freedom. See also A.F. Westin, *Privacy and Freedom* (Bodley Head, London, 1967) and my 'Privacy and Its Legal Protection', pp. 76-84.

24. Some may argue that this is an undesirable function of privacy, since it permits deviation from justified norms and standards of society: Posner, 'The Right to Privacy', p. 407. The argument is valid for some contexts, simplistic for others: see my 'Privacy and the Limits of Law', pp. 451-55.

25. Since the requirements of 'natural justice' apply to legal organs, their exact boundaries, for each legal system, are determined by the courts, on the background of general principles which are universally seen as a part of the requirements of the rule of law and fair trial. For the combination of general principles and particular rulings in England, see e.g. P. Jackson, *Natural Justice*, 2nd edn (Sweet and Maxwell, London, 1979).

26. For a sensitive argument linking this 'right to silence' with the values discussed by me, see R. Gerstein, 'Privacy and Self-Incrimination', *Ethics*, 80 (1970), p. 87.

27. This complex relationship between democracy and freedom has been frequently elaborated in the literature. I still find I. Berlin, 'Two Concepts of Liberty', in *Four Essays on Liberty* (Oxford University Press, London, 1969), very illuminating.

28. 381 U.S. 479 (1965).

29. Patents and copyright may be seen as similar mechanisms, but since they relate to financial activities which have been excluded from discussion, I shall not elaborate on this aspect here. For a discussion of patents as a way of producing useful information, see Posner, 'The Right to Privacy', pp. 397-98, 404.

30. See e.g. the Report of the Younger Committee, *Report of the Committee on Privacy*, Cmnd. 5012, July 1972. The Committee recommended the creation of an offence of surveillance by devices but ruled against a legal duty not to publish privacy-invading material.

31. The publication of the name and picture of an individual who is suffering a rare disease is one obvious example. Courts in the United States are usually very reluctant to limit freedom to publish, yet in some rare cases, including this one, they have done so. See e.g. *Barber* v. *Time Inc.*, 348 Mo. 1199, 159 S.W.2d 291 (1942).

6 PRIVATE SELVES AND PUBLIC PARTS

Alan Ryan

I. The Gap Between Natural Persons and Social Roles

There is no one problem to which this chapter is devoted. Indeed, a good deal of what follows is concerned to draw attention to the multifariousness of the issues sheltered by my title and to the absence of any very compelling way of providing them with a theoretical unity. All the same, these issues cluster together rather naturally, as they have done in the work of sociologists, moralists and literary theorists for several centuries at least.[1] To summarise these concerns, we might say that the crucial question is what more there is to the self than its ability to play social roles, how well adapted or maladapted we naturally are to the social roles we are called upon to play, and how the answers to these questions relate to our concern with 'privacy' in the usual sense.

I want to start with a very commonplace illustration of the kind of event which sparks off a curiosity about the subject at all. A man who has just given a lecture may be told by one of his hearers that he is a very good lecturer; the praise may mean absolutely nothing to him. That is, successful role-performance may not gratify the performer, for reasons of any of three kinds, each addressing a particular kind of problem. The first is that the praise attached to success in the role simply doesn't happen to be one of the objects of desire of the performer; a second is that doing successfully what performing in the role requires (including fulfilling his moral commitments) is not one of the objects of his desires. A third possibility is that *what* he was doing, in successfully doing what his role required, has been misunderstood. Thus, a man might not want any of the things which successful role-performance might help him to achieve — promotion, the goods his salary allows him to purchase, or the good opinion of his colleagues and students; in that case, his role-performance would be instrumentally problematic. Or, he might not think that it mattered that students should understand Mill's analysis of matter as the permanent possibility of sensation, might get no pleasure from seeing their grasp of the subject improve; in this case, his role-performance would be intrinsically problematic. Or, thirdly, he might have hoped, in doing what he

135

did in the way that he did it, to communicate something about *himself*; here the notion of successful performance becomes systematically ambiguous — a subject well dealt with by Erving Goffman.[2] Thus, a wild and romantic young lecturer might feel a great gap opening up between himself and his public performance in all three ways — the praise of the stuffily academic is dust in his nostrils, the receiving of instruction seems to him no fit task for the most vigorous years of his pupils' lives, and he might have *meant* the way he gave his lecture to tell his audience that he was, indeed, just such a Byronic figure, 'mad, bad, and dangerous to know'.

This commonplace example illustrates what I mean by the existence of a 'gap' between the natural person — him, that person, Jones — and the roles he bears — father, teacher, mental patient. The large general question is, then, how his performance in his roles is constrained and facilitated by the demands and aspirations of the natural person. These demands and aspirations can in obvious ways be kept private, that is, knowledge of them can be restricted by the person whose aspirations they are; role performance, by contrast, is at any rate commonly more visible, and in that sense public, and is certainly a matter the success and failure of which are judged by the audience rather than the performer. Whether I get what I want out of my job is something on which my authority is almost absolute; whether I do it properly is something on which my say-so is not at all decisive. Even if my role is one which requires me to act in secret — I may be a spy, a commando, or a private eye — success and failure are in the appropriate sense a public matter.

II. Pre-modern and Modern Conceptions of the Self/Role Relationship

It is sometimes suggested that this 'gap' between a person and the roles he occupies is either a discovery of, or the invention of, the modern world;[3] and it is sometimes held that an acute awareness of it is a discovery or invention of the modern American world.[4] In its extreme form, the suggestion would have to be dismissed as silly. Even a society which held strange views about procreation and therefore labelled people as fathers, mothers, aunts and uncles on, to us, peculiar grounds would still distinguish between *who* one was and *what* one was. Rather, writers have evidently meant that pre-modern societies have generally held much more deterministic views about the relationship between persons and roles than we — or some of us — do.[5] In part, this is to say that people in such societies are born into or pass by age into the network of rights and obligations which marks off the roles they occupy; in part, it is to say that people are not held to have any right to avoid or deflect the obligations ascribed to them, and are not thought of as entitled to adjust the demands of the world to their own characters. Of course, put as briefly as that, the claim is instantly vulnerable to counter-example; Odysseus was certainly a hero, but what he is celebrated for is the cunning and deftness with which he fulfilled the heroic role, and this surely shows that even if *what* one does is laid down by the local standards, *how* one does it is less strictly determined.

Nevertheless, there is still the grosser contrast between a society like our own, where the individual's assumption of a role is very often a matter of choice, and older societies, where it very often is not. Odysseus could not have decided that he did not like fighting, or argued that his talents were better suited to a career as a stand-up comic. This point was insisted on by Hegel,[6] and is closely connected to another point associated with him. Just as the individual person had no right to set the claims of his own personality against the demands of his role, so the highest moral aspirations of the individual were still inevitably couched in terms of fulfilling the duties attached to a role. When Antigone breaks the laws of her city to bury her brother, this is not a piece of pure conscientious action, but the fulfilment of the duties of a sister. What makes *Antigone* not just a tragedy but a Greek tragedy is that she has no room for manoeuvre; it is in a sense bad luck that she is saddled with obligations she cannot fulfil except by breaching other obligations of equal stringency, but she cannot appeal to that as an *excuse*. It is this, the way the duties of the role press upon the private self, that we find so alien and alarming in Greek drama; and it is not surprising that some people have been tempted to deny that the Greeks even had a conception of the individual moral agent. All the same, perhaps the most perspicuous way of making the point is rather to insist, as we have, on the way Greek conceptions of personal success and failure — morally and in terms of honour at least — made almost everything of the objective, role-fulfilling activity and made little of the project of the person who filled the role, save in so far as his project was identical with what the role prescribed.

Still, there are plenty of instances in modern conditions of just the same identification of the person and the role he or she occupies. In Durkheim's *Suicide*, the category of what he calls 'altruistic' suicide covers what at first sight looks like an ill-assorted group of cases — officers who kill themselves because they have dishonoured their regiments, soldiers who do something fatally self-sacrificing in battle, and religious enthusiasts who kill themselves ceremoniously and publicly.[7] Yet these are not such oddly assorted cases as they initially appear; always, the individual who fills the role is so closely identified with it that anything that happens to him *qua* occupant of that role fills his moral and psychological landscape. He cannot stand back from what has happened to him *qua* occupant of the role, in order to decide how to react to it. Durkheim certainly writes as if such a degree of identification is dangerous and 'abnormal', but this, after all, is to some extent a function of the subject matter of the book. What is not at all clear is that 'modernity' has much to do with it. There does not seem to have been anything very un-modern about the captain of the *Graf Spee*, who shot himself when he scuttled his ship.

Conversely, Lévi-Strauss' engaging account of the shaman Quesalid casts doubt on the thought that the ability to stand back and contemplate escape from the duties of one's position is the gift of modern society.[8] Quesalid was a shaman who was taught the tricks of his trade; these tricks were literally such, one of them being a way of producing a physical manifestation of the patient's illness – the knack was to secrete a ball of bark in the mouth, to bite one's cheek, mix bark, blood and saliva together, suck the afflicted area, and then triumphantly produce the 'illness'. Quesalid was disgusted, left his own tribe, wandered among neighbouring tribes, and finally discovered that by using this trick he could genuinely cure people whom the shamans of other tribes had failed with. At this, he made his way home and took up his profession, observing that although he did not know why his cures worked, they evidently did work, and that he was at any rate no fraud.

Perhaps the best explanation of these rather discrepant phenomena is this. In small scale, technologically non-complex societies *kinship* roles in particular inevitably provide a great part of social organisation. People in such societies simultaneously *need* the assistance of kin more continuously and more urgently than we do and are under more continuous pressure to provide such assistance in turn.[9] In simpler societies the 'gap' between the individual self and the demands of one's public roles may well be closed by people identifying very completely with the demands of their roles, not necessarily because of anything about their *conceptual* scheme, or even about their moral outlook and psychological dispositions, which is different from our own, but because of the effectiveness of social pressure of the appropriate sort. If this is plausible, it suggests that modern, more complex societies will often exhibit just the same phenomena – where the same pressures need to be applied and can be. But because it is implausible to suppose that such cultural features are strictly determined, individuals in modern societies could have more room for manoeuvre too.

This sort of contrast between different social settings is, of course, loose. In the hands of anthropologists and ethnographers it is interesting, not because of the theoretical rigour of these disciplines but because the quality of the observation is high, and because we want to know how particular societies cope with the various exigencies to which they are subject. It could hardly be a discovery that a given tribe was faced with the problem of socialising its young men into military tasks; it would be more of a discovery to find out how it was done, especially if one could anticipate difficulties in the way, or if there were some puzzlement about how they did it without making their warriors too arrogant, without putting them off farming, or whatever. Still, what level of generality can we expect of a theory − or any explanation at all − of the way persons relate to the roles they occupy? What I have so far said implies, though it does not yet rest on any argument to that effect, that we shall look in vain for either a psychological theory which would derive predictions about our reactions to roles from a few axioms about the human mind, or a sociological theory with which we could derive predictions about what roles a society would institute and how it would do it. Rather, on my account of it, explanations will be piecemeal, situational and historical.[10]

III. The Problem of 'the Self'

Scepticism about the possibility of a psychological theory of role behaviour sometimes appears to rest on the thought that such a theory requires the positing of a 'substratum' whose existence is conceptually or logically impossible. The thought is something like this: a theory of the way selves relate to roles seems to suppose that selves wear roles, that roles are dispensable properties which can be stripped away, leaving the real self for further description and explanation. But we are familiar with Hume's difficulty when he tried to discover his own 'self'; he tried, so he says, to catch himself without a perception but always failed. Assuming that 'I see' means 'the something or other to which "I" refers' has the experience of seeing, Hume tried to discover what the 'I' was like when it was not having experiences.[11] As Hume very well knew, however, when you remove all the experiences of the self from it, what you are left with is not it but nothing, just as you would be left with nothing if you took away all the properties of a table or a chair. By analogy, there seems to be something amiss with the project of searching for an underlying self. If we took away from Dr Jones everything which either was, or was causally modified by, a property he possessed by virtue of being a General Practitioner, Secretary of the Golf Club, doting father, loving husband and so on, we shouldn't expect to find the real Jones at the end of the process.

The relationship of the conscious subject to its perceptions and actions is quite deeply mysterious. If the self is not a substratum, its exact ontological status is hard to describe in more positive terms. Happily, none of this affects the argument here. When we contrast the role-performance of a given person on a given occasion with what he really wants, we do not ascribe those real wants to a mysterious substratum. Moreover, even though there may be some severe conceptual limitations on what a psychological theory can achieve, there is no conceptual obstacle to producing an account of what sort of thing men really are up to in general, and how this is or is not masked by their performances in a role.

An example here can properly carry more conviction than a good deal of argument. On Freud's view of the social condition of mankind, what we *really* want much of the time is to treat each other in a very unKantian way as resources for our sexual and violent impulses.[12] We begin as *homo homini lupus*, but we learn to wear a friendly face in order to avert the war of all against all. We repress or divert the underlying anti-social impulses and come to enjoy the quieter but more secure pleasures of civilised life. Someone who embarked on the quest for a substratum would find himself in just the same impasse as before; if he thought that the 'I' in 'I am a doctor' referred to some underlying bearer of the role, he would be as likely to think that the 'I' in 'I am sexually and aggressively voracious' referred to some underlying carrier of the impulse to fight and violate. The Freudian, however, is not looking for any such substratum. He is certainly looking for what nature contributes to the person we encounter in everyday life, and this is to look to biology and psychology, but it is not to look beneath or below those disciplines.

The difficulties the Freudian does face are familiar enough. They are difficulties about the relationship between the evidence and the large theoretical claims it is made to support. Is it true that even the most consistently 'good-natured' person is sitting on a volcano and that we cannot trust the appearances? Conversely, when civilised men behave violently on the battlefield, is this a sign of their deep desire to kill and maim or simply panic in the face of unexpected danger?

Such doubts are commonplace, though they are serious. The point, however, is that Freud's account of the relationship between inner and outer experience is in principle exactly what we want, even if it is factually utterly wrong. Freud's account offers not necessarily answers, but a framework for tackling the questions which agitate social theorists and literary critics and others — how far can we square our true natures with our social obligations? Can we be both sociable and 'authentic'? What impulses do we have to 'manage' to fill the social roles we find ourselves in?[13]

IV. Nature, Social Adaptation and 'Authenticity'

I have claimed that there is no difficulty in principle in asking the question whether we are chronically endowed by nature with characteristics which are in a large measure at odds with the demands of the social roles we have to fill. I have also suggested that answers to this question also answer questions about the 'gap' between us and the roles we fill. It is time to admit that this is a disputable claim. Someone committed to a Nietzschean or Sartrean view, that human beings uniquely possess *no* nature, would reject the contrast between nature and convention which is being employed here.[14] The tension between the uncontrollable impulse and the controlled expression of it is one he would explain in other terms, since all he would admit is the contrast between the capacity for choice and the choices actually made. Someone who thought in Aristotelian terms, on the other hand, might reject the contrast just as emphatically, but in this case on the grounds that our natures were pre-adapted to the social roles we are called on to fill. The tension implied in the questions I have asked need not exist. If it does exist, it is because individuals have acquired unnatural wishes — women wanting to take part in politics, for instance; alternatively, society has become disordered — perhaps by the enslavement of Greeks.[15] The nature of tragic conflict as well as everyday disgruntlement is another thing which would be explained in different terms by someone who thought of our 'nature' as pre-adapted to social life and its moral demands.

When Brutus slew his sons, he was faced with a conflict between being a good father and being an utterly scrupulous Consul; he chose to be punctilious in his duties as Consul. On one view of the choice, he subordinated his natural affections to his duties as citizen and Consul; on another, he was faced with a conflict of roles rather than a conflict of nature and duty. Whatever he felt, as a father he ought to, and by nature was designed to, protect and cherish his sons; what he did was choose to act in accordance with the dictates of another role. There is some terminological awkwardness about all this, of course, because the Aristotelian, or teleological, picture insists that fathers will generally and 'naturally' feel spontaneous affection for their sons. Perhaps the crucial point is that in a teleological framework there are 'proper' natural responses, while in the non-teleological framework there are not. What you feel is, so to speak, a brute and basic fact.

The modern version of the self/role gap rests on the rejection of the teleological universe. Once that universe is rejected, some vertiginous prospects open up, as Lionel Trilling's *Sincerity and Authenticity* suggests.[16] We cease to live in a world where we can try to unfeignedly and sincerely take on the obligations and enjoy the benefits of an appropriate social position, in the belief that we shall be at ease and happy in so doing. We acquire a new freedom of choice; we may realise our private ends by going along with the demands of the world, or we may choose a cross-grained existence, exhibiting our freedom precisely by not living up to expectations. Rameau's nephew appeals to commentators just because he displays such a triumphant disaffection, but Camus' 'outsider' is from very much the same stable. It is not that society is ignored: rather, its expectations are not 'internalised'; they are treated as raw materials for a purely private and asocial enterprise.[17]

V. Three Sociological Perspectives on Social Adaptation

Such an enthusiasm for authenticity is not common in the sociological literature. In a manner of speaking, sociology is professionally committed to showing that since human society is of long standing, human nature cannot be fundamentally ill-adapted to social life. This goes some way towards explaining the standing obsession with 'the Hobbesian problem of order'; Hobbes, having considered men as if they were new sprung out of the ground, like mushrooms, explained society as the result of a peace treaty. The difficulty he left dangling — at any rate in the eyes of his sociological critics — was that human nature seemed to prompt men to flout that peace treaty when they safely could. Surely something more was needed than Hobbes could provide.[18] There are three well-known views which may serve to illustrate the possibilities. In essence, Durkheim's view is one which defuses the threat posed by human nature by making that nature very malleable and by insisting on the creative and need-fulfilling aspects of society; Mead's account of socialisation and role-playing allows a good deal of room for natural impulse as well as some room for an 'I' which monitors what I do in my various roles; while Dennis Wrong's attack on what he calls 'the oversocialised conception of man' comes close to telling his colleagues to face the truth that Hobbes's solution to the problem of order is as good a solution as they will find.[19]

A. Durkheim – Individuals with Socialised Motives

Durkheim's career was an example of the territorial imperative in action. Much of his energy went to warning biologists and psychologists off the sociologists' patch, especially in works such as *Suicide*.[20] What seems to emerge is a view of human beings as having very 'thin' natures – reason, morality, even the urge to preserve ourselves, all seem to be imposed on something close to *tabula rasa*. We seem to be little more than raw material for social processes, and sometimes what one would think of as psychological considerations become absorbed by sociological ones. Durkheim's enthusiasm for Rousseau, both the Rousseau of the *Discours* and the Rousseau of the *Contrat social*, rests on his liking for Rousseau's view that society gives us a new nature.[21] And in such a perspective, there is little room for the idea that dissatisfaction arises when the rewards of a role are just of no use to you. Of course, Durkheim acknowledges the phenomena of dissatisfaction, nobody more eloquently than he. But the gap is not a gap between the demands of the real or natural person and what society offers him; rather, it is either the result of an incoherence in the process of socialisation, or it is a gap between the aspirations the person has been taught to have and the actual outcome. So, for instance, Durkheim's account of *anomie*, which stresses the role of economic fluctuation in driving people to suicide, rests on the thought that the way in which rewards and obligations are attached to roles in the productive process inculcates in people the idea that they are entitled to whatever outcome is in question. The social order is a normative order, so that this sense of an entitlement is a matter of justice rather than a mere want; indeed, on Durkheim's view, wants have no natural shape or bound, and it is only because we are constrained by social norms that we can even form a coherent picture of what we want. What maddens us is not misfortune or unhappiness but injustice. The crucial 'gap' which society needs to close is that between the expectations it arouses and what happens to us. It is not that we have *no* nature – it is a natural fact that a bullet in the head or prolonged lack of food will kill us — but that these biological truisms provide nothing more than some raw material for social transformation. Our motivation is social through and through.[22]

In this universe, socialisation effectively replaces the natural preadaptation of Aristotelian social theory. The price is that certain sorts of behaviour become hard to characterise, and tend also to become hard to treat as normal features of social life. All those pieces of behaviour which Goffman discusses under the general heading of *role distance* — behaviour in which we make it clear that we are not to be completely identified with the particular behaviour we are engaging in at the time — become rather mysterious.[23] In Durkheim's world, we can and should find a set of roles waiting for us which we can wholeheartedly and happily fill; there is no suggestion that even a healthy society won't achieve that goal, let alone any suggestion that it is a depressing goal in any case. Surprisingly, Durkheim combines this goal with the claim that the ethos of the modern world is that of individualism, an ethos to which he is himself committed.[24] But this is an individualism which attaches supreme value to the individual's conscientious performance of his or her duty, and which sees society's task as finding an organisational form which will enable everyone to find a niche which employs his or her talents. It is not a concession to the view that society is a device by which we pursue our private ends more effectively; the fully individuated moral agent is fulfilling a public role rather than pursuing a private quest. Even institutions which protect privacy, such as the family and some sorts of property, get their sanctity from society's commitment to moral individualism and not from the individual's personal needs. We are sent by society to engage in small-scale or even solitary activities; we do not seek a shelter from society's demands.[25]

B. Dennis Wrong — Individual Dissatisfactions as 'Normal'

Dennis Wrong has attacked such views as resting on an 'oversocialised' conception of man. The oversocialised picture suggests that the creature which receives its character from the socialisation process is so amenable to whatever indoctrination society undertakes that any tension between the demands of the person and the demands of the role has to be explained in terms of contradictory socialisation. The sceptical view by contrast insists that the conflict is between the demands of society and the 'old Adam'. Society tries to expel nature with a pitchfork, but nature keeps on coming back. Of course, the conflict between the two views need not be as sharp as that; the version of the 'oversocialised' conception which is commonly associated with Talcott Parsons takes for granted a good deal of commonsense psychology and assumes that there is rather more than *tabula rasa* for society to write on. The process of socialisation does not supply affect and allegiance so much as shape it.[26]

Nonetheless, there are two lines of cleavage between the two positions, one explanatory and one evaluative. Unrest or misery is likely to be explained by the 'oversocialised' conception as a failure of social integration; the assumption is that society can and normally does offer a comfortable place for everyone, seeing that everyone wants what he will get and gets what he wants. The opposed view sees dissatisfaction as no less normal than satisfaction and is disinclined to explain it as the breakdown of anything in particular unless the degree of dissatisfaction reaches the sort of pitch we associate with civil war rather than everyday life. Again, the 'oversocialised' conception is likely to condemn rebellion and political radicalism as mistaken, and in some sense a sign of the maladjustment of the rebels. This used to provoke a good deal of resentment among American radicals of the 1960s who felt that their criticisms were being ignored while they themselves were being treated as misfits. The alternative view rather takes it for granted that in any society there will be much to criticise, that rebellion always makes sense even if it may be imprudent or morally dubious, and that society will always fall a good deal short of what it might be. In brief, Kant was right to observe that no straight thing could be made from the crooked timber of humanity.[27]

C. G.H. Mead — *The Self and the Generalised Other*

G.H. Mead can plausibly be thought of as occupying something like a half-way house.[28] He wrote a great deal about the process of socialisation which he thought of primarily as the process whereby we learned to take the point of view of the generalised Other — that is, to see our behaviour from the standpoint of all those to whom we owed the duties associated with a role and from whom we could demand the reciprocal duties they owed to us. Commonsensically, Mead acknowledged the existence of a self that controls and scrutinises the role-performances we learn in play and by more formal means. Yet he makes no great use of it; his eye is always on the process whereby the child learns to adapt to others, not on the way in which the adult person can exploit the gap between the social selves and his underlying self for his private ends, whatever they might be.

There is a natural, biological and psychological basis to social behaviour on Mead's view; his ethical theory, with its emphasis on adjusting our impulses one to another for the sake of maximum satisfaction, presupposes an unsocialised instinctive pressure which it is the ego's task to organise fruitfully. All the same, this does not amount to a stress on what we might think of as the private self, and it does not amount to a stress on the contrast between the tumult of private desire and what it is decorous to admit to in public. I suspect that Mead feared that the search for a private self could turn too easily into the search for a pure substratum and turned aside from it for just that reason. The price, though, is a high one, for it leaves quite unclear what the connection is between ourselves as role-bearers and our selves.

To offer three sociological 'perspectives' in this fashion raises the obvious question of how we are to choose between them. In one way the answer is obvious too – we ought to choose the one which does most justice to most of the facts. The difficulty with that answer is that the facts themselves are not quite the rock-bottom consideration we might hope they would be. That is, when faced by the varied ways in which people respond to social ties and opportunities, we can neither say that 'the facts' unequivocally support Durkheim, Wrong, Mead or whomever, nor content ourselves with saying that people seem to behave as Durkheim expects here and quite differently there. That is, it seems inadequate to say no more than that some societies seem to have a conception of personality and a view of choice which makes their members look for roles to commit themselves to, while other societies have a conception of these things which makes their members engage in the elaborate strategies of Goffman's gamblers, surgeons and other virtuosi of modern social interaction. Yet, to say more than this would require the creation of a psychological theory which we not merely have not got, but which there seems some reason to think we cannot have.[29]

VI. Explanations by 'the Logic of the Situation': Values and Beliefs

Explanations in the social sciences commonly employ what Popper has baptised 'the logic of the situation'; that is, they adduce an agent's situation and wants (in a suitably wide sense of that term), in order to show what is 'the thing to do'. If the agent is rational and suffers no weaknesses of will or other mishaps, he will do the thing to do; his behaviour is then explained. Of course, situations only have a logic for persons with certain wants, and actions are only explained by situations as they are understood by the actor. Much social science is dedicated to working out *how* social actors perceive situations and *what* it is that they want; but this is very largely a piecemeal historical and retrospective exercise. A good deal of social sicence is not like this, but even so it depends on the same 'situational logic'. In economic theory, economic agents' beliefs and wants are taken for granted, and the consequences of their acting on the logic of the situation are then explored. One way and another, then, situational logic seems central to social science.[30] A role provides the person who occupies it with reasons for action, as long as he is committed to achieving the goals the role presupposes; so citing a role is a way of citing what we take to be the reasons which governed the behaviour we explain by appealing to the role.

Even so, if we are to have a general psychological theory capable of explaining when people will see what is 'the thing to do', we need a general theory, a set of causal laws, linking conditions of the world with states of mind, namely desires and beliefs. There are at least two difficulties about producing any such thing. The first is that desires and beliefs are not independent; we desire things in virtue of the beliefs we hold about them. The second is that the intentional character of beliefs makes them implausible candidates for explanation by causal laws. A person who believes that water boils at 100° may not believe that H_2O boils at 100°, though in some sense water boiling is just the very same thing as H_2O boiling. So *what* the state of mind is that is being causally explained is not as straightforward as it looks at first blush.[31]

This slightly arcane point has implications for the social sciences. Take the familiar phenomenon of a bread riot. In the twentieth century, bread riots seem to occur in Eastern Europe when incompetent governments raise the price of bread. The governments seem to think that their subjects will behave like 'economic man'; that is, their subjects will treat an increase in the price of bread as a reason for consuming less of it and will adjust their consumption. 'Economic man' is a useful fiction, but he cannot engage in bread riots and the like, since he is a fiction defined in terms of the sort of reasons that count as good reasons for action. Their subjects, however, often turn out to resemble not economic man but revolutionary man, who regards a price rise as an insult and a reason for revolt. Economic man has no concept of an insult; but this is why the behaviour of economic man is quite often a bad guide to political behaviour.

We might be able, after the event, to discover what it was that made the citizenry decide that enough was enough, and that this price rise was not just a price rise but a declaration of war on the part of the government. But we do not derive this explanation from general causal laws. When we employ our knowledge that people were in a revolutionary frame of mind, we do not so much employ causal laws about their behaviour as employ their conceptual scheme to rationalise their behaving as they do. When we explain how they come to have that conceptual scheme, we can trace its pedigree to other conceptual schemes they have operated in the past, but at present we not merely have no sort of theory about how people have come to conceptualise and evaluate their environment, we have not the least idea what such a theory would be like. Anyone who doubts this can reflect on how we would explain different reactions to some commonplace event — say, being insulted in a pub. One man might see the insult as self-evidently something to reply to with a blow; another might see it as something to reply to with a smile. The first might share factual beliefs with the second, and they might differ in thinking he ought to defend his impugned honour; or they might share that value, and the second differ from the first in believing that the insult was really a symptom of some sort of mental ailment and thus something to be sympathetically treated. We could no doubt make a good fist of explaining why each held the beliefs and values he did; but who could offer any sort of account of what underlying general laws validate that explanation?[32]

VII. Three Models of How People Relate to Their Roles

In the absence of such a general psychological theory as would provide the required backing for a particular sociological perspective on roles and role-playing, what we find is that three sorts of models of how people relate to their parts can plausibly be distinguished. These 'models of man', to adopt Martin Hollis's phrase, do not so much cover questions of motivation — whether men are selfish or altruistic or neither of these — as questions of the sort of explanation of individual action and social organisation we are to look for.[33] We might, in part borrowing from Hollis again, call these models, the 'plastic', the 'autonomous' and the 'theatrical'. Their relation to one another is complicated, and here I shall duck the complexities almost entirely; I ought, however, to say that I do not suggest that they form a jointly complete and mutually exclusive set of models of explanation of behaviour.

A. *The Plastic Model*

Plastic man is generally found in the sort of sociological theory that offers an 'oversocialised' picture of man, since the point about plastic man is that he is just that: malleable. His standards are those society has impressed upon him in allocating him to his social position; and his *vie intérieure* is no more elaborate than his status as a simple stimulus-response mechanism requires. He is not a hedonist — unless he is so programmed — but a programmable device whose outputs reflect the twin influences of his programme and his current input. Critics of functionalism call him the 'cultural dope'. It is not even clear that he is a sincere dope, since sincerity suggests an understanding of the possibilities of fraud and dissimulation, and it is not clear how he can manage that understanding. Life being what it is, and the existence of fraud hard to deny, when plastic man misbehaves, this is usually explained by the invocation of a 'sub-culture' — his frauds upon the wider culture are simply a fulfilment of the requirements of the narrower, but more causally effective, criminal sub-culture.[34]

B. *The Autonomous Model*

A stress on autonomy is often part of an attempt to bring back ideas more at home in the rationalist tradition than in the empiricist tradition which most social scientists take for granted. Autonomy is the capacity for reflection and self-monitoring by the rational self-conscious agent who can take responsibility for his actions.[35] The mere fact of his existence as an autonomous agent tells us nothing about what the autonomous agent wants; but what is clear is that his decision whether to act as his role demands or in some other fashion is a matter of choice. He decides which reasons for action to take as his own reasons for action.[36]

Theories like Freud's can be interpreted according to either model. On the plastic view the promptings of instinct may be shaped or transformed by the process of socialisation, but the mechanisms of their action are not altered. We remain creatures of the pressures upon us, even if those pressures appear in a sublimated form. One could even agree with Wrong that plastic man was not as completely socialised as some sociological theories maintain, while sticking to a plastic conception of the explanation of behaviour — there is no conceptual or logical impossibility about it, though it is an unlikely combination for other reasons. On an autonomist reading, much of the point of Freudian theory is to explain the growth of the autonomous ego whose task is to manage the pressures of id and super-ego so as to maximise the well-being of the agent. The rationalist elements in the theory do not eliminate the non-rational, flatly empirical inputs — we are not disembodied techniques of calculation but *persons*. What they entail, however, is that even a simple decision needs to invoke not just the psychophysical stimulus but the agent's conception of the point of reacting to it one way rather than another.

C. The Theatrical Model and Concern for Privacy

The concern with autonomy recovers a good deal of what we ordinarily know about human behaviour, but not all of it. Some of the rest, at least, is picked up by an emphasis on the theatrical model. Indeed, the sociologists' talk of roles suggests we ought never to have neglected the ability to *play* parts and *manage* appearances, that is, to lay on performances of what Goffman sometimes calls 'strips' of social interaction. That the theatrical metaphor is both inescapable and elusive is not only noticed by the writer with whom it is currently associated, Erving Goffman, but was a matter of some discussion in the eighteenth century and even before.[37] Detaching the idea from any particular writer, we plainly have to begin with the observation that a great deal of behaviour is not just doing but saying. Our actions in a given role do more than merely fulfil whatever requirements of a successful performance they do fulfil; crucially, they tell the audience something about us and how we relate to the role.[38]

Two ideas much at home in this account, and nowhere else, are the concept of role-distance and the explanation of tact — of the sort of forbearance that one might call allowing people some privacy even in public. Armed with these insights we have another way of considering the importance of privacy in general. The kind of phenomenon which role-distance is adduced to illuminate is the behaviour of parents on children's rides at a fairground, say, where parents habitually go to great lengths to make it clear that they are there only *qua* parent, that they wouldn't spend their time on the rides if they weren't compelled to, and so on. In essence, what the parent does is make it clear that he is not really the sort of person who *wants* to do frivolous and childish things. What the parent can do is employ the known obligations of the role to subvert inferences about *him*. The ability to play a role in such a way as to communicate any number of different things about ourselves while we do it may be used for altruistic and public-spirited ends — the surgeon who pretends that he would rather be on the golf course is not trying to get his colleagues to believe that he really is an idle beast who cannot distinguish a scalpel from a niblick.

He is reassuring them that he is so much in control of his bit of the team's task that they can safely relax and not worry about him. Light-heartedness and conscientiousness may, agreeably, be allies.

Now, since people will always draw inferences about *us* from the performances we give, we can finally move to say a little about privacy. I take it that a central element in the idea of privacy is that we have the right to control what information people possess about certain areas of our lives, and that other people have a duty to skirt round those areas — not that they have a duty not to *know* about us, but that they have a duty not to try to find out. And a central concern of the theatrical model is precisely with how we control what others do know about us. The assumption is that other people inevitably want to know a good deal about us, since they have projects at risk if we are unreliable or deviate from their expectations. Much of the time we shall want to make our private selves public for precisely this reason — we shall want to reassure others. Of course, this cannot be done by direct means; people look at our conduct to decide how far they can really trust our direct assurances.

All this, however, is inevitably somewhat wearing. Moreover, everyone knows that not every moment can be spent in whole-hearted commitment to being a sincere and committed player in the social game. Played too rigorously, the whole thing would become impossible, too many lapses would be detected, too large a gap between private profession and public performance. If people were checked and rebuked each time such a gap was suspected, or even known, cooperation would collapse. So we work with a lighter touch than that and avoid impugning the quality of the underlying self except when matters become particularly serious. Just as we affect not to hear the rumblings of guests' stomachs at dinner, treating these as hazards not to be held against them, so a good many quirks of taste and temperament are treated as hazards not to be held against a man. He keeps his self-respect, we keep a partner in social enterprises.

This, pressed a little further, illuminates the need for privacy with friends and families. Although a family *can* be 'the public' before which we enact our roles as fathers and sons or whatever, it is also true that at least in our sort of society the family is private, a sort of backstage area where one can wipe off the greasepaint, complain about the audience, worry about one's performance and so on. In their company we can engage in repairs and rehabilitation, chew over performances and think how to improve them, and even rethink the whole play in which we are engaged. Of course, we *may* wish to do all this even more completely on our own, either merely thinking things through, or fantasising new scripts, or simply engaging in activities we want nobody else to know about, and want to answer to nobody for. Family life and marriage or prolonged affairs are all of them full of examples of this.

One other aspect of the theatrical picture may also be connected with this — though less directly. An emphasis on theatricality is partly an emphasis on style, and a worry about privacy may partly be a recognition that style matters, and that people need to be able to keep at least enough distance between themselves and their audience to plan their performance. A feeling for the essential privacy of the actor and for style as the way that private self comes out into the public arena is something to which the theatrical model calls attention. Whether this is an attractive phenomenon is something on which opinions divide sharply. One (gloomy) view might be that society is so efficient at finding slots for us to fill that we can safely be consoled by being allowed to weave roses round our chains — so where one observer might notice the variety and gaiety of American office-workers' clothes, another might notice that their clothes were the only gay and varied things in their lives. The America-domiciled exiles from the Frankfurt School notoriously went in different directions on this sort of issue.[39]

The elaboration of these remarks is best left for empirical research, of which there is a good deal already available. The final question we ought to address here is whether any of this emphasis on the theatrical capacity of the self raises philosophical or conceptual problems. On one view, it surely cannot. What is mostly at stake is simply the fact that when we discuss the way people set about filling the roles they are called on to fill, we need to invoke information-passing, appearance-managing, self-protecting skills in our analysis. That people do use such skills is indubitable; the question is how they do it. The answer will vary from one situation to another, no doubt, but none of it demands any drastic rethinking of the nature of the self and its capacities.

On another view, we may need to revise our conceptions of the self more drastically. If theatrical skills are central, a great deal of social life will be very poorly explained in 'materialist' terms. It seems likely that human beings will be more concerned to put on a good show, even at the price of a good meal, than most materialist theories can cope with. This suggests that the explanation of human behaviour in human terms may simply stop at the communicative and expressive levels, without there being any pressure to find more basic functions for such behaviour to fulfil.[40] This in turn would detach the human sciences from studies of animal behaviour and cast doubt on the utility of sociobiology. But this would be no bad thing, since it is human beings alone who have the sort of self-consciousness which is a precondition of any idea of privacy. Animals may be said in a loose way to have private lives, but this is either a coy way of talking about their sexual activities or a reference to what they do in hiding from possible predators. The distinctively human conception of privacy is detachable from sexual matters; and the monitoring self we carry about with us wherever we go is clearly a private rather than a hidden possession. [See the discussion of the relation between self-consciousness and privacy, pp. 33-34, above — Eds.] If having such a self is tied in so closely with our ability to act in a particular style, and with our ability to communicate something special about ourselves, then it seems that either in addition to a capacity for autonomy or as an aspect of that capacity, the self's dramatic capacities must be regarded as essential, central and as yet not very well understood.

Notes

1. Lionel Trilling, *Sincerity and Authenticity* (Oxford University Press, London, 1972).
2. Erving Goffman, *The Presentation of Self in Everyday Life* (Doubleday, New York, 1959).
3. Michael Banton, *Roles* (Tavistock, London, 1965), p. 138.
4. Ibid., p. 198.
5. Ibid., p. 6.
6. G.W.F. Hegel, *Phenomenology of Spirit*, A.V. Miller (trans.) (Clarendon Press, Oxford, 1977), pp. 274-75.
7. Emile Durkheim, *Suicide* (Routledge and Kegan Paul, London, 1962), Ch. 4, pp. 217-40.
8. Claude Lévi-Strauss, *Structural Anthropology* (Allen Lane, London, 1968), pp. 175-78.
9. Edmund Leach, *Social Anthropology* (Fontana, London, 1982), pp. 164-66.
10. See Michael Lessnoff, *The Structure of Social Science* (Allen & Unwin, London, 1974), pp. 75-95.
11. David Hume, *A Treatise of Human Nature* (Oxford University Press, Oxford, 1888), pp. 633-36.
12. Sigmund Freud, *Civilisation and Its Discontents* in *Collected Works* (Hogarth Press, London, 1961), vol. 21, pp. 66ff.
13. Trilling, *Sincerity and Authenticity*, pp. 140ff.
14. Jean-Paul Sartre, *Being and Nothingness* (Philosophical Library, New York, 1953), Pt. I, Ch. 2.
15. Aristotle, *Politics* (Oxford University Press, Oxford, 1948), pp. 19, 124-25.
16. Trilling, *Sincerity and Authenticity*, Ch. V.
17. Ibid., pp. 30-31. [The references are to Denis Diderot, *Le Neveu de Rameau*, J. Fabre (ed.) (Geneva, 1950), and to A. Camus, *The Outsider* (Penguin Books, Harmondsworth, 1964) — Eds.]

18. Talcott Parsons, *The Structure of Social Action* (The Free Press, New York, 1968), vol. I, pp. 92-94.

19. Dennis Wrong, *Skeptical Sociology* (The Free Press, New York, 1976), Ch. 2.

20. Durkheim, *Suicide*, Bk. I.

21. Emile Durkheim, *Montesquieu and Rousseau: Forerunners of Sociology* (University of Michigan Press, Ann Arbor, 1961).

22. Durkheim, *Suicide*, p. 300.

23. Erving Goffman, *Encounters* (Bobbs-Merrill, Indianapolis, 1961), pp. 85-152.

24. Emile Durkheim, *Professional Ethics and Civic Morals* (Routledge and Kegan Paul, London, 1957), pp. 172-73.

25. Durkheim, *Suicide*, pp. 378ff.

26. Talcott Parsons, *Essays in Sociological Theory* (The Free Press, New York, 1954), pp. 338ff.

27. Immanuel Kant, *On History* (Bobbs-Merrill, Indianapolis, 1963), pp. 17-18.

28. George H. Mead, *Mind, Self, and Society* (University of Chicago Press, Chicago, 1934).

29. Donald Davidson, *Essays on Actions and Events* (Oxford University Press, Oxford, 1980), pp. 229-39.

30. Ibid., pp. 231-32.

31. Ibid., pp. 236-39.

32. Ibid., p. 230.

33. Martin Hollis, *Models of Man* (Cambridge University Press, Cambridge, 1977).

34. Steven Box, *Deviance, Reality and Society* (Holt Rinehart and Winston, London, 1971), pp. 100ff.

35. Hollis, *Models of Man*, Chs. 4-6.

36. Ibid., pp. 84-85.

37. See Trilling, *Sincerity and Authenticity*, p. 10.

38. Goffman, *Encounters*, pp. 102-3.

39. Herbert Marcuse, *One Dimensional Man* (Routledge and Kegan Paul, London, 1964), pp. 57-77.

40. Rom Harré, *Social Being* (Basil Blackwell, Oxford, 1979), pp. 10ff.

7 PRIVATE AND PUBLIC MORALITY: CLEAN LIVING AND DIRTY HANDS

Stanley I. Benn

I. The Senses in which Morality can be Public or Private

A. Public and Private Aspects of Liberal Morality

The object of this chapter is to exhibit certain tensions in liberal morality which seem to arise from the tensions in the liberal conception of the individual in society, examined in Chapter 2. The conflicts of duties, interests, rights, and principled commitments in which these tensions assert themselves are sometimes referred to in other terms, e.g. as conflicts between 'the personal' and 'the political'. It seems very natural, nevertheless, to see them as conflicts of 'Public and Private Morality', the title chosen for a collection of essays edited by Stuart Hampshire and for an essay of his own in that collection.[1] A leading theme of that book is *the Machiavellian problem*: whether in governing a state and managing its foreign relations a statesman should be prepared to do things that would be grossly immoral if done in private life; whether, as Machiavelli himself put it, the prince must 'learn the ways of evil, and to use his knowledge or to refrain from using it as the need arises'.[2] Can that 'must' be a moral must? And are 'the ways of evil' in public life really evil?

The antithesis of the public and private crops up in other moral contexts, too. In 1957, the U.K. Report of the Committee on Homosexual Offences and Prostitution — the Wolfenden Report — declared, 'There must remain a realm of private morality and immorality which is, in brief and crude terms, not the law's business.'[3] Commenting on this view, Lord Devlin asked: 'Ought there ... to be a public morality, or are morals always a matter for private judgement?'[4] But instead of answering the question, Devlin rejected the distinction: 'I do not think one can talk sensibly of a public and private morality.'[5]

For many liberals there is at least one difficulty in distinguishing the two kinds of morality. They understand morality to be a rational mode of action and judgement, one that provides reasons for action and for assessments of action. All morality must be in principle public; it cannot have the private standing of 'gut feelings', immediate, incommunicable as reasons, invoked at best to explain actions, but unable to justify them except to someone who happens to share those feelings. In as much as we can and do *discuss* what is the right thing to do, we think of moral judgements and decisions as capable of being supported and defended by reasons good for anyone, which any normally rational person would recognise. To that extent a moral argument must be accessible in principle to anyone: so my morals cannot be private to me, as my emotions or my liking for artichokes might be. Morality is public at least in the rather special sense in which Wittgenstein claimed that a language must be public: the principles, the reasons for saying that you have got it right or wrong, must be open to anyone.

Admittedly there are liberals who would not be entirely happy with this account of moral judgement. The sceptical view that moral judgements necessarily rest on non-demonstrable ultimate premises or values has had considerable appeal since Western Europe learnt its advantages as a basis for toleration in the destructive religious wars and persecutions of the sixteenth and seventeenth centuries. Some hold that such ultimates can be grasped only intuitively; others, more damaging still to the publicness of morality, ascribe to values the status of mere basic preferences. Either way, though reasons for action might emerge at a late stage of argument, they could not be relied on to convince someone who happened not to share those fundamental intuitions or preferences. And, given that nothing in such a person's experience or belief structure rationally committed him to accepting them as reasons, his not being convinced by them would not betoken a defect of reason. Morality would then be essentially private, even if contingently shared.

The liberal commitment to the toleration of diversity of moral and religious opinion draws heavily not only on value scepticism but also on a kind of fallibilism that has similar practical consequences, namely, that while there might be moral truths, no one could claim to have found them once and for all. If we cannot demonstrate that our opponents are mistaken in their beliefs, and that they are rationally committed to accept our own, how could we be entitled to persecute them for believing as they do? Moreover, if irreconcilable conflicts are possible in principle, it is prudent for the sake of social peace to encyst them in a private sphere unless they threaten the public interest in law and order. Considerations of this kind make for moral pluralism and for refusing jurisdiction to public authority in areas where the pronouncements of conscience are firm and the chances of agreement through rational discussion particularly unpromising.

The emphasis that liberals place on the role of conscience in the moral life gives rise, however, to a more positive kind of moral privateness. This is a legacy from that element of the Protestant Reformation which insisted on the priesthood of the believer, the divine authority of the Inner Light, on Luther's 'Here I stand', against the claim of ecclesiastical institutions to final moral authority. In liberal ideology the Inner Light has become secularised, of course, as the light of reason. But whatever the claims of authority, custom, convention, or even law, the ultimate liberal source of moral judgement is the individual himself, on whom rests the ultimate responsibility of deciding whether to fall in with their demands. This is the notion of moral autonomy – of living according to a *nomos*, or rule of life, that one prescribes to oneself, the rationalised conscience or the rational will, in obedience to which we find moral freedom. The autonomy of this private moral experience can be quite consistent, however, with the public rationality of what Kant called 'the moral law'; for the autonomous moral agent is conceived as adopting a morality because he sees the point of it, and that is not at all a private point, but one accessible to every rational being.[6] By contrast, the romantic existentialist notion of moral freedom as freedom *from* the moral law, as freedom to choose any *nomos*, repudiates this link between the publicness and the privateness of morality. For the existentialist, the individual's moral choice is altogether private precisely because nonrational; it must be arbitrary because, until it is made, there is nothing that could give it point. So his reasons for action are the outcome of a private choice, a choice not itself governed by public reasons.

The important thing to grasp, however, is that these two characterisations of morality as in one sense public, in another, private, apply to the whole range of morality. There is no suggestion that there are two kinds, or even two sectors, of morality, one public, the other private.

B. *Public and Private Positive Morality*

I have been considering morality from the point of view of the moral agent: as principles, rules, values *in use*. Someone else may *mention* that agent's morality, without thereby committing himself to it. So 'public morality' may mean simply 'the public's morality', i.e. the principles by which the community at large, or perhaps a majority, decides what is right or wrong. A 'private morality' would then refer to whatever rules or principles some particular person might use – or what (we might say) his conscience tells him to do. We might call this his *personal* morality. And that might be quite different from public morality. Mentioning a morality in this sense does not imply endorsement, but only takes note of a social or psychological state, a positive fact in the world, like the fact of positive law. And, like positive law, a morality in this sense can itself be subjected to moral criticism. So this usage would be quite consistent with there being two — or two hundred and two — moralities. But behind them all would then be the morality used in the critique, which, while itself a fact in the world, would also be endorsed and not merely referred to or described.

C. Can There be Two Moralities, a Public and a Private?

A morality in use can be expected not merely to supply reasons for actions — for there may be reasons in abundance for each of many competing courses — but also to order them in such a way that they issue in a moral imperative: that action which is the thing to do. This is part, at least, of what Kant meant by 'the categorical imperative' of pure practical reason, which would be obligatory quite apart from one's inclinations and preferences. Of course, not all liberals are Kantians; running from Bentham to R.M. Hare is a strong utilitarian strain. But it is clear that neither the Kantian nor the utilitarian can have much sympathy for a notion that there might be two co-existent and competing moralities, one public and one private. What would be the thing to do when public and private moralities pronounced differently? The utilitarian requires of us that we act to maximise happiness, and presumably in any given situation there is only one course that would do that. Or if by chance there should be two that would produce exactly equal amounts, then it would be quite rational and quite consistent with utilitarian morality to toss a coin, since which of the two available acts one did would be, morally speaking, immaterial. *Ex hypothesi*, nothing further could count as a reason for doing one rather than the other. It would not amount, therefore, to choosing between moralities. How, then, does talk about 'the ... differences between public morality and the morality of private life'[7] come about?

Publicness and privateness were exhibited in Chapters 1 and 2 of this book as complex-structured concepts, each with several dimensions, and operating on different levels or in different modes within ideological structures. This suggests, despite what I have said above, that morality, or its constituent rules, duties, rights, and so on, might still be public or private in a variety of ways. So we may have duties to the public, i.e. to all our fellow-citizens or to the state, and duties to our family and friends, i.e. the duties of private life. Or an individual may be caught between the claims of his society as a set of moral institutions and the claims of his own personal commitments. Or the claims of his private roles may conflict with those of his public roles,

Private and Public Morality: Clean Living and Dirty Hands 159

as Minister, official, or simply as citizen; and provided that he identifies with such roles — that he does not see them as alien and imposed, as a reluctant conscript might see his role as soldier — he will see such conflicts as moral conflicts. The existence of such conflicts does not refute my claim that liberals cannot consistently endorse two moralities; but it does indicate that the liberal moral universe is divided on a wide range of issues between the claims of the private and the public realms.

In this chapter I shall look particularly at four of liberalism's problem areas, namely, the Machiavellian problem or the problem of 'dirty hands', the problem of conscientious objection, the problem of legal moralism, i.e. of the role of the criminal law in sustaining moral standards, and, finally, at the legitimacy of paternalistic interference by public agencies. I do not pretend to deal adequately in so short a compass with the merits of the various solutions proposed in the complex and extensive literature on these problems. By putting them together in this way, however, I hope to exhibit more clearly the sources of tension in liberal moral judgement that constitute each of them a problem area. It is not just that each involves conflicts of principle — life is full of such conflicts, which we learn to resolve one way or another — but that the conflicts involve notions of publicness and privateness which in turn invoke different and probably irreconcilable models of the individual in society. This may explain why the two-moralities view attracts some liberal moralists, despite its inconsistency with the conception of morality as the thing to do. For it does serve to emphasise that some conflicts are in a sense irresolvable within the liberal moral framework. Liberal morality does not offer, in principle, an open choice between alternative right things to do, but requires the subject to rank the options in a rationally defensible way; yet the criteria with which liberal morality furnishes him are not sufficient for a determinate ranking. Consequently, for some liberals, at any rate, whatever one does, whatever one takes to be the thing to do, a feeling of loss — if not of wrong-doing — is inescapable.

II. Dirty Hands

A. Politics and Morality

Sartre's play 'Dirty Hands' is about the conflict between Hugo, an idealistic young revolutionary intellectual who sets out to assassinate the leader of his party, Hoederer, for — as he believes — betraying the party's principles for opportunistic reasons. Hoederer's contemptuous rejection of such moralism in politics has often been quoted:

> How you cling to your purity, young man! How afraid you are to soil your hands! All right, stay pure! What good will it do? Why did you join us? Purity is an idea for a yogi or a monk. You intellectuals and bourgeois anarchists use it as a pretext for doing nothing. To do nothing, to remain motionless, arms at your sides, wearing kid gloves. Well, I have dirty hands. Right up to the elbows. I've plunged them in filth and blood. But what do you hope? Do you think you can govern innocently?[8]

Or, as Machiavelli put it:

> how we live is so far removed from how we ought to live, that he who abandons what is done for what ought to be done, will rather learn to bring about his own ruin than his preservation. A man who wishes to make a profession of goodness in everything must necessarily come to grief among so many who are not good. Therefore it is necessary for a prince, who wishes to maintain himself, to learn how not to be good, and to use this knowledge and not use it, according to the necessity of the case.

And

> [A] prudent ruler ought not to keep faith when by so doing it would be against his interest, and when the reasons which made him bind himself no longer exist.[10]

Benedetto Croce claimed that Machiavelli was here announcing the 'autonomy' of politics, i.e. that politics was an activity to which moral judgements simply could not apply — a sphere of activity outside or beyond morality. Now it is not clear, in the first place, how an activity could be beyond morality, if moral judgement always pronounces the thing to do. But aside from that, Croce's interpretation is not supported by other passages, in which, for example, Machiavelli writes approvingly of the thirteenth century Florentines, that they had 'a higher regard for their *patria* than for their souls'.[11] It seems much more likely that Machiavelli is asserting that the requirements of political life impose special demands which are not merely different from those of private life, but which oppose and override them. That amounts not to the autonomy of politics, but to the moral claim that political expediency must override the moral proprieties of private life.

Michael Walzer, whose article 'Political Action: The Problem of Dirty Hands' opened up a new debate on this question, has no doubt

Private and Public Morality: Clean Living and Dirty Hands 161

that the problem is one *within* morality. But he is not prepared to accept that political situations are such that sometimes murder, treachery, or lying is simply the morally right thing to do, and there's an end of it. Walzer states the paradox as a tragic dilemma:

> Sometimes it is right to try to succeed, and then it must also be right to get one's hands dirty. But one's hands get dirty from doing what it is wrong to do. And how can it be wrong to do what is right? Or how can we get our hands dirty by doing what we ought to do?[12]

Walzer refers approvingly to Max Weber, who denies the political leader the self-indulgence of an 'ethics of ultimate ends' (i.e. of absolute principles of right and wrong). The statesman's ethics must be the 'ethics of responsibility', even though, like Machiavelli's Florentines, his political vocation may cost him his soul. And Walzer refers, too, to Camus' play, *The Just Assassins*, in which terrorists, feeling the moral compulsion of their political situation, commit murder but accept the guilt for their act and willingly go to their deaths by execution. To Walzer this seems the right way of it: if the political morality demands the sacrifice of private morality, then remorse is in order: it is not for a good man to shrug complacently — even resignedly — and say, 'I made the best of a bad job.'

Walzer's somewhat romantic view has been rejected by several critics. Alan Donagan, for instance,[13] claims that the problem of dirty hands 'dissolves' when strictly analysed. Often the act apparently contrary to 'common morality' (i.e. private morality) simply cannot be justified; but if it can, it will be found that common morality can in fact accommodate it. Donagan suggests, for example, that torturing a captured terrorist to extract information to save the lives of innocent people endangered by hidden bombs is really consistent with common morality, since by practising terror one forfeits the immunity from personal violence that such morality bestows. And Donagan brings against Walzer, if in a qualified way, the testimony of R.B. Brandt and R.M. Hare, who, he says, have

> argued irresistibly . . . that, if no consideration outweighs the ends of good government, and if the ends of good government can be accomplished only by sometimes traversing the precepts of common morality, then, whatever validity common morality has, it has conditionally, within the scope of a more embracing consequentialist system. If they are right [Donagan adds], successful politicians are

not tragic heroes, but simply intelligent men making hard decisions, as good intelligent men must.[14]

If Donagan, Brandt and Hare are right, we should talk, perhaps, not of two moralities but of the different considerations which regulate moral action in the public and private spheres. And this again recalls Max Weber's treatment of the subject:

> We are placed into various life-spheres, each of which is governed by different laws . . . The Hindu order of life made each of the different occupations an object of a specific ethical code, a Dharma . . . This specialization of ethics allowed for the Indian ethic's quite unbroken treatment of politics by following politics' own laws and even radically enhancing this royal art.

The rule is, 'Do what must be done.' Hinduism, he says, 'believes that such conduct does not damage religious salvation but, rather, promotes it.'[15]

B. What Makes Politics Special?

Moral philosophers are perennially concerned with the problem of the rational solution of moral dilemmas. Sometimes, of course, one can resolve them with a clear conscience, confident that one has chosen a greater good at the cost only of a lesser. But according to moralists such as Stuart Hampshire, Bernard Williams and Michael Walzer,[16] we occasionally end up feeling that, while, all things considered, we have done what had to be done, we have nevertheless done a wrong thing; and that it would have been wrong whatever we had done.

Moral conflicts are not restricted, of course, to conflicts between private and public commitments. Nor is the problem of 'dirty hands' peculiarly a public/private dilemma. So if the Machiavellian problem does have a special character, it must come from something besides the mere fact of conflict. Reinhold Niebuhr quotes Hugh Cecil's observation,

> 'that all that department of morality which requires an individual to sacrifice his interests to others, everything which falls under the heading of unselfishness, is inappropriate to the action of a state. No one has a right to be unselfish with other people's interests.'[17]

Is it this, perhaps, that makes public morality special? But Cecil's observation is surely just as true of servants of corporations, trustees, trade union officials, and anyone whose role commits him to promote the interests of someone, or some group, or even some activity like science or art, rather than his own. Yet obligations of that kind only very exceptionally justify setting aside the ordinary decencies of private life. Nor are special attachments to groups or movements — the demands of solidarity — ordinarily enough to do so. By liberal standards neither fraternity among trade unionists nor small group loyalties between members of a club warrant lying or stealing for the benefit either of a fellow member or of the group collectively. A possible exception is an immediate family tie. The humane detective in a TV crime series, however tough with anyone else concealing information, is expected to be merciful towards someone 'covering up' for a member of the family. And though stealing to feed one's own family was once a transportable, even possibly a capital, offence, in more liberal times it would be thought venal enough. With this possible exception, however, no private loyalty, and no private role commitment would warrant setting aside the principles of private life for the sake of a beneficent outcome to so gross a degree as will generally be tolerated in public life. Why then should a statesman's commitment to the national interest, a minister's loyalty to his colleagues, or even a private person's commitment to his public duty as a citizen-soldier, warrant expediently soiling his hands on so much more massive a scale than we should condone in a company director or in a university vice-chancellor promoting the interests for which he is responsible?

It is evident that both reasons of expediency and reasons of principle are types of moral reason. Reasons of the latter type invoke notions such as the inviolability of persons, or of property, respect for truth and promises, and so on. To this area of moral reasoning belong considerations of justice, rights, and freedom, and the principle of legality in punishment. Reasons of expediency, by contrast, appeal directly to the value attached to the consequences of actions, assessing the resultant states of the world. In our private relations, in the family, between friends, in ordinary commerce, between employers and employees, reasons of the first class are generally uppermost, at least in our appraisals of other people's actions, if not always when we decide on our own. Why, then, should reasons of expediency appear, in liberal morality, to override reasons of principle so much more readily in public than in private life? Two features of public life may contribute to this.

In the first place, the interests of the public are commonly presumed to weigh more heavily against principled reasons for action than do private interests. Not that any public interest always outweighs any private interest; if that were so, the expropriation of land 'in the public interest', as against compulsory purchase at a fair market price, would be more widely acceptable than it is. Rather, when a claim is made on behalf of the public, the advantage at stake (or the damage to be avoided) assumes a much more important and far-reaching appearance. Outcomes so weighty are thought properly to override moral principles which normally regulate behaviour between private persons. In private life, by contrast, the interests of an individual or a small group appear to weigh less heavily and rarely justify sacrificing a principle, even if a net loss in utility results. However, the more one leans towards an individualist view of public interest, the more easily eroded is this difference between the weight attached to the interests of society at large, and to the interests of individuals or small groups. So Robert Nozick and Ronald Dworkin − and perhaps John Rawls too − would argue that no one in fairness should be picked out to suffer a heavy sacrifice to provide benefits, however weighty, for the multitude, however numerous. 'It is expedient that one man should die for the people' has never been a very popular liberal individualist principle. Consequently, the language of rights and principles, if not paramount, is generally quite powerful and persuasive in liberal domestic politics, where the individualist model is usually uppermost and that kind of interest confrontation is most evident. (See, however, other discussions of this issue, notably in Ch. 2, pp. 44-47 and 59-61, Ch. 4, pp. 109-10, and Ch. 5, pp. 117-18 above.)

But when the state is viewed as an organic entity, a corporate person confronting other states, the conception of national interest as the state's good, the condition, perhaps, of its very survival, makes an apologetic for unprincipled behaviour seem far more plausible. Moreover, the people who are disadvantaged by it are perceived as foreigners, aliens, external to the whole. This is to put the interests attacked on a different moral footing from the one advantaged − the national interest. Expedient action in the public or the national interest may still incur a moral cost in terms of principle, and the statesman may still be reproached for having told lies or for betraying an ally; but that cost may weigh less heavily if the interests that have suffered are those of aliens, and the interests advantaged by it are those which, in his role of statesman, he is peculiarly bound to promote. Indeed, some liberal writers, especially those who, under the influence of Hegel, have made more of the organic than the individualist model of society, have questioned whether there can be any moral relations between states.[18] Nevertheless, the liberal tradition also includes a strong vein of universalistic, humanitarian moralism, even in its approach to international relations. From Kant's claim that the statesman has a duty to do what is possible in a world of predatory states to create the conditions for perpetual peace,[19] to Gladstone's moralisation of the rhetoric of international relations, through to President Carter's preoccupation with Human Rights, liberals have insisted on the relevance of moral considerations, even in power politics. But they have also retained a strong sense that the citizens of a country have a special stake in a national interest which they have a moral right to defend, as each individual has a right to defend his own interest, subject to due regard to the interests of others; and whatever the statesman's duty to strive to create the conditions for international order, that duty could never override his duty as trustee of the national interest. He would not be entitled to gamble generously for the sake of mankind when the stakes were national interests.

Another reason that will help to explain the different weightings of moral expediency and moral principle in private and public life is that the conditions of public life, the context of public behaviour, are generally less well structured by dependable practices than family life or civil society, i.e. the world of domestic commerce and industry. This comparative lack of structure derives from two of its essential features:

(a) The commodity in contention in political life is the power to mobilise the support of other people and to direct their activities towards goals that the power-holder determines, including the mobilisation of still more support. Consequently the rules for acquiring power and using it are relatively feeble constraints on its exercise. Competitors in this contest can shrug off the constraints of common morality as they cannot in trade and industry, in academic life or medical practice, where the standards of the practices and institutions themselves reinforce the common morality of principles. False company prospectuses or fraudulent applications for funds from a university budget are frowned on by those particular forms of life as well as by the rules of common morality; and though company directors and deans of faculties are expected to get the best results they can for the institutions they represent, and will be thought remiss if they do not put the facts in the best possible light, nevertheless the blatant deceptions that are tolerated in the world of politics would not be acceptable in these other worlds. In politics the stakes are too high, and success enables the winner to overrule the penalties for unprincipled behaviour. Liberals are generally unhappy with these features of public life, but acknowledge, with Machiavelli, that a politician who keeps his hands clean among so many who willingly dirty theirs, can only come to ruin; and no good can come of that for the public at large. Just because politics is the contest for ultimate power, the ruthless dictate the terms on which the game is to be played, even by those who would prefer to play it the principled way. So the rigour of principles is weakened in public life to match the higher risks of complying with them. As Machiavelli made very explicit, to give the appearance of principle can be advantageous in public life; and to be caught out in unprincipled action is always to be taken at a disadvantage. But however much the liberal believes in the moralisation of politics as an ideal, he is forced to act on Niebuhr's maxim:

> Politics will, to the end of history, be an area where conscience and power meet, where the ethical and coercive factors of human life will interpenetrate and work out their tentative and uneasy compromises.[20]

> The selfishness of human communities must be regarded as an inevitability. Where it is inordinate it can be checked only by competing assertions of interest; and these can be effective only if coercive methods are added to moral and rational persuasion.[21]

Liberal indulgence towards reasons of expediency in politics is restricted, however, to unprincipled conduct in the public interest. The grim necessities of the contest for power will excuse a lie for the country's sake. To lie for the government's survival can be acceptable, if embarrassing, to its supporters. To lie for personal advantage alone is not acceptable, and not to be excused merely by an appeal to the Hobbesian rules of the political game. Richard Nixon's error was to continue to lie when it could no longer be plausibly claimed, even by his supporters, that lying was in the public interest. Public life calls for moral flexibility in the public interest; but the politician is doomed who is caught with his private hand in the public till.

(b) The second feature of public life that helps to account for its relative lack of structure by firm moral principles, and for the greater part played in it by consequential considerations, is that in public life there is more novelty — or perhaps less repetition of basically similar patterns of events — than in ordinary daily life, which is consequently rather more predictable. Though there may well be conflicts between principles and consequences in private life, experience and precedent will generally have laid down how they are to be managed. Our moral principles are not simple; 'don't tell lies', 'don't steal', 'don't betray friends' are more complex injunctions than they appear to be; built into them are sets of more or less understood qualifications. Saving notions, such as 'a white lie', lubricate the bearings of private life, preserving harmony and avoiding hurt feelings. One can say without hyprocrisy: 'Certainly it is wrong to lie; but I don't call *that* lying.' Alternatively, 'that isn't the sort of lie that the principle is about'. Our moral principles in daily life are generally adapted to meet the conflicts — both between principles and between principles and valued outcomes — that would otherwise disturb us had they not already cropped up countless times and been duly resolved and accommodated in our moral practice. In daily life, as in the common law, the cases that fit rule and precedent are more common than the hard ones that come to court and for precisely the same reason: that these rules have developed to govern the situation-types that occur regularly. It is significant that when moral philosophers seek examples of moral dilemmas where principles conflict, with no easy resolution, they choose scenarios such as the tragic dilemmas of Orestes and Agamemnon, or Bernard Williams's parable of Jim and Pedro,[22] which could happen only in the unfamiliar worlds of Homer, Euripides, or the Amazon jungle, rather than in the predictable surroundings of a suburban supermarket. Our moral principles have evolved out of the necessities of the latter kind of situation, and little happens there for which they are totally unprepared; the political world is much more like the unstructured relations of a jungle encounter, or the somewhat unpredictable world of Homeric myth.

C. Moral Integrity and Dirty Hands

I have argued, then, that states and their agents are licensed, in liberal theory, to set aside moral principles for the sake of good outcomes (or, more usually, to avoid bad ones), and that the reason for this is that they are the champions and trustees of the public in a jungle world. If one simply stopped at that point, one might decide that liberalism simply endorsed the Machiavellian claim; if so, the politician would behave morally in doing what had to be done, and his virtue would consist in his clear-headedness, his resolution, and his fidelity to the best outcome. The morality of private relations would simply not obtrude into the public sphere; someone who condemned acts of political expediency directed to optimal outcomes would simply be confused. But that does not seem to deal adequately with the uneasiness of many liberals, such as Weber, Williams, and Walzer, who feel a moral tension in the statesman's role.

In 1945, British officials and statesmen decided to accede to Stalin's demands that Russians and Ukrainians, some but not all of whom had fought with the German armies and who had fallen into the hands of the Western Allies as they advanced across Germany, be repatriated, willy-nilly.[23] The decision-makers knew that they were handing them over to forced labour camps, and possibly to die. They believed that the higher interests of good Anglo-Soviet relations, and possibly a future peaceful world order, depended on it and justified it. But there is no doubt that for some of those involved, justifying the act did not redeem the agent, any more than those who worked on the atomic bomb, and those who ended the war by dropping it on Hiroshima, were all able to live easily with their actions. The stain, accepted as a moral necessity, still remained a stain.

A consistent utilitarian would have to dismiss such an attitude as totally irrational, supposing that, in their best judgement, those officials served the greatest good. But utilitarianism in public affairs is only part of the liberal morality. As we saw earlier, there is, besides, a strong commitment to the ideal of personal integrity. Every normal individual is credited with the rational capacity to work out, by a process of critical self-examination, a coherent and consistent self, and by the exercise of autonomous will to remain true to it in his life and conduct. Bernard Williams's parable of Jim and Pedro, alluded to earlier, illustrates how these two strands can generate moral dilemmas. Jim, the traveller in the Amazon jungle, is required to decide whether to save nineteen innocent peasants from Pedro's firing squad by shooting a twentieth with the gun that Pedro generously offers him, or to stand by, with hands still clean, while the squad shoots all twenty. Jim's dilemma is precisely that to kill an innocent peasant in cold blood, even to forestall the killing of nineteen others by someone else, goes against the grain. And though Jim might well reason that it would go just as much against the grain to stand by while twenty were killed, when he might have saved nineteen of them, to be able to kill just one in that way is to discover in himself a horrifying moral possibility, difficult to reconcile with his humanitarian conception of himself.

Similarly, for Weber and Walzer the statesman who sets aside principle for the sake of the public interest is making a personal sacrifice. The price he pays for the valuable outcome is his own moral personality. The unthinkable has not merely been thought, but done — and the agent cannot entertain the same image of himself afterwards as before. For Weber, the acceptance of the necessity is a kind of erosion of moral integrity; for Walzer, that erosion can be prevented only by a kind of admission of guilt, an act of penance that reaffirms the morality which has been prejudiced.

Now it is possible that this is a perverse way of seeing both the politician's and Jim's dilemmas. If the hard decision is indeed morally justified, then, it might be said, the morally strong and well-balanced personality will be able to assimilate it, and emerge, not crippled, but wiser and stronger than before, hardened in the fires of moral experience in a world more painful and more complex than had hitherto appeared. The tempering need not be a coarsening, a suppressing of moral sensibility; the hard choice conscientiously made might be thought to add something to the moral stature of the chooser, who has faced up courageously and honestly to the thing he is called upon to do. But to see the matter in that way is to acknowledge that morality is not only about the evaluation of the publicly accessible consequences of action, but also about character. A moral dilemma is not necessarily terminated by the action in which it issues; it may lead the agent to reassess his own moral nature in the aftermath of such traumatic experiences. Jim may remain a man of principle; but he will never again believe that principles can be simple, or that living by them is a straightforward matter, like obeying Company Orders.

III. Conscience and Public Duty

The dilemma of dirty hands arises when the moral commitments that an individual acknowledges as a private person conflict with those that the same individual acknowledges in his public role in politics and affairs of state. It is a conflict within the individual's own moral consciousness, not between the moral standpoints of different individuals. Conscientious objection to military service (which I take to be the standard case of conscientious objection) can generate similar conflicts; but, as we shall see, it can also generate conflict within the morality of the public confronting the dissident individual.

The objector, we may suppose, recognises the claim upon him of civic duty, to participate in the common enterprises of the nation, to take his share of common burdens, and so on. Moreover, a law, simply as law, creates for him a reason, though not always a conclusive reason, for acting conformably with it. He is, after all, an objector, not a rebel, a revolutionary or a nihilist. His quarrel is not with the regime but with killing, or preparing to kill, or with abetting the killing of people, as a way of settling disputes between nations. But the belief that this is something he ought not to do conflicts with the duty to take up arms required of him by his civic role, which is as valid a part of his moral personality, as he understands it, as is his pacifism. It is not something merely external or imposed: he acknowledges it as part of his complex moral self. But whereas for other people this civic obligation overrides the principle that forbids taking up arms, for him, the commitments are ordered differently. So far we have no special theoretical problem, a conflict of principles, or of principles and role commitments, is common enough in our moral lives. What is more particularly interesting is that many liberals treat this case as an exception to the general claim that the public may legitimately coerce not only every member whose participation in collective action is necessary to what it perceives as its vital interest, but that it may, in the name of fairness, call on everyone, without inquiring whether this one or that one could be let off without endangering the whole enterprise. Since self-interest would not be accepted as grounds for exemption, why are conscientious scruples that are not shared by the public, either in the sense of the state and its policy, or in the sense of the ordinary run of people, who form the vast majority?

It is often said that the law ought not to violate a person's conscience. Gerald C. MacCallum Jr. has challenged this ground for exemption.[24]

> [T]he law's demand for compliance can neither violate nor threaten to violate a person's conscience. It can, however, lead a person to violate his own conscience in a way revealing to him his failure to live up to his own aspiration for himself. When we ask what stake we could possibly have in protecting people from finding themselves in such situations, we uncover a model of personal integrity underwriting the importance generally attached to giving conscience (some) priority over law, a model whose acceptability is open to serious questioning.[25]

> Why should we think that these persons *merit* or *have a right to* protection against such states of affairs, or ... why should we want to protect them from being put in such a situation?[26]

MacCallum claims that the model of personal integrity is of 'something sufficiently unified to count as a single person and sufficiently well-bounded to distinguish as one separable thing in an environment of other things'.[27] Moreover, 'in its inward-looking aspect, the person's integrity thus is seen to be a function of the extent to which his impulses, needs, wants, thoughts, etc. are harmoniously and "coherently" integrated vis-à-vis one another'.[28] According to MacCallum, the liberal objection to coercion in cases of conscience is that it disrupts, disorganises this integrity, presumably by inducing the person to do what he believes he ought not to do. MacCallum refers to, but does not develop, objections that might be made to this conception of 'the self as a *bounded* domain', and which dismiss it as 'atomistic individualism'.

Whatever the objections, it seems to me that MacCallum has grasped only part of the liberal's concern for the coercion of conscience. His account of the liberal's attitude to conscientious objection cannot be correct because it does not explain the latter's discomfort when coercion fails, and the objector goes heroically to gaol. On MacCallum's account, that should leave the liberal happy, since the integrity of the objector has clearly survived the test. But the contrary is the case. To be sure, the objectors who succumb to pressure would be thought of less account because their principles were less well formed. But the martyr is often held to be a victim of injustice.

The source of this sense of injustice is the moral point that MacCallum has missed. Two fundamental liberal principles bear on the case of conscientious objection: (i) the law ought to punish only people who do wrong; (ii) to act unlawfully is not necessarily to act immorally. Consequently, a government that punishes people who rightly disobey immoral laws acts unjustly and oppressively, for they do no wrong. Suppose, however, that an observer believes that in the present case the public, or the government on its behalf, is justified, that it is both within its legitimate powers and not demanding immoral actions in pressuring free-riders to bear their share of the burden. Nevertheless there are dissidents who conscientiously but mistakenly take a different view of the morality of the acts required of them. What, in the liberal observer's view, is the public entitled to do? Even if the observer believes that in the present case the government's injunction should be obeyed, and that not to obey would be to do wrong, he may also think that someone who obeyed while believing it to be wrong to obey would be doing wrong in acting against his conscience. For the liberal, morality does not consist only in the public fact of doing the right thing; it is the conjunction of the right act done, if not as Kant would have it for the sake of duty, at least for reasons that are not unworthy. Consequently, the liberal's resolution in pressing the recalcitrant to conform to the public's morality is always liable to be undermined by the questions whether the conformity is worth having if grudgingly given, and, still more, whether it can be right to pressure someone else to do what that person believes to be wrong. The interesting moral conflict in the case of conscientious objection is not the conflict within the conscience of the objector so much as the conflict within the widely shared liberal morality, between the moral power of the public to insist on conformity and the moral immunity of the individual by virtue of his duty to follow the Inner Light.

There are, however, limits to liberal indulgence. The values to which the dissident is committed will tell against his duty to conform only if the liberal observer has some commitment to them, though, in the case in point, he rates them less highly. The pacifist and his liberal critic differ, after all, not in valuing peace but in the weight they attach to it. The racist and the cult murderer, by contrast, are attached to values that amount, for the liberal, to wickedness; invoking such values does not earn indulgence and consideration, but increases the heinousness of offences committed for their sake.

IV. Legal Moralism: The Conflict of Public Moral Concern and Private Liberties

Conscientious objection is the standard case of the conflict of the public's claim to enforce civic duty and the individual's liberty to do his duty according to his inner light. Homosexual acts between consenting adults, prostitution and pornography are, correspondingly, the standard cases of conflict between the public's claim to uphold standards of morality in social relations, and the individual's liberty to do whatever he pleases without interference, even when that is an immoral thing.

All liberals agree that in principle the state, through the criminal law, may properly interfere with the acts of individuals to prevent harm to others. In particular cases or in particular areas, overriding reasons may make such interference undesirable; but the expectation of harm to others always constitutes at least a prima facie ground for regulation. The question posed by homosexuality, prostitution, and pornography is whether, supposing such practices to be immoral, it is legitimate for the state to exert the power of the criminal law to prevent them, given that if harm is done at all, it is to the individual alone, or to a group of consenting individuals, each of whom can be thought of as the author of whatever harm falls upon him.

Now there is one short answer to this question. It may be said that if such acts do no harm to anyone but the agent in question, they are not immoral, and present no problem. If the common morality condemns them, it is merely displaying irrational prejudice, which cannot in reason be a moral ground for interference with individuals' preferred occupations. But the premise of this short answer is unreliable: it may not be true that only actions that do harm to others can be immoral. A recurring theme of the individualist morality, which has already been alluded to in this chapter, is that the individual has a duty in respect of his own person, to develop his capacities, to engage his talents in some commendable way, to strive for personal integrity and autonomy, and so on. Anyone failing in this could presumably be considered a moral failure, as alcoholics and drug addicts often are, and not necessarily for failing in their duties to others, or in putting a burden of care on others. Suicide in such a case, though putting an end to society's burden, might be thought only to set the seal on a lifetime of moral failure, not to redeem it. Other kinds of immorality, too, such as ingratitude, and lack of charity, may not harm anyone else, though they may withhold some supererogatory good that a more benevolent attitude might have bestowed. Of course, what constitutes harm is itself very problematic; but the notion of harm would surely be stretched to breaking point if harming someone were taken to include withholding from him any benefit which it was within one's power to bestow, even if he were in no actual need, and had no special right to it. Yet not to bestow a benefit, even under those conditions, might still be mean or selfish. And these are terms of moral condemnation.

Again, it is not clear that people who are offended, shocked, or disgusted by obscene and blasphemous acts are actually harmed by them. In an extreme instance, of course, they might be — as hearing bad news might bring on a heart attack. But to give someone bad news is not in itself to do him harm, any more than a giver who suffers distress in the telling thereby inflicts harm on himself. Imbedded in the doctrine that the only immoral acts are those that harm others, and that only acts that harm others are properly subject to state regulation, is a theory about the nature of harm: either that merely offensive acts are neither harmful nor immoral, and therefore not properly criminal, or that anything that causes distress to anyone else — however unreasonably sensitive that person may be — counts as harm, and therefore could be criminal. Neither view seems very plausible.

Libertarians have been properly suspicious of the second possibility, since it leaves any kind of deviance from accepted life styles vulnerable to interference. On the other hand, some very reputable liberals – among them J.S. Mill and H.L.A. Hart – have been unwilling to go so far as to say that offensive behaviour was a matter of no public concern – or at least, that the public in its institutional mode, the criminal law, had no business with it. A possible way out of the dilemma is to appeal to the concept of nuisance. Everyone, it might be said, has an interest in being able to go about his business without offensive and distracting sensations, smells, noises and perhaps sights, obtruding upon him, interfering with, or preventing him from giving his full attention to his projects, or simply marring an otherwise pleasant experience. Just as some noises are so loud or unpleasant that it would be unreasonable to expect people simply to accept them as natural and inevitable consequences of sharing a social environment with others who have different interests and activities, so some deviations from accepted decency might be so gross that a passer-by's attention would be compelled to them, however distressing they might be to him. According to this view, we all have a right not to have our indignation stimulated to a disquieting degree, provided that we have no convenient way of avoiding the stimulus, that our indignation is not excessive by the standards of our culture, and is not aroused by things that most people in our culture take in their stride.

However the liberal individualist handles such cases (and he rarely does so very confidently), there is always an initial presumption that the individual can ask of the public: What business is it of yours? His private life – whatever he does that cannot be represented as fulfilling a civic duty or the duties of an official role, or as a participation with the rest of his community in a common enterprise where fairness calls for a sharing of burdens – is a residual category where the public's only right of entry is the protection of other people. Not that liberal individualism is indifferent to the quality of people's private lives: I suggested earlier that it distinguishes between good and bad lives, and between good and bad characters. Moreover, as Mill himself makes very clear, anyone with liberal sentiments may properly make a judgement on the life of anyone else. He has, however, no standing to interfere to change it except in self-defence or, as a member of the aggregated public, as that person's acts have a more or less direct impact on some third party. As a simple observer, he is an outsider. And, though he may disapprove, he has no licence to interfere. Neither, in consequence, has the public, the polity, or its agent the state, all of which the individualist takes as essentially a conglomeration of persons with rights of interference no greater than his own. So if gross obscenity is immoral, that alone would not constitute ground enough for public interference. It would have to be shown that the liberty of third parties to go about their legitimate business free of nuisance and disturbance was being denied. And this, of course, is an individualist's account of what constitutes a public nuisance.

Lord Devlin's attack on the Wolfenden Committee's reasoning denied the individualist premise that there is a residual area of private life in which the public could never have right of entry, whether that area be defined in terms of acts doing 'no harm to others', 'causing no nuisance to others', or in any other terms that supposed that the people's interests in other people's lives must be confined to their overflow effects. According to Devlin (and in this Devlin's arguments correspond closely to James Fitzjames Stephen's attack on J.S. Mill), the cohesion of a society requires a moral consensus, in defence of which it is entitled to examine and condemn, by force of law, any kind of action whatsoever. Because Devlin was enough of a liberal to feel the force of the argument from a right to privacy, he acknowledged that invading privacy could, in some instances, be too high a price to pay even for sustaining public morals.[29] But while the private interests in privacy might reasonably be weighed against the public interest in law enforcement, he firmly rejected the individualist's more far-reaching claim that there was a sphere of private morality in which the criminal law had no business.

The difference between Mill's individualism and Devlin's and Stephen's organicism can be put in this way: according to the individualists, the state and the criminal law exist only to protect individual members from being harmed by other members or by outsiders, to coordinate action to that end, and to ensure that burdens are fairly divided. There is, accordingly, a kind of action, a sphere of life, where the state has no standing: intrusion into that sphere cannot be justified since the use of the state's coercive power there would not further those ends, and it is not entitled to use it to further any other. Devlin and Stephen, by contrast, deny that society needs that kind of standing. A society is not simply an aggregate of individuals: 'society means a community of ideas; without shared ideas on politics, morals and ethics no society can exist. Each one of us has ideas about what is good and what is evil; they cannot be kept private from the society in which we live.' A society is sustained by a common agreement about good and evil; 'if . . . the agreement goes, the society will disintegrate'.[30] So 'society may use the law to preserve morality'.[31]

Now an individualist, too, might argue that every individual has an interest in preventing the disintegration of his society. And if, as Devlin believes, moral consensus is necessary to prevent it, and the stern prohibitions of the criminal law are necessary to maintain the consensus, then every individual has an interest in legal moralism. But that kind of instrumentalist argument invites Hart's retort that morality is not a 'seamless web': surely not every detail of the society's code must be preserved intact on pain of social dissolution. That kind of retort comes very naturally to an individualist like Hart; but if Devlin allowed himself to be pushed in that direction, he would have to admit, what he clearly means to resist, that the onus of justification in every case of interference with private conduct rests with the public and has to be met by showing the advantages for specifiable individuals, or for the aggregate of individuals, for each particular interference. Devlin is more inclined to the view that moral consensus is not a causally but a logically necessary condition for society's existence. It is part of the very nature of social life that a common morality shall be sustained. If no moral consensus, then no society, only an aggregation of individuals living alongside one another. The criminal law is at least one mode of social action whereby that consensus is asserted. Devlin would say that, while there may be practical reasons for holding back at particular points, the onus lies, not where Mill and Hart want to put it, but rather upon the morally deviant, to show reasons why society should not exercise its right to protect its collective self against subversion.

V. Paternalism

Paternalist interference with individuals' freedom of choice raises parallel problems. Over the last century or so, public authorities — whether through regulatory agencies or the courts — have come increasingly to restrict individuals' options in order to prevent their doing themselves harm or knowingly entering into arrangements by which others might harm them, and have aspired to promote their good in more positive ways as well, irrespective of their own wishes. Examples of such interference are seat belt and safety helmet legislation, control over the sale of dangerous drugs, compulsory prophylaxis of various kinds, and enforcing safety standards on manufacturers, thereby preventing consumers from choosing cheaper but riskier products. True, the object of the regulation is not always the individual's own well-being alone; some public interest may also be involved (compulsory vaccination is a case in point). In the case of protective clothing and seat belts, however, the well-being of the subject himself does seem to be the dominant consideration, even if a supplementary case could be made out in terms of the use of scarce medical resources; and it is doubtful whether even in the other cases public rather than individual protection loomed largest in legislators' minds.

The liberal's problem with paternalism can be broken down into two questions: (a) Does the public have a reason to interfere? (b) Does it have the right to interfere? As to the first, there seems little room to doubt that it has a reason. Whether we set a value on human beings as such, or, like utilitarians, we value their experiences and states of consciousness, such as happiness, we have reasons, as individuals, for preventing people from hurting themselves or giving themselves pain. This is not a reason that applies especially to people collectively, as the public, or institutionally, as the state; it applies to us severally, as individuals. But if we can act effectively in concert, through legal and administrative institutions, to maximise well-being or minimise suffering, then there is a reason for doing so. This we may call the reason of benevolence.

There may be counter-reasons, also of benevolence. It might be argued, for instance, that to interfere to promote someone else's good is to claim to know his interests better than he does himself, and that it is so easy to be wrong that it is on balance best not to interfere. Yet in cases such as seat belts and safety helmets, the objective evidence in favour of wearing them seems pretty conclusive, unless one credits those who do not wear them with rather special interests, akin to a mountaineer's or a racing driver's interest in thrilling experiences. There is little reason to think that people who do not buckle their seat belts are so motivated, or have in mind some good greater than safety which regulation would block. Again, it might be argued that if individuals as such were in the habit of imposing upon one another their ideas of what would be their respective advantages, there would be a good deal of very clumsy and damaging interference and a great deal of conflict too. But this argument is less cogent if one envisages interference by experts only, perhaps by trained social workers or medical officers. Or the interference might take the form of setting expert standards to which goods must conform, based on technical knowledge that individual consumers rarely possess. In such cases, the benevolent counter-reasons would apply less to interference by public authorities than to indiscriminate private interference.

The question whether the public has a *right* to interfere is less easily answered. To begin with, it is necessary to note the distinction generally made between children and normally rational adults. The term 'paternalism' is used of benevolent constraint precisely because it is a form of action paradigmatically appropriate as between father and child; a parent would be remiss if he did not safeguard a young child's interests against his inexperience and untutored desires. But that is not the way liberals regard relations between adults.

The reasons and counter-reasons of benevolence take no account of a quite separate and distinct element in liberal individualist morality. No doubt everyone has a duty to aim at the greatest good; but set against this is a constraint on interference with another person's liberty to pursue his own projects, deriving not from the good outcome of non-interference but from the respect that persons owe to one another. This respect amounts to a recognition that every person has his own conception of the life he wants to live, of the things that are important for that life, and the right to pursue them as he thinks appropriate, short of invading the like freedom of others, or inflicting harm upon them. This principle of respect for persons acts as a block against the exercise of benevolence, at least towards persons competent to make rational and informed decisions. To impose restraints upon a person for his own good, one has to have some special standing, some right to interfere that makes his welfare our business, beyond the reasons of benevolence. To try to alter a person's life against his wishes and for no better reason than that it is for his own good is to make him the object of a project of one's own, albeit one for his advantage, without regard to his view of the matter. This is to treat him as one might treat a valued — or valuable — animal or art object, not a person. And if people severally are not entitled to deal that way with one another, there is no reason why they should be so entitled collectively. That is not to say that a liberal could never rightly interfere with another's action. But he would always have to show that he acted to protect either his own interests or those of a third party, or that he had some special authority or standing to interfere. 'What business is it of yours?' is the most characteristic of all liberal challenges to would-be interferers.

A justification often used for interference is that an injured person's family, or the community at large, also suffers from his imprudence. Such a reason implicitly acknowledges the need for a reason for interference beyond the good of the agent himself. A child or an insane person may properly be restrained in his own interest precisely to the extent that he lacks the capacities necessary to be a rational chooser, for these capacities alone warrant the forbearance due to a moral person and exclude paternalistic interference. But constraining rational persons (who will not be a charge on the community or a burden on their families if they become paraplegics) to wear seat belts or give up contact sports is a policy which leaves a humane, benevolently disposed liberal in two minds — torn between the private rights of the person as a project maker, and the duties of the public to make the best world it can for everyone.

I have argued too exclusively, perhaps, from the individualist standpoint. Liberalism, as we have seen in Chapter 2, has an organicist fallback position which is as often apparent in discussions of paternalism as of other matters. One form of argument denies that harm done to an individual, even by himself, could ever be of concern only to himself. 'No man is an island, entire of itself,' wrote John Donne; 'any man's death diminishes me, because I am involved in mankind.' But what kind of involvement is it? At its weakest, it might be that because I have a deep, benevolent concern for all mankind, a loss grieves me, as when I lose a friend. But if I do have a right to prevent my friend taking risks with his life, it is surely not to guard my interest, but his. Though in hurting or destroying himself my friend causes me pain, the individualist would deny that he has done me harm; for I had no right to his continuing well-being, nor even to his existence. An organicist, by contrast, would quite reject that way of putting it. As friends, he might say, we have built together a way of life, a small community perhaps, to which each has made a commitment. The harm and the wrong done is not so much to me as an individual, but to the whole — the idea — in which we have both (or all) participated, which has a collective right to that participation, and which is diminished by any member's wilful withdrawal. Substitute, now, the whole community for the group of friends, and we come close to the organic conception of a common good or public interest for the sake of which the community or its agencies might interfere to protect its due, as the medieval king might interfere to prevent or punish self-mutilation which deprived him, and the people, of a soldier.

*   *   *   *   *   *   *

I have dealt, somewhat summarily it is true, with four problem areas for liberal moralists, each of which, in its own way, points up the conflict in liberalism between the individual, equipped with a conscience that, at its most liberal, will stand no gainsaying, and the claims of the public to loyalty, to a committed concern for its collective interest, as an overriding moral end. On the one hand the individual as a citadel, autonomous, possessed of liberties that only he himself can waive, by consent; on the other, the state, which overrides perverse, wilful obstacles in the way of the general will. I have tried to relate this ambiguous model of the individual and society not only to conceptions of what belongs to the private and what to the public, but also to the tension between a morality of principles and one of valued outcomes, which, in my view, is very closely connected with the ambiguity of the model.

Notes

The author would like to thank friends and colleagues who have made helpful comments on this chapter, notably G.F. Gaus, John Kleinig, Miriam Benn, Mohammad Nawawi and Brenda Cohen.

1. *Public and Private Morality*, S. Hampshire (ed.) (Cambridge University Press, Cambridge, 1978).
2. Niccolò Machiavelli, *'The Prince' and 'The Discourses'* (Modern Library New York, 1950), Ch. XV.
3. Cmd. 247, §61.
4. Lord Devlin, *The Enforcement of Morals* (Oxford University Press, London, 1965).
5. Ibid., p. 16.
6. In a recent article ('Kant's Conception of the Private Sphere', *The Philosophical Forum*, XII (1981), pp. 295-310), Thomas Auxter challenges what he claims is the general impression, at least in the English-speaking world, that

> Kant has created an ethic neatly dividing the world into public and private domains and that for the public domain of social relations we must establish a social and political system within which each person has the opportunity to concentrate on the private, individual activities and decisions which are properly the major concern of life (p. 295).

Auxter claims, on the contrary, that 'in the *Grundlegung* Kant makes continual reference to the framework of "the systematic union of different rational beings," i.e. "a whole of all ends in systematic connection," or "a whole of rational beings" ' (p. 303); he quotes the following passage from the *Critique of Judgement*:

> In such a whole every member should surely be end as well as means, and because all work together toward the possibility of the whole, each should be determined as regards place and function by means of the idea of the whole.

Immanuel Kant, *Kritik der Urteilskraft, Kgs* Band V, §65, quoted by Auxter, 'Kant's Conception of the Private Sphere', p. 304.

7. Hampshire, *Public and Private Morality*, p. 48.
8. In J.-P. Sartre, *No Exit and Three Other Plays*, Lionel Abel (trans.) (Vintage Books, New York, 1955), p. 224.
9. Machiavelli, *The Prince*, Ch. XV.
10. Ibid., Ch. XVIII.

11. *Florentine Histories* III, vii, quoted in F. Chabod, *Machiavelli and the Renaissance* (Bowes and Bowes, London, 1958), p. 141. See also Machiavelli, *The Discourses*, Bk. III, Ch. xli, pp. 527-28.
12. M. Walzer, 'Political Action: The Problem of Dirty Hands', *Philosophy and Public Affairs*, 2 (1973), p. 164.
13. Alan Donagan, *The Theory of Morality* (University of Chicago Press, Chicago, 1977), pp. 184-89.
14. Ibid., p. 184.
15. Max Weber, 'Politics as a Vocation', in *From Max Weber: Essays in Sociology*, H.H. Gerth and C. Wright Mills (eds.) (Kegan Paul, Trench, Trubner & Co., Ltd., London, 1948), p. 123.
16. S. Hampshire, 'Public and Private Morality', in Hampshire (ed.), *Public and Private Morality*, pp. 23-53; Bernard Williams, 'Politics and Moral Character', in ibid., pp. 55-74, and his 'Conflicts of Value', in *The Idea of Freedom*, A. Ryan (ed.) (Oxford University Press, Oxford, 1979), pp. 221-32; and Walzer, 'Political Action'.
17. Hugh Cecil, *Conservatism*, p. 182, as quoted in Reinhold Niebuhr, *Moral Man and Immoral Society* (Student Christian Movement Press, London, 1963), p. 267.
18. In his discussion of 'the morality of public and private action', Bosanquet insisted that 'Moral relations presuppose an organised life; but such a life is only within the State, not in relations between the State and other communities.' *The Philosophical Theory of the State*, 4th edn (Macmillan, London, 1951), p. 302.
19. Immanuel Kant, *The Metaphysical Elements of Justice*, John Ladd (trans. and ed.) (Bobbs-Merrill, Indianapolis, 1965), pp. 127-29.
20. Niebuhr, *Moral Man and Immoral Society*, p. 4.
21. Ibid., p. 272.
22. Bernard Williams, 'A Critique of Utilitarianism', in J.J.C. Smart and Bernard Williams, *Utilitarianism: For and Against* (Cambridge University Press, London, 1973), pp. 98ff.
23. For a detailed study of this unhappy episode, see Nikolai Tolstoy, *Victims of Yalta* (Hodder and Stoughton, London, 1977).
24. Gerald C. MacCallum Jr., 'Law, Conscience, and Integrity', in *Issues in Law and Morality*, N.S. Care and T.K. Trelogan (eds.) (Case Western Reserve University Press, Cleveland, 1973), pp. 141-59.
25. Ibid., p. 141.
26. Ibid., p. 147.
27. Ibid., p. 155.
28. Ibid., p. 156.
29. Devlin, *Enforcement of Morals*, p. 18. Cf. *Griswold v. Connecticut*, 381 U.S. 479 (1965), where legislation regulating marital intimacy, by prohibiting the use of contraceptive devices, was invalidated, not because such regulation was held to be intrinsically objectionable, but because it could be done only by resorting to objectionable means of collecting information.
30. Devlin, *Enforcement of Morals*, p. 10. Cf. Thomas Auxter's interpretation of Kant, cited above, note 6. Auxter comments:
A moral whole is the ideal of an organically unified society which requires a differentiated functioning of individual members. [O]ne's choice of a private end – or one's abandonment of a private end – is a *social* question which deserves *moral* scrutiny. Private ends should undergo constant adjustment and improvement in accordance with the ideal of human (organic) solidarity.
'Kant's Conception of the Private Sphere', pp. 304-5.
31. Devlin, *Enforcement of Morals*, p. 11.

8 PUBLIC AND PRIVATE INTERESTS IN LIBERAL POLITICAL ECONOMY, OLD AND NEW

Gerald F. Gaus

I. Introduction

No facet of liberal theory relies more on the public/private distinction than its political economy.[1] At the heart of classical political economy is a theory of the market order according to which the pursuit by each of his private interests engenders a network of voluntary co-operation that is beneficial to all. From Adam Smith to Milton and Rose Friedman, classical liberal political economists have insisted that in a properly structured market

> an individual who 'intends only his own gain' is 'led by an invisible hand to promote an end which was no part of his intention ... By pursuing his own interest he frequently promotes that of the society more effectually than when he intends to promote it'.[2]

It was precisely this political economy that was criticised and reformulated by the 'new liberalism' that began to take shape in the last years of the nineteenth century. As John Dewey emphasised, while this 'renascent liberalism' stood by the older liberalism's devotion to individual freedom, it could not accept the *laissez-faire* political economy which the 'new liberals' attributed to classical theory.[3] To a new liberal like Dewey, the classical doctrine rested on an almost religious faith in a competitive market order premised on the pursuit of private interests. In its stead the new liberals advocated an economic order based upon an interventionist state, guiding and supervising private interests so as to achieve the public good.

The main aim of this chapter is to examine this shift in the competencies and functions of private agents and public authorities in liberal political economy. In particular, I shall focus on the changing conceptions of, and relations among: (1) the public interest, (2) the market order of private interests and (3) public authorities. Section II considers the position of the classical liberal political economists on these three points, while section III takes up the new liberal political economy.

184 *Gerald F. Gaus*

The new liberal critique of the classical system, I will argue, by no means constitutes a radical break with the classical perspective. Rather, it involves a balance of revisions and retentions and is best understood as an outgrowth of the classical tradition. I then turn to three criticisms of the new liberal position (section IV), which charge that the public/ private balance endorsed by the new liberals is either inadequate or illusory. I close in section V by briefly suggesting that underlying the many changes in liberal political economy is a basic consistency in aims and concerns.

II. Classical Political Economy

A. *The Public Interest as the Aim of Economic Policy*

The classical liberal political economists[4] were widely agreed that a basic, perhaps the basic, aim of legislation was the public welfare. 'Freedom', wrote J.R. McCulloch, 'is not, as some appear to think, the end of government; the advancement of the public prosperity and happiness is its end.'[5] And by 'public prosperity' the classical economists generally meant the increase of aggregate wealth or income. Of course, as Nassau Senior pointed out, the growth of wealth and happiness need not go together, but, like others, he was convinced that, as a matter of fact, 'wealth and happiness are very seldom opposed'.[6] So in practice the devotion of the classical political economists to the public welfare translated into the conviction that the creation of wealth ought to be the object of economic policy. Moreover, because they thought the accumulation of capital was the key to growth — we shall see later that nearly all of them thought over-saving impossible — the more specific practical conclusion was that 'the public interest requires that the national capital should, if possible, be kept constantly on the increase'.[7]

One of the things we saw in Chapter 2, however, is that it is difficult to make much of the idea of a public interest without resorting to the organic model. Now the classical liberals certainly did not entertain any organic notion of the public interest as the interest of 'society as a whole', where that means anything but the interests of a number of individuals. Indeed, J.-B. Say was very explicit that a nation 'is but an aggregate of many individuals' and thus 'there is no truth in the argument, that perhaps the state may gain, though individuals cannot; for how can the state gain, except through the medium of individuals?'[8] Given, then, that the classical liberals were no organicists, what options existed? Well, most obviously, they might, as they undoubtedly sometimes did, conceive of the public interest simply as the (net) interest of *everyone*. But as we saw in our analysis of this conception of the public interest (Ch. 2, §II.E, above), it implies that in most circumstances no public interest exists: as long as the (net) interests of a significant number oppose the rest, no public interest can emerge. Moreover, given that classical theories like those of Smith and Ricardo imply significant divergence of class interests,[9] the 'everyone' conception seems particularly unfitting. Not surprisingly, then, we can discern in classical liberal writings at least two other understandings of the public interest.

The class of consumers, wrote Say, 'is always the most important class, because it is the most numerous; because it comprehends every description of producer whatever; and because the welfare of this class, wherein all others are comprised, constitutes the general well-being and prospering of a nation'.[10] Within this sentence Say suggests both classical liberal conceptions of the public and its interest. (1) The primary classical understanding of the public interest, and that stressed by Say, is the public interest as the interest of consumers because, as Ricardo said, 'all classes are consumers'.[11] This, of course, is an example of the role analysis of the public interest that we analysed in Chapter 2: the public interest is the interest of everyone *qua* consumer. And because the interests of everyone *qua* consumer are generally harmonious, i.e. a plentiful supply of inexpensive quality goods, there will be a good number of cases in which the interest of the public (everyone as a consumer) will be advanced or retarded by a particular policy or measure. Thus, unlike the simple 'net interests of everyone' conception, it provides a useful test for economic policy. In particular, it indicates in a more specific way how an increase, to use Ricardo's phrase, in the 'general mass of productions' furthers the interest of the public.

(2) Yet, as was also suggested by Say, classical political economists were sometimes apt to identify the public, or at least the crucial part of it, with 'the most important class because it is the most numerous'. And while in the quoted sentence Say is referring to consumers, classical political economists usually pointed to the labourers. To Ricardo, the workers were 'by far the most important class in society', to McCulloch 'the largest and not least valuable portion of society' and, to Malthus, 'it is most desirable that the labouring classes should be well paid, for a much more important reason than any that can relate to wealth, namely the happiness of the great mass of society'.[12] Hence, as one scholar has noted, classical economists strongly supported all measures that might be reasonably expected to raise real wages and were extremely critical of middle-class influence on legislation.[13] However, this is not to say

that they favoured systematically suppressing the interests of other classes to further that of workers. As we will see later, one of the objections of a liberal like Adam Smith to government interference in economic life was that it usually acted as a vehicle for class interests. And while the size of the working class gave it a special status in classical liberal political economy (we saw in Chapter 2, at pp. 35-36, that the mass is sometimes equated with the public), they resisted class legislation. Classical liberal political economy — indeed, we will see, all liberal political economy — ultimately aims at policies that benefit everyone, i.e. the public.

Lord Robbins points to yet another reason why the classical economists would not have supported legislative attempts to set either a minimum or maximum level of wages: viz. they violate the principles of security and property. More generally Robbins also tells us that the ultimate value of classical political economy was liberty.[14] This appears to raise an important question: were the classical political economists aiming primarily at the public interest or were considerations of justice (e.g. rights of property and liberty) uppermost in their minds? To put the issue thus is, I think, distorting, for classical political economists did not entertain the possibility of a sustained conflict between the demands of justice (including the protection of 'Natural Liberty' and private property) and the pursuit of the public interest. A central tenet of classical economics is, of course, that security of private property and the protection of liberty are essential to the growth of wealth. Indeed, secure them and, as we are about to see, the creation of wealth will very largely take care of itself. So if you insist on justice, you end up promoting the public interest; and if you aim at the public interest, you must secure justice. 'At bottom there is no real distinction between what is just and what is useful.'[15]

This is not to say that they thought the two never conflict. And when they do, a case apparently can be made out for the priority of the public interest. This seems even to be true for Smith, who, unlike so many other classical liberals, was no utilitarian. Thus, for example, although he is certainly very suspicious of public officials' sacrificing 'the rights of a private man' to state interests, Smith refrains from outright condemnation. Rather, he insists that only 'urgent necessity' can justify the sacrifice of 'the ordinary laws of justice to an idea of publick utility'.[16] Faced with the possibility of such a conflict, Smith is willing to make his choice, but he is clearly uneasy about it.

B. The Spontaneous Order of Private Interests

According to Lord Robbins:

The essence of Classical Liberalism was the belief that, within a suitable system of general rules and institutions, there will arise spontaneous relationships also deserving the term 'order' but which are self-sustaining and, within the limits prescribed by the rules, need no detailed and specific regulation.[17]

Four aspects of this 'spontaneous order' require consideration here: (1) its appropriateness to human nature, (2) its self-regulation, (3) its justification and (4) its supporting framework.

Appropriateness. Although Robbins has argued that the classical economists thought the market was an artificial mechanism,[18] running throughout their writings is the idea that an economic system grounded on private property and the pursuit of private interests is especially appropriate to human nature and in that sense natural, and hence stable. Thus, in response to Rousseau's contention that private property is the source of unnatural inequality, McCulloch insists:

> The truth, however, is, that differences of fortune are as consonant to the nature of things, and are as really a part of the order of Providence, as differences of sex, complexion, or strength. No two individuals will ever be equally fortunate, frugal, and industrious; and supposing an equality of fortunes were forcibly established, it could not be maintained for a week ... By attacking that security which is a *sine qua non* of all industry, the success of the levelers would be destructive alike of wealth and civilization. The establishment of a right of property enables exertion, invention and enterprise, forethought and economy, to reap their due reward ... To enjoy immediately — to enjoy without labour, is the natural inclination of every man. This inclination must be restrained: for its obvious tendency is to arm all those who have nothing against those who have something.[19]

McCulloch, then, suggests three lines of argument for the naturalness of private property. (1) The *anti-egalitarian* argument contends that inequality of talents naturally leads to inequality of outcomes (fortunes); the system of private property recognises this and, by protecting the differential outcomes, tends towards stability. (2) The *incentive* argument maintains that only by ensuring each his 'due reward' will wealth be created and thus, as we have seen, the public interest be advanced. (3) Lastly, McCulloch stresses what might be called the

Augustinian argument for property as necessary to compensate for the weaknesses of human nature. Although McCulloch was disturbed by the desire to enjoy without labour, uppermost in the minds of many of the classical political economists from the time of Malthus onwards was the human desire to reproduce. As Ricardo saw it, 'so great are the delights of domestic society' that increases in the wages of labourers 'invariably' lead to an increase of population.[20] Now, as J.S. Mill argued, an economic system based on the pursuit of private interests (as institutionalised in private property) makes clear to each that his welfare depends on his own effort and restraint: if one wants to breed, he must pay for it. A scheme based on the public provision of needs would thus be all too likely to undermine this restraining force, resulting in 'a greater number of people, in as great poverty and as great liability to destitution as now'.[21]

Self-regulation. The cornerstone of the classical conception of the market order, however, was not merely that the market was in some sense natural, but that it was very largely self-regulating or, more precisely, self-equilibrating. The claim of self-equilibration that J.S. Mill thought 'fundamental' and Keynes saw as the foundation of classical economics was, in James Mill's words, 'that most important doctrine, that the aggregate demand and supply of a nation are always equal, that production can never be too rapid for the market; in other words, that there never can be a general glut of commodities'.[22] According to this 'Law of Markets' or 'Say's Law',

> there is no amount of capital which may not be employed in a country because demand is only limited by production. No man produces, but with a view to consume or sell, and he never sells, but with an intention to purchase some other commodity, which may either be immediately useful to him, or which may contribute to future production.[23]

Production creates its own demand. And, for nearly all the classical economists, savings are always used to finance more production, which, necessarily, will be consumed. So neither over-saving nor over-production was thought possible.

Malthus was the great heretic of classical economics, finding Say's Law 'to be utterly unfounded, and completely to contradict the great principles which regulate supply and demand'.[24] Consumption, Malthus argued, could exceed production, leading to the consumption of capital and eventual impoverishment. Or effectual demand might not be sufficient. And if production can be in excess, so too can savings (investment). For Malthus, then, an equilibrium of production and consumption, as well as an optimum level of savings, are goals to be sought rather than automatic outcomes of the market mechanism. As we shall see later, this heresy leads Malthus to depart from the orthodox classical understanding of the role of the state in economic life.

The Market and the Public Interest. Although conformity to human nature and self-equilibration are desirable features of an economic order, alone they would not be sufficient to recommend the market system. For the public interest was the true test of economic policy in classical theory. The system of economic liberty, it repeatedly argued, promoted the public interest better than an alternative system based on extensive state regulation and supervision of economic life. As illustrated by my opening quotation from the Friedmans, the obvious point of departure here is Smith's 'invisible hand' metaphor. Though the importance of the metaphor to classical economics is usually exaggerated, it does convey a basic tenet of classical theory. Smith's thesis was that 'the private interests and passions of individuals'[25] lead them to seek the safest and most profitable employments of their capital and industry. Now, Smith argued, this means that each will endeavour to employ his capital and industry domestically (which was safer than overseas), where it will produce the greatest value. And since the aggregate revenue of a society is equal to the exchangeable value of the produce of its industry, Smith's conclusion was that each individual was, in fact, working to maximise the aggregate revenue of society. It was in this sense that, according to Smith, the pursuit by each of his private interest promotes 'the publick interest'.[26] McCulloch put much the same argument in terms of the creation of wealth (rather than revenue or value):

> When individuals are left to be guided by their sense of what is best for themselves in the employment of their stock and industry, their interests are identified with those of the public; and those who are most successful in increasing their own wealth, necessarily, also, contribute most effectually to increase the wealth of the state to which they belong.[27]

This classical doctrine — that the public interest is best promoted by each pursuing his private interest — is neither miraculous nor tautologous. It is not particularly miraculous since, in the argument, the public interest is identified with the increase of wealth. And since for the classical political economists 'the wealth of any community is the sum of the portions of wealth belonging to the several individuals of which that community is composed',[28] the claim that 'if each seeks to maximise his private interest, the public interest is maximised' translates into the claim that 'if each seeks to maximise his own gains, the total aggregate of individual gains will be maximised'. But if that does not seem miraculous, it certainly is not tautologous either. We can easily imagine situations like Hobbes's state of nature in which the attempt by each to maximise his own position leads to an outcome in which everyone is worse off than if some less competitive strategy were pursued. Instead of a Hobbesian war of all against all, classical theory supposes a rule-governed framework in which one gains through voluntary (and so, it is assumed, mutually beneficial) exchanges. Within this order, the effort by each to maximise his own gains is not self-defeating, and so the sum of individual gains is maximised.

I have been stressing that in practice classical theory identified the public interest with the increase of the community's aggregate wealth or revenue. Moreover, since, in general, classical theory defines 'wealth' as something like the 'material objects necessary, useful or agreeable to man, which have required some portion of human exertion to appropriate or produce',[29] it is easy to see how its increase benefits the public *qua* consumers. However, all this concern with increasing the total aggregate of wealth does not mean that classical political economists were blind to issues of distribution. For example, it was Say who noted that though Europe was flourishing, much was left to be desired:

> The haggardness of poverty, is everywhere seen contrasted with the sleekness of wealth, the extorted labour of some compensating for the idleness of others, wretched hovels by the side of stately colonnades, the rags of indigence blended with the ensigns of opulence; in a word, the most useless profusion in the midst of the most urgent wants.[30]

But Bentham's position on this subject characterises classical political economy. The concern with equality of wealth, he argued, is not a concern distinct from opulence: the aim, 'whatever may be done in the design of favouring equality', is not to make the rich poorer, but the poor richer.[31] The classical practical identification of the public interest with an increase of aggregate wealth was thus related to their commitment to the interests of the working class. Indeed, Smith insisted that 'the lowest ranks of the people' had already gained by the progression of 'opulence'. Even a workman 'of the lowest and poorest order, if he is frugal and industrious, may enjoy a greater share of the necessaries and conveniences of life than it is possible for any savage to acquire'.[32]

We must, though, be cautious here for it is very easy indeed to caricature rather than characterise classical political economy. Although, all things considered, they certainly believed that workers' interests were advanced by economic growth, classical liberals were not unaware of the costs incurred by the labouring class for these gains. We thus find, for example, Say maintaining that while the division of labour greatly increased productivity, it nevertheless blunted or extinguished many of the workman's capacities upon which his narrow routine never called.[33] Smith, in an oft-quoted passage, is even more emphatic:

> The man whose whole life is spent in performing a few simple operations, of which the effects too are, perhaps, always the same, or very nearly the same, has no occasion to exert his understanding, or to exercise his invention in finding out expedients for removing difficulties which never occur. He naturally loses, therefore, the habit of such exertion, and generally becomes as stupid and ignorant as it is possible for a human creature to become.[34]

Nor was that the only problem recognised with the system of natural liberty in achieving the public interest. Indeed, the doctrine of the inevitable advance of the stationary state, fundamental to classical economics, is hardly unobjectionable from the perspective of the public interest. As J.S. Mill observed:

> It must always have been seen, more or less distinctly, by political economists, that the increase of wealth is not boundless: that at the end of what they term the progressive state lies the stationary state, that all progress in wealth is but a postponement of this, and that each step in advance is an approach to it.[35]

Eventually, the classical economists held, the rate of profit would fall so low that net accumulation, and hence the growth of wealth, would cease. And though the younger Mill saw opportunities in the stationary state, the other economists feared this inevitable halt. The condition of the labouring poor, said Smith, 'is hard in the stationary, and miserable in the declining state. The progressive state is in reality the cheerful and the hearty state to all the different orders of the society. The stationary is dull; the declining, melancholy.'[36]

Lastly, it needs to be emphasised that classical economists recognised that the market, by its very nature, failed to secure many things essential to the public interest. It was generally seen, for example, that 'public goods' would not be sufficiently provided by the market as they envisaged it. In the market, a private agent provides goods to a consumer because the consumer is willing and able to remunerate the producer sufficiently for them. The consumer is only willing to pay for the benefits he receives, and the producer provides benefits only for those who pay. But, as the classical economists realised, discrimination in organising the flow of benefits is impossible for some goods. A lighthouse, for example, benefits all passing ships; and because each benefits whether or not he has paid for it, each is tempted not to pay his 'share' of the costs of production. Consequently, a market economy tends to supply such goods inadequately. We can find, then, classical economists endorsing public, i.e. state, provision of many such goods affording indiscriminate benefit, from lighthouses to scientific research and exploration.[37] More generally, J.S. Mill allows for government intervention in two broad cases of market failures: (1) when the assumption that each knows his own interest best does not hold and (2) when the actions of an individual have adverse effects on third parties (i.e. what are now called externalities or external effects).[38] In addition to these theory-based interventions, classical writings offer abundant examples of a largely pragmatic support for government action on poor relief, assistance to those displaced by mechanisation, education (J.S. Mill argued for it in terms of market failure) and limitations on the working hours of women and children.[39]

The Political Framework. Underlying the claims that the market is self-equilibrating and promotes the public interest is the assumption that economic life is structured by a framework of rules and institutions. Most important to the classical liberals, of course, were the laws of property and contract and the criminal law. But beyond this, classical liberals were prepared to endorse a number of other measures aimed at structuring the pursuit of private interests so as to achieve the public interest. The licensing of professionals,[40] health, safety and fire regulations[41] and banking regulations[42] are just some of the rules that we find classical liberal economists accepting in order to achieve a harmony of public and private interests. Moreover, in addition to the political-legal framework, all our classical liberals except McCulloch advocated the public development of what we would now call the economic framework or infrastructure (e.g. roads, harbours, canals) in order to 'facilitate commerce'.[43] It is thus quite clear that the so-called 'night-watchman state of classical liberal theory',[44] whatever else it may have been, was most certainly not the state endorsed by classical liberal political economy.

C. The Limitations of the State

Writing on the causes of the retardation of the progress of wealth, Say emphasised two characteristics that, unfortunately, men in power share with the rest of mankind. They were both 'too slow in their intellectual progress' and 'impelled by interested motives'.[45] This twofold attack on the state, not only by Say but by classical economists as a group,[46] provides a basis for the insistence that government's role in economic life be kept as small as possible.

(1) Smith was the most vehement in arguing that the state is usually the vehicle of private rather than public interests. 'All for ourselves, and nothing for the people, seems, in every age of the world, to have been the vile maxim of the masters of mankind.'[47] Every nation, he tells us, has a governing 'private interest'.[48] And in his day it was the interest of the merchants and masters, because, of all the classes, they were by far the most adept at passing off their private interests in the guise of the public interest. Not surprisingly, moreover, they were the counsellors of governments.[49] The upshot of all this, as Smith saw it, was a wide range of regulations and legislation intended to advance private (middle-class) interests at the expense of the public:

> the cruellest of our revenue laws, I will venture to affirm, are mild and gentle, in comparison of some of those which the clamour of our merchants and manufacturers has extorted from the legislature, for the support of their own absurd and oppressive monopolies. Like the laws of Draco, these laws may be said to be all written in blood.[50]

We might note here in passing that, despite the condemnation by the classical liberals of monopolies and combinations intended to restrict trade, they were generally prepared to accept combinations by workers seeking to raise wages,[51] yet another instance of the special status of the labouring class in classical liberal theory.

(2) The conviction that government is merely a tool of private interests is not as strong in all the classical economists as it is in Smith.

'In despotisms', wrote Senior, 'the principal evils arise partly from the ignorance, and partly from the bad passions of the rulers. In representative governments, they arise principally from their unskilfulness.'[52] At least two criticisms of governments' intellectual competency were made. First, they operated on false economic theories; on this count, accepting the classical analysis would do much to raise their competency. But, more significantly, it is a tenet of classical analysis that even the most enlightened government can usually do little good by interfering with the spontaneous order of the market. 'A first Lord of the Treasury, or of Trade, or any other Member of the Legislature', Bentham argued, will never be able to make as good choices as to the conduct of trades or the employment of capital as those intimately acquainted with the trades. Not only will the official have insufficient information but he will be far less interested in each transaction and decision than those directly involved.[53] Governments, classical liberals thus insisted, were inattentive spendthrifts: 'when works are carried on at the public expense, they are never performed so economically and well, as when carried on at the risk of private individuals, watching over the expenditure of their individual fortunes'.[54] The upshot of all this, as Smith put it, was that:

> The sovereign is completely discharged from a duty, in the attempting to perform which he must always be exposed to innumerable delusions, and for the proper performance of which no human wisdom or knowledge could ever be sufficient; the duty of superintending the industry of private people, and of directing it towards the employments most suitable to the interest of the society.[55]

D. *The State and Economy in Classical Liberalism*

A fairly clear picture thus emerges of classical liberal political economy's view of the relation of state and economy. But, while clear, it is not so simple as is usually thought. Although Torrens at one time appeared to insist that the state should entirely restrict itself to police functions, J.S. Mill's position that *laissez-faire* is but a general rule admitting of numerous exceptions is far more typical.[56] Despite their praise of the market and attacks on the state, they realised that the economic order required a significant amount of regulation if it was to work in the interest of the public. And even then it would fail to secure some things necessary to the public interest.

The competency of the market contrasted with the incompetency of the state thus provides a strong presumption against state interference, albeit one that can be rebutted. Now if either the competency of the market or the incompetency of the state in securing the public interest is questioned, the presumption against state action will be weakened. Among the classical political economists, the strongest attack on the competency of the market was launched by Malthus. If, as Malthus maintained, aggregate consumption did not automatically match aggregate production, a serious inefficiency is introduced into the market. Goods may be produced but lie unsold in storage or else by running down stocks the nation's net capital may be diminished, perhaps endangering future growth. Not surprisingly, therefore, Malthus's attitude towards various state economic activities departed from the orthodox position. He was, for example, considerably less hostile than other classical economists to taxes and the national debt: government spending spurred consumption and hence alleviated what he saw as persistent under-consumption.[57] Moreover, Malthus endorsed public works projects for the unemployed: by employing those who did not produce goods, consumption could be raised without increasing production.[58] But, though he attacked the market's competency to promote the public interest, Malthus retained the classical liberal's doubts about the ability of the state to do much better. It was an increase in private, not public, (unproductive) consumption that Malthus ultimately hoped would bring about economic equilibrium.

Malthus foreshadows one attack that the new liberalism will make on classical political economy: viz., that the market is not self-equilibrating and hence does not best promote the public interest with minimal state interference. But, as we see with Malthus, that line of attack alone is not sufficient. If the state is still largely incompetent to correct the mechanism's failings, the door to government action is only slightly opened. Hence we shall find that the new liberal political economy elevates the competency of the state at the same time as it disparages that of the market. The first stage of this critique is a partial reformulation of the very notion of the public interest. It is to that first attack of the new liberal political economy that I now turn.

III. The New Liberal Political Economy

A. The Public Interest: Revisions and Retentions

We saw that classical liberal political economy operated with a strictly aggregative conception of the public, and hence of the public interest. With the rise of the new liberalism in the latter part of the nineteenth century we witness the injection of a distinctively organic strain. In one of the earliest new liberal critiques of the classical system, A.F. Mummery and J.A. Hobson charged that '[t] his view, that a community means nothing more than the addition of a number of individual units, and that the interests of Society can be obtained by adding together the interests of individual members, has led to as grave errors in Economics as in other branches of Sociology.'[59] To Hobson, this conceptual error was a fundamental flaw in the classical system and, so, 45 years later we still find him stressing the importance of policies that are in the interests of 'the social organism as a whole'.[60] To be sure, not all new liberals were as ready as Hobson to employ the organic metaphor, but it was clearly a view of social life with which nearly all had considerable sympathy.[61] Even J.M. Keynes, in a refutation of '*laissez-faire*' individualism not unlike Hobson's, appeals to the 'organized society as a whole'.[62] Indeed, a recent analysis of Franklin Roosevelt's economic policies sees fit to call to our attention his 'organic view of society'.[63]

This is not to say that organic notions of the public interest simply displace more traditional views. To a very large extent, the new liberals still endorse the market order on the grounds that it functions in the consumers' — that is, the public's — interest. And certainly they did not forsake classical liberalism's special devotion to the working class.[64] But the new liberals do tend to recast some of these ideas in organic terms. Thus, for example, Hobson supported a wide range of working class interests by arguing that they were 'ultimately consistent with and conducive to the interests of society as a whole'.[65] In this vein J.S. Mill — who is a bridge between the classical and new liberal traditions — contended that if 'greater fellow-feeling and community of interest' were to be achieved, i.e. if social harmony were to be advanced, the 'claims of labour' must be recognised and secured.[66] 'Misery generates hate' is thus appropriately the motto of William Beveridge's *Full Employment in a Free Society*.[67] Nevertheless, like their classical counterparts, the new liberals are reluctant to simply equate the public interest with the interest of any single class, even labour's. Their aim is to promote the public good, and although that includes labour's good, it transcends it.[68]

When we descend from these heights to consider the practical economic goals of the new liberals, we again find a change, but by no means a revolutionary one, from the classical perspective. The promotion of economic growth, so central to classical political economy, undergoes something of a demotion in the new liberal outlook for at least two reasons. (1) We saw that the classical economists were aware of the detrimental effects of industrial life on the working population; but, since they were convinced that only an increase in wealth could improve the lot of the workers, they thought it a necessary cost. The new liberalism adopts and extends this critique of the industrial system: the development and welfare of all, it is charged, is impaired by obsession with money-making and production. J.S. Mill insists on this point: the existing type of social life, consumed with the pursuit of riches, was, he hoped, only a temporary and passing phase of industrial progress.

> In the mean time, those who do not accept the present very early stage of human improvement as its ultimate type may be excused for being comparatively indifferent to the kind of economical progress which excites the congratulations of ordinary politicians; the mere increase of production and accumulation.[69]

Although not all the new liberals were quite so ready to proclaim that we have had enough of such 'economical progress', L.T. Hobhouse, John Dewey, D.G. Ritchie, Keynes and John Rawls all acknowledge at one place or another that the pursuit of wealth can, if pushed too far, detract from individual welfare or the public good.[70]

(2) The second factor behind the new liberalism's cooling towards economic growth is an increasing scepticism as to just how much growth alone actually bettered the lot of the working class. Echoing Mill, Hobhouse insisted that 'if the economic basis of social life is to be sound, not increased production, but a better distribution of wealth, is essential'.[71] At this point, though, we encounter an interesting twist in the new liberal argument. Hobson, Hobhouse, Dewey and others were committed to the idea that a redistribution of wealth would not only benefit the workers — and hence through them society — but also increase industrial efficiency and economic growth! 'Thus', said Hobson, 'we recognize the problem of greater productivity to be, in fact, inseparable from that of a better distribution.'[72] In a similar way, Dewey heralded the approach of a ' "new economy" based on the identity of high wages with industrial prosperity'.[73] And Keynes, who did not share Hobson's view that equality always increased efficiency, was ready to agree that for practical purposes redistribution and increased productivity did indeed (at the time) go together.[74] Even Rawls, who is widely known for his insistence on the priority of justice over efficiency, emphasises that, as he defines it, justice is 'consistent with efficiency'.[75] This means that, especially among the early new liberals, the insistence that redistribution is more important than production amounted in practice to a strategy to increase productivity.

To a surprising extent, then, the new liberal political economy persists in the classical belief in the essential convergence of justice and the public interest. Of course 'justice' as well as 'public interest' are differently understood. The classical liberal economist's focus on the protection of natural liberty and private property rights gives way in the new liberalism to emphasis on distributive justice. And while the new liberal does not deny the importance of property, he is inclined to worry less about its security than its distribution. Moreover, he is apt to think some sorts of private property — e.g. in social assets such as land and mineral wealth — unjust. In sum, the classical faith that public interest and justice converged was premised on the conviction that increased wealth would follow from protecting private property and natural liberty; whereas many new liberals held that while the public interest did indeed converge with social justice, they called for a more equal distribution, which, in turn, would be likely to increase productivity.

But while we tend to think of the classical political economy as essentially utilitarian — and thus generally more concerned with considerations of interest than justice[76] — the new liberal political economy seems to demonstrate a shift in emphasis towards justice. As Bertrand de Jouvenel has said, social justice appears to be 'the obsession of our time'.[77] And perhaps one of the marks of this 'obsession' is what would seem to be a growing insistence among some liberals that justice — particularly social justice — should be achieved even if it conflicts with the general welfare or public interest. Now if we combine this principle of the priority of social justice with the belief of many welfare economists today that equity and efficiency very often do not converge — that one must be traded for the other[78] — we seem to have the basis for a marked divergence of (social) justice and the public interest. So perhaps we are witnessing the beginnings of a breakdown of the long-standing liberal conviction in the essential convergence of justice and the public interest. Yet alternative accounts are possible too. It might be argued, for instance, that as liberals lose their enthusiasm for economic growth,[79] they become more willing to trade efficiency for equity; but this still need not amount to trading the public interest for justice since, on this account, efficiency is even less an element of the public interest than the earlier new liberals believed. Regardless of which account one accepts, however, theories that insist on persistent and widespread conflicts between efficiency and equity represent a significant departure not only from the classical but from the earlier new liberal political economy as well.

B. The Spontaneous Order Attacked

A central focus of new liberal attacks on classical political economy was the idea that the market order is somehow 'natural'.[80] J.S. Mill, in the famous discussion of socialism in his *Principles*, rejected the idea that an economic order based on the pursuit of private interest was somehow especially appropriate to human nature and, thus, stable. 'Mankind', he believed, 'are capable of a far greater amount of public spirit than the present age is accustomed to suppose possible.'[81] Hobhouse, too, emphasised the latent strength of social service as a productive motive.[82] Yet, though the new liberals have thought public spirit a more potent motivational force than did the classical liberals, they are usually at pains to point out its limitations. Rawls thus emphasises that his theory 'assumes a definite limit on the strength of social and altruistic motivation. It supposes that individuals and groups put forward competing claims, and while they are willing to act justly, they are not prepared to abandon their interests.'[83] The new liberal political economy thus has by no means endorsed a wholesale abandonment of an economic order based on private interest; but it has insisted that pursuit of private interest is not an iron law of human nature, and, hence, that various schemes of redistribution for the public good are indeed conformable to human nature and, in this way, stable.

The importance of the new liberal critiques of the classical claim of a self-regulating market is part of the lore of political economy. 'By making it impossible to believe any longer in an automatic reconciliation of conflicting interests into a harmonious whole', says Joan Robinson, 'the General Theory brought out into the open the problem of choice and judgement that the neo-classicals had managed to smother. The ideology to end ideologies broke down. Economics once more become Political Economy.'[84] Keynes himself saw his theory as the final break away from Say, showing that demand could indeed be deficient.[85] But though Keynes's was the first generally accepted liberal critique of the classical system, new liberals had been attacking the self-regulating claims of the classical political economists for some time. From 1899 into the 1930s Hobson 'flung himself with unflagging, but almost unavailing, ardour and courage against the ranks of orthodoxy'.[86] Like Keynes, the object of Hobson's attack was Say's Law and its implicit claim that the levels of production and consumption could be left to take care of themselves. But whereas Keynes's thesis was that money savings were not automatically transformed into real investment (thus allowing for an equilibrium of investment and consumption with substantial unemployment), Hobson's theory was straightforwardly underconsumptionist. Real investment, he said, was itself too high in relation to total consumption. This difference, of course, may well be critical in respect to policy prescriptions: whereas Keynes might endorse an increase in investment to raise employment levels, for Hobson this would be precisely the wrong policy, further adding to surplus investment.[87] On Hobson's analysis the desideratum was an increase of consumption, effected chiefly by a redistribution of income from savers to spenders. But both analyses are at one on the inability of the market order to regulate itself, and hence on the need for some conscious control of aggregate production and investment levels.

Unlike Hobson's analysis, Keynes's does not really deny that the market is self-equilibrating; for Keynes the problem was not that the economy would fail to reach an equilibrium, but that it would do so at very high levels of unemployment. But this sort of self-equilibration hardly amounted to a justification of the market order. What was wanted, as Beveridge put it, was a 'prosperous equilibrium'.[88] Equilibrium or no, in the eyes of the new liberals an unregulated market is so permeated by 'waste and error'[89] as to be, in Keynes's words, a 'public scandal'.[90] Thus, whereas classical political economy could recommend a free market system based on private property as the most efficient way to further the public interest, understood as economic growth, the new liberalism not only challenged so impoverished an understanding of the public interest but denied, in any case, that it could even efficiently promote growth. 'Many people', said Hobson in something of an understatement, 'hold that this system no longer works with a reasonable degree of efficiency.'[91]

Inefficiency, of course, is not the only modern liberal complaint about a regime of unregulated private enterprise. 'With the organization of the principal lines of business and industry in great corporations, which frequently control the supply of resources', Dewey wrote, 'it is increasingly difficult to suppose that competition automatically turns the seeker for profits to methods which supply public needs.'[92] Indeed, one of the driving forces behind the development of the new liberal outlook was the conviction that the classical world of individual capitalist entrepreneurs had given way to a system of powerful bureaucratic organisations able to defy the discipline of the market and whose individual decisions greatly affected the public welfare. As Franklin Roosevelt saw it, the president of General Motors held 'a private office with a public trust'.[93] Moreover, to those like Hobhouse, the breakdown of the individual capitalist world not only resulted in large concentrated corporations but also in an opposing camp of organised labour. And so in place of a spontaneous order based on the competition of a multitude of individual agents, new liberals were prone to see a war between powerful opposing camps, engendering economic anarchy. 'Competition failed and we live among its debris with no established freedom of social co-operation to take its place, but with the struggles of organized capital and labour confronting us.'[94] Nevertheless, despite such flights of rhetoric, the new liberal critique is only a partial one. As Hobson, one of the most vehement new liberal critics of the classical system, concluded, 'a good deal of order emerges in the working of the whole. This order, however, is attended also by a good deal of disorder.'[95]

Given their attacks on the market, it is not surprising that the new liberals are critical of the classical 'idea of a divine harmony between private advantage and the public good'.[96] While their criticism stems in part from their conclusion that the pursuit of private advantage very often does not best promote the public interest even when understood as economic growth, their wonder at classical harmony stems also from the shift in the meaning of public interest. If the public interest calls for an increase in aggregate wealth, it does not seem to require much call on the divine to maintain that the public interest is furthered by each seeking to employ his wealth in the most privately profitable way. Of course such pursuit need not maximise the accumulation of wealth, but that it does so is not so improbable that we need to look for the invisible hand of God. But if the public interest is defined to include not only the accumulation of wealth but also a fairly equal distribution, an interesting and challenging life for all, and social harmony as well, then it will really need prayer to obtain all this from the pursuit of private advantage. Interestingly enough, Hobson – whose liberalism generally emphasised his economic theory – makes just this point: viz. that the invisible hand promoted the public interest only because classical liberalism presupposes an impoverished, individualist theory that 'leaves out of account the claims of society, as an organic whole, expressed through the State'.[97]

C. The Rise of the Public and Competent State

We saw earlier that classical liberal political economists were by no means unaware of imperfections in the market order and that, in particular, Malthus could be very critical of it. But any suggestion that government might intervene to correct things was restrained by the two-pronged critique of the state as both biased and incompetent. The new liberals recognised this, supplementing their analysis of the market with a re-evaluation of public authorities. The most obvious element of this new evaluation was the insistence that public authorities could be, indeed increasingly were (to use Hobson's phrase), 'representatives of the community'[98] rather than tools of private interests. Without doubt, the main reason for this new faith in the publicness of the state was the extension of suffrage to the working class. In terms of the analysis of Chapter 2, the rise of democratic government gave credibility to the claim that the state was the institutionalisation of the public, i.e. of everyone in the society. Though a liberal like J.S. Mill worried that universal manhood suffrage might merely hand over the state to a new class, he nevertheless thought a democratic state to be a necessary (if not a sufficient) condition of a public state: alone it might not prevent class rule, but in the absence of a democratic state it was most unlikely that the nation would be governed in the interests of all. To be sure, the democratic movement was well under way in the classical era, and, as we have seen, not all the classical political economists were as convinced as Smith that private interests controlled the levers of state action. But it is only with the new liberals that the democratic, public nature of the state becomes a dominating theme. It is not only that the state is now seen as the friend of the public, but it is conceived as the institutionalisation of the public itself. Thus, said D.G. Ritchie,

> be it observed that arguments used against 'government' action, where the government is entirely or mainly in the hands of a ruling class or caste, exercising wisely or unwisely a paternal or grandmotherly authority — such arguments lose their force just in proportion as the government becomes more and more genuinely the government of the people by the people themselves.[99]

Complementing this new perception of the state as the 'supreme organ of the community'[100] is a revised evaluation of its competency. To some extent, perhaps, the loss of faith in the market itself raised the perception of the state's competency. If one is not to simply counsel despair, i.e. that the public interest cannot be secured to the extent traditionally thought imperative, then something must be done and the state may well be the agency to do it. But as we saw with Malthus, it is equally plausible to insist that whatever the problems with the market, the state can do no better. Where the classical liberals were sceptical of any attempt at conscious control of the economy, the new liberals, with their faith in human intelligence and purpose, thought the state could indeed do better. The experience of World War I seemed a decisive factor: at least as the new liberals understood it, it proved once and for all that the economy could be consciously managed to achieve collective goals.[101] And when the post-war depressions of the 1920s and 1930s hit, the memory of wartime management was contrasted with the subsequent 'economic anarchy'. Conscious control, continued drift or, ultimately, violence were the alternatives that liberals of Dewey's mould envisaged.[102] 'The transition from economic anarchy', wrote Keynes, 'to a regime which deliberately aims at controlling and directing economic forces in the interests of social justice and social stability, will present enormous difficulties both technical and political. I suggest, nevertheless, that the true destiny of New Liberalism is to seek their solution.'[103]

D. The Public and Private Sectors

In their most critical moments, it sometimes seems as if the new liberals thought the market 'order' to be a hopeless, chaotic failure premised on greed gone rampant, while, in contrast, the state was a potentially omnipotent and omniscient force for rational economic control and the public good. Along this path lies a completely socialist command economy. If the market is anarchic and hopelessly inefficient while the state is competent and good, the obvious course is to absorb the economy into the state, with central planning replacing the (non-existent) spontaneous co-ordination of the market. The new liberals, except perhaps in their most polemical moods, do not endorse this complete reversal of the judgements of classical political economy. Despite their criticisms, the new liberals persist in the classical belief that the market order of private interests does many things well. Thus, as Keynes put it (borrowing from Bentham), the 'Agenda' for the state is not to take over those activities already adequately performed by private individuals, but to undertake tasks required by the public interest that are not being performed at all.[104] The new liberal aim, then, is not to replace the market, but to manage and supplement it so as to promote the public interest (and justice). Hobhouse nicely described the new liberal position as endorsing a 'Social Liberalism' or 'semi-Socialism' striving for 'public control' of economic life rather than a 'State Socialism' that aims at direct 'public management' of all industries.[105] Even Dewey, probably the most socialist of the new liberals, seemed (at least at times) to call more for public supervision of the economy than for state ownership.[106] This is not to say that the new liberals are opposed to nationalisation of industry when in the public interest, but rather that their goal is typically to rectify the system of private ownership rather than to replace it.

Robbins quite rightly points out that this goal is very much in the spirit of classical political economy.[107] But conjoined with the far-reaching critique of the market, it endorses a multitude of governmental economic acitivities that the classical economists would hardly have accepted. The regulation of investment and aggregate demand (through both fiscal and monetary policies) and redistribution to spur consumption require an overall regulative role for the state that was both unnecessary and impossible to achieve in the eyes of the classical political economists. Moreover, given the revised conception of the public interest and the rise of the public and competent state, the health and welfare measures that classical liberals were prepared to accept become expanded and enthusiastically endorsed by the new liberals. Not only are they much more convinced than their classical counterparts that growth alone will not promote the general welfare (and they are less worried about over-population), but they have fewer doubts about granting the state the necessary power and resources to perform these welfare functions.

In sum, then, the new liberal political economy substitutes the notion of 'public and private sectors' for the classical liberal's distinction between 'state and economy'. Though by now it should be clear that it is simply false to say that the state stood entirely aloof from economic life in classical theory, its economic functions were pretty strictly circumscribed by its own incompetency and the efficiency of the spontaneous order of private agents. By relaxing both these judgements the new liberal political economy has made the state a major, perhaps the major, economic agent. But by only relaxing and not abandoning those judgements it has prevented the state from usurping all of economic life. For the new liberals believe that a market system based on private property still does many things (e.g. promote technical progress and productive efficiency) considerably better than state-socialist or centrally planned economies.

> For my part [said Keynes], I think that capitalism, wisely managed, can probably be made more efficient for attaining economic ends than any alternative system yet in sight, but that in itself it is in many ways extremely objectionable. Our problem is to work out a social organization which shall be as efficient as possible without offending our notions of a satisfactory way of life.[108]

IV. The Public/Private Divide Challenged

The new liberal solution to Keynes's problem has thus been a mix of a spontaneous order of private interests and public intervention in, and supervision of, economic life. Today, this solution is under attack on a wide variety of fronts, not only by critics of liberalism but by liberal critics too. Most well known, of course, are the neoclassical critiques of liberals like F.A. Hayek and Milton Friedman. Now although these are important critiques, and I do not wish to underestimate them, for our purposes they do not seem the most interesting ones. For their essence is a reassertion of the classical conception of the state and economy, a story with which we are already well acquainted. Of course they break new ground too as we shall see presently. But rather than focusing on these well-known criticisms, I wish to concentrate here on three other critiques of the new liberalism that directly challenge, albeit in different ways, its division between a market order of private interests and a public state acting as guardian of the public interest. I shall call these the *pluralist, corporatist* and *radical democratic critiques.*

A. Pluralism and the Balkanisation of the State

The pluralist, or interest group, analysis of politics has never accorded well with the essentially organic perspective of the new liberalism, according to which the state is the institutionalisation of the social whole and the guardian of the public interest. Even Keynes talked of 'the common will, embodied in the will of the State'.[109] But classical pluralists such as David B. Truman had little patience with the very idea of the public interest. While he was willing to acknowledge that claims based on the public interest are part of the data of politics, Truman was adamant in maintaining that 'they do not describe any actual or possible political situation within a complex modern nation'.[110] As the 'group pluralist' sees it, the only interests are those of 'the many social aggregates encompassed within the boundaries of the nation'.[111] Although it would be a mistake to say that such pluralists adopted the 'individualist' rather than the 'organic' model of society described in Chapter 2 (indeed, they constantly stressed that political life was premised on groups, not individuals),[112] they nevertheless share the typically individualist view of politics as a competition of private or special interests rather than a search for a common will or public interest. Consequently, pluralists tend to perceive the state as essentially reactive — responding to 'pressure groups' — a view that does not cohere well with the new liberal ideal of an active state, guiding private and sectional interests along the path to the public good.

Still, although the pluralist analysis of politics was essentially at odds with the new liberal perspective, a reconciliation seemed possible. Even though the early pluralists would have denied it, the public interest might be seen as a resultant of forces brought to bear on the state by private pressure groups. The public interest, then, would be 'the diagonal of the forces that constantly struggle for advantage'.[113] And if the resulting vector of forces leaves some groups disadvantaged, that only shows that they too should be organised so that the outcome accommodates the interests of all. Moreover, the goal of ensuring fair representation of all interests can easily lead to policy prescriptions that converge with those of the new liberals. Thus, for example, we find Robert Dahl advocating a redistribution of wealth and income to overcome inequalities of political influence.[114]

Recent criticisms of 'new liberal pluralism', however, suggest that the accommodation is even less persuasive than it might at first seem. Rather than governments being pushed along the path of the public interest by private interest groups, it has been argued that the state has been broken up into a number of fiefdoms, each lorded over by some private interest. The paradigmatic instance here is that of regulative agencies, a prime element of most new liberal prescriptions. Referring to the American experience of the 1930s, Otis Graham writes:

> The agency would enter upon its duties accompanied by many claims of the triumph of the public interest, perhaps even with zeal. But if regulation was not always in its initial phases completely satisfactory to the regulated interests, the passage of time enhanced the influence of organized groups and reduced the abstract zeal of the regulators. Usually without clear policy guidelines from Congress, the agency would soon adopt a cooperative spirit, consulting with affected groups of private citizens who had economic stake and expertise, often seeking further constituent support by decentralizing some of its decision-making processes.[115]

Hence, Graham concludes, 'By the end of the 1930s, the State, which Planners had intended to use to establish sufficient control over the fundamental affairs of the nation, was thoroughly Balkanized, its sovereignty compromised by the invasion along the edges of public policy by private groups with regular and often legalized roles in policy-making.'[116]

Leaving aside the question whether such an outcome could plausibly be said to be in the public interest, it entirely undermines the new liberal conception of the state. Unlike the new liberal compromise with pluralism, the 'state' (as a unity) can no longer be seen as reacting to pressure groups; instead, it is conquered and divided up among the various private interests. And as a consequence of this Balkanisation, as Milton and Rose Friedman point out, 'there is hardly an issue on which government is not on both sides'.[117] In such a situation, it is charged, it is impossible to make any sense of the new liberal ideal of 'public' authorities guiding and controlling — or even being pushed by — private interests to achieve a public good. One department or agency controlled by its 'client' group is deployed against another directed by an opposing private interest. In the face of pressure group politics, the state dissolves and all that remains are private interests and their particular governmental allies.

B. *Corporatism: The Integration of the Public and Private*

Interestingly, many of the same developments that have led some to conclude that the 'new liberal state' has been broken up and divided among private pressure groups has led others to the very different conclusion that the state and sectional interests are being integrated into a co-operative structure designed to promote social stability. And very often such 'corporatist' analyses attribute to the state, and not to private interests, the leading role in producing the integration.

In the past decade a number of writers have described the interventionist state of the new liberalism as corporatist, or developing towards some form of corporatism. According to J.T. Winkler, whose paper on 'Corporatism' is one of the classics of the recent renaissance in corporatist theory, 'Corporatism is an economic system in which the state directs and controls predominantly privately-owned business according to four principles: unity, order, nationalism and success.'[118] 'Directs' is a crucial term in Winkler's definition, for his thesis is that the state in 'advanced capitalist countries' is moving from a *supportive* to a *directive* role in the economy. Indeed, Winkler goes so far as to argue that corporatism constitutes a unique economic system, characterised by *private* ownership but *public* control and as such is to be distinguished from both capitalism (under which both ownership and control are private) and socialism (under which both are public). So, as Winkler depicts it, in a corporatist order the state goes beyond macroeconomic management to assume 'control over the *internal decision-making* of privately-owned businesses'.[119]

In many ways the corporatist analysis of advanced liberal industrial states is more in accordance with the new liberal outlook than is pluralism. According to Philippe Schmitter, who views corporatism as a mode of 'interest representation' rather than an economic system, the corporatist analysis sees the contemporary liberal state as premised on 'the functional adjustment of an organically interdependent whole' rather than the pluralist's 'shifting balance of mechanically intersecting forces'.[120] Or, as Winkler puts it, the emphasis of a corporatist structure is on integration and co-ordination in place of the bargaining and compromise that is so central to pluralism.[121] To the corporatist, then, the distinctive feature of contemporary liberal political economy is not the competition of interests but rather the calls for an 'America Inc.' or for economic social contracts, calls which are being made by liberal economists, business leaders and even labour unions.[122] Indeed, as Leo Panitch has stressed, labour relations appear to best fit the corporatist paradigm of state-induced collaboration between interest associations.[123]

Panitch's reference to *state-induced* collaboration is important as it draws attention to two distinct types of corporatism. As corporatists like Winkler, Schmitter and Panitch see it, the state takes a leading role in collaboration between functional interests. This is not to say that they think the state is acting to further some general public interest: Panitch in particular makes much of the class-bias of the state. But, according to such corporatists, the state certainly is not simply the tool of private interests. Even on Panitch's account the state does not always do what business wants. Although the resulting collaborative framework may be in the long-run best interests of business, the state may have to apply pressure to ensure that business interests act in the required co-operative manner. In contrast, J.K. Galbraith, who adopts much of the corporatist analysis, seems to reject the leading role of the state. Indeed, Galbraith supports much of the 'pluralist Balkanization' thesis, asserting that 'public regulatory bodies, it has long been observed, tend to become the captives of the firms that ostensibly they regulate.'[124] But instead of the multiplicity of warring fiefdoms observed by such critics as Friedman, Galbraith sees a more co-ordinated control of the state by private interests. The 'technostructure' (a large group that includes all who contribute information to group decisions in the great firms) ultimately directs the state for the overall benefit of the large corporations. 'The modern state, we may remind ourselves . . . is not the executive committee of the bourgeoisie, but it *is* more nearly the executive committee of the technostructure.'[125] Moreover, in Galbraith's most recent writings, he no longer sees the trade unions as a countervailing power to that of the corporations but instead finds that they collaborate with the great corporations to pursue common goals, thus reinforcing his essentially corporatist analysis.[126]

It is not difficult to see why Galbraith finds all this objectionable. Being a liberal, he insists that the state should serve the interests of the public at large.[127] As long as the state remains the captive of the

Public & Private Interests in Liberal Political Economy, Old & New 209

large corporations — even with the consent of the unions — the interests of many, in particular those owning and working for small businesses and the consumer, are ignored. Thus, in the true new liberal fashion, Galbraith calls for a 'public state'.[128] However, in contrast with the typical new liberal solution (Dewey, at least in some moods, is probably another exception), Galbraith believes that the liberation of the state from domination by powerful private corporations requires an explicit and radical public control over them, i.e. some form of state socialism. In similar vein Charles E. Lindblom concludes his *Politics and Markets* by suggesting that the power of large corporations is inconsistent with democracy. 'The large private corporation fits oddly into democratic theory and vision. Indeed, it does not fit.'[129] The consistent appeal of fairly radical sorts of socialism to liberal democrats like Dewey, Galbraith and Lindblom, who want an active and powerful state but are so worried about the influence of powerful private interests, suggests the possibility of an instability in the new liberal position. The new liberal seeks to combine general public regulation with a spontaneous order of private interests; but according to liberal democrats like Galbraith and Lindblom, the private sector poses a constant threat to the publicness of the state. Unlike classical theory in which the state is not such an attractive prize, or state socialism which attempts to absorb the economy into the state, the new liberal creates a state that can dispense great benefits and burdens while allowing the continued existence of large private corporations that can seek to capture it.

Winkler's analysis also suggests an instability in the new liberal position, albeit in a different way. As he sees it, the new liberal vision does not call for socialisation to liberate the state from domination by private interests, but has already led to a much more intense interference with the market than the new liberals expected. In fact, Winkler believes that modern liberal states have adopted an anti-market ideology. 'Corporatist controls destroy the autonomy of economic actors technically necessary for a market to operate — the ability to employ or withdraw resources as one sees fit, to adjust asking or offering prices, to buy from and sell to whom one chooses, to consume, invest or save as one prefers.'[130] According to Winkler, then, the new liberal ideal of control and co-operation to advance the good of the organic whole has led the contemporary liberal state to abandon the spontaneous order of the market, retaining the vestige of private ownership without private control.

Although the Winkler/Schmitter and Galbraith/Lindblom theses offer very different accounts of the co-operative relation between business, labour and government, all would agree with Galbraith's conclusion that the public/private divide is 'nearly imperceptible' in practice.[131] For Galbraith and Lindblom, who maintain that private interests wield immense power to shape the actions of 'public' authorities, the public/private divide would seem to be an ideology in the sense that it masks reality to the advantage of some. If business interests were seen for what they really were — i.e. the hidden government — their claims to freely pursue their goals as private agents would be undermined and some form of public accountability would be imposed. For Schmitter and Winkler, however, the public/private distinction would seem to be more a leftover from the past and now neither describes social reality nor the dominant ideology. As Schmitter understands it, it is not the separation of public and private that characterises the corporatist state and its ideology; rather the stress is on the integration of the various functional interests into state-recognised (if not state-created) organs.[132] As such, 'labour', 'business', 'agriculture' etc. are perceived not so much as private interests to be contrasted with the public interest but as sections whose interests are constituents of the larger public interest. To the analytically minded corporatist, the private/public dichotomy would seem to give way to the trichotomy of private (i.e. personal) interests, institutionalised sectional interests and the public interest. This accords, moreover, with our analysis of the organic model in Chapter 2 (§III.C, pp. 52-56) in which it was observed that the grand interests and sections of civil society seem to be neither public nor straightforwardly private. It may well be, then, that a thoroughgoing organic theory of society, not being premised on the opposition of 'individual' and 'society' but admitting a wide variety of mediating institutions that integrate individuals into the whole, tends to replace the public/private opposition with a more complex classification. Certainly this is so in Hegelian thought in which, as Bosanquet said, the '[c]orporation' is 'the very root of ethical connection between the private and the general interest.'[133] Now while I certainly do not wish to deny that new liberal writings evince nascent corporatist traits (e.g. Hobhouse's endorsement of the trade boards),[134] the new liberals did not pursue their organicism this far. Although they stressed the unity of the whole, they generally saw the social organism, as did Rousseau, as composed of interconnected individual persons, and they typically insisted, as did he, that particular subgroups are as private as individual persons and, indeed, are often threats to the public good. In sum, as with Rousseau's organicism, that of the new liberals has a strong individualist bent, persisting in the individualist's contrast between the 'individual' and 'society' while providing an organic account of their relation. If corporatism is to be seen as the outcome of new liberal organicism, it must be admitted that it is an outcome that emphasises its Hegelian over its Rousseauian sides.

C. Radical Democracy: The Politicisation of the Economy

As I said, one of Lindblom's complaints about large corporations is that they wield immense power and so have inordinate influence on supposedly public authorities. Apart from their adverse effects on the integrity of public decision-making, however, Lindblom objects to the giant corporations just because they possess the discretion to make decisions that determine many of the main features of a modern industrial economy. Thus, for example, he tells us that '[w]hether to tie workers to an often stultifying technology or try to organize them in possibly more humane processes is a discretionary corporate decision not popularly controlled.'[135] The target here is not the corrupting power of the great corporations but simply their discretion. Whatever might have been true of small-scale capitalists, Lindblom — and a great many other liberal democrats — insists that today's corporate leviathans are not subject to the iron discipline of the market but rather that, in a wide range of areas, they exercise discretion.

Much of this, of course, is itself central to the new liberal critique of classical liberal political economy. If large corporations exercise a discretion unrestrained by the discipline of the market, the new liberals insisted, they must be regulated in the public interest. Lindblom's argument, however, seems to be a change of emphasis from that of new liberals like Keynes. Lindblom not only objects that corporations do not act in the public interest, but that they are not popularly controlled. The focus for Lindblom is on public *control* more than public *interest*. Put differently, Lindblom seems more concerned with process — how decisions are made — than that the outcomes of those decisions are in the public interest. It is partly because of this, I think, that he is so attracted to Yugoslav market socialism. While Lindblom acknowledges that 'worker control remains in large part an aspiration',[136] he clearly thinks that it is an aspiration more in tune with the democratic ideal than the hierarchical corporation. Of course the democratic aspiration for popular control of economic life can also lead to more traditional, centralised forms of socialism. Galbraith's advocacy of a 'new socialism' is explicitly based on a demand for public control of the economy.[137] So too with C.B. Macpherson, who argues:

A fully democratic society requires democratic political control over the uses to which the amassed capital and the remaining natural resources of the society are put. It probably does not matter whether this takes the form of social ownership of all capital, or a social control of it so thorough as to be virtually the same as ownership. But more welfare-state redistribution of the national income is not enough.[138]

As Amy Gutmann has observed in the case of industrial democracy, such proposals urge that 'what liberal theorists have traditionally considered a private sphere should become a political sphere, controllable (at least in part) by its now subordinate constituents'.[139] Again, the emphasis on control is central. As I have been arguing throughout, both the classical and new liberal political economists maintain that the economic sphere is subject to public (i.e. political) regulation to ensure that it operates in the public interest. Radical liberal democrats like Lindblom go beyond this to assert that the economy itself should become politicised. And, as a consequence, an important element of the public/private divide in liberal political economy — between the political order and the spontaneous order of private interests — is undermined in a much more radical way than indicated by the limited new liberal critique.

While I wish to argue that both classical and new liberal political economy have been much more concerned with ensuring that outcomes are in the public interest rather than that the public makes the decisions, it has to be admitted that the idea of public control of economic life is not without roots in the liberal tradition. In particular the idea of 'consumer sovereignty' has often been invoked to support claims that the economy is 'popularly controlled'. Economic actors, it is said must respond to consumer demands just as politicians must respond to votes. Milton and Rose Friedman make a great deal of this voting analogy, stressing that the daily vote of the marketplace is superior to that of the ballot box, as the former produces 'unanimity without conformity' whereas the latter requires 'conformity without unanimity'.[140] Not surprisingly, the theory of consumer sovereignty is a central target of both Macpherson's and Galbraith's critiques. According to Galbraith, for various reasons consumer control is ineffective, and, in fact, a 'revised sequence' obtains, according to which the seller controls the buyer.[141] Given this, Galbraith can, and does, argue that the goal of popular control of the economy can no longer be achieved through the market and so the public *qua* the state must take charge.[142]

Calls for the democratisation and politicisation of the economy thus seem to get more purchase on those parts of liberal political economy that have asserted the existence of popular control of the economy through the marketplace. And as I have depicted liberal political economy in this chapter, neither the classical nor the new liberal version has made such control the primary value. However, a case can be made for industrial democracy that has closer ties to typically liberal concerns. Rather than building simply upon the intrinsic merit of popular control, liberals such as Mill have focused on the happy consequences of institutions that encourage worker participation in industrial decisions.[143] Liberal political economy has always been devoted to workers' interests, and if it can be shown that such institutions promote their well-being, a strong liberal case for them exists. However, if industrial democracy is to be urged as a natural development of liberal political economy (and in particular the new liberalism), it needs to be shown not only that it benefits the workers but also that it is in the interest of the public — conceived either as the class of consumers or the community as a whole. Thus, in contrast to many radical democrats, the liberal proponent of industrial democracy generally will be concerned with its efficiency as well as its personality-enriched properties. While, I think, it is going too far to say that '[t]he only question is whether authority is efficient or not',[144] it has been a fundamental question within liberal political economy.

V. Conclusion

The history of liberal political economy has largely centred on the problem of the relation of private and public interests. And of course the market mechanism is the linch-pin of the liberal solution. The insight of the classical political economists was that a system of exchange relations arising out of the pursuit of private interests could be so structured as to advance the public interest. Given the legal and political framework, an essentially self-regulating market order would promote consumer and worker interests, requiring only modest interventions by public authority in a limited range of areas in which the spontaneous order failed to promote the public interest. Consequently, classical liberal theory is characterised by a fairly distinct public/private divide along the lines of the state and the economy. The new liberals retain the essentials of this solution but simultaneously depreciate the competency of the market to promote the public interest and elevate that of the state. The state thus becomes a major economic actor, with the result that the economy itself becomes divided into public and private sectors. But this settlement can be challenged from a number of directions. It assumes that a strong 'public state' can coexist with a semi-independent order of private interests, intervening judiciously and selectively to promote the public good. However, if it is maintained that powerful private interests capture the state or that the state really controls them, the distinction appears *illusory*. But if the state is economically omniscient, or if the market is not an order but a chaos, the distinction is *untenable*. And if it is insisted that the market does not function in the public interest and indeed is merely the field of unbridled corporate discretion that must be democratised, the distinction will be thought *morally unacceptable*.

I wish to stress in this account, then, that the new liberal political economy is not only historically the outgrowth of classical theory but is also theoretically tied to it. From the classical liberals through Keynes to Rawls, liberal political economists have maintained that the play of private interests, when properly structured and regulated, does much to promote the public weal. But they have recognised, too, not merely that the order of private interests assumes a legal and political framework but also that it sometimes fails to promote the public good. And when the market does fail, liberal political economy, old and new, has acknowledged the case for state intervention in economic life.

Notes

I would like to thank Stanley Benn, John Chapman, Knud Haakonssen, J. Roland Pennock and Fred Whalen for their comments and suggestions.

1. 'Political economy' is used in a multitude of ways. In my vocabulary, as in Lord Robbins's, 'political economy'

is not scientific economics, a collection of value-free generalisations about the way in which economic systems work. It is a discussion of principles of public policy in the economic field: and while it makes appeal to the findings of economic science, it also involves assumptions which, in the nature of things, lie outside positive science and which are essentially normative in character.

Political Economy: Past and Present (Macmillan, London, 1977), pp. 2-3.

2. Adam Smith, quoted in Milton and Rose Friedman, *Free to Choose* (Secker and Warburg, London, 1980), p. 2.

3. See John Dewey, 'The Economic Basis of the New Society' in Joseph Ratner (ed.), *Intelligence in the Modern World: John Dewey's Philosophy* (Modern Library, New York, 1939), pp. 416-33; and his *Liberalism and Social Action* (G.P. Putnam's Sons, New York, 1935).

4. My classical economists are for the most part those of Lord Robbins: Smith, Say, Malthus, Torrens, Senior, McCulloch, Bentham and James Mill. Apart from the inclusion of Say (who was omitted from Robbins's study because he was not British), and the exclusion of Hume, the main difference is that I do not place J.S. Mill squarely within the ranks of the classical political economists, seeing him rather as a transition figure between the old and the new liberalisms. Robbins, *The Theory of Economic Policy in English Classical Political Economy* (Macmillan, London, 1961), p. 2.

5. J.R. McCulloch, *Principles of Political Economy*, 5th edn (Adam and Charles Black, Edinburgh, 1864), pp. 187-88.

6. Nassau William Senior, *An Outline of the Science of Political Economy*, 7th edn (Allen and Unwin, London, 1951), pp. 4, 152. John Austin objected that 'writers on the science of political oeconomy [sic], whenever they meddle incidentally with the connected science of legislation . . . forget that the wealth of the community is not the weal of the community, though wealth is one of the means requisite to the attainment of happiness'. W. Jethro Brown (ed.), *The Austinian Theory of Law* (John Murray, London, 1906), pp. 196-97.

7. McCulloch, *Principles*, p. 491.

8. J.-B. Say, *A Treatise on Political Economy* (Kelley, New York, 1964), pp. 228, 172.

9. Adam Smith, *An Inquiry into the Nature and Causes of the Wealth of Nations*, W.B. Todd (ed.) (Clarendon Press, Oxford, 1976), p. 264; David Ricardo, *On the Principles of Political Economy and Taxation*, Piero Sraffa (ed.) (Cambridge University Press, Cambridge, 1951), pp. 335 ff. McCulloch, however, sought to minimise the disharmonies of Ricardo's system. *Principles*, pp. 350ff. On the disharmony of classes in classical economics, see Elie Halévy, *The Growth of Philosophical Radicalism* (Faber and Faber, London, 1949), p. 424.

10. Say, *Treatise*, p. 89.

11. Ricardo, *Principles*, p. 133.

12. See ibid., p. 425; McCulloch, *Principles*, p. 315; T.R. Malthus, *Principles of Political Economy*, 2nd edn (Kelley, New York, 1951), p. 405. Malthus makes the distinction here between wealth and happiness since he believes that an increase in wages can diminish the growth of wealth.

13. D.P. O'Brien, *The Classical Economists* (Clarendon Press, Oxford, 1975), p. 274. O'Brien cites Senior as a possible exception to the general classical support of high wages (p. 284).

14. Robbins, *The Theory of Economic Policy*, p. 104; and his *Political Economy*, p. 124.

15. McCulloch, *Principles*, p. 480.

16. Smith, *The Wealth of Nations*, pp. 722, 539. See also Malthus, *Principles*, p. 431.

17. Robbins, *Political Economy*, p. 9. For a recent and detailed analysis of this market order, see F.A. Hayek, *Law, Legislation and Liberty*, vol. 2: *The Mirage of Social Justice* (Routledge and Kegan Paul, London, 1976), Ch. 10, 'The Market Order or Catallaxy'.

18. Robbins, *The Theory of Economic Policy*, p. 57.

19. McCulloch, *Principles*, pp. 35-36. Compare Milton and Rose Friedman: The drive for equality [in Britain] failed for a . . . fundamental reason. It went against one of the most basic instincts of all human beings. In the words of Adam Smith, 'The uniform, constant, and uninterrupted effort of every man to better his condition' — and, one may add, the condition of his children and his children's children. *Free to Choose*, pp. 144-45.

20. Ricardo, *Principles*, p. 407. On the attitudes of classical economists towards population growth, see Pedro Schwartz, *The New Political Economy of*

J.S. Mill (Weidenfield and Nicolson, London, 1968), pp. 26-30; O'Brien, *The Classical Economists*, pp. 55-66.

21. J.S. Mill, 'The Claims of Labour' in his *Dissertations and Discussions* (Haskell House, New York, 1973), vol. 2, p. 197. See also his *Principles of Political Economy*, 7th edn, Sir William Ashley (ed.) (Kelley, Fairfield, N.J., 1976), pp. 363-66.

22. James Mill, *Elements of Political Economy* in Donald Winch (ed.), *James Mill: Selected Economic Writings* (Oliver and Boyd, London, 1966), p. 205. For J.S. Mill, see his *Principles*, p. 562. For Keynes, see *The General Theory of Employment, Interest and Money* (Macmillan and Cambridge University Press, London and Cambridge, 1973), p. 19. For classical theory's development of the Law of Markets, see J.S. Mill's 'On the Influence of Consumption on Production' in his *Essays on Some Unsettled Questions of Political Economy* (Kelley, Clifton, N.J., 1974), pp. 47-74.

23. Ricardo, *Principles*, p. 290.
24. Malthus, *Principles*, p. 315.
25. Smith, *The Wealth of Nations*, p. 630.
26. Ibid., p. 456.
27. McCulloch, *Principles*, p. 125.
28. Jeremy Bentham, *Manual of Political Economy* in W. Stark (ed.), *Jeremy Bentham's Economic Writings* (Allen and Unwin, London, 1952), vol. I, p. 226. See also Say, *Treatise*, pp. 304-5n.

29. T.R. Malthus, *Definitions in Political Economy* (Kelley and Millman, New York, 1954), p. 234; for a definition of 'revenue', see ibid., p. 238. Although classical economists had some disagreements as to the proper definition of wealth (e.g. whether immaterial things could count as wealth, see ibid., pp. 249-50), their association of wealth with useful things separates them from mercantilists who, while not neglecting goods, emphasised the connection between wealth and precious metals. See Eli F. Heckscher, *Mercantilism*, Mendel Shapiro (trans.) (Allen and Unwin, London, 1934), Pt. IV, Ch. II.

30. Say, *Treatise*, Introduction, p. l.
31. Bentham, *Manual of Political Economy*, p. 226n. According to Amy Gutmann, Bentham's utilitarianism 'may sanction inegalitarian distributive policies in some contexts and egalitarian ones in others'. *Liberal Equality* (Cambridge University Press, Cambridge, 1980), p. 26.

32. Smith, *The Wealth of Nations*, pp. 22, 10. See also Say, *Treatise*, p. 334.
33. Say, *Treatise*, p. 98. He adds:
Nor is it to be imagined that this degeneracy from the dignity of human nature is confined to the labourer, that plies all his life at the file or the hammer; men, whose professional duties call into play the finest faculties of the mind, are subject to similar degradation.

34. Smith, *The Wealth of Nations*, p. 782.
35. J.S. Mill, *Principles*, p. 746. See also McCulloch, *Principles*, pp. 52-54; Senior, *Science of Political Economy*, pp. 192-93; Schwartz, *The New Political Economy*, pp. 210-12; O'Brien, *The Classical Economists*, Ch. 8; Robbins, *Political Economy*, p. 25.

36. Smith, *The Wealth of Nations*, p. 99.
37. See McCulloch, *Principles*, p. 226; J.S. Mill, *Principles*, p. 976; Say, *Treatise*, p. 201; Robbins, *Political Economy*, pp. 12-14.

38. See Schwartz, *The New Political Economy*, pp. 129-39.
39. See O'Brien, *The Classical Economists*, Ch. 10; Robbins, *The Theory of Economic Policy*, pp. 68-110.

40. Say, *Treatise*, p. 181; McCulloch, *Principles*, p. 228.
41. McCulloch, *Principles*, pp. 129, 226-30. See also Robbins, *The Theory of Economic Policy*, pp. 89-93.

42. Ricardo, *Principles*, pp. 356-57. See O'Brien, *The Classical Economists*, pp. 274-75.

43. It might be thought that these are examples of public goods. However, as Smith pointed out:
> It does not seem necessary that the expence of those publick works should be defrayed from that publick revenue, as it is commonly called, of which the collection and application is in most countries assigned to the executive power. The greater part of such publick works may easily be so managed, as to afford a particular revenue sufficient for defraying their own expence, without bringing any burden upon the general revenue of the society.

The Wealth of Nations, p. 724. See also O'Brien, *The Classical Economists*, pp. 275-76.

44. Robert Nozick, *Anarchy, State, and Utopia* (Basil Blackwell, Oxford, 1974), p. 26.

45. Say, *Treatise*, p. 213.

46. Robbins, *The Theory of Economic Policy*, p. 184.

47. Smith, *The Wealth of Nations*, p. 418.

48. Ibid., p. 617.

49. Ibid., pp. 144, 157, 266-67.

50. Ibid., p. 648. See Robbins, *Political Economy*, pp. 49-51.

51. Senior is the notable exception. See O'Brien, *The Classical Economists*, pp. 284-85. Robbins's analysis suggests a somewhat less favourable attitude towards unions, likening them more to other 'monopolies'. *The Theory of Economic Policy*, pp. 103-10. For a detailed treatment of J.S. Mill's changing views, see Schwartz, *The New Political Economy*, Ch. 5.

52. Senior, *Science of Political Economy*, p. 76.

53. Bentham, *Manual of Political Economy*, pp. 229-30. See also McCulloch, *Principles*, p. 97.

54. Robert Torrens, *An Essay on the Production of Wealth* (Kelley, New York, 1965), p. 226.

55. Smith, *The Wealth of Nations*, p. 687.

56. Torrens, *The Production of Wealth*, p. 208. Robbins points out that he later made clear that this was not his position. *The Theory of Economic Policy*, p. 44n. As O'Brien notes, the flexible attitude of the classical political economists on *laissez-faire* is often confused with the much more rigid position of the Manchester school. *The Classical Economists*, pp. 72-74.

57. Malthus, *Principles*, pp. 410, 426.

58. In a letter to Ricardo, Malthus agreed with him 'in thinking that the funds raised for the support of the poor (though perhaps necessary at the moment) essentially interfere with other employments'. (Letter from Malthus to Ricardo in *The Works and Correspondence of David Ricardo*, Piero Sraffa (ed.) (Cambridge University Press, Cambridge, 1973), vol. XI, pp. x-xi.) Somewhat puzzlingly, Robbins cites this as his sole ground for maintaining that Malthus was only lukewarm to public expenditure. (*Political Economy*, p. 69.) Of course Malthus was indeed lukewarm, but that is the point: i.e. he was not cold to it. Senior was in favour of public works in Ireland both to promote economic development and as a means of famine relief. O'Brien, *The Classical Economists*, p. 287.

59. A.F. Mummery and J.A. Hobson, *The Physiology of Industry* (Kelley and Millman, New York, 1956), p. 106.

60. J.A. Hobson, *The Science of Wealth*, 4th edn, rev. by R.F. Harrod (Oxford University Press, London, 1950), pp. 168-69.

61. See Peter Clarke, *Liberals and Social Democrats* (Cambridge University Press, Cambridge, 1978), pp. 149-50; Michael Freeden, *The New Liberalism: An Ideology of Social Reform* (Clarendon Press, Oxford, 1978), pp. 94-116.

62. John Maynard Keynes, 'The End of Laissez-Faire' in his *Essays in Persuasion* (Macmillan, London, 1972), p. 275.

63. Otis L. Graham, Jr., *Toward a Planned Society: From Roosevelt to Nixon* (Oxford University Press, New York, 1976), p. 20. By 'organic' Graham seems to mean a complex system in which all elements are interrelated, certainly one element of the 'traditional' understanding of a society as an organism.

64. 'But the essential point here is that Keynes's justification [of capitalism in the nineteenth century], whether or not its premises are sound, can be made to turn solely on improving the situation of the working class.' John Rawls, *A Theory of Justice* (The Belknap Press of Harvard University Press, Cambridge, Mass., 1971), p. 299.

65. Hobson, *The Science of Wealth*, p. 165.

66. J.S. Mill, 'The Claims of Labour', p. 205.

67. 'It comes from the account given by Charlotte Bronte, in the second chapter of *Shirley*, of the hand-loom weavers who one hundred and twenty-five years ago were being driven into unemployment and miserable revolt by the introduction of knitting frames. "Misery generates hate. These sufferers hated the machines which they believed took their bread from them; they hated the buildings which contained the machines; they hated the manufacturers who owned the buildings." ' William Beveridge, *Full Employment in a Free Society* (Allen and Unwin, London, 1944), p. 15. Classical economists generally were not blind to this hate; McCulloch, for example, argued that the Poor Law helped relieve working class 'outrage'; *Principles*, pp. 134-39. For a discussion of the classical economists' attitudes towards mechanisation, and specifically hand-loom weavers, see O'Brien, *The Classical Economists*, pp. 279-80.

68. See Freeden, *The New Liberalism*, pp. 150-53; J.M. Keynes, 'Am I a Liberal?' in his *Essays in Persuasion*, pp. 295-306. According to Graham:

In a Jefferson Day speech . . . [Roosevelt] expressed admiration for a Jefferson somewhat unfamiliar to the Virginian's admirers, a man who stressed the universality of the national interest and who concentrated men's thoughts upon 'the shared common life' rather than the predicament of individuals. In that address Roosevelt spoke for 'a true concert of interests' rather than class rule.

Toward a Planned Society, p. 19.

69. Mill, *Principles*, p. 749.

70. L.T. Hobhouse, *The Labour Movement*, 3rd edn (Harvester Press, Brighton, 1974), p. 14; Dewey, *Liberalism and Social Action*, pp. 59, 89-90; D.G. Ritchie, *Principles of State Interference*, 2nd edn (Swan Sonnenschein, London, 1896), p. 150; Keynes, *The General Theory*, p. 325; Rawls, *A Theory of Justice*, p. 290. See also my *Modern Liberal Theory of Man* (Croom Helm, London, 1982), pp. 239ff, 256ff.

71. Hobhouse, *The Labour Movement*, p. 14. See Mill, *Principles*, p. 749. Beveridge provides a different sort of distributive argument:

Abolition of want cannot be brought about merely by increasing production, without seeing to correct distribution of the product; but correct distribution does not mean what it has often been taken to mean in the past — distribution between the different agents in production, between land, capital, management and labour. Better distribution of purchasing power is required among wage earners themselves, as between times of earning and not earning, and between times of heavy family responsibilities and of light or no family responsibilities.

Social Insurance and Allied Services (Her Majesty's Stationery Office, London, 1942), p. 167.

72. J.A. Hobson, *The Economics of Unemployment* (Allen and Unwin, London, 1922), p. 117.

73. Dewey, *Individualism — Old and New* (Allen and Unwin, London, 1931), p. 45. See also L.T. Hobhouse, *The Elements of Social Justice* (Allen and Unwin, London, 1949), Ch. VII.

74. See Clarke, *Liberals and Social Democrats*, p. 268.
75. Rawls, *A Theory of Justice*, p. 79.
76. Robbins, *The Theory of Economic Policy*, pp. 46-48. As Robbins notes, Adam Smith cannot be called a thoroughgoing utilitarian, although his arguments in political economy are 'consistently utilitarian in character'.
77. Bertrand de Jouvenel, quoted in John W. Chapman, 'Justice, Freedom and Property' in J. Roland Pennock and John W. Chapman (eds.), *NOMOS XXII: Property* (New York University Press, New York, 1980), p. 289. Chapman provides an excellent overview of the spectrum of theories of social justice.
78. See Arthur M. Okun, *Equality and Efficiency: The Big Tradeoff* (The Brookings Institution, Washington D.C., 1975); J.E. Meade, *The Just Economy* (Allen and Unwin, London, 1976), Ch. III.
79. See E.J. Mishan, *The Costs of Economic Growth* (Penguin, Harmondsworth, 1967). See also Ronald Dworkin, 'Liberalism' in Stuart Hampshire (ed.), *Public and Private Morality* (Cambridge University Press, Cambridge, 1978), pp. 118 ff.
80. A favourite, though confused, line of attack contended that 'to intervene is to interfere; to interfere is to invite the disaster that comes from any attempt to "violate" natural law. This is the uniform intellectual background of the *laissez-faire* philosophy of society.' As we have seen, however, classical liberals like McCulloch and Malthus were very worried about how to successfully interfere with some natural human tendencies. See John Dewey, *Characters and Events: Popular Essays in Social and Political Philosophy*, Joseph Ratner (ed.) (Henry Holt, New York, 1929), pp. 728-29. See also Ritchie, *Principles of State Interference*, p. 48; L.T. Hobhouse, *Liberalism* (Oxford University Press, London, 1964), pp. 32-33.
81. Mill, *Principles*, p. 206.
82. L.T. Hobhouse: 'The Historical Evolution of Property, in Fact and in Idea' in his *Sociology and Philosophy: Centenary Collection of Essays and Articles* (G. Bell and Sons, London, 1966), pp. 104-5; 'Industry and the State' in ibid., pp. 212-13.
83. Rawls, *A Theory of Justice*, p. 281.
84. Joan Robinson quoted in Vic George and Paul Wilding, *Ideology and Social Welfare* (Routledge and Kegan Paul, London, 1976), p. 46.
85. Keynes, *The General Theory*, p. xxxv.
86. Ibid., pp. 364-65. See also Freeden, *The New Liberalism*, p. 19.
87. Lord Robbins in Clarke, *Liberals and Social Democrats*, p. 234.
88. Beveridge, *Full Employment in a Free Society*, p. 96.
89. Hobson, *The Science of Wealth*, p. 40.
90. Keynes, *The General Theory*, p. 381.
91. Hobson, *The Science of Wealth*, p. 41.
92. John Dewey and James H. Tufts, *Ethics*, rev. edn (Henry Holt, New York, 1932), p. 451. See also Hobhouse, *The Elements of Social Justice*, p. 170; Joan Robinson, *The Economics of Imperfect Competition* (Macmillan, London, 1961), Ch. 27.
93. Roosevelt quoted in Graham, *Toward a Planned Society*, p. 46.
94. Hobhouse, 'Industry and the State', p. 216.
95. Hobson, *The Science of Wealth*, p. 196.
96. Keynes, 'The End of Laissez-Faire', p. 274.
97. Hobson, *The Science of Wealth*, p. 198. See also Mummery and Hobson, *The Physiology of Industry*, p. 105.
98. Hobson, *The Economics of Unemployment*, p. 49.
99. Ritchie, *Principles of State Interference*, p. 64.
100. Beveridge, *Full Employment in a Free Society*, p. 35.
101. See Graham, *Toward a Planned Society*, pp. 9-13; Dewey, 'The Social Possibilities of War' in his *Characters and Events*, pp. 551-60.

102. See Dewey, *Liberalism and Social Action*, p. 87.
103. Keynes, 'Am I a Liberal?', p. 305. In a similar vein, Hobson argued that '[t]he necessity of some policy of general conscious control, in order to secure the full productivity of national and world resources for the production and consumption of wealth, is winning recognition everywhere.' *The Science of Wealth*, p. 200.
104. Keynes, 'The End of Laissez-Faire', p. 291. See also Beveridge, *Full Employment in a Free Society*, p. 36.
105. Hobhouse, *The Elements of Social Justice*, p. 172.
106. Dewey, 'Elements of Social Reorganization' in *Characters and Events*, p. 758. However, Dewey could also sound much more 'state socialist' as, for example, in *Liberalism and Social Action*, p. 88, and *Individualism – Old and New*, Ch. VI.
107. Robbins, *Political Economy*, p. 179.
108. Keynes, 'The End of Laissez-Faire', p. 294.
109. Keynes, *The General Theory*, p. 377.
110. David B. Truman, *The Governmental Process*, 2nd edn (Alfred A. Knopf, New York, 1971), pp. 50-51.
111. Harmon Zeigler, *Interest Groups in American Society* (Prentice-Hall, Englewood Cliffs, N.J., 1964), p. 23.
112. See Truman, *The Governmental Process*, Ch. 2; Arthur F. Bentley, *The Process of Government* (Principia Press, Bloomington, Ind., 1949), Ch. VI.
113. R.M. MacIver, *The Web of Government* (Macmillan, New York, 1947), p. 220. This is the conception of the public interest which, MacIver suggests, follows from the pluralism of people like Bentley. It is *not* MacIver's notion of the public interest which, instead, insists on the existence of a common welfare above and beyond the play of private interests. See C.B. Macpherson, *The Life and Times of Liberal Democracy* (Oxford University Press, Oxford, 1977), pp. 72-73.
114. Robert A. Dahl, *Democracy in the United States: Promise and Performance*, 3rd edn (Rand McNally, Chicago, 1976), pp. 493-97.
115. Graham, *Toward a Planned Society*, p. 66.
116. Ibid., p. 67.
117. Milton and Rose Friedman, *Free to Choose*, p. 291.
118. J.T. Winkler, 'Corporatism', *Archives Européennes de Sociologie*, vol. 17 (1976), p. 103. The corporatist ideal was, of course, a central feature of Fascist ideology. According to Herman Finer:
> It grew out of Mussolini's repudiation of the 'class' organisations of the proletariat, his sense of nationalism and order, and the practical need felt by an absolutism of destroying the autonomy of any natural grouping, including economic groupings, and among these especially the associations of workers, which afford their members the daily opportunity of information, discussion, and resistance.

Mussolini's Italy (Victor Gollancz, London, 1935), p. 493.
119. Winkler, 'Corporatism', p. 104.
120. Philippe C. Schmitter, 'Still the Century of Corporatism?', *Review of Politics*, 36 (Jan. 1974), p. 97.
121. Winkler, 'Corporatism', p. 106.
122. According to Trish Evans, 'New York labor leader, Mr Victor Gotbaum, argues that business, labor and government should join in a new social contract in which consensus would replace conflict.' *Weekend Australian*, 6-7 June 1981, p. 12. And, according to Lester Thurow, 'Major investment decisions have become too important to be left to the private market alone, but a way must be found to incorporate private corporate planning into this process in a nonadversary way. Japan Inc. needs to be met with U.S.A. Inc.' *The Zero-Sum Society* (Basic Books, New York, 1980), p. 192.

123. Leo Panitch, 'Recent Theorizations of Corporatism: Reflections on a Growth Industry', *British Journal of Sociology*, vol. 31 (June 1980), pp. 159-87. See also his *Social Democracy and Industrial Militancy* (Cambridge University Press, Cambridge, 1976), pp. 245 ff.

124. J.K. Galbraith, *Economics and the Public Purpose* (Penguin, Harmondsworth, 1975), p. 176.

125. Ibid., p. 188. On the technostructure, see J.K. Galbraith, *The New Industrial State*, 2nd rev. edn (Andre Deutsch, London, 1972), Ch. 6.

126. Reginald J. Harrison, *Pluralism and Corporatism: The Political Evolution of Modern Democracies* (Allen and Unwin, London, 1980), pp. 55-56.

127. See Galbraith, *Economics and the Public Purpose*, p. 314.

128. Ibid., Ch. 29.

129. Charles E. Lindblom, *Politics and Markets* (Basic Books, New York, 1977), p. 356.

130. Winkler, 'Corporatism', p. 111.

131. Galbraith, *The New Industrial State*, p. 395.

132. Schmitter, 'Still the Century of Corporatism?', pp. 93-94.

133. Bernard Bosanquet, *The Philosophical Theory of the State*, 4th edn (Macmillan, London, 1951), pp. 259-60.

134. Hobhouse, *The Elements of Social Justice*, pp. 137-38n. See also J.A. Hobson, 'L.T. Hobhouse, A Memoir' in J.A. Hobson and Morris Ginsberg (eds.), *L.T. Hobhouse: His Life and Work* (Allen and Unwin, London, 1931), pp. 53-58.

135. Lindblom, *Politics and Markets*, p. 155.

136. Ibid., p. 337.

137. Galbraith, *Economics and the Public Purpose*, Ch. 27.

138. Macpherson, *The Life and Times of Liberal Democracy*, p. 111.

139. Gutmann, *Liberal Equality*, p. 178.

140. Milton and Rose Friedman, *Free to Choose*, p. 66.

141. Galbraith, *The New Industrial State*, Ch. 19. See Macpherson's essay on 'Revisionist Liberalism' in his *Democratic Theory: Essays in Retrieval* (Clarendon Press, Oxford, 1973), pp. 77-94.

142. Galbraith, *Economics and the Public Purpose*, pp. 114, 333-34.

143. Mill, *Principles*, pp. 752-94. See also Gutmann, *Liberal Equality*, Ch. 2. See my *Modern Liberal Theory of Man*, Ch. VII, §D.

144. Chapman, 'Justice, Freedom and Property', p. 314. See also P.J.D. Wiles, *Economic Institutions Compared* (Wiley, New York, 1977), Ch. 10, pp. 259-65; Ch. 14, pp. 378-81; Abram Bergson, 'The Politics of Socialist Efficiency', *American Economist*, 24 (Fall 1980), pp. 5-11.

9 PUBLIC AND PRIVATE PROPERTY

Alan Ryan

In this Chapter I discuss some of the arguments for and against private and public ownership — of the means of production, distribution and exchange for the most part, but not only these, as we shall see. In so doing I rely quite heavily on a simple distinction between different approaches to the analysis of ownership, a distinction which I elsewhere called a distinction between instrumental and self-developmental approaches.[1] I also offer a few suggestions, more or less as a coda, about the implications of a 'dramaturgical' approach to the analysis of social interaction for the analysis of ownership, thus to some extent tying this paper to my account in Chapter 6 of the self and its social faces.

As we shall see, instrumental and self-developmental theories stand in an awkward relationship to natural rights theories of ownership. Both repudiate the view that property rights are themselves natural rights, but both possess more than adequate resources to show how property institutions are natural to human beings, why Roman Law is warranted in distinguishing the 'natural modes of acquisition', and why non-natural rights matter. Moreover, considerations which animate natural rights theorists — a concern for personal inviolability, or for individual freedom, say — can, as we shall see, find room within these theories. I cannot hope to demonstrate that under pressure natural rights theories collapse into instrumental or self-developmental theories, but I offer the thought that in a godless universe the status of natural rights is insecure, and that arguments for their existence rather readily turn into arguments of an instrumental[2] or developmental kind for conventionally recognised rights.

Both forms of argument bear on the merits of private versus public ownership. Instrumental arguments are inevitably the simplest and most straightforward — since they treat property rights as matters of legal fact, they treat arguments about private and public ownership as technical arguments. The question is always which system of legal or quasi-legal ownership rights will best achieve the ends proposed. The self-developmental theory is more complicated to elucidate; characteristically, it is concerned with conceptual as well as technical questions — in effect, to ask whether *ownership* is the same thing in private and public hands, or whether public property *belongs* to the public. These questions can be rephrased up to a point in more instrumental terms, but not without remainder.

The dramaturgical account offered as a coda does not exactly compete on the same ground. In concentrating on the way people employ property rather as stage properties — 'props' — it emphasises the way property can be an aid to privacy, the way we can manage our appearance to the various publics we have to deal with, if we can control a certain space and some of the objects in that space. It also emphasises the way property of a certain sort and social status are implicated with one another — all of these being familiar themes in the sociological literature, and having perhaps some repercussions on practical political issues too.[3]

I. Instrumental Justifications of Rights of Property

Instrumental, particularly utilitarian, justifications of property rights have generally been conjoined with a positivist approach to the definition of property. That is 'A owns x' is held to be elliptical, meaning 'A owns x according to the legal or quasi-legal rules of community o'. Whether somebody does or does not own a given object is in the last analysis a factual question about his relationship to a particular legal or quasi-legal system. The justification of a particular property right is a matter of showing what good would be done by the existence of such a relationship; the justification of private versus public ownership or vice versa is a matter of showing what good would be done by vesting these rights in the hands of private persons or official bodies.[4]

Instrumental theories are not committed to the view that there are no natural rights at all; indeed, they may well hold that positive law should primarily aim to render natural rights secure. They are, however, committed to the view that there are no natural rights of ownership, or, more mildly, that the rights people might plausibly be said to have over things, in the absence of explicit property-rights-creating conventions, would not amount to property rights.[5]

The extreme instrumental position is enshrined in Bentham's account of rights. In this account, there can be no natural property rights because there can be no natural rights at all, since all rights are creatures of law. Combined with the imperative theory of law, this yields the view that A's rights are as it were the shadow cast by the sovereign's orders to B, C, etc. to refrain from interfering with A. In the absence of government, *A* would be free to do what he liked, use what he liked, destroy what he liked, and so on. He would be free to hang on to whatever he could. By the same token *B*, *C*, etc. would be free to stop him, seize it from him, and so on. What the law does is to create property by leaving one person or body of persons with the freedom everyone formerly had but could not use, while removing that freedom from everyone else.[6]

As an account of rights in general this seems defective twice over. Firstly it begs the question whether we might be entitled to various immunities in the absence of government by simply assuming that terms such as 'entitled' and its moral equivalents must either be interpreted positivistically or be meaningless. This is not just perverse, however; Locke and Hobbes had both held that for natural law to impose obligations on us, it had to be the legislation of one 'who by right hath command'.[7] Natural rights seemed to presuppose a supernatural legislator; if there were no such being, could there be natural rights? It is not wholly fair to complain of Bentham, when he was working within just the same framework as his opponents. All the same, one can properly object that there seem to be good grounds for saying that people are *entitled* to various immunities, that they have rights to life and liberty, even in the absence of either God or an earthly legislator.

Secondly, however, Bentham seems to err in reducing all rights to immunities. This comes interestingly to grief at a crucial point. Of course many rights are primarily immunities; the right to life is primarily an immunity against wanton attack or murder, for instance, and much more dubiously a claim right against some person or institution for the means of survival.[8] Take promising, however. If I promise a student that I will turn up at 10 o'clock tomorrow, the student has a right to my turning up, and I violate her rights if I fail to come. Here her right is evidently not a mere immunity, it is a claim right against me. In making the promise I have transferred to someone else the right I formerly had to say where I would be tomorrow at 10 o'clock. Now she has the right, for she, not I, can release me from my promise, and it is with her not me that you must deal if you want me to do something other than turn up to see her at 10 o'clock.

The similarity between my rights over my own actions and my rights over property is quite marked. It looks almost as if promising makes sense as a transfer of proprietorship. The future action was formerly one of my possessions and it has now become one of her possessions. Nevertheless, and in spite of some impressive support for a view very like this in Kant's *Elements of Justice*,[9] I take it that promising is more importantly unlike the transfer of property rights, in the sense that what is given is only a right good against one person, a *jus ad personam* and not a *jus ad rem*, and that unless there were additional powerful reasons for supposing that our fundamental rights over ourselves are proprietary in nature we should not try to elucidate promising by reference to such property rights.

However, if promises do give rights to the promisee, Bentham's claim that there can be no non-legal or quasi-legal property rights because there are no non-legal rights at all cannot be accepted. Can an argument for the same conclusion be founded on different premises? The obvious source of such an argument is J.S. Mill, whose essay *On Liberty* defends the view that we have a right to harmless activities of any kind, as well as rights stemming from agreement with others, while Mill remains adamant that property rights are a matter of positive social institution.[10] That is, the rights over things which can be generated from these ingredients are not property rights.

The right to harmless action would no doubt mean that if I picked and ate an unowned apple, I ought not to be interfered with; again, if I am in possession of an object, and harm nobody, I ought not to be interfered with. If I promise someone an object I possess and it will harm nobody if she has it, then if I succeed in handing it over, her possession ought not to be interfered with. But, my right to hand it over owes nothing to my ownership, and everything to the harmlessness of my and her possession. Equally, her rights are not rights she has by grant from me – her rights to my fulfilling my promise was a right against *me* and is extinguished when she receives the things I promised her; but her rights over the things themselves rest on the same foundation as ever, that of harmless occupation and use.

The point here is that we rely on rights which amount to an immunity against interference with what we can naturally do, plus rights of a promissory kind. The interesting thing about fully paid up property rights, however, is that they allow the property owner to alter the status of others in ways he cannot himself physically control – the freeholder grants a 99-year lease, the elderly parent makes a will with provision for his children's unborn children – and such powers seem to be a social invention.[11] This, I think, is what Mill's case amounts to, and it is compelling in a way Bentham's is not.

The claim that property rights are not natural rights seems perhaps to license the view that the existence or non-existence of a system of positive property rights could not violate people's rights. This does not follow, however, we need to distinguish three views. The first is that although people have no natural property rights, they do have rights which a system of property rights must respect, and which it can certainly violate. The second is that although people have no natural property rights, they have a right to the existence of some (yet-to-be specified) system of property rights. The last is that they have natural property rights.

The distinction is easy enough to see in obvious cases, and the plausibility of the view that a system of property rights can violate rights but not property rights emerges clearly. Thus we may (i) object to slavery that it is a violation of rights in the first sense because the slave is used as a mere means, and his human right to equal concern and respect has been violated.[12] We might (ii) hold that it was a violation of rights in the second sense because the slave had a right to the existence of some positive system of property rights inconsistent with slavery. One might hold, say, that people have a right to self-actualisation in a system of legal relations which uniquely requires the ownership of one's own labour, and thus not slavery. Finally, we might (iii) claim that slavery is a violation of rights in the third sense, because all men are by nature their own owners, and the slave is in a manner of speaking stolen from himself. It seems to me that arguments for the second view will probably amount to saying either that when we put in all the rights-based constraints suggested in (i), people in effect have a right to some particular system, or else, as in (iii), that people own themselves and their abilities and that only one system properly reflects this. This is not inevitable, however, and there is certainly a clear position to be occupied between the view that positive property institutions must not violate rights and the view that they must reflect pre-legal property rights. Suppose some system of property rights — or some small class of systems — were uniquely defensible as a way of protecting people's rights. Theorists who hold that our duty is to *protect*, and not merely to avoid violating, the rights of others, would then hold that we had a duty to institute this system or one of these systems, and that the beneficiaries had a right to its existence.[13]

Although utilitarianism is not the only instrumental theory of property, it is the most extreme in its consequentialism, and when it is held that instrumental theories outrage our moral intuitions, it is usually utilitarianism that is the object of attack. Now, we have seen that even if we have to invoke rights to account for the illicitness of, say, slavery, these are not themselves possessory or proprietary rights. Perhaps we *should* say that slavery is just wrong, and not begin to calculate the slave's losses and society's gains; we do not need to suppose that the right violated in the slave's person is the slave's property in his own person.[14]

An analogous argument deals with the recently popular hypothetical case of compulsory transplant surgery. The utilitarian, it is sometimes said, ought to treat the bodies of members of society as a pool of medical resources. Once surgical techniques are good enough, we should not flinch at dismembering Jones in order to provide new lungs for Smith, new kidneys for Williams, and so on. The proposal is often felt to be peculiarly repulsive, and yet hard to dismiss.[15] As so often, however, the utilitarian has very good resources for dealing with the case. As a proposal for making the best use of available human resources, it suffers from the vice of creating a 'moral hazard'. The scheme gives us all an incentive to neglect our bodies — if we fall ill, we shall be repaired, and the likelihood of our being cannibalised for spare parts is diminished too. So no utilitarian would propose it.[16] Moreover, even a utilitarian can agree that our relationship to our own bodies is not like our relationship to other external objects. The proper control and management of them from toilet training up, is almost our ticket of admission to the human race.[17] In none of this, do we need to rely on the thought that this is *my* body; and, again, if it is held that the utilitarian objections still miss the point about the violation of the rights of the compelled donor, it remains true that these rights are not property rights.

Almost always, however, those who want to defend property rights as conventions to be justified instrumentally have something other than the protection of individual rights in mind, at any rate as a primary justification. The most common arguments for systems of ownership rest on considerations of the general welfare, allied to notions of incentive and security — or perhaps it is more accurate to say, incentive based on security. The argument of James Mill and Bentham runs much as follows: men's needs outrun what nature readily provides, for which reason they have to work to procure both bare necessities and anything better.[18] Some men will be tempted to take what others have created or gathered or found. Failure to ensure that a man can generally keep what he has worked to produce is a threat to incentive, for who will work to acquire what he has no certainty of keeping? Beyond the very barest subsistence — gathering enough to live on from the bushes as we pass, where we can be certain of eating it before someone else intervenes — we must institute a system of enforced rules which provide security and therefore incentive. From this comes both the need for government to protect our possessions, and the problem of controlling it.[19]

How, then, are we to judge what system of rules to adopt, and how do these considerations bear on the issue of private and public ownership? Briefly, legislators ought to aim at abundance, together with whatever bias in distribution maximises the real welfare of the community. They do not need, strictly, to *provide* incentives to individuals to pursue their own welfare, since individuals generally do so as best they can anyway.[20] But they do need to make sure that disincentives such as uncertainty over legal titles are cleared away; if land is subject to the vagaries of the common law, buyers may be unsure whether they have a sound title, and be deterred from making the most of the land for fear of seeing their efforts go for nothing. Another disincentive is sudden or unforseeable changes in taxation especially if they fall unpredictably on different sorts of property and income. There must almost inevitably be an initial presumption in favour of private ownership where possible, since this connects good management of resources with reaping the benefits, and thus provides maximum incentive to good management.

Since the aim of the system is to promote abundance, there is nothing sacrosanct about existing property rights, nor is there any principled limit on the degree to which governments may create, extinguish and adjust property rights. Suppose, for instance, that a government decided that shareholding of the sort we presently observe in Britain was simply inefficient — that it did nothing to direct capital towards productive investment and encouraged companies to engage in sterile manoeuvres to manipulate share prices at the expense of their shareholders. There would then be no reason of principle why the government should not force companies to pension off their shareholders with fixed interest stock, or perhaps with fixed price stocks which bore some sort of profits-related dividend, but which could not be sold on a stock exchange.[21] There would, however, be plenty of practical reasons motivating governments: the shift itself should not so interfere with people's motivation that the second state would be worse than the first, and the costs of the transition should not be so high that they would wipe out the subsequent gains. There are issues of what one might term secondary justice: although it is not intrinsically unjust to abolish a property right for good reason, it is unjust to do so without compensation; one important point of a property right is to secure an expectation of reward, and to defeat that expectation is an injustice to the expectant property-owner.[22] On a large scale such injustice would be an instrumentally bad thing, since it would be unsettling and so defeat the point of instituting property rights at all. The issue of justice arises particularly and awkwardly in the narrower case where we need to ensure that the person who has legitimately and non-fraudulently acquired the right receives something equivalent to it, and that if his former property rights have been abolished he will not think that he has been picked on without sufficient reason. All the general problems attending attempts to give an instrumental or utilitarian account of justice will plague the analysis of this case too. Hume's view that justice and property are coeval social institutions, as much as Mill's view that the conventional character of property entails a government's absolute discretion about its amendment, runs into difficulties in accounting (save in terms of habit) for our belief that a person whose rights are extinguished without his consent is unjustly treated, even if there was indeed a good reason for picking on him.[23]

Theories of ownership tackle two questions above all: the first is the question of how we obtain a title to whatever sorts of property are at issue; the second is the question of what rights we obtain and over what – how extensive our rights over property are, and over what things we can have such rights. The attraction of natural rights theories is that they answer both questions at once and in intuitively compelling ways: that is, they start by announcing our self-ownership, and derive our ownership of things external to us by extension – usually by resting on our having 'mixed' our labour with the external object. My body is mine, and what I made out of otherwise unowned stuff is also mine. Thereafter, the natural rights theorist and everyone else agree that rights pass by and arise from contract, gift, sale, bequest and the like.

A. How Title Is Obtained

While the instrumental theorist will, of course, wish to say that all modes of acquisition are questions of legal right, he can agree that it is possible nevertheless to distinguish, as Roman lawyers do, a 'natural' mode of acquisition, such as the acquisition of a title by unopposed occupation, because it can be defended as a good utilitarian rule.[24] Where something is not otherwise owned, the efforts of someone who either digs it up, or fashions it into something useful, or cultivates it, ought to be encouraged by recognising his ownership of it. Arguments from simple possession, of an apple, for instance, picked from an unowned tree tend correspondingly towards not frustrating desires. *De facto* and uncontested possession ought often to be allowed to create *de jure* ownership, for utilitarian reasons. There is a difference between possession and ownership, and between occupancy and ownership, but the overarching point of all property rights together with some truisms about human nature justify the conventional recognition of these 'natural' titles.

Beyond these natural titles to natural objects lie the thoroughly artificial titles and objects of ownership. Since the greatest of all resources is human labour, mental as well as physical, there will be particular reason for creating property rights which encourage people to exercise ingenuity as well as strength and perseverance. This is all the more necessary since with many results of human ingenuity, the things to which ownership rights are at issue would not exist if it were not for the labour that had gone into them.[25] The man who invents a new drug, say, invents something whose ownership is not interesting as a matter of his owning or not owning the original chemical constituents — this flask full of stuff, so to speak — but in terms of his having the right to say whether others may copy the process.[26] The utilitarian claim is that people should be given ownership of patents and the like, not because they are the 'natural owners' of their own ideas, but to encourage thought and its employment in useful projects.[27]

B. *The Exclusiveness and Extent of Ownership Rights*

Now if this is enough for the moment to settle the question of how a person gets initial property rights in an object — or gets ownership of an artificial object like a patent — the question still arises of how extensive such rights are, and how this bears on the question whether the rights of ownership ought to be held by natural individuals or by public bodies of some sort. In an instrumental conception of ownership, it is easy to justify very extensive property rights, but always as a matter of convenience. There is no initial thought that when an individual acquires a piece of property, he enters into a relationship with it which brings it under his arbitrary or despotic control, or one in which he somehow permeates it with his will — both suggestions which we find in Kant and Hegel and in the 'volitional' account of ownership in general.[28] It is rather that life will go on more briskly and more comfortably if individuals can usually dispense of *all* possible rights in a thing, that is, if someone or other is both the absolute and the outright owner, so that people wishing to make contracts with each other, say, can know exactly whom to turn to, and can know that when he gives his word, that disposes of everything there is to dispose of. Encumbering property with secondary claims increases insecurity in contract — it becomes harder to be sure that we have really acquired the rights we thought we had, and harder to be sure that we have managed to transfer the rights we meant to transfer. To simplify all this is a great step forward. It is, however, a creative act.

In spite of Adam Smith's talk of the system of 'natural liberty',[29] full, freehold ownership subject to absolute freedom of contract is an invention, not something that nature revealed after people regained their liberty. And arguments for it are arguments of convenience; in principle, one could devise any number of coherent, though no doubt increasingly complex, schemes to spread around the ownership of whatever is at issue. The person who occupies and cultivates a patch of ground, for instance, could be given a freehold in it, or a seven-year lease with an option to renew, or a lease to him and his family, the freehold reverting to the state, to an agriculture board, to a village cooperative or any other legal owner one cared to make up.[30] The advantages of freehold are to be assessed in terms of convenience rather than of right.[31] There is not, therefore, something natural or special about vesting all ownership rights in a single natural individual. But, then, if single natural individuals do not automatically get all the rights of ownership, we can think of ownership as a bundle of separable rights — to an income, to dispose of the capital, to appoint managers of the capital, and so on — and some of these may fall into private hands and some may fall into the hands of public bodies.

Moreover, it is also characteristic of this way of looking at the subject that the argument between private and public ownership will often dissolve into arguments about different sorts of rights, some of them not property rights. This is not a matter of great surprise; one way of giving the public a voice in how railways are run, say, might be by nationalising the railways, giving the ownership of track, buildings and the rolling stock to a public corporation, thereby establishing political control answerable to the public in the usual way. It would then be up to the government of the day to set the general framework within which management operated the railways and charged for their services. Almost exactly the same thing could be achieved without ownership changing hands from private shareholders to a public corporation; the government could simply legislate itself the necessary powers to appoint managers, or to require the railways to operate in a particular fashion; or the government might choose to purchase services from the railways on social grounds, or to do any number of different things to achieve its objectives. Always the general point would hold: that much which could be achieved by transferring ownership could also be achieved by other means. Indeed, the popularity of what has been called the Morrisonian pattern of nationalisation attests to this, since in that scheme, nationalised industries have been run by publicly owned corporations which have behaved for most purposes as commercial enterprises aiming at a return on their capital, but some of whose services have either been performed at an agreed loss or have been hived off for accounting purposes and covered by a specific subsidy.

The point can obviously be applied generally. A health service might be run with government-owned medical facilities, with the doctors and surgeons making private contracts for the use of them. The whole service might be run by insurance companies, or by the government with a medical staff of civil servants. It is likely, of course, that the advantages of one scheme would be decisively in its favour. Within a generally instrumental framework there might be other values, such as personal responsibility, social equality, or community, that one might want to pursue, additional to efficiency of service; but however that may be, it is the balance of instrumental advantage that ought to set the choice between different schemes of ownership rights and of the hands in which to vest them.[32] So an instrumentalist is not likely to be very passionate in defence of private or public ownership; he ought to think that ownership itself is interesting only because the whole bundle of rights involved in it is significant. There is no relationship between men and their world which either demands private ownership of things, or is threatened by it.

II. The Self-developmental or Self-expressive Justifications of Ownership

It is time, therefore, to turn to an opposed view in which ownership is important for its own sake. Whereas on the instrumental view of property rights there is nothing special about ownership, or, we might say, 'owning' is phenomenologically thin, the opposed position is concerned with the special relationship between owner and owned. It might be called a self-developmental or self-expressive view, or perhaps an intrinsic justification view. On my account, what is important about intrinsic justifications is their emphasis on the relationship between the owning subject and the owned object. But just as utilitarian arguments which generally favour private property turn out to be arguments against it under some conditions, so non-instrumental justifications of private property can provide the terms in which the 'owner-owned' relationship is attacked as intrinsically evil — as occurs in Marx's *Economic-Philosophical Manuscripts* with their denunciation of *having*.[33]

Hegel: Ownership as the Assertion of Human Will in the Material World

The central thought of the self-developmental or self-expressive view of ownership is that human beings are essentially subjects, possessors of free will, agents with plans and projects, who introduce value into the world of brute material things by incorporating that world into their plans. The thought is most fully expressed in Hegel's writings on work and ownership, but as with so much of Hegel's social thought, many of the ingredients are to be found in Kant, though they are found there in an exaggeratedly individualist framework which Hegel repudiates.[34] The derivation of property rights starts with some latent premises about rights; the most important of these are the claims that rights depend for their existence upon recognition — they can to some extent exist implicitly in a given social order without being fully recognised, but this, especially for Hegel, is a rather impoverished and second-rate existence — and that an individual who claims a right claims to be able to exercise a portion of his freedom as a person and claims it on the basis of his own existence as a person.[35] To be a person in the fully-fledged sense requires the recognition of one's personality as an object demanding respect by others. Others are under an obligation to recognise claims — we cannot agree by majority vote that Jones is not a person and then legitimately treat him as a mere thing. Ownership is not, then, primarily a question of utility; rather, individuals are seen as asserting the right of their wills to become the wills of otherwise will-less matter. To claim to be the owner of something is to claim sovereignty over it.[36] This view resists the attempt to dissolve ownership into a series of rights which might be parcelled out among different people; the owner, being sovereign over what he owns, can create lesser rights in those things by quasi-legislative action, but this is conceptually different from thinking of ownership as 'built up' by putting together claims which might have different grounds, such as the right to use, the right to control, the right to bequeath and so on.

It might seem odd to start from a complex notion like that of ownership in explaining rights over things. Anyone brought up on a Lockean picture of the state of nature is almost certain to start by thinking of the Indian wandering in the woods of America taking fruit from the trees and drinking water from the streams; a right to undisturbed use seems more 'natural' or 'basic' than fully fledged ownership.[37] But this is to misunderstand the thrust of Hegel's argument. In Hegel's view, the Indian who simply takes and uses the fruit and water is *asserting* his ownership, even, so far as I can see, if he has no concept of ownership in his vocabulary. For, in taking and using what is merely there, he presupposes the right to destroy mere stuff for his own purposes.[38] The thrust of the argument can better be appreciated if we ask the question, What might make us say that the Indian *could not* appropriate the things he wanted to consume? The obvious answer would be that he could not do so if they were already someone else's. Being 'someone else's' would mean that the objects were already occupied by another human will, and *ex hypothesi* objects in their unowned state are not so occupied.[39] In these early pages of *The Philosophy of Right*, where this argument occurs, Hegel does not enquire whether other sorts of claim on unowned things might amount to an occupation by a prior human will. The later portions of *The Philosophy of Right* show clearly enough, however, that an organised political society may have all sorts of regulations about when our attempt to acquire something as our property should be recognised as successful. But the question at the beginning of the argument is whether an action which implies my sovereignty over some material thing or things is legitimate. The material thing itself has no claim to autonomy; and there is a *ceteris paribus* assumption that in using, altering, or consuming things we rightly treat them as if we own them. The intrinsic value of ownership is thus that it expresses our status as sources of value in the world, and permeates otherwise pointless inanimate matter with our purposes. We give a soul to the world.[40] The individual cannot do this singlehandedly, though. Although one might say, as we have, that even without a concept of ownership the man who turns the world to his purposes behaves towards it as its owner, for this relationship to be fully realised he requires communal endorsement of his ownership. Only in a community can he acquire the habits and even the intelligence which it is the point of property to express.

All the same, property in Hegel's view is essentially private property.[41] The reason is not that it is conceptually impossible that there should be public property; Hegel recognises that modern individual ownership is a recent development. Monasteries, universities and the like owned property in the past, and private rights were carved out of traditional, collective, family or communal ownership. He recognises too that in the case of entailed estates, say, the extent of the present individual owner's rights over his property might also be limited.[42] Rather, Hegel is making a twofold point: first, that property is tied to the will, and we increasingly see that it is individuals who are the source of will — perhaps because they are increasingly able to will as individuals — and, second, that the supreme value of the modern world is individual liberty, that of a socialised individual no doubt, but nonetheless, the liberty of individuals.[43] This means that except for overriding good reasons, we recognise that the ownership rights of the present generation ought not to be restricted by entails and unbreakable covenants — 'feudal remains in the course of disappearing', says Hegel — and that individuals ought to possess over things all the rights that may properly be possessed over them.[44] The modern limited liability company, which is created when individual owners get together to pool resources, is a fundamentally different moral entity from a medieval corporation.

Does this mean that Hegel's arguments imply outright, absolute, unimpeded ownership? The answer is plainly that in Hegel's own eyes they do not. They imply absolute ownership in the technical Roman Law sense: someone or other can be identified as *the owner* of any piece of property, in contrast to the common law condition where there might be nobody who was so identifiable, but where several persons held different estates, all anchored in one piece of ground.[45] But they do not imply the extensive powers involved in 'the liberal conception of ownership'.[46] Hegel, for instance, is adamant that English law allows far too much licence in testamentary disposition; he does not accept that we should say, 'It's his property, he can leave it to whomever he chooses', for his view about bequest seems to be that in invoking the aid of others in realising our wishes about the destiny of things which we are naturally no longer able to control, we cannot claim their assistance in realising mere wilfulness and arbitrariness.[47] There is also a strong hint that since the sort of individuals we become in society depends upon the social roles we occupy, we become stewards rather than despots. As parents, responsible for our families, we are stewards of what is morally family property, and we cannot claim an arbitrary freedom of testamentary disposition.

Use, work, incentives and the familiar ingredients of the utilitarian view are not left out of this argument; but their role is greatly changed. We are not asked to think about designing institutions for maximising the general welfare; rather, we are asked to think about institutions which express the idea that moral personalities live in a law-governed community. But it is taken for granted that we are embodied personalities, that we need to eat, drink, clothe and shelter ourselves; we are inevitably *prompted* by instrumental and utilitarian goals. Similarly, the intransigence of natural objects in their natural state means that we must work, must acquire the skills needed to bring about long term changes in things.[48] But these utilitarian promptings are not the *point* of the institutions to which they give rise; that point lies in the rational, moral existence we lead in operating them. This existence, for Hegel, expresses the modern view of the moral individual. He is a fully participating member of his community, but he is not lost or swallowed up in it. So the bias is towards private ownership, private initiative and private responsibility, with a substantial measure of governmental supervision though not of public ownership.

Marx: Private Property as the Enemy of Personal Autonomy and Self-development

Just as the utilitarian argument can be turned round to argue that the actual legal institutions of a society ought to be altered in the direction of taking into public ownership what is now in private hands, so the self-expressive, intrinsic argument is turned round in a most striking fashion in Marx's *Economic-Philosophical Manuscripts*.[49] What is striking about Marx's attack on private ownership in those essays is that he rests his case on just the considerations from which Hegel derived the rational necessity of private property. That is, where Hegel saw property as expressing the individual's control over things, and the affirmation of individual ownership as the basis for individuals' recognising one another as persons with rational plans for their lives, Marx attacks private property as the enemy of such recognition, and as frustrating that contol. In the famous theory of alienation, the key claim is that, paradoxically, the individual owner who may legally do what he likes with his own, in practice is compelled to do whatever will yield him enough profit to go on owning it; if you own a shop and would like to sell vegetables, but only car parts will yield a profit, you must sell car parts or go broke. Again, so far from property creating an incentive to develop abilities which expand your personality, the need to work for a living implies that you must develop whatever abilities the market demands; they are in a crucial way less yours than the market's. The starting point is the claim that the essence of ownership is control; if the market has no use for your talents as a poet, which you *would* want to develop, but only for your ability to shovel coal which you would not, you have no control over your abilities after all. They 'belong' to the market rather than you. If the abilities in demand are ones you don't enjoy using, yet have to use to stay alive, they tyrannise over you, as if their development is achieved by exploiting you.[50] Under capitalism our humanity is a misfortune: on account of our need to stay alive, clothed and sheltered, we find ourselves forced to treat our own abilities and the like as mere commodities in the market place.[51] Nothing could be further from the sovereignty of mind over matter that Hegel envisages as the point of property.

Marx is apparently saying that private property is internally contradictory, that the legal and economic arrangements which we properly call those of a system of private property make it impossible to really own things; indeed, they create a state of affairs in which we are dominated by things which have come to take on a life of their own. *Le mort saisit le vif* is Marx's constant cry against capitalism; it sustains his analysis of the nature of commodity production, and it plainly implies that with private property there is no true appropriation of the world. But, what is true appropriation like? To this, Marx's reply in the early essays is that it is a matter of enjoyment, not of having: the eye can appropriate the beauty of a painting; merely purchasing it cannot.[52] Real appropriation is only possible when developed human beings enjoy their own activities and their own creations.

It is quite unclear that this has any very determinate implications for property institutions. It is, of course, plain enough that it entails the abolition of private ownership of capital goods, as well as abolishing exchange made through the market; what one might call exclusionary property, the whole point of which is that its owner can employ it as a weapon in the struggle for survival in a capitalist economy, is clearly to be abolished. But so too would be what we ordinarily think of as public ownership; if we were all employed by state corporations run by enlightened managers, we might be more prosperous, but we would not be any freer. For if we preserved all the attitudes we have developed under a competitive capitalism, we should still be forced to treat our abilities as means to an end, still produce things we took no real interest in, and we might still measure our quality as human beings by how much money we earned or by how many goods we had got hold of. A debased Stakhanovite view of the world is all too compatible with state ownership.

Appropriation is only possible when the concept of ownership has been rendered inapplicable. And this can only occur when some kind of communal decision-making system has been established which makes it possible for us all to decide what to produce and how, and to come to such a decision by some process other than bargaining and by some procedure other than simple majority rule. The great lacuna in Marx's work is the absence of any serious attempt to elaborate on this claim and spell out what sort of collective decision-making system a communist society would operate. Nonetheless, it is plain enough that for Marx's arguments against private property to be fully convincing, we need some picture, however rough, of what it would be like to have utterly abolished it. Apart from remarks which suggest that the problem would solve itself, Marx gives us nothing.[53] Indeed, things are worse than that. For Marx has two different complaints against capitalism. One is that capitalism is chaotic, because the market is an inefficient way of coordinating production decisions; it lurches from boom to slump and back again, with waste, unemployment and instability. This complaint can be put in terms intelligible to the most diehard utilitarian or instrumental thinker.[54] The socialists' claim is that the ownership or control of capital goods needs to be vested in public bodies which could take planning decisions by-passing the market place; private ownership of the means of production would be abolished for good instrumental reasons. This would not entail that private ownership of consumer goods, consumer durables, or even of houses or small patches of land would be abolished. Roughly, we need abolish only those forms of ownership which would threaten to reintroduce chaos. Of course, there is a vast amount to be said about the plausibility of the idea that central planning is more efficient, and almost as much about the way to draw a boundary between harmless ownership and harmful ownership: the moment we ask whether a person who owns a house is allowed to rent it out, we start raising difficulties. But these are questions of a technical kind about the legal arrangements and political control that will bring about certain economic results.

Marx's second complaint against capitalism, that it is a form of alienated existence, is not susceptible to this treatment. Its attractions lie in the global, moral character of the indictment, in the picture of the depraved state of human character under capitalism. [For a fuller development of this aspect of Marx's thought, see Eugene Kamenka's account below in Ch. 11 — Eds.] Merely making the life of capitalists and workers less chaotic is not much good; what we must do is abolish the capitalist mentality, abolish the proletarian mentality, re-establish humanity in place of alienation. This seems to have little or no direct bearing on legal arrangements. Rather, it raises the much larger issue of whether we could envisage any decision-making system whatever which would meet Marx's requirements. And my own view is that *we* cannot. Roughly, what Marx seems to envisage is that we should lose any sense of having separate interests, and that we should identify ourselves so completely with the welfare of everyone else that our greatest desire is to convey to others our sense of the importance of their lives and happiness. This seems to me to be possible, if anywhere, only in very small, very intimate groups, where people know one another so well that both the knowledge and the emotional commitment required for Marx's picture to come true can be relied on. For larger groups, the project is utopian. It is implausible that a non-manufactured version of the appropriate emotional commitment would arise spontaneously.

Moreover, it is not clear how, without the existence of *some* conflicts of interest, we could ever arrive at a decision about what to do. We need some basic likes and dislikes to give a decision-making scheme something to bite on; people wholly committed to each other's wants would be like over-polite people trying to get through a door. On any large scale, however, it is hard to see how time, information and all the obvious things which are in short supply for non-human reasons would permit a system fulfilling Marx's requirements. And, if that is right, the application of Hegel's account of property rights for Marx's radical purposes is at one level misconceived.[55]

It is only at this level, however, that I should want to complain of it. It is at least plausible that without something like Hegel's account to start from, Marx's insights into the deficiencies of capitalism would have been thinner and less engrossing than they are. If the idea of real communal appropriation is too slippery to make much use of, the individual complaints against capitalism are not; there is surely something to be said for the view that the painting *qua* painting 'belongs' more to the artist and the appreciative spectator than to the ignorant plutocrat who has paid half a million dollars to show off how rich he is. But although there is a good deal to be said for it, it is not a view which readily sustains an analysis of what institutional arrangements count as genuine socialism.

III. Dramaturgical Approaches to Private Property

I hinted at the beginning that one thought sustaining this chapter was that the legal positivism which seems a natural conceptual ally of instrumentalism is the best way to approach institutional issues, but that the stress on the nature of *owning*, on the relationship between owner and owned, offered insights of a sociological and psychological sort that instrumental accounts of property were prone to pass over. I shall conclude by suggesting that the usual discussion of property in terms of capital goods and consumer goods, property for use versus property for power, and so on, should be extended to cover one more aspect of our dealings with the outside world, that is, our use of things as stage sets, and our use of clothes, consumer goods and the rest as 'props'.

There have, of course, been many discussions of 'conspicuous consumption', and there has been a great deal of slightly silly discussion about the way people acquire things less for use than for status. An aspect of private property which is less attended to is the importance of people being able to control how their immediate intimate environment is to look and what information it is to transmit to others.[56] There are, of course, lots of arguments in favour of such control. One such argument is from the importance of friendship; if we lived always in public space there would be no boundaries which we could allow people to cross as a sign that they and we were friends rather than mere acquaintances. The insurance salesman who tries to push his way into one's house is in essence taking advantage of the fact that to allow someone across that boundary is to accept him as a friend, so that turning down his sales pitch thereafter is so much the more difficult. Again, if there were no goods or services to which we had exclusive title, we could not give them to others, and could not cement relationships by so doing. Another argument rests on the same general considerations about security that motivate most discussions of privacy. We need some territory which is physically ours, protected from the casual intrusions of others, and even from their merely looking at us. The familiar complaint that much modern architecture induces the sensation that we are living in the street, in full view of everyone walking past, is a complaint against the physical inability of some buildings to provide such shelter;[57] if we do not have rights of exclusion of others of the sort which go along with (though, of course, they neither add up to, nor are only to be had with) private ownership of homes and the like, we suffer insecurity, we constantly need to think about how we appear to an audience, and are ill at ease. I do not at all wish to suggest that it is only through individual home ownership that such privacy can be secured; many men at least feel that their privacy is a great deal more secure in an office whose door will not be opened by every Tom, Dick and Harry than it is in their own homes, where young Samantha may come bursting through the bedroom or bathroom door at any moment. Nevertheless, a concern for ownership of one's own space is one branch of a concern for control of that space, and the ground for wanting control is much the same as the ground for wanting any sort of privacy.

Of course, publicly owned housing which was humanely organised so that people had security of tenure, to which officials could not gain access without permission, and so on, would meet most of what was needed. However, there is a more positive side to the story, which goes beyond the need for immunities against intrusion. This is the argument that we need spaces and objects which we can control so as to tell the world a story about ourselves. The prisoner's pin-ups on the wall of his cell announce what his sexual tastes are, but more importantly remind him and his jailers that he is still a man, even when incarcerated. His pictures announce that he is still attached to the outside world, only in jail for a limited period and, as it were, by accident. The point is not that any particular message has to be conveyed, so much as the fact that people need the sort of control that having some personal possessions gives them if they are to be able to give an account of themselves at all.[58]

Again, the characteristic area in which this tends to be obvious is clothes, homes and — in England anyway — gardens. Allegiances can be declared, aspirations tried out, character displayed in colours, shapes and the rest. Here is an area where it is quite likely that even humane and rational public ownership of things like houses will leave important needs unfilled — unless tenants' rights to decorate as they wish, keep pets, and all the other things that cause contention, are so guaranteed and so taken for granted that the distinction between public and private ownership begins to wither away. Different cultures and groups will treat all this very differently of course. There are, if writers like Tom Wolfe are any guide, bits of American society where life is lived almost wholly in the street, and a bright blue Buick is the precondition of viability in the local scene; the aristocrats of the underclass might well regard the most comfortable apartment as scarcely better than prison, being committed to a lifestyle with a low probability of survival beyond the age of thirty, but with a very high premium on showing oneself to be a hell of a fellow before the grim reaper strikes. In such situations, it would be difficult to call the bright blue Buick a consumer good, even a consumer durable, since it would be both a stage set for whatever dramas we enacted and a property which we made use of on the larger stage set of the street. Certainly it would not be readily analysable as a store of utilities. In soberer or grayer societies, with longer time horizons, the drawing room would be a central asset in conducting our lives as drawing-room comedies or tragedies, and the various bits and pieces of equipment which members of the family possessed would all be used to express and assist the moving forward of the everyday drama.

This amounts not to an argument for or against private property or public property, but to a small plea that when larger issues of the virtues of public and private ownership are discussed, we ought not to forget that when it comes down to making a large social theory work in some particular environment, we may find that people are using their property for all sorts of subtle purposes which we ignore at our peril. When we try to persuade a Zulu family to grow vegetables rather than keep cows, we are likely to be ignored, and if we try to browbeat them into doing as we suggest we are likely to cause great misery, simply because keeping cattle is a man's business, tending vegetables is a woman's business, and to suggest that women's business is more important than men's business is to insult the head of the family. In many societies a cow is a cow and a man who farms cows will cheerfully move into pigs if pigs sell better; but we cannot rely on this being universally so, and any discussion of property can be no more general or universal in its aims than any other part of social theory.

Notes

1. Alan Ryan, 'Two Concepts of Politics and Democracy' in M. Fleisher (ed.), *Machiavelli and the Nature of Political Thought* (Atheneum Press, New York, 1972), pp. 76-113.
2. Cf. David Lyons, 'The New Indian Claims and Original Rights to Land' in Jeffrey Paul (ed.), *Reading Nozick* (Basil Blackwell, Oxford, 1982), pp. 355-79.
3. Rom Harré, *Social Being* (Basil Blackwell, Oxford, 1979), Chs. 10, 17.
4. C.A.R. Crosland, *The Future of Socialism* (Cape, London, 1964), pp. 312-40.
5. Lyons, 'New Indian Claims', p. 363ff.
6. Jeremy Bentham, *Bentham's Theory of Legislation* (ed. Dumont) (Trubner, London, 1887), p. 113.
7. Thomas Hobbes, *Leviathan* (Dent, London, 1914), p. 83.
8. Maurice Cranston, *What are Human Rights?* (Bodley Head, London, 1973).
9. Immanuel Kant, *The Metaphysical Elements of Justice* (Bobbs-Merrill, Indianapolis, 1965), pp. 54-55.
10. J.S. Mill, *The Principles of Political Economy* in *The Collected Works of John Stuart Mill*, vols. II, III (University of Toronto Press, Toronto, 1963), pp. 199-203.
11. A.M. Honoré, 'Ownership' in A.G. Guest (ed.), *Oxford Essays in Jurisprudence* (Oxford University Press, Oxford, 1961), pp. 108ff.
12. Kant, *Elements of Justice*, pp. 47, 98-99.
13. John Rawls, *A Theory of Justice* (The Belknap Press of Harvard University Press, Cambridge, Mass., 1971), p. 334ff.
14. Bentham, *Theory of Legislation*, pp. 201-9.
15. John Harris, 'The Survival Lottery', *Philosophy*, 50 (1975), pp. 81-87.
16. Peter Singer, 'Utility and the Survival Lottery', *Philosophy*, 52 (1977), pp. 219-21.
17. Harris, 'Survival Lottery', pp. 86-87.
18. James Mill, *An Essay on Government* (Bobbs-Merrill, Indianapolis, 1955), p. 48.
19. Ibid., pp. 49-50.
20. Bentham, *Theory of Legislation*, p. 100.
21. Crosland, *Future of Socialism*, pp. 265-71.

22. Bentham, *Theory of Legislation*, Ch. XV.
23. Rawls, *Theory of Justice*, pp. 175-92.
24. Barry Nicholas, *An Introduction to Roman Law* (Oxford University Press, Oxford, 1962), pp. 130-40.
25. Robert Nozick, *Anarchy, State, and Utopia* (Basic Books, New York, 1974), pp. 198-99.
26. Ibid., p. 181.
27. Ibid., p. 182.
28. G.W.F. Hegel, *The Philosophy of Right*, T.M. Knox (trans.) (Clarendon Press, Oxford, 1942), see §44.
29. Adam Smith, *An Inquiry into the Nature and Causes of the Wealth of Nations* (Methuen, London, 1960), vol. II, p. 208.
30. Mill, *Principles of Political Economy*, pp. 228-33.
31. This argument, it ought to be noticed at once, is rather readily employed as an anti-landlord argument. Utilitarians in the 19th century were almost unanimous in favour of reforming the law of landlord and tenant in agriculture, for they saw that both in terms of income and in terms of capital gains the system was anti-progressive; the tenant knew that if he farmed well, got the land in good heart, and put up its yield, the result would be that his rent would go up; equally, so would the capital value of the land. Extreme arguments met at this point. One could argue, on the one hand, that the state ought to become the sole landlord and should adjust its rents so as to maximise the efficiency of farming. That would presumably mean charging higher rents for land of better natural fertility, but allowing good tenants to keep the benefit of improvements they had made, and perhaps allowing them to charge some sort of premium when they parted with their leases. Alternatively, one could argue that there should be no landlords at all and that all land should be owned by those who farmed it. At that point there would be no rents and no capital gains accruing to anyone other than those who had made the improvements for which the appropriate price was being asked.
32. Crosland, *Future of Socialism*, pp. 35-42, 312-40.
33. Karl Marx, *Early Writings* (Penguin Books, Harmondsworth, 1975), p. 352.
34. Hegel, *Philosophy of Right*, §33.
35. Ibid., §36.
36. Ibid., §44.
37. John Locke, *Two Treatises on Government* (Cambridge University Press, Cambridge, 1967), Bk. 2, Ch. V, para. 26, pp. 304-6.
38. Hegel, *Philosophy of Right*, §44.
39. Ibid., §§50, 52.
40. Ibid., §44.
41. Ibid., §46.
42. Ibid., p. 293, addition to §306.
43. Ibid., p. 236, addition to §46.
44. Ibid., p. 240, addition to §63.
45. F.H. Lawson, *The Law of Property* (Oxford University Press, Oxford, 1958), pp. 68-73.
46. Honoré, *Ownership*, p. 108.
47. Hegel, *Philosophy of Right*, §180.
48. Ibid., §§196, 197, and p. 270, addition to §§196, 197.
49. Marx, *Early Writings*, pp. 279-400.
50. Ibid., pp. 322ff.
51. Ibid., pp. 360-61.
52. Ibid., pp. 352-53.
53. John Plamenatz, *Karl Marx's Philosophy of Man* (Clarendon Press, Oxford, 1975), p. 472.

54. Peter Singer, *Marx* (Oxford University Press, Oxford, 1980), pp. 61-62.
55. Charles Taylor, *Hegel and Modern Society* (Cambridge University Press, Cambridge, 1979), pp. 149-50.
56. Harré, *Social Being*, pp. 226-31.
57. Richard Sennett, *The Fall of Public Man* (Cambridge University Press, Cambridge, 1976), pp. 13ff.
58. Cf. Erving Goffman, *Asylums* (Doubleday, New York, 1967), Ch. 1.

PART TWO

CRITIQUES OF THE LIBERAL CONCEPTION OF PUBLIC AND PRIVATE

10 PUBLIC AND PRIVATE INTERESTS: HEGEL ON CIVIL SOCIETY AND THE STATE

Anthony S. Walton

I. Introduction

Political theory has largely been dominated by liberal individualism. This tradition has been important in staking out and expressing the claims of individuals and groups, and it has rightly insisted on the respects in which the determination of the public interest must in some way be tied to a consideration of private interests. However, as we shall see, there are a number of theoretical difficulties which individualist theories of the public interest cannot deal with which suggest that concepts and categories of a different order are required, not in order to displace totally those of individualism, but to go beyond them by integrating them into a more comprehensive and adequate analysis. It is useful for this purpose to draw on Hegel's contribution to discourse on the character of public and private interests, their relationship, and the implications of that relationship for the state. Hegel's contribution suggests a blending of two apparently rival traditions of political theory: what Benn and Gaus have called the 'individualist' and 'organic' perspectives.

In Chapter 2, Benn and Gaus suggested that these were two independent perspectives, and that liberalism had to draw on the latter in order to make up certain shortcomings in the former. On the Hegelian view, however, these are not two independent perspectives, the organic merely supplementing the individualist. On the contrary, they are two mutually dependent perspectives which, when adequately integrated, provide the key to a coherent and comprehensive grasp of society in general and of concepts such as the public interest in particular. Benn and Gaus argue that a number of tensions are generated within liberalism because of the relationship between the two — independent — perspectives. From an Hegelian point of view, these tensions arise because of a failure to see the essential relatedness and interdependence of the two perspectives; and this issues in the further failure to grasp individualism as a distinct and crucial moment *within* a broader and more comprehensive theoretical framework. Whether Hegel is successful in his integration remains a large question, particularly since it is not self-evidently the case that social reality can be a vehicle for the kind of coherence in social and political life which Hegel envisages.[1] Nevertheless, he embarks on an intriguing project of searching for connections between theories rather than emphasising their discontinuities; and in particular, he fruitfully pursues the line of revealing how what is apparently individual turns out to have an underlying social aspect which is important for both explanatory and ethical reasons.

One consequence of Hegel's approach is that it gives greater prominence to one particular concept which is almost absent from liberal individualist theory, namely, that of the *state*. The liberal individualist preoccupation with the state as a reflection of, or means to, the securing of the private interests of civil society, has given the state a drastically minimal role in political theory.[2] Hegel's theory of the state may have a number of defects,[3] but it does at the very least direct attention to the importance of the state and to the role of political authority in ways lacking in liberal individualism.

II. The Ontology of the Social World

I have suggested that in Hegel's view the individualist and organic traditions in political theory can be brought together to provide a more powerful and comprehensive account of the character of society. These two traditions have their underlying ontologies, and it would be as well to begin by considering their differences and potential integration. Given Benn and Gaus's claim that trying to bring the two traditions together results in a 'puzzle'[4] as far as understanding the relationship between the individual and society is concerned, I shall concentrate particularly on Hegel's attempted reconciliation of the two views.

Fundamental to individualism is a claim in respect of the logical priority of the individual as opposed to society. A society is taken to be an aggregate of individuals, contrasting with the organicist's claim that the whole is in some sense greater than the parts.[5] Indeed, 'whereas the individualist model takes the individual person as logically the most primitive notion, the organic model takes it to be the social group'.[6] And it is this claim which has given rise to the individualist's argument that organicism wrongly fails to treat individual interests and rights as primary, but rather treats as primary the rights and interests of social wholes which are over and above individuals and to which individual interests should be subordinated.[7] This view has frequently been advanced in relation to theories such as Hegel's, and it involves the general claim, issuing from a broadly individualist view of social reality, that a non-individualist account is necessarily anti-individualist to the extent that a rejection of the major propositions of individualism entails arguments which drastically subvert claims in respect of the importance of individual rights and interests.[8]

Much of Hegel's social theory is devoted to explaining the interdependence of the two models of society, and hence also involves unpacking the claim that a rejection of individualism does not necessarily imply anti-individualism, but does, rather, imply its integration within a more encompassing theory. In this respect the following quotation from the *Philosophy of Right* indicates Hegel's general stance.

> The result is that the universal does not prevail or achieve completion except along with particular interests and through the cooperation of particular knowing and willing; and individuals likewise do not live as private persons for their own ends alone, but in the very act of willing these they will the universal ... The principle of modern states has prodigious strength and depth because it allows the principle of subjectivity to progress to its culmination in the extreme of self-subsistent personal particularity.[9]

The core of Hegel's analysis lies in a complex set of arguments concerning the *dialectical* relationship between universality and particularity, the social context and the individual. The idea of dialectic in Hegel is extremely difficult, compounded by the fact that it operates in different ways and at different levels of his philosophy. Consequently, little more can be done here than to indicate a restricted range of features of the idea of the dialectic, which are of importance to Hegel's social and political theory.

In rather formal terms, the following is meant by the dialectical relationship between universality and particularity:
(1) Particularity is dependent upon universality;
(2) Particularity has its own characteristics and properties;
(3) Universality exists in and through particularity;
(4) Universality has its own characteristics and properties.
In the above, (1) and (3) indicate the mutual dependence of universality and particularity. Neither is reducible to the other. Hence a dialectical relationship is to be distinguished from a *reductionist* one. Propositions (3) and (4) indicate the potential tension between the two

'moments' of particularity and universality. While each moment strives in its own direction, its striving is *aufgehoben* in so far as they are mutually dependent. The idea of dialectic implies, thus, both tension and reconciliation, conflict and consensus.

We can supplement this rather formal presentation of the dialectic with the more concrete analysis to be found in the philosophical anthropology at the root of Hegel's social theory. Hegel takes the view that an explanation of individuals' beliefs, actions and essential capacities must necessarily make reference to their constitutive social context. In this sense all individuals are universal beings. Consequently, in all his writings Hegel is concerned with analysing the various kinds of *relations* holding between individuals, and the different modes they take in specific historical forms and phenomenological stages. This argument has its corollary in an emphasis on the importance of socialisation, by which we come to accept the norms and values of a social context. Thus, 'the positive aspect and the essence of the child is that it is suckled at the breast of universal life'.[10] To become a member of a society is to internalise the norms and values of a form of life which is anterior to the individual.

If it is true that (1) the social context is in some fundamental sense constitutive of individuals; (2) that an account of individuals must necessarily make reference to social relations; and (3) that socialisation into an already existing social context is necessarily part of the individual's experience of living in a society, then it follows that it is difficult to sustain the individualist claim that social groupings are simply aggregations and, so, are reducible to their individual components. On the contrary we are driven to place greater explanatory weight on the *relations* holding between individuals; and the Benthamite claim, which Benn and Gaus cite, that the 'community is a fictitious *body*, composed of the individual members',[11] begins to look weak. It might, of course, be rejoined by the individualist that while there are, obviously, established practices into which individuals are socialised, nevertheless the process of socialisation is something one experiences at the hands of other individuals.[12] But this reply will not do since, while it is true that socialisation takes place through the agency of particular individuals, what one is socialised into are the norms and values characterising social *relations*.

It is not, however, only the issue of socialisation that is relevant here. The limitations of the individualist model are revealed in Hegel's explanation of private rights and interests. To enjoy the right to property, for example, is to live in a society in which the concept of private property is understood and recognised. So a society of property owners is not just an aggregate of individuals enjoying the right to property. The ownership of property expresses a complex of shared concepts which are definitive of the social context. Similarly, to speak about one's interests is necessarily to draw upon shared concepts which give meaning to conceptions of interests. There is a public, social, aspect to one's interests which both constitutes them and makes them intelligible to others.[13]

It is important, however, to recognise that the Hegelian argument does not involve an assertion that social wholes are autonomous entities. It involves only the claim that private rights and interests, together with essential human capacities, are acquired in society, and so significantly that close attention need be paid to social relations[14] which, on this view, cannot be simply *reduced* to individual beliefs and actions.

It is, however, also Hegel's view that the universal is dependent upon the particular. The idea of a social mind existing autonomously, independent of particular minds, would be quite inconsistent, therefore, with Hegel's understanding of the relation between the universal and the particular. But, as we shall see later, a society's ethical life could well be understood as a kind of social mind existing through, and only through, the mediation of individual minds. Like the rules and conventions of language which exist only in and through their intelligent use by individual language users, the social context exists only through the medium of the consciousness and agency of individuals. That is not to say that people will necessarily be capable of full discursive reasoning as to what they do, or that they will necessarily fully understand the point of the practices in which they are involved. But it is to say that practices exist only in so far as people understand the point of actions in terms of those practices.[15] Thus the knowing and willing of individual agents is a necessary condition for the existence and reproduction of the social context.

Hegel found the roots of such self-conscious agency in the development of Christianity, where the self-awareness of the reflective subject begins to emerge, with momentous implications for subsequent social and political development. With the development of subjectivity the individual's self-consciousness and rationality are articulated only in actions for which the individual can have reasons for performing. That is to say, it is not sufficient justification for an action that it is stipulated by custom or political authority.

> But from the reflection which here breaks in, it no longer satisfies man to obey law as an authority and external necessity, for he

desires to satisfy himself in himself, to convince himself, through his reflection, of what is binding upon him and what he has to do for this end.[16]

Of course, to show that claims in respect of subjectivity are made by Hegel is one thing, but to show that the claims are sustainable in non-individualist terms is another. An individualist might insist that Hegel's arguments are inconsistent with one another in so far as claims about subjectivity cannot be made consistent with non-individualist arguments. But, as has already been argued, the capacities which individuals acquire as rational agents they acquire only by virtue of being members of a society, as participants in institutions and practices, something only the most abstract, unsociological, and ahistorical individualist could ignore.

The individualist may still retort, however, that because for Hegelians the criteria of rationality and self-consciousness are supplied by a particular social context, that context itself becomes *a priori* uncriticisable. The Hegelian must concede that his conception of rationality is tied to contextually determinate criteria; but this is not really a damaging concession. First of all, there is something intuitively compelling about the claim that rationality is in at least some minimal sense relative to a particular context of shared concepts and meanings, standards of appropriateness, and so on. Conversely, there is something counterintuitive in the claim advanced, for example, by utilitarians, that the criteria of rationality are objective and acontextually determinate. Secondly, the social context is not *a priori* uncriticisable if that context itself supplies criteria of criticism and self-assessment. Modern social life, which has developed the principle of subjectivity, does precisely this. The contemporary world, unlike the Greek world, supplies critical concepts and categories which can be drawn upon and invoked by individual subjects in the assessment of the beliefs and practices of their society. The capacity for subjectivity – reflective judgement – is itself generated in modern society and is not just the personal internalisation of whatever norms happen to exist. Because it is a reflective, critical capacity, it is not reducible to the content of a society's ethical life.

A discussion of public and private interests in Hegelian political theory, then, must be set against the following background: (1) Hegel's philosophical anthropology involves the view that individuals have both a universal and a particular dimension; (2) neither dimension is reducible to the other, but each is dependent upon the other; and (3) both dimensions have their own expression: the universal in shared norms and values acquired by the individual in becoming a member of society; the particular in the pursuit of private rights and interests, and in the expression of subjective judgement.

III. Civil Society

In suggesting that for Hegel private interests and rights have relational properties, I have indicated an argument about the essential sociality of what is ostensibly private, and this should be taken as part of the broader argument that, contrary to Benn and Gaus, individualism and organicism are not mutually exclusive but, rather, mutually dependent. However, the idea that there is a private sphere is not radically undermined by the fact of its relational character. Indeed, central to Hegel's conception of modern society is the recognition of the private, of the importance of individual rights and interests, and of the need for social and political organisation to take account of the individual as a being making claims in respect of his personhood. In this respect Hegel frequently distinguishes the modern from the Greek worlds on the grounds that the latter expressed an undifferentiated universality in which the specific claims of particularity were not recognised.[17] [But see Ch. 15, below, for a different view of the Greeks' understandings of their societies – Eds.]

The claims of particularity cannot, however, be established on the basis of natural rights or individual needs *per se*, if these are taken to be distinct from the processes of their social construction and legitimation. Such rights and needs are an expression of a particular kind of society which is the source of both the construction and legitimation of the private sphere. They are social as well as private. Consequently these notions are not rejected but included in a broader conception. In this respect Hegel takes up and embraces the individualist conception of personhood, but insists that it cannot be made sense of except in terms of mutually recognitive social relations. Thus, claims made in respect of personhood are not discontinuous with organicist claims but are, rather, dependent upon them. Hegel expressed both the relational character of particularity and also the respects in which it has claims of its own in the following passage: 'The right of individuals to their *particular* satisfaction is also contained in the ethical substantial order, since particularity is the outward appearance of the ethical order – a mode in which that order is existent.'[18] And in his Berlin University lectures on the philosophy of right he claimed: 'The ethical substantiality must exist in the particularity of the subjects.'[19] Thus civil society is integral to the expression of particularity, but also bounded by, and an expression of, the organic ethical order.

The starting point of Hegel's analysis of civil society is the claim that it is integral to the expression of particularity: it is in civil society that particularity has 'the right to develop and launch forth in all directions'.[20] Hegel paints a picture of free individuals making choices in respect of their private interests, interacting with others as a means to achieving their personal goals, and being free from excessive institutional pressures. In his early political writings Hegel had anticipated his subsequent concern for the claims of particularity:

> It is one great virtue of the old states of Europe that while the public authority is secure so far as its needs and its progress are concerned, it leaves free scope to its citizens' own activity in details of administration of law and customary usages.[21]

In the later theory of civil society, there is developed a systematic account of the right to property, relative freedom of economic activity, and free scope to pursue personal interests. The 'system of needs' is taken to be central to civil society in which particularity 'is in the first instance characterized in general by its contrast with the universal principle of the will and thus is subjective need'.[22]

In many respects this characterisation of civil society shares much with individualism; it is a view of social activity as involving the pursuit of personal interests, and the need for co-operation with others as a means to that end. Like the individualists, Hegel recognises that there is a fundamental problem of co-ordination, the problem to which contractarians and utilitarians have perennially addressed themselves: how can the competing interests and aspirations of individuals be harmonised and co-ordinated? What must individuals be prepared to sacrifice in the interests of co-ordination? And what institutional mechanisms are necessary for co-ordination? Consistent with individualist assumptions, Hegel argues that individuals must rationally seek satisfaction; that is to say, they must recognise that others, too, have interests which they wish to satisfy. As Hegel expresses it: 'individuals can attain their ends only in so far as they themselves determine their knowing, willing, and acting in a universal way and make themselves links in this chain of social connexions'.[23] On this view, the public interest is what is necessary for the co-ordination of private interests. Further, on this view, the role of the state is that of securing private interests in so far as it enforces the public interest.[24] This is what Hegel calls the state 'based on need',[25] the state which is a *means* to securing private interests. 'Individuals in their capacity as burghers in this state are private persons whose end is their own interest. This end is *mediated* through the universal which thus *appears* as a *means* to its realization.'[26] In the modern community civil society has emerged as a distinct and integral moment, and in a way which renders inconceivable the organic unity of Greek society. The identity of man and citizen to be found in Plato's *Republic* can no longer be sustained since man is also a burgher, a private person with rights and interests. Co-ordination and integration cannot be achieved, as they were for Plato, merely by appeal to specified roles and functions. Modern society, too, is a system of roles and functions, and in ways frequently ignored by individualists. But it is also a system of free persons[27] making claims in respect of their individual rights and interests. These rights and interests potentially conflict and consequently require co-ordination, and this is one of the functions of the state.

The individualist conception of the state which has developed as a consequence of the recognition of the need for the co-ordination of an essentially atomistic society has a long history. It rests on the assumption that the state is a reflection of, or a response to, the rights and interests of the aggregate elements of society. In the liberal, as opposed to the Hobbesian, strand of the individualist tradition, this conception of the state has resulted in what is, arguably, an emasculated conception of the nature and scope of political authority. What is primary, on this view, is civil society and its diverse interests, and the state can be conceived as nothing other than an elaborate institutional mechanism for co-ordinating those interests.

In its most naive form, individualism has conceived of individual interests as subjective preferences and the state as a means of converting subjective preferences into policies. In the language of modern pluralist political science, the state converts inputs (subjective preferences) into outputs (policies). Hegel is criticising something like this view in the following passage:

> If the principle of the individual will is taken as the sole determination of political freedom, and it is accepted that all individuals should consent to everything that is done by and for the state, there is ... no constitution. The only institution required would be a central body with no will of its own, which took note of what appeared to be the needs of the state and made its opinion known; and then a

mechanism would have to be set up to call the individuals together to register their votes, and to perform the arithmetical operation of counting and comparing the number of votes in favour of the different propositions, at which point the decision would already have been taken.[28]

However, individualists have not always held to the view that interests are constituted by subjective preferences. Hobbes provides the most striking example by arguing that individuals should give up their right to pursue every whim, and allow their actions to be checked by the superordinate political authority of Leviathan, which would have the sole power to determine interests and the means to achieving them. The state has the task of defining the rules governing relations between individuals, staking out the limits of individual acquisitiveness, and imposing rules with whatever power is necessary. The public interest is embodied in the rules promulgated by Leviathan as necessary to the maintenance of peace and order.

This begins to get us closer to the Hegelian view of the state since it gives the state an active and authoritative role in the determination of public policy and a fundamentally creative part to play in the constitution of civil society. The state is not merely a response to the professed demands of civil society; it has a creative role in shaping and organising those demands, locating them within a coherent system of rules, indeed making their very existence possible, and in ways not appreciated by much subsequent liberal theory.[29] However, from the Hegelian point of view, we have not yet reached the notion of the state as the 'actuality of the ethical Idea',[30] and in the following section an attempt will be made to see what is involved in Hegel's account of the state by considering in more detail what questions individualism leaves unanswered.

IV. The Limits of Individualism — the Hegelian State

The first difficulty which individualism confronts is the question of how, exactly, private interests are to be co-ordinated. That is to say, which interests should be favoured, and what criteria are available for determining the relative merits of competing interests? Do some interests have stronger claims than others? From an Hegelian point of view individualism is unable to supply the relevant criteria, and the argument can be most forcefully presented by taking utilitarianism as an instance of individualism. The utilitarian response to the problem of co-ordination is to make claims in respect of the adequacy of empirical and analytic criteria, and at their crudest these are to be found in Bentham's principle of the greatest happiness of the greatest number. In more sophisticated formulations in modern rational choice theory[31] and welfare economics, empirical and analytic criteria are invoked with some power.[32] However, despite the sophistication and elegance of these formulations, they remain inadequate from an Hegelian perspective because they reduce practical reasoning to empirical and analytic criteria, and in doing so make moral and political judgement an essentially technical matter. As Bernard Williams has put it, utilitarianism is a 'one-principle system', which, regrettably, makes little reference to 'ancillary principles and moral notions'.[33]

Arguments implying a critique of utilitarian individualism are offered by Hegel in his account of the will. In the 'Introduction' to the *Philosophy of Right* he speaks of the arbitrary will (*Willkür*), the will that is concerned only with considerations of personal desires and satisfactions. This is the utilitarian conception of a person as a bundle of wants which require ordering and co-ordination. He argues, however, that the language of desires and interests is radically incomplete since any amount of empirical information about the relative strength of people's wants is going to drastically underdetermine conclusions concerning the rational co-ordination of people's desires and interests. All that the 'arbitrary will' can yield is a 'dialectic of impulses and inclinations'[34] which, in Hegel's view, can only be coherently and rationally ordered through the application of principles of an essentially normative kind, and of a sort not reducible to empirical and analytic criteria. What is required is that 'the impulses should become the rational system of the will's volitions',[35] and these are to be found, as the later arguments of the *Philosophy of Right* indicate, in the norms of ethical life (*Sittlichkeit*) which enter into, inform, and mediate the individual's conceptions of his interests,[36] and which provide a normative framework within which various desires and interests can be rationally ordered.

With the notion of ethical life we can begin to see more clearly both how Hegel conceives of the public interest and also how he conceptualises the role of the state. On the one hand, ethical life consists of a complex of shared norms and values; and on the other, the state has the task of articulating those norms and values in policies. Thus, the state is the institutional expression of the common will of the community.

Hobbes, too, had supposed that the state was founded on a common will; indeed that was the source of its legitimacy. But Hobbes's common will, while consistent with his own individualist premises, drastically undermines claims in respect of individual interests since it gives to Leviathan a degree of arbitrary power inconsistent with the usual claims of individualism. Hobbes's theory provides a reliable basis for coordination, namely, the arbitrary will of the sovereign, and in doing so avoids some of the difficulties generated by liberal individualism. But it avoids those difficulties in such a way as to undermine individualist claims in respect of the importance and integrity of individual rights and interests. The Hegelian way of avoiding this difficulty is to invoke the dialectic of particularity and universality. On the one hand, particularity has specific claims and legitimacy expressed in the opportunity to pursue one's interests and enjoy one's rights within the framework provided by civil society. On the other hand, universality is expressed in the ethical life of the community. In this respect there are some crucial distinctions between Hobbes and Hegel. First, the norms and values of ethical life derive from the common, historically nurtured, experience of people living together in a shared culture. The common will of the community cannot, on this view, be determined exclusively by the will of the sovereign. Second, the norms and values of ethical life exist only through the consciousness and agency of individuals[37] and not exclusively through the stipulative will of Leviathan. Moreover, the principles of ethical life, and their articulation in the policies of the state, are subject to the reflective critical judgement of citizens,[38] thus creating a social and political environment a world away from the austerity of Hobbes's 'sovereign definer'.

V. Ethical Life, the Public Interest and the State

The social dimension of individual experience, constituted more particularly by ethical life, gives rise to, and provides the foundation for, the Hegelian theory of the state. It has already been suggested here that the state is in some sense an expression of ethical life in so far as its policies and activities embody the historically emergent norms and values of the community. And in the *Philosophy of Right*, the state is treated as a subsection of the section on ethical life, and is described as the 'actuality of the ethical Idea'.[39] That is to say, the terms in which it is conceived are not consistent with its being merely a means to individual interests.[40]

However, what is also at stake here is a set of arguments about the nature and extent of political authority. It has already been argued that liberal individualism is unable to provide an adequate account of the state. And we have also seen that while the Hobbesian view of the state more adequately establishes the scope of political authority, it does so at severe costs to the individual interests it is supposed to protect. We can see how Hegel connects the notion of ethical life with those of the state and common interest through his account of the welfare functions of the state.[41] Hegel was greatly exercised by the phenomenon of poverty and inequality in contemporary industrial society,[42] and the thrust of his argument implies a moral condemnation of the fact of gross inequality produced by economic upheaval, and a corresponding commitment to state activity as an ameliorative process. This commitment derives from a rejection of private charity and almsgiving as a means to helping the poor. Helping the poor cannot be left to 'private sympathy'[43] and the 'charitable disposition'[44] of particular individuals. On the contrary, it is the obligation of the community as a whole, acting through the state, to provide for the needs of those afflicted by the consequences of economic crisis. The remedying of poverty is thus a 'universal' as opposed to a 'particular' activity, and as such it expresses the ethical life of the community. Modern ethical life embodies generally shared norms and values governing relations between individuals and groups; it embraces shared principles of justice and reasonable equality, and these are concretised in state action. In taking measures to deal with the poor the state expresses the common will, a set of expectations about how relations between individuals and groups should be arranged, and what the limits of differentiation should be.

In adopting a line of argument of this order Hegel is distanced from extreme liberal — libertarian — conceptions of the state according to which, as Nozick,[45] for example, has argued, the just distribution of resources within a society is that which is the historical outcome of purportedly free negotiations between private individuals with the right to dispose of their property as they wish. With greater realism, Hegel recognises that the 'structural' conditions of civil society substantially undermine the condition of free competition and negotiation; consequently standards of justice and equality stand opposed to the 'natural' outcome of the competitive process, and the means to securing those standards requires extensive state power.

Of course, liberal individualists have also been concerned with the phenomenon of equality,[46] and have been concerned, sometimes, with showing that principles of liberal freedom are closely bound up with notions of equality, and in ways not recognised by other liberals. Hegel's arguments are not unconnected with claims about what individuals have a right to expect and what it is reasonable for society to do on their behalf. But these justifying grounds are closely tied to more general — universal — claims about the *form of life* it is rational to enjoy. The regulation of inequalities constitutes an adjustment in the relations holding between individuals and groups and is an expression of a universal ethical concern for living under one form of life as opposed to another. The justification for a particular policy rests upon the claim that it is consistent with a set of values and norms embodying the common will. A policy is justified by reference to criteria of appropriateness in respect of one form of life against another. This clearly establishes the obligation of citizens to recognise and respect the principles of that form of life, even when their own interests are adversely affected. In this respect Hegel established the independent moral claims of the public interest, something which individualists find hard to do[47] since they are disposed to think of the public interest as reducible to private interests and as a means to them.

Nevertheless, despite the independent moral claims of the public interest, it has no force independent of, or in abstraction from, particular interests and opinions. The conduct of the state, and indeed its organisation, is dependent upon this principle. Thus,

> a state will be well constituted and internally powerful if the private interest of its citizens coincides with the general end of the state, so that the one can be satisfied and realised through the other; this proposition is an extremely important one. But for the state to achieve this unity, numerous institutions must be set up and appropriate mechanisms invented and the understanding must go through prolonged struggles before it discovers what is in fact appropriate.[48]

Hegel does not develop a theory of parties and pressure groups, and on some grounds is opposed to them. However, his argument moves in that direction. For example, he supports representative institutions as a medium for the expression of people's opinions. In the *Proceedings of the Estates Assembly in Wurtemberg* he claims:

> There surely cannot be a greater spectacle on earth than that of a monarch's adding to the public authority, which *ab initio* is entirely in his hands, another foundation, indeed *the* foundation, by bringing his people into it as an essentially effective ingredient.[49]

What is at work here is a principle that can, simply, be referred to as the principle of *taking into account*. That is to say, the determination of the public interest must take into account a consideration of private interests and opinions. From a liberal individualist point of view the principle of taking into account is clearly not sufficiently strong since it does not make the public interest a means to private interests, but rather takes the latter as an aspect of the determination of the former. But it does meet, to some extent, the typical individualist objection that Hegelianism is not, and cannot be, concerned with private interests, and that it subordinates them to some trans-subjective purpose. And if we accept the view, argued for by Hegel, that individualism is conspicuously unsuccessful in generating workable notions of the public interest, then the principle of taking into account does have some minimal intuitive appeal, and is consistent with ordinary conceptions of what it means, at least in part, to recognise the importance of individual interests.[50]

VI. Conclusion

In Chapter 2 above, Benn and Gaus identify what are taken to be certain organicist elements within the liberal tradition, existing uneasily alongside liberalism's dominant individualist orientation. I have attempted to show, however, that while Hegel's position is fundamentally non-individualist, it does depend upon, and involves the integration of, a number of ostensibly individualist claims. This, in turn, implies a criticism of the classification, to be found in Benn and Gaus, of Hegel as an organicist when by that is meant a position opposed to and discontinuous with individualism. While Hegel's philosophy has organicist elements, his theory of society cannot be depicted exclusively in those terms, as if he was concerned only with the 'wholeness' of a society, with the organic relations holding between individuals, and with the relational as opposed to aggregative aspects of society. Although he is indeed deeply concerned with these, he is also concerned with the respects in which the organic aspect of society is meshed with the individualistic, with the independent claims of private interests, and with the expression of subjective opinion. The aggregative conception of society is not entirely dispensed with, but is rather incorporated into a broader conception. Particularity is not eliminated, but rather integrated, as an essential 'moment' of the whole. Society is as much an association of free persons as it is an integrated organic whole. Thus, on this view, individualism and organicism are not two opposed and discontinuous theoretical perspectives. They are, on the contrary, both aspects of, and necessary conditions for, a more comprehensive, and thereby more adequate, conceptualisation of society.

Notes

I am indebted to S.I. Benn and G.F. Gaus for their careful and constructive comments on an earlier draft of this chapter.

1. Isaiah Berlin has, in his various writings, stressed what he takes to be the incommensurability of human values and the need to recognise the value, in a liberal society, of a plurality of values. See Bernard Williams's 'Introduction' to I. Berlin, *Concepts and Categories* (Hogarth Press, London, 1978), p. xvii.

2. It is one of the theses of Sheldon S. Wolin's admirable book *Politics and Vision* (Little, Brown and Co., Boston and Toronto, 1960) that the liberal tradition has undermined the concept of the state. See also C.B. Macpherson, 'Do We Need a Theory of the State?', *Archives européennes de sociologie*, XVIII, no. 2 (1977), pp. 223-44.

3. For example, the idea of functional representation is difficult to square with Hegel's views on subjectivity and the rights of particularity, and renders his ideas uncongenial to those insisting on the need for a full franchise and the full expression of individual political equality.

4. See Benn and Gaus, above, Ch. 2, §IV (4), at p. 61.

5. See the citations from Hegel and Hobhouse by Benn and Gaus, ibid., §III.A, at p. 50.

6. Ibid.

7. Ibid., §III.E, at p. 57.

8. For a recent restatement of the individualist position see Philip Pettit, *Judging Justice* (Routledge and Kegan Paul, London 1980), Pt. II, Chs. 5-7.

9. G.W.F. Hegel, *Philosophy of Right*, T.M. Knox (trans.) (Clarendon Press, Oxford, 1967), § 260.

10. G.W.F. Hegel, *Natural Law* (Pennsylvania, 1975), p. 119.

11. See Ch. 2, above, §II.D, p. 41. Steven Lukes has expressed objections to individualism in the following way: 'The abstract conception of the individual ... directly contradicts all the accumulated lessons of sociology and social anthropology and of social psychology', *Individualism* (Basil Blackwell, Oxford, 1973), p. 151.

12. See Pettit, *Judging Justice*, p. 62.

13. The social, and also evaluative, character of interests is stressed by W.E. Connolly in *The Terms of Political Discourse* (D.C. Heath, Ontario, 1974), Ch. 2.

14. For a discussion of Hegel on the relational character of reality, see Bertell Ollman, *Alienation: Marx's Conception of Man in Capitalist Society* (Cambridge University Press, Cambridge, 1971), pp. 32-34.

15. For example, I can claim to be acting as a self-conscious agent when putting a cross on a ballot paper as long as I understand the meaning of voting. But this need not involve understanding the full implications and complexities of democratic theory and practice. (I am indebted to S.I. Benn and G.F. Gaus for this example, and for their help in clarifying the issues involved.)

16. G.W.F. Hegel, *History of Philosophy* (London, 1896), vol. 1, p. 358.

17. See, for example, Hegel, *Philosophy of Right*, §184. In this respect Hegel shares much with the individualist tradition. Benn and Gaus indicate how 'the notion of specifiable individuals, each going about his own business ... leads naturally to a conception of a network of private relations developing among them'. Consequently, the idea of civil society becomes important (Ch. 2, above, §II.D, p. 41). And for Hegel, civil society is a crucial aspect of contemporary social experience because of the emergence of the private person with recognisable rights and interests.
18. Hegel, *Philosophy of Right*, §154.
19. G.W.F. Hegel, *Rechtsphilosophie* (4 vols., Fromann-Holzboog, Stuttgart-Bach Cannstaat, 1974), vol. 3, p. 501.
20. Hegel, *Philosophy of Right*, §184.
21. G.W.F. Hegel, *Political Writings* (Clarendon Press, Oxford, 1964), p. 159.
22. Hegel, *Philosophy of Right*, §189.
23. Ibid., §187.
24. See Benn and Gaus, above, Ch. 2, §II.D, p. 42.
25. Hegel, *Philosophy of Right*, §183.
26. Ibid., §187.
27. See Benn and Gaus, above, Ch. 2, §II.A, pp. 33-34, for the importance of personhood in individualism.
28. G.W.F. Hegel, *Lectures on the Philosophy of World History*, H.B. Nisbet (trans.) (Cambridge University Press, 1975), p. 116.
29. See Wolin, *Politics and Vision*, Ch. IX.
30. Hegel, *Philosophy of Right*, §257.
31. For a full discussion see A.K. Sen, *Collective Choice and Social Welfare* (Holden Day, San Francisco, 1970).
32. See G.W. Mortimore, 'Rational Social Choice', in *Rationality and the Social Sciences*, S.I. Benn and G.W. Mortimore (eds.) (Routledge and Kegan Paul, London, 1976).
33. J.J.C. Smart and B. Williams, *Utilitarianism: For and Against* (Cambridge University Press, Cambridge, 1973), pp. 136-37. Utilitarianism's commitment to treating moral disputes as essentially factual ones is identified by Alan Ryan in his discussion of John Stuart Mill, *J.S. Mill* (Routledge and Kegan Paul, London, 1974), p. 130.
34. Hegel, *Philosophy of Right*, §17.
35. Ibid. §19.
36. The connection between interests and morality, against utilitarianism, is discussed by John Plamenatz, 'Interests', *Political Studies*, II (1954), pp. 1-8.
37. See above, p. 253.
38. Ibid.
39. Hegel, *Philosophy of Right*, §257.
40. Ibid., §187.
41. I am indebted to Professor K.-H. Ilting of the University of the Saarland for drawing my attention to the possibility of a 'welfarist' reading of Hegel's conception of the state.
42. Hegel, *Philosophy of Right*, §244.
43. Ibid., §242.
44. Ibid.
45. Robert Nozick, *Anarchy, State, and Utopia* (Basil Blackwell, Oxford, 1980).
46. See Amy Gutmann, *Liberal Equality* (Cambridge University Press, Cambridge, 1980).
47. For discussion of some of the problems confronted by individualists, see Benn and Gaus, above, Ch. 2, §II.E.

48. Hegel, *Lectures on the Philosophy of World History*, p. 73. See also Shlomo Avineri, *Hegel's Theory of the Modern State* (Cambridge University Press, London, 1973), p. 163.

49. Hegel, *Political Writings*, p. 251.

50. The paradigm historical example of the failure to recognise the claims of individuals and to subordinate them unremittingly to the power of the state is, in Hegel's view, the Roman World. The most reliable and full source of Hegel's views on this period is to be found in K.-H. Ilting's as-yet-unpublished edition of the *Philosophy of History*, based upon the lecture notes of a number of Hegel's students. There it is made clear that the Roman World exhibits 'abstract universality'; that is, a universality which is not rooted in and integrated with particular interests and subjective judgements, but, rather, imposed upon them by the power of the state.

11 PUBLIC/PRIVATE IN MARXIST THEORY AND MARXIST PRACTICE

Eugene Kamenka

I. Overcoming Man's Alienation

'Man is born free; and everywhere he is in chains. One thinks himself the master of others, and still remains a greater slave than they.' So Rousseau wrote in *The Social Contract*. It was for the sake of liberating men from these chains (chains which Rousseau thought could be made 'legitimate') that Marx became a radical critic of society; it was in the name of freedom, and not of security, that Marx turned to communism. The vision before his eyes, from his youth onward, was that of the creative, self-determined man, master of his environment, of the universe, and of himself, co-operating, spontaneously and harmoniously, with all other men as 'aspects' of the human spirit liberated within him. 'Dignity', the young Marx wrote in a secondary school essay, 'can be afforded only by that position in which we do not appear as servile instruments';[1] 'the criticism of religion', he said in the *Deutsch-französische Jahrbücher* nine years later (1844), 'ends in the teaching that *man is the highest being for man*, it ends, i.e., with the categorical imperative to overthrow all conditions in which man is a debased, forsaken, contemptible being forced into servitude'.[2] Communism, for Marx, meant neither the mere abolition of poverty nor that abstract application of fairness which he rejected so scathingly in his *Critique of the Gotha Programme* (1875) — the triumph of distributive justice in social affairs. Least of all did Marx see communism as a form of state socialism in which governmental or 'representative' power and authority replaced individual power and authority over men. Ultimately more consistent than Rousseau, Marx implicitly rejected any possible justification for the 'chains' that bind men together; in the belief that Rousseau's general, universal will could and would flower in history, Marx confidently predicted that all social chains would wither away. Communism would be the society of freedom, in which man became the subject and ceased to be the object of power. No longer would man's nature and actions be determined by something outside himself, either by the state, society, man's social situation, his animal needs, or by other men. No longer would man's fellow human beings confront him as competitors, enslaving him and themselves to the inexorable demands of competitive economic life. For the first time in human history, society, technology and the whole range of human conduct and relations would become expressions of man's true being and cease to be limitations upon that being. In his own life, man would find that true and ultimate freedom which is the necessary destiny of man; in other men he would find partners in that spontaneous but cooperative creativity that distinguishes man as a universal and social being from the animal as a limited and particular one. Man would become praxis – the subject and not the object of history.

'The critique of society which forms the substance of Marx's work', the French Marxologist Maximilien Rubel has reminded us, 'has, essentially, two targets: the State and Money.'[3] The state, for Marx, was the visible, institutionalised expression of political power over men; money, both the visible means and the secret but indispensable ground of the more fundamental and pervasive economic power over men. If Marx was concerned with the critique of politics and economics, it was because he saw in these critiques the key to understanding the human condition and grasping the necessary foundations for the elimination of power over men.

In Marx's earlier works, especially in his contributions to the *Deutsch-französische Jahrbücher*, in his *Economic and Philosophical Manuscripts* of 1844 and in the *German Ideology* that he wrote with Engels in 1845-46, we are presented with an analysis of the nature and foundations of human dependence that many socialist humanists see as subtler and less dated than the crude class theory of human dependence which Marx's vulgarising disciples drew out of his popular political pamphlets. In these earlier works, Marx made it clear that he did not see man enslaved simply by other men: the citizen by a dictatorial police state, the worker by a greedy and grasping capitalist. All past and present social systems may resolve themselves, from one point of view, into systems made up of masters and slaves – but the masters are no more free than the slaves; both live in a relationship of mutual hostility and of insurmountable mutual dependence; both are governed by the system that makes them play out their allotted roles, whether they will or not. Marx saw this dependence as arising 'naturally' from the division of labour and the consequent introduction of private ownership. But the possibilities of intensifying dependence, of alienating man from his work, his products and his fellow human beings, were vastly increased with the rise of money as a universal medium of exchange. Money –

into which everything can be converted — made everything saleable, and enabled man to separate from himself not only his goods, the product of his work, but even his work itself, which he could now sell to another.

> Money lowers all the gods of mankind and transforms them into a commodity. Money is the universal, self-constituting value of all things. It has therefore robbed the whole world, both the human world and nature, of its own peculiar value. Money is the essence of man's work and existence, alienated from man, and this alien essence dominates him and he prays to it.[4]

Man's alienation, for Marx, was expressed in the fact that man's forces, products and creations — all those things that are extensions of man's personality and should serve directly to enrich it — are split off from man; they acquire independent status and power and turn back on man to dominate him as his master. It is he who becomes their servant. As the division of labour, the use of money and the growth of private property increase, man's alienation becomes more acute, reaching its highest point in modern capitalist society. Here the worker is alienated from his product, from the work that he sells on the 'labour market', from other men who confront him as capitalists exploiting his labour or as workers competing for jobs, and from nature and society which confront him as limitations and not as fulfilments of his personality. [For a development of this aspect of Marx's critique of private property, see Alan Ryan's Ch. 9, above, pp. 237ff. — Eds.] It is this alienation — expressed in the intellectual field by the compartmentalisation of the science of man and society into the 'abstract' study of economic man, legal man, ethical man, etc. which Marx portrays vividly in his *Economic and Philosophical Manuscripts*:

> The more riches the worker produces, the more his production increases in power and scope, the poorer he becomes. The more commodities a worker produces, the cheaper a commodity he becomes. The devaluation of the world of men proceeds in direct proportion to the exploitation of the values of the world of things. Labour not only produces commodities, but it turns itself and the worker into commodities.[5]

Not only the products of man's work, but the very activity of this work are alienated from man. The source of all the distinctions between the savage and the civilised man, Rousseau wrote, 'is that the savage lives within himself, while social man lives constantly outside himself, and only knows how to live in the opinion of others, so that he seems to receive the consciousness of his own existence from the judgement of others concerning him'.[6] Marx, in his early (and, I would argue, in his later) work sought to show the necessary foundation of this alienation in economic life, in a division of labour organised on the basis of private property, in the use of money that makes it possible to convert all things, even labour and care and affection and love, into commodities that are bought and sold. For Marx the division of labour and private property was, of course, inevitable, even necessary, at a certain period of history — only through it could man develop his capacities and realise his limitless potentialities. The savage had not yet separated his labour from himself, had not yet learned to produce for any purpose but use; but in his desperate struggle to satisfy his basic (animal) needs, in his pitiful dependence on nature, he was also man in bondage. To master nature and to overcome human alienation — in these achievements lies the key to the freedom of man. Capitalism has done the former; socialism, Marx believed, would accomplish the latter.

At the end of his *Economic and Philosophical Manuscripts* of 1844, Marx painted a picture of the communist society, the society of true and ultimate human freedom. Sympathetic critics have called it the picture of a society of artists, creating freely and consciously, working together in spontaneous and perfect harmony. In such a society, Marx believed, there would be no state, no criminals, no conflicts, no need for punitive authority and coercive rules. Each man would be 'caught up' in productive labour with other men, fulfilling himself in social, co-operative creation. The struggle would be a common struggle: in his work, and in other men, man would find not dependence and unpleasantness, but freedom and satisfaction, just as artists find inspiration and satisfaction in their own work and in the work of other artists. Truly free men rising above the very conception of property will thus need no rules imposed from above, no moral exhortations to do their duty, no 'authorities' laying down what is to be done. Art cannot be created by plans imposed from outside; it knows no authorities and no discipline except the authority and discipline of art itself. What is true of art, Marx believed, is true of all free, productive labour. Just as true communism, for Marx, is not that crude 'communism' which 'is so much under the sway of *material* property, that it wants to destroy everything which cannot be owned by everybody as *private property*; it wants *forcibly* to cut away talent, etc.';[7] so 'free labour', for Marx, is not 'mere fun, mere amusement, as Fourier thinks with all the naïveté of a *grisette*. Truly free labour, e.g. composition, is every bit as much damned serious labour, is the most intensive exertion'.[8]

The vision of communism outlined here, I believe, remained with Marx all his life. It comes out clearly in the *German Ideology* of 1845-46, in the notes and drafts he made between 1850 and 1859, in his *Critique of the Gotha Programme* in 1875. It runs through all three volumes of *Das Kapital*. It is a vision of freedom, of spontaneous co-operation, of men's conscious self-determination once they are freed from dependence and need. It is not merely a vision of economic plenty or social security.

II. Marx's Theory of Communism – Transcending the Public/Private Distinction

The concept of alienation underlies Marx's treatment of the distinction between private and public as it underlies much of the rest of his work. Marx himself does not discuss the issue directly and systematically; his references are generally to the distinction between the individual and the social and, in his early work, to the distinction between the particular and the universal. Even then, they are references rather than discussions. But a coherent position emerges – a position that takes its departure from the philosophy of Hegel, which sees particularity as a form of incompleteness, dependence, lack of 'true' reality.

The vindication of man, for Marx, meant the vindication of man as a universal being, as sharing a common character or essence with all other human beings. Being free for Marx meant being self-determined, that is, determined by this universal human character which, because it was universal, could be developed harmoniously and without contradiction or conflict, internally or with other human beings. Particularity, that which distinguished one human being from another, was, according to the young Marx, the product of external determination, of limitation, failure to develop fully differences in social location. Freedom meant the overcoming of that sort of particularity and the recognition of all human activities as in principle possible to every human being and as in fact conducive to his welfare and development even when performed by others 'on his behalf'. The general will, which was not the sum of particular wills but the outcome of man's essential and universal character, would determine all man's actions and relationships. The tension, even the very distinction between the individual and the social, between the private and the public, would disappear. So would the distinction between one person and another as a distinction important for social theory. Man would be replaced by mankind.

This is the view of the young, in many ways still naïvely philosophical, Marx. It is not repeated in that form in his later work, though there are many echoes of this view that make it clear that an unexamined version of it continued to underlie some of his most basic beliefs and hopes. In 1843-44, as his philosophical critique of society acquired more social content, he developed two additional lines of approach. The first, drawing to some extent on the work of Ludwig Feuerbach, rejected the concept of man as an abstract individual, capable of being understood without reference to other human beings. Feuerbach had argued that the three most basic human activities – love, reasoning and speech – all depended on the recognition of and relation to other human beings. Marx insisted, with equal plausibility, that Robinson Crusoe was conceivable only as a social product, as someone reared in society and *then* cast away. A human being raised outside society would not be recognisably human. Man is always social. Nothing is private in the sense of being outside society or of no social concern.

Much of Marx's social criticism in 1843 and 1844 was concerned with the question of the state as an alleged or self-proclaimed public power confronting the individualism and egoism of man in his 'private' pursuits, in the 'civil society' of industry and trade. Hegel had argued that the state and its bureaucracy as bearers of public rationality were needed to prevent the egoism of man and civil society from ending in mutual self-destruction: the state was thus the necessary completion and complementation of civil society; the public was necessary to secure, guarantee and order the private. Marx argued on the one hand that there could be no completion of civil society by an external repressive state; civil society could become coherent only by becoming itself rational, human, universal, through being transformed into the human community. The alienation of civil society was made worse and not better by driving this alienation further and separating man's public being – the state – from man's private pursuits and setting one against the other. At the same time, the separating out of the public as a specific, partial power – the state and its bureaucracy, distinct from the rest of society – enabled the state and its bureaucracy to become or to be captured by sectional interests. The state, in short, was only an illusory semblance of public power; it was in fact another, partial, particular, private power. By 1845, Marx had developed this into the view that the state was merely the representative of the ruling class in society and helpless before civil society, before the economic life of man. With the abolition of private property and the division of labour, with the overcoming of alienation, the separation between state and civil society, between the public and the private, would disappear. The contradiction between the individual and the social, Marx wrote, was a contradiction that belonged to bourgeois society — for even feudalism had not yet perfected alienation to the extent of consummating a divorce between the private and the public, the individual and the social. Thirty years later, he still believed that true communism would mean the overcoming of the narrow horizons of bourgeois right (or law).

There are two senses in which Marx and his collaborator Engels, and many subsequent Marxists, totally rejected the postulation of a distinction between the public and the private. They did not believe that anything was private in the sense of not being socially conditioned and of not impinging on others in society — though Engels inclined to the view that the exclusiveness or non-exclusiveness of sexual relations between adults were in a socialist society of no concern to others: a view not shared by the rulers of any Marxist-socialist society since and not endorsed by Marx. They also believed that public power as a coercive power confronting individuals as something external would disappear. The state and law would wither away; rational self-regulation by working groups, teams, communities would take their place. Lenin's *State and Revolution* is the *locus classicus* for the enthusiastic development of this view of the ultimate communist society — a view totally out of step with Lenin's subsequent practice, in its very real concern with and understanding for state power and his constant rejection of decentralisation, worker-control or utopian experiments as a *path* toward communism.

Even many of those who have had a nagging suspicion that Marx's view of ultimate communism may be excessively utopian have found force and point in Marx's use of the concept of alienation to characterise modern commercial society, with its elevation of the abstract individual and its tendency toward the 'privatisation' of all social relations. The German sociologist Ferdinand Tönnies,[9] in part consciously influenced by Marx, strikingly developed Marx's contrast between the commercial, divisive society of capitalism and the unalienated society of communism into a sociological category, the contrast between the commercial, divisive *Gesellschaft* and the organic fellowship of the *Gemeinschaft*. *Gesellschaft* is the bourgeois commercial society in which the cash nexus tends to drive out all other social ties and relationships, in which men become bound only by contract and commercial exchange, in which the city dominates the country and the trading class converts the whole land into a market, in which the 'common, social sphere' is based on the fleeting moment when men meet in barter, when they have what the law of contract calls 'a [transitory] meeting of minds'. The 'common sphere' of the *Gemeinschaft*, on the other hand, rests on a natural harmony, on the ties of tradition, friendship, and the common acceptance of a religious order; production is primarily agricultural and for use, society is based on status relations that prevent any man from treating another 'abstractly'. In the *Gemeinschaft* men are essentially united in spite of all separating factors; they act on each other's behalf. In the *Gesellschaft* they are essentially separated in spite of all uniting factors; here every man is isolated and by himself, other men confront him as competitors and alien intruders.

The conception of *anything* as private, as standing outside society or as prior to it, as unrelated to other people and of no concern to them, or as resting on the rights and claims of single persons, most Marxists and many socialists have believed is a dangerous illusion, theoretically confused and vicious in its practical consequences.

III. Marxist Practice

The development of Marxism since Marx, and the coming to power, in various countries, of Marxist-Leninist regimes, have not been accompanied by any deepening or extended working out of Marxist conceptions or critiques of the distinction between public and private. The main thrust has been to continue rejecting the elevation of any socially important conception of the private at all. Socialism began as a critique of 'bourgeois' individualism and insisted that property must be converted from a private right to a public function. Marxists, more than most socialists, also elevated the collective — giving it moral and historical primacy over the individual and arguing that it was only in and through the collective that any individual could realise his potentialities. In the period of War Communism after the Russian Revolution, from 1918 to 1921, there were theoreticians and ideological militants who took these doctrines very seriously indeed. A concern with privacy, let alone with private rights or individual satisfactions, was condemned as a bourgeois hangover (if not worse) and as totally alien to the collective spirit, culture and morality of peasants and workers. One extremist, professing to be inspired by the thought of Lenin and Trotsky, argued that housing for the people should contain no divisions into separate rooms; the, according to him admittedly necessary, privacy for the act of love could be catered for in specially designed accommodation to be placed in public parks. Communes, both urban and rural, in which members shared all possessions were extolled, though they never became an important feature of Soviet life. Educational theory, especially that of A.N. Makarenko, emphasised the social character of learning and the moral importance of teaching the child to subordinate its will to that of the collective. Moral theory emphasised selfless devotion to things outside the individual – the collective, the Party, the Fatherland, the international proletariat, the coming worldwide Revolution. Means and individuals were consistently subordinated to ends – except in and through the collective struggle for those ends, the individual was nothing.

Ideology is one thing, reality and the consequent practice another. The period of War Communism, with its Civil War, anarchy and disorder, was followed by a New Economic Policy which, as a transitional means of building socialism, restored a form of licensed and limited capitalism, recognising private property – if not in the major factors of production – and private rights, though always insisting that these guarantees were conditional upon support for the socialist system and upon these not being used to subvert its social purpose. The rights of the individual guaranteed by the new law codes of 1922-26 and by subsequent constitutions and codes were all seen as granted by the state, as derived from society and its purposes and not from the nature or integrity of the individual. While a code of private law – the Civil Code of 1922 – was one of the first codes promulgated, and while it followed fairly closely the provisions of 'bourgeois' European codes, Soviet theoreticians insisted that these codes were transitional and that the distinction between private and public law could not be central or lasting in Soviet society. Private law, E.B. Pashukanis argued, was based on the fundamental conception of a conflict of interests; in a fully socialist society, there would be unity of purpose and a need for policies and administration, but not for law. (See Ch. 3, above, pp. 80 and 84-86, for a more extended account of Pashukanis's theory of law.)

In China under Mao, and especially in the period of the Great Proletarian Cultural Revolution from 1966 to 1969, these views were promulgated just as strongly, if not even more so. The individual could find himself only through the collective. A radical egalitarianism must be pushed, and pushed by force and violence, even after the revolution, to prevent the re-emergence of classes, inequalities and private interest. Communes were organised on a grand scale, for a time indeed with the enforced separation of sexes in separate mass sleeping areas for at least six days out of seven, to break up the individualistic and bourgeois family; in some communes special cubicles were built so that couples could meet briefly for sex and not require separate sleeping accommodation. The taunting, physical beating and 'sending to the country' of those who displayed individualistic traits, reservations or preferences in the face of this radical levelling are well known.

The distinctive character of Marxism as a political philosophy, apart from its insistence on the revolution as the only path to socialism and its more systematic ambitions, lay in its principled and thoroughgoing rejection of individualism and of any private realm in social affairs. Many, indeed, saw the revolution as not only inevitable but as necessary for the wholesale destruction of the bourgeois individualist values of the old world. There was, as George Kline has remarked,[10] a Nietzschean strain in Marxism, especially in Russian Marxism, which called for the transformation and reassessment of all values. Some of the Nietzscheans emphasised the element of individual self-expression, others that of immersion in the collective. In the hours of revolutionary enthusiasm in Russia, in the Germany of 1919, in the China of 1949, 1958 and 1966, the collectivists always won.

Marxist-Leninist regimes, nevertheless, have been concerned with maintaining power in actual, historical societies. None have found a thoroughgoing collectivism or the communitarian ideal a maintainable basis for policy over more than a few years. The collectivism in both Russia and China, and in communist parties generally, quickly became a means of disciplining and mobilising the masses for goals external to them, rather than a means for achieving communal self-expression. The Kronstadt sailors and workers who had played a heroic role in the Revolution of 1917 were ruthlessly suppressed in 1921 when they called for the rule of Soviets and not of parties. Mao is no longer a prophet honoured in his own country and he himself had drawn back from the consequences of his policies.

The development of ideology in communist regimes is a complex story, closely tied to internal economic, social and political problems, faction fights, personalities and a constantly changing external situation. Nevertheless, certain general trends are clear. No communist theoreticians, let alone rulers, now believe that law and the state will wither away in a historical future and be replaced by communal self-administration. All communist regimes in the last twenty-five years have made important concessions to 'private' realms in society. In the Soviet Union, the thoroughgoing commune was never favoured by the authorities. The people attracted to communes tended to be unstable and have poor work habits; in any case, their lifestyle offended the peasants the regime was trying to win to its cause or to acquiescence in the new social order. The collective farm favoured by the authorities, and in the horrible years of 1929-32 imposed by force, maintained the integrity of the private peasant household, with its furniture and personal possessions, including basic tools, and conceded a small plot of land as a kitchen garden. The story of Soviet and Chinese agriculture has been the story of increasing attempts to raise agricultural productivity by increasing the size of private plots and extending the right to sell in the private free market. Marxist theory has been amended or 'clarified' to explain that the abolition of private property under communism did not mean the abolition of personal property – which can be owned, sold and inherited and which includes housing for use, savings, tools and machines the owner works himself and, with certain limitations, private plots for agricultural purposes. More important in a theoretical sense were the developments associated with de-Stalinisation – an elevation, partly by Khrushchev himself and even more so by Soviet writers and moral theorists, of the importance of the individual and of intra-personal relations: kindliness, sincerity, compassion, love of truth.[11] The same path is being followed by the Chinese today. The view that the individual finds himself and can only find himself in the collective is not promulgated even at official level, where theoreticians call for a balance – rather than a harmony – between social and individual considerations. Marxist ethics has been reinterpreted to allow for certain ethical values that are all-human, not class-based, though they may be class-distorted, and which are ultimate values, not to be justified as means to an end.[12] The same view is now being taken by an increasing number of theorists about law and even about the state which is seen as serving, in any age, certain public moral and administrative functions that cannot simply be reduced to class interest and class rule. (See the discussion of recent trends in Soviet and Chinese legal theory, in Ch. 3, above, pp. 80-81.) The stage for a much more conventional 'liberal' discussion of the relation between public and private is set – though the discussion is certainly not encouraged and though there are strong countervailing trends in the direction of seeing both law and morality as means of social administration, of securing the pre-eminence of the alleged 'public' interests over now-recognised but still-subordinated 'private' interests. The Eurocommunists, under fewer constraints than Soviet theoreticians or Polish Party leaders, proclaim with the Spanish Communist Manuel Azcárate that 'capitalist society should be transformed into socialist society with full respect for political freedoms, human rights, trade union freedom, religious and cultural freedom. Moreover, this change should be made through universal suffrage, which means obviously that if a coalition in favour of socialism is defeated in elections, it must resign.'[13] The socialist transformation envisaged by Azcárate will bring about an end to the oligarchy of banking and financial interests; it will put emphasis on self-management and bringing democracy into social and economic life, and not only into politics, as with capitalism. But the economic transformation, according to him, will be based on the coexistence of a public sector and a sector of private enterprise consisting mainly of small and medium-size enterprises, necessary for the efficient delivery of certain products and services.

With that, any distinctive Marxist contribution to the question of distinguishing public and private realms in the economy, in law, morals and politics, is indeed at an end and intelligent Marxists are back where we all are: balancing interests, whether public, private or sectional, and usually a mixture of all of these.

Notes

1. From 'Considerations of a Young Man on Choosing a Career', in *Marx-Engels Werke [MEW]* (Dietz Verlag, Berlin, 1957-68), Ergänzungsbd. pt. 1, p. 523.

2. From 'Contribution to the Critique of Hegel's Philosophy of Right: Introduction', *MEW*, vol. 1, p. 385. Cf. also *The Portable Karl Marx*, E. Kamenka (ed.) (Viking-Penguin, New York, in press), p. 119.

3. Maximilien Rubel, 'Le concept de démocratie chez Marx', in *Contrat Social*, vol. VI, no. 4 (1960).

4. 'On the Jewish Question', in *MEW*, vol. 1, pp. 374-75.

5. 'Economic and Philosophical Manuscripts of 1844', First Manuscript, in *MEW*, Ergänzungsbd. 1, p. 511. Cf. also *Portable Karl Marx*, p. 133.

6. J.-J. Rousseau, 'A Discourse on the Origin of Inequality', pt. 2, in *The Social Contract & Discourses*, trans. with introduction by G.D.H. Cole (Everyman's Library, London, 1913), p. 237.

7. 'Economic and Philosophical Manuscripts', Third Manuscript, in *MEW*, p. 534. Cf. also *Portable Karl Marx*, p. 147.

8. *Grundrisse der Kritik der politischen Ökonomie* (Dietz Verlag, Berlin, 1953), p. 505.

9. F. Tönnies, *Gemeinschaft und Gesellschaft* (1887), trans. and supplemented by Charles P. Loomis as *Community and Association* (Routledge & Kegan Paul, London, 1955).

10. See G.L. Kline, 'Changing Attitudes Toward the Individual', in C.E. Black (ed.), *The Transformation of Russian Society* (Harvard University Press, Cambridge, Mass., 1960), pp. 606-25; and G.L. Kline, 'Theoretische Ethik im russischen Frühmarxismus', in *Forschungen zur osteuropäischen Geschichte* 9 (1963), pp. 269-79.

11. See, e.g., Eugene Kamenka, 'Soviet Writing and the Party', in *Current Affairs Bulletin* 32 (1963), pp. 67-80.

12. See Eugene Kamenka, *Marxism and Ethics* (Macmillan, London, and St. Martin's Press, New York, 1969), Ch. VI.

13. Manuel Azcárate, 'The Present State of Eurocommunism: Its Main Features, Political and Theoretical', in Richard Kindersley (ed.), *In Search of Eurocommunism* (Macmillan, London, 1981), pp. 24-25.

12 FEMINIST CRITIQUES OF THE PUBLIC/PRIVATE DICHOTOMY

Carole Pateman

The dichotomy between the private and the public is central to almost two centuries of feminist writing and political struggle; it is, ultimately, what the feminist movement is about. Although some feminists treat the dichotomy as a universal, trans-historical and trans-cultural feature of human existence, feminist criticism is primarily directed at the separation and opposition between the public and private spheres in liberal theory and practice.

The relationship between feminism and liberalism is extremely close but also exceedingly complex. The roots of both doctrines lie in the emergence of individualism as a general theory of social life; neither liberalism nor feminism is conceivable without some conception of individuals as free and equal beings, emancipated from the ascribed, hierarchical bonds of traditional society. But if liberalism and feminism share a common origin, their adherents have often been opposed over the past two hundred years. The direction and scope of feminist criticism of liberal conceptions of the public and the private have varied greatly in different phases of the feminist movement. An analysis of this criticism is made more complicated because liberalism is inherently ambiguous about the 'public' and the 'private', and feminists and liberals disagree about where and why the dividing line is to be drawn between the two spheres, or, according to certain contemporary feminist arguments, whether it should be drawn at all.

Feminism is often seen as nothing more than the completion of the liberal or bourgeois revolution, as an extension of liberal principles and rights to women as well as men. The demand for equal rights has, of course, always been an important part of feminism. However, the attempt to universalise liberalism has more far-reaching consequences than is often appreciated because, in the end, it inevitably challenges liberalism itself.[1] Liberal feminism has radical implications, not least in challenging the separation and opposition between the private and public spheres that is fundamental to liberal theory and practice. The liberal contrast between private and public is more than a distinction between two kinds of social activities. The public sphere, and the principles that govern it, are seen as separate from, or independent of, the relationships in the private sphere. A familiar illustration of this claim is the long controversy between liberal and radical political scientists about participation, the radicals denying the liberal claim that the social inequalities of the private sphere are irrelevant to questions about the political equality, universal suffrage and associated civil liberties of the public realm.

Not all feminists, however, are liberals; 'feminism' goes far beyond liberal-feminism. Other feminists explicitly reject liberal conceptions of the private and public and see the social structure of liberalism as the political problem, not a starting point from which equal rights can be claimed. They have much in common with the radical and socialist critics of liberalism who rely on 'organic' theories (to use Benn and Gaus's terminology) but they differ sharply in their analysis of the liberal state. In short, feminists, unlike other radicals, raise the generally neglected problem of the patriarchal character of liberalism.

I. Liberalism and Patriarchalism

Benn and Gaus's account of the liberal conception of the public and the private (see Ch. 2, above) illustrates very nicely some major problems in liberal theory. They accept that the private and the public are central categories of liberalism, but they do not explain why these two terms are crucial or why the private sphere is contrasted with and opposed to the 'public' rather than the 'political' realm. Similarly, they note that liberal arguments leave it unclear whether civil society is private or public but, although they state that in both of their liberal models the family is paradigmatically private, they fail to pursue the question why, in this case, liberals usually also see civil society as private. Benn and Gaus's account of liberalism also illustrates its abstract, ahistorical character and, in what is omitted and taken for granted, provides a good example of the theoretical discussions that feminists are now sharply criticising. The account bears out Eisenstein's claim that 'the ideology of public and private life' invariably presents 'the division between public and private life, . . . as reflecting the development of the bourgeois liberal state, not the patriarchal ordering of the bourgeois state'.[2]

The term 'ideology' is appropriate here because the profound ambiguity of the liberal conception of the private and public obscures and mystifies the social reality it helps constitute. Feminists argue that liberalism is structured by patriarchal as well as class relations, and that the dichotomy between the private and the public obscures the subjection of women to men within an apparently universal, egalitarian and individualist order. Benn and Gaus's account assumes that the reality of our social life is more or less adequately captured in liberal conceptions. They do not recognise that 'liberalism' is patriarchal-liberalism and that the separation and opposition of the public and private spheres is an unequal opposition between women and men. They thus take the talk of 'individuals' in liberal theory at face value although, from the period when the social contract theorists attacked the patriarchalists, liberal theorists have excluded women from the scope of their apparently universal arguments.[3] One reason why the exclusion goes unnoticed is that the separation of the private and public is presented in liberal theory as if it applied to all individuals in the same way. It is often claimed — by anti-feminists today, but by feminists in the nineteenth century, most of whom accepted the doctrine of 'separate spheres' — that the two spheres are separate, but equally important and valuable. The way in which women and men are differentially located within private life and the public world is, as I shall indicate, a complex matter, but underlying a complicated reality is the belief that women's natures are such that they are properly subject to men and their proper place is in the private, domestic sphere. Men properly inhabit, and rule within, both spheres. The essential feminist argument is that the doctrine of 'separate but equal', and the ostensible individualism and egalitarianism of liberal theory, obscure the patriarchal reality of a social structure of inequality and the domination of women by men.

In theory, liberalism and patriarchalism stand irrevocably opposed to each other. Liberalism is an individualist, egalitarian, conventionalist doctrine; patriarchalism claims that hierarchical relations of subordination necessarily follow from the natural characteristics of men and women. In fact, the two doctrines were successfully reconciled through the answer given by the contract theorists in the seventeenth century to the subversive question of who counted as free and equal individuals. The conflict with the patriarchalists did not extend to women or conjugal relations; the latter were excluded from individualist arguments and the battle was fought out over the relation of adult sons to their fathers.

The theoretical basis for the liberal separation of the public and the private was provided in Locke's *Second Treatise*. He argued against Filmer that political power is conventional and can justifiably be exercised over free and equal adult individuals only with their consent. Political power must not be confused with paternal power over children in the private, family sphere, which is a natural relationship that ends at the maturity, and hence freedom and equality, of (male) children. Commentators usually fail to notice that Locke's separation of the family and the political is also a sexual division. Although he argued that natural differences between men, such as age or talents, are irrelevant to their political equality, he agrees with Filmer's patriarchal claim that the natural differences between men and women entail the subjection of women to men or, more specifically, wives to husbands. Indeed, in Locke's statement at the beginning of the *Second Treatise* that he will show why political power is distinctive, he takes it for granted that the rule of husbands over wives is included in other (non-political) forms of power. He explicitly agrees with Filmer that a wife's subordination to her husband has a 'Foundation in Nature' and that the husband's will must prevail in the household as he is naturally 'the abler and the stronger'.[4] But a natural subordinate cannot at the same time be free and equal. Thus women (wives) are excluded from the status of 'individual' and so from participating in the public world of equality, consent and convention.

It may appear that Locke's separation of paternal from political power can also be characterised as a separation of the private from the public. In one sense this is so; the public sphere can be seen as encompassing all social life apart from domestic life. Locke's theory also shows how the private and public spheres are grounded in opposing principles of association which are exemplified in the conflicting status of women and men; natural subordination stands opposed to free individualism. The family is based on natural ties of sentiment and blood and on the sexually ascribed status of wife and husband (mother and father). Participation in the public sphere is governed by universal, impersonal and conventional criteria of achievement, interests, rights, equality and property – liberal criteria, applicable only to men. An important consequence of this conception of private and public is that the public world, or civil society, is conceptualised and discussed in liberal theory (indeed, in almost all political theory) in abstraction from, or as separate from, the private domestic sphere.

It is important to emphasise at this point that the contemporary feminist critique of the public-private dichotomy is based on the same Lockean view of the two categories; domestic life is as paradigmatically private for feminists as it is in (this interpretation of) Locke's theory. However, feminists reject the claim that the separation of the private and the public follows inevitably from the natural characteristics of the sexes. They argue that a proper understanding of liberal social life is possible only when it is accepted that the two spheres, the domestic (private) and civil society (public), held to be separate and opposed, are inextricably interrelated; they are the two sides of the single coin of liberal-patriarchalism.

If, at one theoretical level, feminists and liberals are in conflict over a shared conception of the public and the private, at another level they are at odds about these very categories. There is another sense in which the private and public are far from synonymous with Locke's paternal and political power. Precisely because liberalism conceptualises civil society in abstraction from ascriptive domestic life, the latter remains 'forgotten' in theoretical discussion. The separation between private and public is thus re-established as a division *within* civil society itself, within the world of men. The separation is then expressed in a number of different ways, not only private and public but also, for example, 'society' and 'state'; or 'economy' and 'politics'; or 'freedom' and 'coercion'; or 'social' and 'political'.[5] Moreover, in *this* version of the separation of private and public, one category, the private, begins to wear the trousers (to adapt J.L. Austin's patriarchal metaphor for once in an appropriate context). The public or political aspect of civil society tends to get lost, as, for example, Wolin points out in *Politics and Vision*.[6]

The uncertain position of the public sphere develops for very good reason; the apparently universal criteria governing civil society are actually those associated with the liberal conception of the male individual, a conception which is presented as that of *the* individual. The individual is the owner of the property in his person, that is to say, he is seen in abstraction from his ascribed familial relations and those with his fellow men. He is a 'private' individual, but he needs a sphere in which he can exercise his rights and opportunities, pursue his (private) interests and protect and increase his (private) property. If all men ('individuals') are so to act in an orderly fashion, then, as Locke is aware, a public 'umpire' (rather than a hidden – private? – hand), or a representative, liberal state, is required to make and enforce publicly known, equitable laws. Because individualism is, as Benn and Gaus remark, 'the dominant mode of liberal theory and discourse', it is not surprising either that the private and the public appear as the 'obvious' pair of liberal categories, or that the public gets stripped of its trousers and civil society is seen, above all else, as the sphere of private interest, private enterprise and private individuals.[7]

In the late twentieth century the relation between the capitalist economy and the state no longer looks like that between Locke's umpire and civil society and confusion abounds about the boundary between the private and public. But the confusion is unlikely to be remedied from within a theory which 'forgets' that it includes another boundary between private and public. One solution is to reinstate the political in public life. This is the response of Wolin or of Habermas in his rather opaque discussion of the 'principle' of the public sphere, where citizens can form reasoned political judgements.[8] Unlike these theorists, feminist critiques insist that an alternative to the liberal conception must also encompass the relationship between public and domestic life. The question that feminists raise is why the patriarchal character of the separation of a depoliticised public sphere from private life is so easily 'forgotten'; why is the separation of the two worlds located within civil society so that public life is implicitly conceptualised as the sphere of men?

The answer to this question can be found only by examining the history of the connection between the separation of production from the household and the emergence of the family as paradigmatically private. When Locke attacked (one aspect of) patriarchalism, husbands were heads of households but their wives played an active, independent part in numerous areas of production. As capitalism and its specific form of sexual as well as class division of labour developed, however, wives were pushed into a few, low-status areas of employment or kept out of economic life altogether, relegated to their 'natural', dependent, place in the private, familial sphere.[9] Today, despite a large measure of civil equality, it appears natural that wives are subordinate just because they are dependent on their husbands for subsistence, and it is taken for granted that liberal social life can be understood without reference to the sphere of subordination, natural relations and women. The old patriarchal argument from nature and women's nature was thus transformed as it was modernised and incorporated into liberal-capitalism. Theoretical and practical attention became fixed exclusively on the public area, on civil society — on 'the social' or on 'the economy' — and domestic life was assumed irrelevant to social and political theory or the concerns of men of affairs. The fact that patriarchalism is an essential, indeed constitutive, part of the theory and practice of liberalism remains obscured by the apparently impersonal, universal dichotomy between private and public within civil society itself.

The intimate relation between the private and the natural is obscured when, as in Benn and Gaus's account, the private and the public are discussed in abstraction from their historical development and also from other ways of expressing this fundamental structural separation within liberalism. I have already observed that, when the separation is located within civil society, the dichotomy between private and public is referred to in a variety of ways (and a full account of liberalism would have to explain these variations). Similarly, the feminist understanding of the private and the public, and the feminist critique of their separation and opposition, are sometimes presented in these terms, but the argument is also formulated using the categories of nature and culture, or personal and political, or morality and power, and, of course, women and men and female and male. In popular (and academic) consciousness the duality of female and male often serves to encapsulate or represent the series (or circle) of liberal separations and oppositions: female, or − nature, personal, emotional, love, private, intuition, morality, ascription, particular, subjection; male, or − culture, political, reason, justice, public, philosophy, power, achievement, universal, freedom. The most fundamental and general of these oppositions associates women with nature and men with culture, and several contemporary feminists have framed their critiques in these terms.

II. Nature and Culture

Patriarchalism rests on the appeal to nature and the claim that women's natural function of childbearing prescribes their domestic and subordinate place in the order of things. J.S. Mill wrote in the nineteenth century that the depth of the feelings surrounding the appeal to nature was 'the most intense and most deeply-rooted of all those which gather round and protect old institutions and customs'.[10] In the 1980s, when women in the liberal democracies have won citizenship and a large measure of legal equality with men, the arguments of the organised anti-feminist movement illustrate that the appeal to nature has lost none of its resonance. From the seventeenth century a question has been persistently asked by a few female voices: 'If all men are born free, how is it that all women are born slaves?'[11] The usual answer, vigorously presented by Mary Wollstonecraft in the *Vindication of the Rights of Women* in 1792, and today by feminist critics of the sexism of children's books, schooling and the media, is that what are called women's natural characteristics are actually, in Wollstonecraft's phrase, 'artificial', a product of women's education or lack of it. However, even the most radical changes in educational practice will not affect women's natural, biological capacity to bear children. This difference between the sexes is independent of history and culture, and so it is perhaps not surprising that the natural difference, and the opposition between (women's) nature and (men's) culture, has been central to some well-known feminist attempts to explain the apparently universal subordination of women. Arguments focusing on nature/culture fall into two broad categories, the anthropological and the radical feminist.[12]

In one of the most influential anthropological discussions, Ortner argues that the only way to explain why the value universally assigned to women and their activities is lower than that assigned to men and their pursuits is that women are 'a symbol' of all 'that every culture defines as being of a lower order of existence than itself'.[13] That is, women and domestic life symbolise nature. Humankind attempts to transcend a merely natural existence so that nature is always seen as of a lower order than culture. Culture becomes identified as the creation and the world of men because women's biology and bodies place them closer to nature than men, and because their childrearing and domestic tasks, dealing with unsocialised infants and with raw materials, bring them into closer contact with nature. Women and the domestic sphere thus appear inferior to the cultural sphere and male activities, and women are seen as necessarily subordinate to men.

It is unclear whether Ortner is arguing that women's domestic activities symbolise nature, are part of nature or, rather, place women in a mediating position between nature and culture. She argues that the opposition between women/nature and men/culture is itself a cultural construct and not given in nature; 'Woman is not "in reality" any closer to (or further from) nature than man — both have consciousness, both are mortal. But there are certainly reasons why she appears that way.'[14] However, Ortner fails to give sufficient weight to the fundamental fact that men and women are social and cultural beings, or to its corollary that 'nature' always has a social meaning, a meaning that, moreover, varies widely in different societies and in different historical periods. Even if women and their tasks have been universally devalued, it does not follow that we can understand this important fact of human existence by asking questions in universal terms and looking for general answers formulated in terms of universal dichotomies. The distinction between domestic, private women's life and the public world of men does not have the same meaning in pre-modern European society as in present liberal-capitalism, and to see both the latter and hunter-gatherer societies from the perspective of a general opposition between nature and culture, or public and private, can lead only to an emphasis on biology or 'nature'. Rosaldo recently criticised arguments about women's subordination that, like Ortner's, implicitly rest on the question,

'How did it begin?' She points out that to seek a universally applicable answer inevitably opposes 'woman' to 'man', and gives rise to a separation of domestic life from 'culture' or 'society' because of the 'presumably panhuman functions' thus attributed to women.[15]

The most thorough attempt to find a universal answer to the question of why it is that women are in subjection to men, and the most stark opposition between nature and culture, can be found in the writings of the radical feminists who argue that nature is the single cause of men's domination. The best known version of this argument is Firestone's *The Dialectic of Sex*, which also provides an example of how one form of feminist argument, while attacking the liberal separation of private and public, remains within the abstractly individualist framework which helps constitute this division of social life. Firestone reduces the history of the relation between nature and culture or private and public to an opposition between female and male. She argues that the origin of the dualism lies in 'biology itself — procreation',[16] a natural or original inequality that is the basis of the oppression of women and the source of male power. Men, by confining women to reproduction (nature), have freed themselves 'for the business of the world'[17] and so have created and controlled culture. The proposed solution is to eliminate natural differences (inequalities) between the sexes by introducing artificial reproduction. 'Nature' and the private sphere of the family will then be abolished and individuals, of all ages, will interact as equals in an undifferentiated cultural (or public) order.

The popular success of *The Dialectic of Sex* owes more to the need for women to continue to fight for control of their bodies and reproductive capacity than to its philosophical argument. The key assumption of the book is that women necessarily suffer from 'a fundamentally oppressive biological condition',[18] but biology, in itself, is neither oppressive nor liberating; biology, or nature, becomes either a source of subjection or free creativity for women only because it has meaning within specific social relationships. Firestone's argument reduces the social conceptions of 'women' and 'men' to the biological categories of 'female' and 'male', and thus denies any significance to the complex history of the relationship between men and women or between the private and public spheres. She relies on an abstract conception of a natural, biological female individual with a reproductive capacity which puts her at the mercy of a male individual, who is assumed to have a natural drive to subjugate her.[19] This contemporary version of a thorough Hobbesian reduction of individuals to their natural state leads to a theoretical dead-end, not perhaps a surprising conclusion to an argument that implicitly accepts the patriarchal claim that women's subordination is decreed by nature. The way forward will not be found in a universal dichotomy between nature and culture, or between female and male individuals. Rather, as Rosaldo argues, it is necessary to develop a feminist theoretical perspective that takes account of the social relationships between women and men in historically specific structures of domination and subordination; and, it might be added, within the context of specific interpretations of the 'public' and 'private'.

III. Morality and Power

The long struggle to enfranchise women is one of the most important theoretical and practical examples of feminist attacks on the dichotomy between the private and public. Suffragist arguments show how the attempt to universalise liberal principles leads to a challenge to liberalism itself, and this is particularly well, if implicitly, illustrated in the writing of J.S. Mill. Despite the enormous amount of attention given to voting over the past thirty years, remarkably little attention has been paid by either theoretical or empirical students of politics to the political meaning and consequences of manhood and womanhood suffrage. In recent feminist literature, however, two different views can be found about the implications of the enfranchisement of women for the separation between the public and the private. There is disagreement whether the suffrage movement served to reinforce the sexual separation in social life or whether, rather despite itself, it was one means of undermining it. In the mid-nineteenth century, when feminism emerged as an organised social and political movement, the argument from nature had been elaborated into the doctrine of separate spheres; men and women, it was claimed, each naturally had a separate but complementary and equally valuable social place. The most striking difference between the early feminists and suffragists and contemporary feminists is that almost everyone in the nineteenth century accepted the doctrine of separate spheres.

The early feminists bitterly opposed the grossly unequal position of women but the reforms they struggled to achieve, such as an end to the legal powers of husbands that made their wives into private property and civil non-persons, and the opportunity to obtain an education so that single women could support themselves, were usually seen as means to equality for women who would remain within their own private sphere. The implicit assumption was that the suffrage, too, meant different things to men and women. This comes out clearly in one of the most passionately sentimental, and anti-feminist, statements of the doctrine of separate spheres. In 'Of Queens' Gardens', Ruskin argues that,

> the man's duty, as a member of the commonwealth, is to assist in the maintenance, in the advance, in the defence of the state. The woman's duty, as a member of the commonwealth, is to assist in the ordering, in the comforting, and in the beautiful adornment of the state.[20]

Citizenship for women could thus be seen as an elaboration of their private, domestic tasks and one of the suffragists' main arguments was that the vote was a necessary means to protect and strengthen women's special sphere (an argument that gained weight at the end of the century as legislatures increasingly interested themselves in social issues related to women's sphere). Moreover, both the most ardent anti-suffragists and vehement suffragists agreed that women were weaker, but more moral and virtuous, than men. The anti-suffragists argued that, therefore, enfranchisement would fatally weaken the state because women could not bear arms or use force; the suffragists countered by claiming that women's superior morality and rectitude would transform the state and usher in a reign of peace. All this has led Elshtain to argue that it was precisely because the suffragists accepted the assumptions of the doctrine of separate spheres that they 'failed, even on their own terms'. Far from raising a challenge to the separation of the public and private, they merely 'perpetuated the very mystifications and unexamined presumptions which served to rig the system against them'.[21]

Much of Elshtain's argument is conducted in terms of the duality of morality and power, one way of formulating the separation of private and public when this is located *within* civil society. Liberal theorists often contrast the political sphere (the state), the sphere of power, force and violence, with the society (the private realm), the sphere of voluntarism, freedom and spontaneous regulation.[22] However, the argument about the implications of women's moral superiority, and Elshtain's use of the duality of morality and power, refer rather to the more fundamental separation of the private, domestic sphere from public life or civil society. The opposition between morality and power then counterposes physical force and aggression, the natural attributes of manliness, which are seen as exemplified in the military force of the state, against love and altruism, the natural attributes of womanhood, which are, paradigmatically, displayed in domestic life where the wife and mother stands as the guardian of morality.[23] Was the struggle for womanhood suffrage locked in the separation and dichotomies of patriarchal-liberalism, within the duality of morality and power (which, again, is one way of expressing the doctrine of separate spheres), to the extent suggested by Elshtain? To vote is, after all, a political act. Indeed, it has come to be seen as *the* political act of a liberal-democratic citizen, and citizenship is a status of formal civil or public equality.

A different assessment of the suffrage movement is presented in recent work by DuBois, who argues that the reason that both sides of the struggle for enfranchisement saw the vote as the key feminist demand was that the vote gave women

> a connection with the social order not based on the institution of the family and their subordination within it . . . As citizens and voters, women would participate directly in society as individuals, not indirectly through their subordinate position as wives and mothers.[24]

DuBois emphasises that the suffragists did not question women's 'peculiar suitability' for domestic life, but the demand for the vote constituted a denial that women were naturally fit *only* for private life. The demand for the suffrage thus reached to the heart of the mutual accommodation between patriarchalism and liberalism since to win the vote meant that, in one respect at least, women must be admitted as 'individuals'. This is why DuBois can argue that women's claim for a public, equal status with men, 'exposed and challenged the assumption of male authority over women'.[25] An important long-term consequence of women's enfranchisement, and the other reforms that have led to women's present position of (almost) formal political and legal equality with men, is that the contradiction between civil equality and social, especially familial, subjection, including the beliefs that help constitute it, is now starkly revealed. The liberal-patriarchal separation of the public and private spheres has become a political problem.

The dimensions of the problem are set out — very clearly with the benefit of hindsight — in John Stuart Mill's feminist essay *The Subjection of Women* and his arguments for womanhood suffrage. Mill's essay shows that the assumption that an individual political status can be added to women's ascribed place in the private sphere and leave the latter intact, or even strengthened, is ultimately untenable. Or, to make this point another way, liberal principles cannot simply be universalised to extend to women in the public sphere without raising an acute problem about the patriarchal structure of private life. Mill shows theoretically, as the feminist movement has revealed in practice, that the spheres are integrally related and that women's full and equal membership in public life is impossible without changes in the domestic sphere.

In the *Subjection*, Mill argues that the relation between men and women, or more specifically between husbands and wives, forms an unjustified and unjustifiable exception to the liberal principles of individual freedom and equality, free choice, equality of opportunity and allocation of occupations by merit that (he believes) govern other social and political institutions in nineteenth-century Britain. The social subordination of women is 'a single relic of an old world of thought and practice exploded in everything else'.[26] At the beginning of the essay Mill attacks the appeal to nature and argues that nothing can be known about the natural differences, if any, between women and men until evidence is available about their respective attributes within relationships and institutions where they interact as equals instead of as superiors and inferiors. Much of Mill's argument is directed against the legally sanctioned powers of husbands which placed them in the position of slave-masters over their wives. Legal reform should turn the family from a 'school of despotism' into a 'school of sympathy in equality' and a 'real school of the virtues of freedom'.[27] However, as recent feminist critics have pointed out, in the end he falls back on the same argument from nature that he criticises. Although Mill argues that in the prevailing circumstances of women's upbringing, lack of education and occupational opportunities, and legal and social pressures, they do not have a free choice whether or not to marry, he also assumes that, even after social reform, most women will still choose marital dependence. He states that it will generally be understood that when a woman marries she has chosen her 'career', just like a man entering a profession:

> she makes choice of the management of a household, and the bringing up of a family, as the first call upon her exertions ... She renounces [all occupations] not consistent with the requirements of this.[28]

The question why, if marriage is a 'career', liberal arguments about (public) equality of opportunity have any relevance to women, is thus neatly begged.

Mill introduced the first measure for womanhood suffrage into the House of Commons in 1867. He advocated votes for women for the same two reasons that he supported manhood suffrage; because it was necessary for self-protection or the protection of interests and because political participation would enlarge the capacities of women. However, it is not usually appreciated that Mill's acceptance of a sexually ascribed division of labour, or the separation of domestic from public life, cuts the ground from under his argument for enfranchisement. The obvious difficulty for his argument is that women as wives will be largely confined to the small circle of the family so they will find it hard to use their votes to protect their interests. Women will not be able to learn what their interests are without experience outside domestic life. This point is even more crucial for Mill's argument about individual development and education through political participation. Mill, in what Benn and Gaus call his 'representative liberal text', refers to the development of a 'public spirit' by citizens.[29] In the *Subjection* he writes of the elevation of the individual 'as a moral, spiritual and social being' that occurs under 'the ennobling influence' of free government.[30] This is a large claim to make for the periodic casting of a ballot and Mill did not think that such consequences would arise from the suffrage alone. He writes that 'citizenship', and here I take him to be referring to universal suffrage, 'fills only a small place in modern life, and does not come near the daily habits or inmost sentiments'.[31] He goes on to argue that the (reformed) family is the real school of freedom. However, this is no more plausible than the claim about liberal democratic voting. A despotic, patriarchal family is no school for democratic citizenship; but neither can the egalitarian family, on its own, substitute for participation in a wide variety of social institutions (especially the workplace) that Mill, in his other social and political writings, argues is the necessary education for citizenship. How can wives who have 'chosen' private life develop a public spirit? Women will thus exemplify the selfish, private beings, lacking a sense of justice, who result, according to Mill, when individuals have no experience of public life.

Mill's ultimate failure to question the 'natural' sexual division of labour undermines his argument for an equal public status for women. His argument in the *Subjection* rests on an extension of liberal principles to the domestic sphere — which immediately brings the separation of the private and public, and the opposition between the principles of association in the two spheres into question. He would not have remained Benn and Gaus's 'exemplary' liberal theorist if he had not, at least in part, upheld the patriarchal-liberal ideology of the separation between public and private. On the other hand, by throwing doubt on the original Lockean separation of paternal and political power, and by arguing that the same political principles apply to the structure of family life as to political life, Mill also raises a large question about the status of the family. The language of 'slaves', 'masters', 'equality', 'freedom' and 'justice' implies that the family is a conventional not a natural association. Mill would not want to draw the conclusion that the family is political, but many contemporary feminists have done so. The most popular slogan of today's feminist movement is 'the personal is the political', which not only explicitly rejects the liberal separation of the private and public, but also implies that no distinction can or should be drawn between the two spheres.

IV. 'The Personal Is the Political'

The slogan 'the personal is the political' provides a useful point from which to comment on some of the ambiguities of the public and private in liberal-patriarchalism and also, in the light of some of its more literal feminist interpretations, to comment further on an alternative feminist conception of the political. Its major impact has been to unmask the ideological character of liberal claims about the private and public. 'The personal is the political' has drawn women's attention to the way in which we are encouraged to see social life in personal terms, as a matter of individual ability or luck in finding a decent man to marry or an appropriate place to live. Feminists have emphasised how personal circumstances are structured by public factors, by laws about rape and abortion, by the status of 'wife', by policies on childcare and the allocation of welfare benefits and the sexual division of labour in the home and workplace. 'Personal' problems can thus be solved only through political means and political action.

The popularity of the slogan and its strength for feminists arises from the complexity of women's position in contemporary liberal-patriarchal societies. The private or personal and the public or political are held to be separate from and irrelevant to each other; women's everyday experience confirms this separation yet, simultaneously, it denies it and affirms the integral connection between the two spheres. The separation of the private and public is both part of our actual lives and an ideological mystification of liberal-patriarchal reality.

The separation of the private domestic life of women from the public world of men has been constitutive of patriarchal-liberalism from its origins and, since the mid-nineteenth century, the economically dependent wife has been presented as the ideal for all respectable classes of society. The identification of women and the domestic sphere is now also being reinforced by the revival of anti-feminist organisations and the 'scientific' reformulation of the argument from nature by the sociobiologists.[32] Women have never been completely excluded, of course, from public life; but the way in which women are included is grounded, as firmly as their position in the domestic sphere, in patriarchal beliefs and practices. For example, even many anti-suffragists were willing for women to be educated, so that they could be good mothers, and for them to engage in local politics and philanthropy because these activities could be seen, as voting could not, as a direct extension of their domestic tasks. Today, women still have, at best, merely token representation in authoritative public bodies; public life, while not entirely empty of women, is still the world of men and dominated by them.

Again, large numbers of working class wives have always had to enter the public world of paid employment to ensure the survival of their families, and one of the most striking features of post-war capitalism has been the employment of a steadily increasing number of married women. However, their presence serves to highlight the patriarchal continuity that exists between the sexual division of labour in the family and the sexual division of labour in the workplace. Feminist research has shown how women workers are concentrated into a few occupational areas ('women's work') in low-paid, low-status and non-supervisory jobs.[33] Feminists have also drawn attention to the fact that discussions of worklife, whether by *laissez-faire* liberals or Marxists, always assume that it is possible to understand economic activity in abstraction from domestic life. It is 'forgotten' that the worker, invariably taken to be a man, can appear ready for work and concentrate on his work free from the everyday demands of providing food, washing and cleaning, and care of children, only because these tasks are performed unpaid by his wife. And if she is also a paid worker she works a further shift at these 'natural' activities. A complete analysis and explanation of the structure and operation of capitalism will be forthcoming only when the figure of the worker is accompanied by that of the housewife.

Feminists conclude that the 'separate' liberal worlds of private and public life are actually interrelated, connected by a patriarchal structure. This conclusion again highlights the problem of the status of the 'natural' sphere of the family, which is presupposed by, yet seen as separate from and irrelevant to, the conventional relations of civil society. The sphere of domestic life is at the heart of civil society rather than apart or separate from it. A widespread conviction that this is so is revealed by contemporary concern about the crisis, the decline, the distintegration of the nuclear family that is seen as the bulwark of civilised moral life. That the family is a major 'social problem' is significant, for the 'social' is a category that belongs in civil society, not outside it, or, more accurately, it is one of the two sides into which civil society can be divided; the social (private) and the political (public). Donzelot has recently explored how the emergence of the social is also the emergence of 'social work' and a wide variety of ways of (politically) 'policing' the family, giving mothers a social status, and controlling children.[34] Feminists, too, have been investigating how personal and family life is politically regulated, an investigation which denies the conventional liberal claim that the writ of the state runs out at the gate to the family home. They have shown how the family is a major concern of the state and how, through legislation concerning marriage and sexuality and the policies of the welfare state, the subordinate status of women is presupposed by and maintained by the power of the state.[35]

These feminist critiques of the dichotomy between private and public stress that the categories refer to two interrelated dimensions of the structure of liberal-patriarchalism; they do not necessarily suggest that no distinction can or should be drawn between the personal and political aspects of social life. The slogan 'the personal is the political' can, however, be taken literally. For example, Millett, in *Sexual Politics*, implicitly rejects Locke's distinction between paternal and political power. In political science the political is frequently defined in terms of power, but political scientists invariably fail to take their definition to its logical conclusion. Millett agrees with the definition but, in contrast, argues that all power is political so that, because men exercise power over women in a multitude of ways in personal life, it makes sense to talk of 'sexual politics' and 'sexual dominion . . . provides [the] most fundamental concept of power'.[36] The personal becomes the political. This approach illuminates many unpalatable aspects of sexual and domestic life, in particular its violence, that too frequently remain hidden, but it does not greatly advance the critique of patriarchal-liberalism. As the radical feminist attempts to eliminate nature, as one side of the dichotomy, so Millett seeks to eliminate power, thus echoing the suffragist vision of a moral transformation of politics. But this does nothing to question the liberal association (or identification) of the political with power, or to question the association of women with the 'moral' side of the duality.

Other feminists have also rejected the identification of the political with power. Sometimes, by standing liberal-patriarchalism on its head, it is merely claimed that, properly understood, political life is thus intrinsically feminine.[37] More fruitfully, the feminist rejection of 'masculine' power also rests on an alternative conception of the political. It is argued that the political is the 'area of shared values and citizenship',[38] or that it 'includes shared values and civic concerns in which power is only one aspect'.[39] These conceptions remain undeveloped in feminist writings, but they are closely related to the arguments of the critics of liberalism who deplore the depoliticisation of civil society or liberalism's loss of distinctive sense of the political. For instance, Habermas argues for public, shared communication so that substantive political problems can be rationally evaluated, and Wolin states that the 'public' and the 'common' are 'synonyms for what is political', so that 'one of the essential qualities of what is political . . . is its relationship to what is "public" '.[40] These critics and some feminists agree that what is not personal is public — and that what is public is political. The implication is that there is no division within civil society, which is the realm of the public, collective, common political life of the community. The argument is usually developed, however, without any consideration of how this conception of the public-political sphere is related to domestic life, or any indication that such a problem arises. The feminists have posed, but have not yet answered, this fundamental question. What can be said is that although the personal is not the political, the two spheres are interrelated, necessary dimensions of a future, democratic feminist social order.

V. Conditions for a Feminist Alternative to Liberal-Patriarchalism

Feminist critiques of the liberal-patriarchal opposition of private and public raise fundamental theoretical questions, as well as the complex practical problems of creating a radical social transformation. But one objection to feminist arguments denies that our project is even sensible. Wolff has recently claimed, from a position sympathetic to feminism, that overcoming the separation of the two spheres presents an inherently insoluble problem. To 'struggle against the split' is pointless; the best that can be achieved is ad hoc adjustments to the existing order. The separation of public and private derives from two 'equally plausible and totally incompatible conceptions of human nature'. One is that of 'man [sic] as essentially rational, atemporal, ahistorical', and the second is of 'man as essentially time bound, historically, culturally and biologically conditioned'.[41] To argue that everyone should be treated in the public world as if the facts of sex, class, colour, age and religion do not count, is to insist that we should deny the most basic human facts about ourselves and thus accentuate the inhumanity and alienation of the present. But Wolff's two conceptions are not of a single 'human' nature, and they are far from equally plausible; they represent the liberal-patriarchal view of the true natures of (private) women and (public) men. Human beings *are* time bound, biological and culturally specific creatures. Only from a liberal individualist perspective (one failing to see itself as a patriarchalist perspective) that abstracts the male individual from the sphere where his wife remains in natural subjection, then generalises this abstraction as public man, can such an opposition of 'human' nature, of women and men, private and public, appear philosophically or sociologically plausible.

Feminists are trying to develop a theory of a social practice that, for the first time in the western world, would be a truly general theory — including women and men equally — grounded in the interrelationship of the individual to collective life, or personal to political life, instead of their separation and opposition. At the immediately practical level, this demand is expressed in what is perhaps the most clear conclusion of feminist critiques; that if women are to participate fully, as equals, in social life, men have to share equally in childrearing and other domestic tasks. While women are identified with this 'private' work, their public status is always undermined. This conclusion does not, as is often alleged, deny the natural biological fact that women not men *bear* children; it does deny the patriarchal assertion that this natural fact entails that only women can *rear* children. Equal parenting and equal participation in the other activities of domestic life presuppose some radical changes in the public sphere, in the organisation of production, in what we mean by 'work', and in the practice of citizenship. The feminist critique of the sexual division of labour in the workplace and in political organisations of all ideological persuasions, and its rejection of the liberal-patriarchal conception of the political, extends and deepens the challenge to liberal-capitalism posed by the participatory democratic and Marxist criticism of the past two decades, but also goes well beyond it.

The temptation, as Wolff's argument shows, is to suppose that if women are to take their place as public 'individuals' then the conflict is about the universalisation of liberalism. But that is to ignore the feminist achievement in bringing to light the patriarchal character of liberalism and the ambiguities and contradictions of its conception of the private and public. A full analysis of the various expressions of the dichotomy between the private and the public has yet to be provided, together with a deeper exploration than is possible in this essay of the implications of the double separation of domestic life from civil society and the separation of the private from public within civil society itself. Feminist critiques imply a dialectical perspective upon social life as an alternative to the dichotomies and oppositions of patriarchal-liberalism. It is tempting, as shown by feminists themselves, either to replace opposition by negation (to deny that nature has any place in a feminist order) or to assume that the alternative to opposition is harmony and identification (the personal is the political; the family is political). The assumptions of patriarchal-liberalism allow only these two alternatives, but feminist critiques assume that there is a third.

Feminism looks toward a differentiated social order within which the various dimensions are distinct but not separate or opposed, and which rests on a social conception of individuality, which includes both women and men as biologically differentiated but not unequal creatures. Nevertheless, women and men, and the private and the public, are not necessarily in harmony. Given the social implications of women's reproductive capacities,[42] it is surely Utopian to suppose that tension between the personal and the political, between love and justice, between individuality and communality will disappear with patriarchal-liberalism.

The range of philosophical and political problems that are encompassed, implicitly or explicitly, in feminist critiques indicates that a fully developed feminist alternative to patriarchal-liberalism would provide its first truly 'total critique'.[43] Three great male critics of abstractly individualist liberalism already claim to have offered such a critique, but their claim must be rejected. Rousseau, Hegel and Marx each argued that they had left behind the abstractions and dichotomies of liberalism and retained individuality within communality. Rousseau and Hegel explicitly excluded women from this endeavour, confining these politically dangerous beings to the obscurity of the natural world of the family; Marx also failed to free himself and his philosophy from patriarchal assumptions. The feminist total critique of the liberal opposition of private and public still awaits its philosopher.

Notes

I am grateful to Stanley Benn and Jerry Gaus for the care with which they read and criticised my arguments.

1. The subversive character of liberal-feminism has recently been uncovered by Z. Eisenstein, *The Radical Future of Liberal Feminism* (Longman, New York, 1981).
2. Ibid., p. 223.
3. J.S. Mill is an exception to this generalisation, but Benn and Gaus do not mention *The Subjection of Women*. It might be objected that B. Bosanquet, for example, refers in *The Philosophical Theory of the State* (Ch. X, 6), to 'the two persons who are [the] head' of the family. However, Bosanquet is discussing Hegel, and he shows no understanding that Hegel's philosophy rests on the explicit, and philosophically justified, exclusion of women from headship of a family or from participating in civil society or the state. Bosanquet's reference to 'two persons' thus requires a major critique of Hegel, not mere exposition. Liberal arguments cannot be universalised by a token reference to 'women and men' instead of 'men'. On Hegel see P. Mills, 'Hegel and "The Woman Question": Recognition and Intersubjectivity', in L. Clark and L. Lange (eds.), *The Sexism of Social and Political Theory* (University of Toronto Press, Toronto, 1979). (I am grateful to Jerry Gaus for drawing my attention to Bosanquet's remarks.)
4. J. Locke, *Two Treatises of Government*, 2nd edn, P. Lastlett (ed.) (Cambridge University Press, Cambridge, 1967), Bk. I, Ch. 47; Bk. II, Ch. 82. The conflict between the social contract theorists and the patriarchalists is more fully discussed in T. Brennan and C. Pateman, ' "Mere Auxiliaries to the Commonwealth": Women and the Origins of Liberalism', *Political Studies*, XXVII (1979), pp. 183-200.
5. Rawls's two principles of justice provide an example of this division. He states that the principles 'presuppose that the social structure can be divided into two more or less distinct parts'. He does not call these private and public, but the 'equal liberties of citizenship' are usually called 'political' liberties and the 'social and economic inequalities' of the second part are usually seen as part of the 'private' sphere. In Rawls's final formulation it is clear that the principles refer to civil society and that the family is outside their scope. Part (b) of the second principle, equality of opportunity, cannot apply to the family, and part (a), the difference principle, may not apply. A clever son, say, may be sent to university at the expense of other family members. (I owe this last point to my student Deborah Kearns.) John Rawls, *A Theory of Justice* (The Belknap Press of Harvard University Press, Cambridge, Mass., 1971), pp. 61, 302.
6. Wolin, *Politics and Vision* (Little Brown, Boston, 1960).
7. It is also the sphere of privacy. J. Reiman, 'Privacy, Intimacy, and Personhood', *Philosophy and Public Affairs*, 6 (1976), p. 39, links 'owning' one's body to the idea of a 'self' and argues this is why privacy is needed. My comments in the text do not explain why liberal theorists typically write of the private and the public rather than the political. An explanation could only be found in a full examination of liberal ambiguities about the public and the political, which takes us far from the purpose of this essay, although the problem arises again below in the context of the feminist slogan 'the personal is the political'.
8. J. Habermas, 'The Public Sphere', *New German Critique*, VI, no. 3 (1974), pp. 49-55. However, Habermas, like other writers, ignores the fact that women are conventionally held to be deficient in reason and so unfit to participate in a public body.
9. In the present context these remarks must be very condensed. For amplification see Brennan and Pateman, ' "Mere Auxiliaries to the Commonwealth":

Women and the Origins of Liberalism'; R. Hamilton, *The Liberation of Women: A Study of Patriarchy and Capitalism* (Allen and Unwin, London, 1978); H. Hartmann, 'Capitalism, Patriarchy and Job Segregation by Sex', *Signs*, 1, no. 3, Pt. 2 (Supp. Spring 1976) pp. 137-70; A.Oakley, *Housewife* (A. Lane, London, 1974), Chs. 2 and 3.

10. J.S. Mill, *The Subjection of Women* in A. Rossi (ed.), *Essays on Sex Equality* (University of Chicago Press, Chicago, 1970), pp. 125-242, at p. 126.

11. M. Astell, 'Reflections on Marriage' (published 1706), cited in L. Stone, *The Family, Sex and Marriage in England: 1500-1800* (Weidenfeld & Nicolson, London, 1977), p. 240.

12. 'Radical feminists' is the term used to distinguish the feminists who argue that the male-female opposition is the cause of women's oppression from 'liberal feminists' and 'socialist feminists'.

13. S.B. Ortner, 'Is Female to Male as Nature is to Culture?' in M.Z. Rosaldo and L. Lamphere (eds.), *Women, Culture and Society* (Stanford University Press, Stanford, 1974), p. 72. Ortner says nothing about the writers over the past two centuries who have glorified nature and seen culture as the cause of vice and inequality. However, the meaning of 'nature' in these arguments is extremely complex and the relationship of women to nature is far from clear. Rousseau, for instance, segregates women and men even in domestic life because women's natures are seen as a threat to civil life (culture). For some comments on this question see my ' "The Disorder of Women": Women, Love and the Sense of Justice', *Ethics*, 91 (1980), pp. 20-34.

14. Ortner, 'Is Female to Male as Nature is to Culture', p. 87.

15. M.Z. Rosaldo, 'The Use and Abuse of Anthropology: Reflections on Feminism, and Cross-Cultural Understanding', *Signs*, 5, no. 3 (1980), p. 409. Compare D. Haraway, 'Animal Sociology and a Natural Economy of the Body Politic, Part I: A Political Physiology of Dominance', *Signs*, 4, no. 1 (1978), esp. pp. 24-25.

16. S. Firestone, *The Dialectic of Sex* (W. Morrow, New York, 1970), p. 8.

17. Ibid., p. 232. She also fails to distinguish 'culture' as art, technology etc. from 'culture' as the general form of life of humankind.

18. Ibid., p. 255.

19. I owe the last point to J.B. Elshtain, 'Liberal Heresies: Existentialism and Repressive Feminism' in M. McGrath (ed.), *Liberalism and the Modern Polity* (Marcel Dekker, New York, 1978), p. 53.

20. J. Ruskin, 'Of Queens' Gardens', in C. Bauer and L. Pitt (eds.), *Free and Ennobled* (Pergamon Press, Oxford, 1979), p. 17.

21. J.B. Elshtain, 'Moral Woman and Immoral Man: A Consideration of the Public-Private Split and its Political Ramifications', *Politics and Society*, 4 (1974), pp. 453-61.

22. A recent argument that relies on this contrast is J. Steinberg, *Locke, Rousseau and the Idea of Consent* (Greenwood Press, Westport, Conn., 1978), esp. Chs. 5-7. Emphasis on consent gives an appearance of morality to the private sphere, which is far less evident when, as is usually the case, self-interest is seen as the governing principle of (private) civil society. If the division within civil society is seen as freedom (as self-interest) opposing power, the location of morality within domestic life is more pointed but poses a serious problem of order for liberal public or civil society.

23. An acute problem about 'nature' and women's 'nature' now emerges because women are seen both as natural guardians of morality and as naturally politically subversive: see my ' "Disorder of Women" '.

24. E. DuBois, 'The Radicalism of the Woman Suffrage Movement', *Feminist Studies*, 3, no. 1/2 (1975), pp. 64, 66.

25. E. DuBois, *Feminism and Suffrage* (Cornell University Press, Ithaca, N.Y., 1978), p. 46.

26. Mill, *Subjection*, p. 146.
27. Ibid., pp. 174-75.
28. Ibid., p. 179.
29. See Ch. 2, p. 303 above, referring to Mill's *Considerations on Representative Government*.
30. Mill, *Subjection*, p. 237.
31. Ibid., p. 174.
32. On sociobiology see, e.g., E.O. Wilson, *Sociobiology: The New Synthesis* (Harvard University Press, Cambridge, Mass., 1975), and S. Goldberg, *The Inevitability of Patriarchy*, 2nd edn (W. Morrow, New York, 1974). For a critique, see, e.g., P. Green, *The Pursuit of Inequality* (Martin Robertson, Oxford, 1981), Ch. 5.
33. See, e.g., for Australia, K. Hargreaves, *Women at Work* (Penguin Books, Harmondsworth, 1982); for England, J. West (ed.), *Women, Work and the Labour Market* (Routledge and Kegan Paul, London, 1982); for America, Eisenstein, *The Radical Future of Liberal Feminism*, Ch. 9.
34. J. Donzelot, *The Policing of Families* (Pantheon Books, New York, 1979). 'The most surprising thing is the status "the social" has won in our heads, as something we take for granted' (p. xxvi).
35. On marriage see, e.g., D.L. Barker, 'The Regulation of Marriage: Repressive Benevolence' in G. Littlejohn et al. (eds.), *Power and the State* (Croom Helm, London, 1978); on rape see my 'Women and Consent', *Political Theory*, 8 (1980), pp. 149-68, and A.G. Johnson, 'On the Prevalence of Rape in the United States', *Signs*, 6, no. 1 (1980), pp. 136-46; on the welfare state see, e.g., E. Wilson, *Women and the Welfare State* (Tavistock, London, 1977).
36. K. Millett, *Sexual Politics* (Hart-Davis, London, 1971), pp. 25, 26.
37. N. McWilliams, 'Contemporary Feminism, Consciousness Raising and Changing Views of the Political' in J. Jaquette (ed.), *Women in Politics* (Wiley, New York, 1974), p. 161.
38. Ibid.
39. L.B. Iglitzin, 'The Making of the Apolitical Woman: Femininity and Sex-Stereotyping in Girls' in Jaquette, *Women in Politics*, p. 34.
40. J. Habermas, 'The Public Sphere', and Wolin, *Politics and Vision*, pp. 9, 2.
41. R.P. Wolff, 'There's Nobody Here but Us Persons' in C. Gould and M. Wartofsky (eds.), *Women and Philosophy* (Putnam's, New York, 1976), pp. 137, 142-43. Wolff also objects to the feminist struggle against the separation of private and public because it builds normative assumptions about human nature into the advocacy of new forms of social institutions – an oddly misplaced objection in the light of the assumption about women's and men's nature embodied in patriarchal-liberalism.
42. See R.P. Petchesky, 'Reproductive Freedom: Beyond "A Woman's Right to Choose",' *Signs*, 5, no. 4 (1980), pp. 661-85.
43 I have taken the phrase from R.M. Unger, *Knowledge and Politics* (Free Press, New York, 1975). Unger's claim to have provided a total critique of liberalism must also be rejected. He fails to see that the antinomies of theory and fact, reason and desire, and rules and values are, at the same time, expressions of the patriarchal antinomy between man and woman. He states (p. 59) that 'the political form of the opposition of formal reason to arbitrary desire is the contrast between public and private existence' – but it is also the opposition between the 'nature' of men and women.

PART THREE

PUBLIC AND PRIVATE IN NON-LIBERAL CULTURES

13 PUBLICNESS, PRIVATENESS AND 'PRIMITIVE LAW'

Martin Krygier

When familiar conceptions, such as the public/private distinction, are in widespread and common use, it is rarely simple to sort out which of their elements are related logically, which presuppose contingent but universal phenomena, and which simply take as given, and relate to, phenomena or ideological traditions found in one society or type of society, perhaps at one period in the history of such a society. In this essay, I hope to provide some material for such sorting, by examining whether some of the central notions we have in mind when speaking of publicness and privateness have any purchase in discussion of activities in societies rather different from our own. For the distinction, I have found useful Benn and Gaus's disambiguation of publicness and privateness in terms of distinctions along the three dimensions of agency, access and interest (see Ch. 1, above). For the activities I have focused on law. For the societies, I have concentrated on those often called 'stateless' since, as Bronislaw Malinowski observed: 'in the study of communities where law is neither codified nor administered before courts, nor yet enforced by constabulary, certain problems arise which can be easily overlooked in a jurisprudence based on our own formal and crystallized systems'.[1]

I. Public and Private Law

No one, even amongst those who doubt the value or clarity of the public/private distinction, would deny its pervasiveness in western discourse and social life. And, as Benn and Gaus remark:

> because, in western culture at any rate, we apprehend a great deal of our social world by distinguishing things that are public and things that are private, how those concepts are structured necessarily informs not only what we ourselves say and do but also what responses to our actions we expect from others, how we assess their actions, and so on.[2]

As earlier chapters in this volume have shown, this remark is particularly relevant to discussions of law.

On the liberal view of the matter, for example, law is a paradigmatically public enterprise. It is made, applied and enforced by public officials; it is in liberal principle, if rarely in fact, accessible to all; it is to serve the public interest or at least public interests. Among such interests is that in the legal vindication of private rights through public institutions rather than by private self-help. In fact, public institutions are usually invoked only as a last resort; but liberals consider the existence of such a resort particularly important.

In liberal democracies, legal officials are required to distinguish the public interests they allegedly serve from their private interests; and considerable efforts are made, for example, with rules disqualifying judges from sitting on cases in which they have an interest to ensure that officials do separate their public and private concerns. Of course, the rules are often broken but, so a realistic liberal might argue, that is neither surprising nor more significant than the scandal which customarily follows revelation of such malfeasance.

Equally revealing of the distinction's importance in contemporary western views of law is what radical critics of liberalism take as the target of their attempts at 'demystification' of law: pre-eminently it is the claim that law and legal officials are *public* servants, agents of public rather than private, or at least sectional, interests.

Apart from discussion of the purposes and functions of legal systems as a whole, many important distinctions *within* contemporary legal systems rest on or involve that between publicness and privateness. The same activities carry different legal consequences, depending on whether they are done in public or in private; the same agents carry differing responsibilities, depending on whether they are regarded as acting in a public or in a private capacity (see Ch. 4, §III, above); similar organisations must comply with differing legal requirements, depending on whether they are considered to be public, open to the public or a section of it, or private (see Ch. 2, §II.B, above). And the law itself, especially in continental Europe, can be viewed as being divided between public law, which has to do with the activities of state agencies, and private law, which is centrally concerned with relationships among private persons (see Ch. 3, above, for an extended discussion). There are, of course, many areas of overlap, and in Anglo-Australian law the distinction has a far shallower pedigree and less importance than in civil law countries; nevertheless it is often made and there is reason to believe that its use will increase rather than decrease, as attempts are made to supervise and control the enormously varied and frequently novel activities of modern states.

Given its importance in discussions of contemporary Western law, it is not surprising that the public/private distinction has also been pressed into service in comparisons between such law and that of societies very different from our own; in particular, early law and the law-like processes of small-scale pre-industrial and pre-literate societies are often regarded by evolutionary theorists as akin to the ancestors of our own.

To some extent such comparisons derive from Durkheim, even though he was in fact careful *not* to adopt the distinction 'utilized by the jurisconsults',[3] between public and private law. Durkheim made the important point, too often overlooked, that 'law is, above all, a social thing and has a totally different object than the interest of the pleaders',[4] and he rejected the distinction between public and private law as inappropriate for sociology, on the grounds that:

> All law is private in the sense that it is always about individuals who are present and acting; but so, too, all law is public, in the sense that it is a social function and that all individuals are, whatever their varying titles, functionaries of society.[5]

On the other hand, Durkheim did insist on a sharp distinction between primitive and modern law: the former being wholly 'repressive' or 'penal'; the latter also, and predominantly, 'restitutive'. The significance of this for our purposes is that repressive law is an expression of what Durkheim at one point calls *la colère publique* (public anger) and, more often, collective or social sentiments:

> [Because] the offended sentiments . . . are found in all consciences, the infraction committed arouses in those who have evidence of it or who learn of its existence the same indignation. Everybody is attacked; consequently, everybody opposes the attack. Not only is the reaction general, but it is collective.[6]

The relations determined by modern, restitutive law, however, though society regulates them by special organs, 'are established immediately, not between the individual and society, but between restricted, special parties in society whom they bind'.[7] Thus primitive penal law is the direct and immediate concern of all; modern restitutive law is not.

Given the basis of the distinction he *did* make and the tendency of the public/private distinction to abhor a vacuum, it is not surprising that Durkheim's terminological preferences have been overlooked by later writers, and that he should have been taken to argue that penal law is public, restitutive law private, and that public law precedes private law in evolutionary development.[8] Indeed A.R. Radcliffe-Brown, seeking to make a distinction between *types* of law rather than legal *systems*, explicitly substituted for the terms Durkheim chose, the public/private distinction he rejected. According to Radcliffe-Brown:

> The confusion which has resulted [from] the attempt to apply to preliterate societies the modern distinction between criminal law and civil law can be avoided by making instead the distinction between the law of public delicts and the law of private delicts. In any society a deed is a public delict if its occurrence normally leads to an organised and regular procedure by the whole community or by the constituted representatives of social authority, which results in the fixing of responsibility upon some person within the community and the infliction by the community or by its representatives of some hurt or punishment upon the responsible person. This procedure, which may be called the penal sanction, is in its basic form a reaction by the community against an action of one of its own members which offends some strong and definite moral sentiment ... A private delict is ... an action which is subject to what may be called a restitutive sanction. The law of private delicts in preliterate societies corresponds [with certain important differences] to the civil law of modern times.[9]

In contrast to Durkheim, a number of authors have argued that the evolutionary development of law was from private to public law. The focus here usually has been on *agency*, with sharp distinctions being made between justice which was individually vindicated and that pursued by institutionalised public agents. Thus, according to L.T. Hobhouse, the development of 'public justice' took the following pattern:

> In the beginning, self-redress by the individual, by his kindred, or some other small group is the predominating fact. Hence we ascend by many small gradations to the impartial justice of a public tribunal, investigating each case by rational process, distinguishing crimes from civil wrongs and limiting the responsibility for a wrong to the individual perpetrator.[10]

Similarly, the Oxford anthropologist R.R. Marett distinguished between early 'law of blood-revenge as purely an affair between the clans concerned; the rest of the tribal public keeping aloof' and subsequent legal developments in which 'with the development of a central authority, whether in the shape of the rule of many or of one, the public control of the blood-feud begins to assert itself'.[11] More recently, the highly influential American legal anthropologist E.A. Hoebel made the central evolutionary message of his account of *The Law of Primitive Man* the move from private law, which 'predominates on the primitive scene', to public law. Thus he observes: 'The trend of the law . . . is to shift the privilege-rights of prosecution and imposition of legal sanctions from the individual and his kinship group over to clearly defined public officials representing the society as such.'[12]

While contemporary legal anthropologists go in less for this sort of comparison, non-anthropologists, seeking to draw on anthropology for contrasts between modern and primitive law, continue to find the public/private distinction useful. Here again the suggestion is that without a state there cannot be public law. Thus Richard Posner, one of the most influential proponents of the economic analysis of law, argues that in primitive societies,'*Virtually the entire burden of deterrence is placed on the tort (private) law.* There is no criminal law to punish acts such as murder or theft, because there is no state; criminal law as we know it is a branch of public law.'[13] And Roberto Unger claims:

> Until one can distinguish among the institutions of the society a body that overpowers other social groups and limits their interaction, it is impossible to speak of public rules. Only after the establishment of an identifiable government will there be a contrast between two kinds of standards of conduct, one public and the other private. Hence, the problem of explaining the public nature of rules merges into that of accounting for the phenomenon of government.[14]

Apart from such use of the public/private distinction to distinguish between systems of law or types of law, there is a good deal of unreflective talk of public opinion, public and private domains, publicity, privacy or its absence in anthropological literature. Yet unlike other fields of anthropology, where authors' conceptual choices are relentlessly, at times over-zealously, investigated for traces of ethnocentric assumptions and biases, use of the public/private distinction has rarely been the subject of self-conscious reflection and criticism. It is certainly not a 'topic' in anthropology. One can search long and fruitlessly through anthropological indexes without hitting upon it.

This is odd, for as the contributions to this volume make abundantly clear, the distinction is almost spectacular for its ambiguity. Moreover, our many different uses of the distinction are likely to be of varying applicability to and usefulness in the discussion of other societies. Benn and Gaus suggest (Ch. 1, §II, above) that there is a semantic continuity linking the senses of publicness in English which derives not from logical entailment but from certain principles, presuppositions and beliefs about the nature of individuals and societies, of collective agents and collective action, embedded in the culture and its language. Other cultures have radically different conceptions, or perhaps none at all. It is not obvious, then, that the public/private distinction will do effectively all that the authors I have discussed ask it to. On the other hand, given its centrality to our ordinary ways of thinking, particularly about law, it is also not plain that we could easily discard it, even if we should.

II. Public and Private Agency

As we have seen, several writers who have sought to contrast 'public' western law with 'private' primitive law have had in mind the character of the *agents* of legal activity. Whatever the merits of their distinction, it is not at all surprising that it should have suggested itself. For in contemporary western societies, most people think of law as necessarily borne by clearly identifiable institutional 'carriers' or embodiments: legal institutions and officials. This association is no accident: in industrialised western societies, legal institutions are structurally differentiated from other institutions, and the responsibilities and authority of legal office-holders are also, in principle, differentiated between those with authority to legislate, others with binding authority to adjudicate disputes, and others again concerned with the execution and enforcement of the law. Law has seemed to many, therefore, to be inextricably intertwined with, and dependent upon, the existence of public agents.[15]

Certainly this was Hobbes's view. For him, without an institutionalised (and centralised) public agency, there could not be positive law, public affairs nor, indeed, society. The sovereign is a public agent in a complete sense: he embodies and represents the interests of all, and his actions as sovereign are authorised by all.

The dimension of agency has, then, played a special role in post-Renaissance discussions of law and politics. And, still, in one important strain of contemporary liberalism, as Benn and Gaus observe,

[p]ublic life tends to be equated with political life, because the idea of political organisation exhausts the understanding of the social whole. What is often called civil society, as distinct from the polity, is then firmly privatised; it is an area in which, whatever one's role, it is not like that of a state official, so one ought not to be held accountable for it to society at large.[16]

Benn and Gaus themselves assume similar structures in their account of agency as a dimension of the public/private distinction. 'The basic distinction', they explain,

> is between an agent acting privately, i.e. on his own account, or publicly, i.e. as an officer of the city, community, commonwealth, state, etc.... A public official may be able to do precisely equivalent things [to those done by a private agent], but only by virtue of a warrant or authorisation deriving from his office.[17]

Now the notion of public office is not at all peculiar to modern or western polities. Many African states, not to mention Polynesian, Fijian, Southeast Asian, chieftainships and kingdoms, have possessed highly differentiated polities, political institutions and notions of public office. However, whilst many societies have possessed structurally differentiated public institutions, many others have not. These are the so-called 'stateless societies'. Among the Australian Aborigines, 'The polity . . . was a kind of anarchy, in which it was open to active and enterprising men to obtain some degree of influence with age, but in which none were sovereign.'[18] In Melanesia, too, with but few exceptions, most societies lacked 'the concept of power being vested in an office . . . In most parts of Melanesia power is essentially personal and transitory . . . '[19] Unlike Polynesian societies, 'complete with public governments and public law, monarchs and taxes, ministers and minions',

> [Melanesian] [b]ig-men do not come to office; they do not succeed to, nor are they installed in, existing positions of leadership over political groups. The attainment of big-man status is rather the outcome of a series of acts which elevate a person above the common herd and attract about him a coterie of loyal, lesser men. It is not accurate to speak of 'big-man' as a political title, for it is but an acknowledged standing in interpersonal relations — a 'prince among men' so to speak as opposed to 'The Prince of Danes'. In particular Melanesian tribes the phrase might be 'man of importance' or 'man of renown', 'generous rich-man', or 'centre-man', as well as 'big-man'.[20]

Similarly, the Comanche Indians, like many other American Indian and Eskimo societies, had 'no public officials endowed with law-speaking or law-enforcing authority'.[21]

Thus, the conception of public agency, so important to liberal democratic theory *inter alia*, has no obvious parallel in the 'law' of many small, 'stateless' societies. In such societies, there are no agents who even in principle are regarded as embodying or safeguarding 'public', as distinct from 'private', interests, no persons whose claim to authority rests on a public rather than a private basis. Of course, in such societies, power, even authority, is frequently exercised, but even where such exercise is generally regarded as legitimate, there is no reason to believe that, say, the Melanesian 'big-man' so well described by Marshall Sahlins thinks himself to be, or is thought to be, a *public* agent.

Western observers were long perplexed by this apparent absence of public agents in many societies, as the persistent interest in Malinowski's essentially Hobbesian question — how societies could exist without 'central authority, codes, courts and constables' — attests. Often observers of stateless societies 'discovered' public officials where it does not appear that they existed: of Australian Aborigines, it used to be suggested that tribal elders exercised such powers; in Africa and New Guinea colonial administrators sought to identify, and came more than once to invent, local 'chiefs' in order to augment their hitherto non-existent local sovereignty with the power of the Colonial Office. Along with grants of 'public' (for example, judicial) authority went attacks on 'nepotism'; a strange combination of virtue and vice for the hapless members of small societies, where links with and obligations to relatives had traditionally been of monumental moral and political significance.[22]

There have been, then, many societies without public officials or the concept of public officialdom, that is, of persons expected and empowered to act as representatives of distinguishably public interests in, among other things, maintaining order and damping down disputes. Nonetheless, in most such societies, order *is* maintained and disputes *are* damped down. And this is anything but a purely private affair.

III. Public and Private Access

One of the difficulties which flows from the ambiguity of the public/private distinction is that on the basis of a rather small claim, which may be true merely by definition, one might be taken to be making larger, more interesting claims, which, however, are not true at all. Thus, if public law has to do with the activities of public agencies, and certain types of societies lack such agencies, then, of course, they lack public law. However, quite apart from whether it is at all enlightening to build contrasts between legal systems or forms of law on this trivial truth, there is something very strange about describing the law of small societies as private. One reason for this can be seen if we move from the dimension of public and private *agency* to that of public and private *access*.

Although stateless societies do not possess public officers whose task is to maintain order, their members are not the asocial and antisocial atoms of Hobbes's state of nature. Widely understood norms of proper conduct exist and are enforced; one of the central aids to such enforcement is the extraordinary publicity of daily life. Many preindustrial societies, and almost all stateless ones, are small in scale or broken into small segments, and their members are in constant face-to-face contact. Information about one's identity and activities is far more accessible to all significant others than it is in large societies, where anonymity is in many circumstances possible; and even where it is not, one can often separate the contexts in which one plays different social roles without fear, for example, of one's public 'self' being undermined by the face one exposes in private. The situation is radically different in small, face-to-face societies. As Fredrik Barth observes of the Baktaman of New Guinea, for example:

> One hundred and eighty-three people plus a scatter of known persons in neighbouring groups make a very diminutive social world where every person is known by all for his or her personality failings, and predilections, and where there is no escape from social sanctions through anonymity.[23]

As a consequence:

> Essentially, unless particular precautions are taken, all behaviour among the Baktaman is public behaviour. There are no recognised and respected ways in which the public gaze can be cut off, no way of separating oneself out from others present. Any conversation between two may be freely invaded, interrupted, or redirected by anyone present or arriving on the scene; sleep (e.g. in the communal men's house) may be interrupted by an alter for any purpose of his

own choosing. Privacy can only be achieved by hiding from others; sexual gratification, peace to defecate, and the opportunity to eat without sharing (except as protected by rules of taboo) can only be obtained that way.[24]

Many features of small societies, besides their size, combine to make life highly public. One of the centrally important characteristics of relationships among members of small societies is that they are what Max Gluckman called 'multiplex', rather than single-interest, relationships. People are linked to each other by many ties of kinship and mutual dependence, and they are exposed to, and interested in, many more facets of each other than is common outside the family in developed western societies. And, as John Roberts and Thomas Gregor have pointed out, 'It is likely that this wide range of curiosity will be satisfied, because social relationships are not only diffuse in the setting of a small community but they also tend to be highly observable.' Among the elements producing the public character of social life, they stress the compactness of settlements, which increases individuals' visibility; technological simplicity, which results in 'building materials [which] are not wholly effective barriers to sound'; the quietness, relative to modern society, of small communities, as a result of which '[t]he sounds that do occur — crying children, conversations, disputes — are socially relevant sounds, contributing to the deprivatization of those who utter them'; and the highly efficient gossip networks which exist in intimate, face-to-face communities.[25] Among the Mehinaku, the Brazilian Indians that Gregor studied:

> It is apparent that privacy is a scarce commodity . . . Wherever a person goes in the village he can be seen or heard. When he speaks there is a chance that a third person is listening, and that in a short time everyone else will know what he said. Even the most intimate details of his sex life often become a matter of public knowledge.[26]

The Baktaman and Mehinaku societies are particularly small, but the high level of public exposure which exists in them is far from unique. Roberts and Gregor have reported a cross-cultural study of privacy patterns in which they participated, which focused on a sample of 42 societies classed as having 'no political integration even at the local level or as having autonomous local communities (not exceeding 1,500 population)'.[27] The societies were classed into one of five 'privacy categories' on the basis of permeability to sight and sound, presence or absence of closable windows, doors and internal partitions, number of persons living together, and openness of the settlement pattern. The majority of the societies chosen were judged to provide 'low' or 'very low' privacy for their members. On the basis of the detailed findings of this study, Gregor suggests that 'many small-scale communities, perhaps a majority of them, render the individual highly observable, making his whereabouts and activities a matter of common knowledge'.[28]

It would, however, be a mistake to conclude from the observability of social life in small societies that there is no privacy in them. And it would be an ethnocentric mistake to conclude, as Posner does, that:

> [T]he concept of privacy, in anything like the senses in which we use it today, is a Western cultural artifact. The idea that it might be pleasant to be off the public stage was hardly meaningful in a society in which physical privacy was essentially nonexistent — was not only prohibitively costly, but also extremely dangerous. Privacy then was the lot of the pariah.[29]

On the contrary, I would hazard a guess that of Benn and Gaus's three dimensions of publicness and privateness — agency, access and interest — privacy of access is the most likely to find counterparts in all societies. Societies differ widely in what they choose to regulate access to, what sorts of behaviour constitute trespass or invasion, what means are available and used to prohibit unauthorised access and in the reasons for which access is considered legitimately restricted. But even the smallest society has norms regulating access to individuals, to domestic units and to significant rituals and ceremonies. It may be, as Simmel and writers influenced by him argue,[30] that maintenance of some degree of privacy and social distance among individuals is necessary in every social relationship. Certainly in small societies, where relationships are multiplex and face-to-face and where many of the physical constraints on observability familiar to us are absent, people frequently take careful, at times quite elaborate, measures to remove certain matters from the public domain. Among the Baktaman:

> Occasions differ radically as to whether they are public, private, or secret, i.e. with respect to the nature of the audience present; and the management of information as one passes between these kinds of audiences is a major concern of the Baktaman.[31]

Among the Mehinaku:

> The dramaturgical problems and opportunities for the actors are very different from those in our own society with its emphasis on privacy and other barriers to communication. In the Mehinaku village everyday conduct — whether gossip, formal speeches, extramarital affairs or children's play — is shaped by a spatial setting that compels each individual to become a master of stagecraft and information control.[32]

The Mehinaku have striking, and even for small societies unusually elaborate, seclusion practices whereby a Mehinaku might during his lifetime spend up to eight years in relative isolation, maintained by both real and symbolic barriers. Among the Tuareg of northern Africa, men cover their faces with a veil so that only areas around the eyes can be seen, and they conceal their faces most completely among those closest to them.[33]

As the materials which Alan Westin summarises make clear, 'Norms of privacy are also found in the family-household settings of primitive life' and '[w]hatever the reasons given, virtually every society holds ceremonies for special groups from which various segments of the whole tribe or community will be barred ... Strict sanctions are imposed on invasion of the privacy of these occasions.'[34] It is significant that in many small societies, information is regarded as an extremely dangerous commodity. Thus the extreme publicity of life in small societies can produce an extreme concern with demarcating zones of privacy and/or secrecy. What Benn and Gaus identify as the tactful recognition of private spaces even within public spaces is also widely reported in small societies.

Nevertheless, in societies where privacy and *anonymity* are so radically unconnected and where there are no public officials, the ways in which order is maintained and disputes, nuisance and deviance dealt with involve publicity and 'publics' of a kind, in several important ways. In such societies 'social life means the submission of an individual to the constant judgement of peers';[35] one is faced always with the 'difficulty of "living down" one's reputation in a close-knit tribal or village society'.[36] It is rarely easy to change one's village, job or social circle. Thus, Richard Sennett's emphasis on the phrase 'out in public' as involving reference to a world of strangers — 'where moral violation occurred and was tolerated; in public one could break the laws of respectability'[37] — presupposes a world unknown to the inhabitant of a small society.

In small societies, being in public has consequences precisely opposite to those that Sennett suggests, and the special importance of good reputation, and fear of its loss, in the lives of small societies becomes comprehensible. The !Kung Bushmen in the Kalahari 'cannot bear the sense of rejection which even mild disapproval makes them feel'.[38] The Mehinaku 'feel shame in a wide variety of circumstances':

> Whatever the source of shame, the villager who experiences it separates himself from his comrades. 'When you are ashamed it hurts to be seen', the Mehinaku say, so the shamed man keeps out of the public eye ... The shamed person physically and symbolically establishes a private world for himself.[39]

Among the Busama of north-eastern New Guinea:

> The attitude of the inhabitants to a breach of custom is summed up in the expression *maya*, the term used for the shame and embarrassment of a person whose unorthodox behaviour has been found out. Asked the reason why he has behaved in a certain way, a Busama usually volunteers the answer that he would have been *maya* ashamed, had he done anything else. If pressed further, he goes on to explain that any failure on his part to take the customary course would have resulted in unpleasant remarks being made about him.[40]

Indeed, Young observes of literature on New Guinea generally that:

> Writers dealing with social control and social conformity in New Guinea find it impossible to avoid mentioning 'shame', though this term is usually an inadequate translation of an indigenous concept which tends to embrace a wide range of affect ... I would endorse Langness's observation ... that 'shame for the natives of New Guinea is an exceedingly powerful emotion', as close to guilt and 'losing face' as it is to the Western concept of shame, 'which is trivial by comparison'.[41]

Examples of 'shaming' used as a device to ensure conformity and reprimand deviance could easily be multiplied. The absence of public agents with a monopoly of legitimate force, combined with the publicity of everyday life, make shaming both a more important and a more potent force than it is in mass societies. Indeed, Posner speculates that the transition from 'shame' to 'guilt' culture is correlated with the ease of maintaining privacy:

Primitive and ancient societies tend to approximate the shame model, more advanced societies (including our own) the guilt model. This pattern may reflect the lack of privacy in primitive and ancient societies. If one is being watched all the time by one's neighbors and relatives, there is no reason to have a sense of being watched all the time by God.[42]

As with several of Posner's speculations, it is difficult to know what to make of this one, but he is not wrong in emphasising the importance of shame in small societies. Ridicule, public harangues, public songs which recount a villain's misdeeds, are widely reported ways in which people in small societies make grievances public, seek public support, shame an opponent in public.

Apart from the use of shame to induce conformity, disputes and dispute settlement are public in a number of other ways. In many small societies lacking officials with power to prevent disputes from escalating or continuing indefinitely, a high value is placed on bringing grievances into the open to avoid having them fester and lead to continued friction. For example, Kenneth Maddock explains that, although aboriginal societies lacked a state, 'The outcome was no Hobbesian war of each against all, for the polity was imbued with juridical and political quality' by a number of features, the first of which is 'the convention whereby issues were aired publicly'.[43] While not all small societies have such a convention, many do, and similar conventions are reported of many societies in New Guinea.

Finally, the multiplexity and density of social networks, and their importance for individual and group survival, have significant effects on what is considered appropriate, indeed essential, to investigate and make public in processes of dispute settlement. In Western courts, especially superior courts, there is often, and deliberately, considerable disparity between what is legally admissible, provable or relevant and what we would consider appropriate to a thorough moral evaluation of, say, the conduct of a criminal accused. Among the things excluded from public scrutiny unless an accused himself chooses to make an issue of them are his personal history, past misdeeds, character. Justice is to be blind to these things. In small societies, however, as in families, small towns and neighbourhoods in large societies, maintenance of mutually dependent relationships is frequently considered as important as, or more important than, the rights and wrongs of specific offences. Moreover, the parties cannot simply avoid each other after guilt or innocence is established. A common consequence is that what our superior courts treat as private is not only regarded as wholly within the public domain, but frequently as more important than the specific acts which might have precipitated a dispute. Thus, even in the highly developed 'legalistic' Lozi courts in (then) Northern Rhodesia, Gluckman observes:

> ... disputes arising out of multiplex relationships have to be settled by broadening the scope of enquiry to cover a long history of relations between the parties and their kin and neighbours, and perhaps their forebears [sic] ... The concept of 'relevant evidence' may therefore be very wide. The kuta [court] attempts to reconcile parties in permanent relationships ... In these cases a litigant comes before the judges not only as a right-and-duty bearing *persona*, but also as an individual involved in a complex of relations with many other persons. Correspondingly, there is no such thing as judicial ignorance, and any judge who knows the parties will volunteer evidence and use his knowledge in judgment ... [T]he kuta ... may also at any point consider any public interests involved; and it may therefore levy a fine in a civil suit, in effect converting it into a criminal trial.
> ... It is clear that were the demands of some British officers, that the kuta should follow English legal procedure, to be successful, the kuta would be prevented from fulfilling one of its main functions — the settlement of disputes arising out of the multiplex relationships which are still basic in tribal life.[44]

IV. Public and Private Interest

Societies can exist, then, without public agents and apparently without a conception of public agency (or at least with no apparent role for such a conception to play). It is also conceivable, though I have denied that it is likely to be the case, for there to be societies with no concerns about questions of access. Is it, however, conceivable for there to be *societies* without any conception analogous to that of public interest? Here the distinction Benn and Gaus draw between two models of social life — individualist and organicist — is particularly useful.

On the individualist model, 'society' is merely the sum of its individual members; nothing more. An individualist might allow talk of a public interest, in the sense of the aggregated individual interests of the members of that society; but he will not be comfortable with the notion, for the reasons that Benn and Gaus have discussed in Chapter 2. They point out that a good many of the ways in which liberal western cultures use the notion of public interest assume a public as a collective entity with its own interests, more in keeping with an organic model. What this suggests, for our purposes, is that if we are seeking in small societies concepts onto which our notions of 'public interest' might latch, we need to find conceptions of the social world which allow for the existence of a social whole which is supra-individual, supra-domestic and is thought of as encompassing, but not reducible to, the interests of individuals. Many anthropologists claim to have discovered just such conceptions and have indeed argued that the cohesion of many small societies depends upon them.

Much of my discussion, and much anthropological discussion of stateless societies, has been prompted by Malinowski's Hobbesian question, how a society could exist without central authority — what structures could support its legal and political processes. In the 1940s British anthropology, particularly in the work of Meyer Fortes and E.E. Evans-Pritchard, made an important theoretical advance in the analysis of the political and legal processes of stateless societies. In their introduction to an extremely influential collection of essays,[45] Fortes and Evans-Pritchard distinguished sharply between two classes of political systems: those which have and those which lack government and sharp divisions of rank, status or wealth. What gave cohesion to the latter and was the basis of identity of and relations between groups was the part played by the lineage system in political structure.[46] In such societies, Fortes and Evans-Pritchard argued, people belonged to 'lineages', that is, groups reckoned on the basis of common descent from a named ancestor: all those and only those descended from this ancestor belonged to the lineage. Most such lineage systems, Fortes and Evans-Pritchard believed, were 'unilineal', that is, descent was reckoned exclusively down either the male line (patrilineal) or, less commonly, the female line (matrilineal). The system of relationships so formed was called a 'segmentary lineage system', for it was composed of numerous small segments related to immediate ancestors ('minimal lineages'), encompassed by fewer larger segments of people connected by descent from more and more remote ancestors, until the one segment including all unilineal descendants of the apical ancestor was reached (the 'maximal lineage'). A maximal lineage is therefore made up of a hierarchy of lower level segments, sentiment within which is more intensely corporate than between those whose only connection is via common descent from a remote ancestor.

In contrast to the public political order regulating relations between groups and established by lineage, private domestic matters were the business of kin, that is, parents, children and the networks of relationship built out of those links. Thus Fortes and Evans-Pritchard explain:

> One of the outstanding differences between the two groups [states and stateless societies] is the part played by the lineage system in political structure . . . In both groups of societies kinship and domestic ties have an important role in the lives of individuals, but their relation to the political system is of a secondary order. In the societies of Group A [i.e. states] it is the administrative organisation, in societies of Group B [i.e. stateless] the segmentary lineage system, which primarily regulates political relations between territorial segments.[47]

In later works, Fortes repeatedly distinguished between the domestic domain on the one hand and the 'politico-jural domain' on the other.

In the works they wrote separately, there was an important, if often overlooked, difference between Evans-Pritchard and Fortes. In *The Nuer*, Evans-Pritchard denied that Nuer lineages formed the basis of corporate groups; 'clans, and even their lineages have no corporate life'.[48] Rather, political groupings were primarily territorially based, though they were associated with and ideologised in terms of lineage doctrine. And even in dogma, members of lineages did not form corporate entities. Rather, as L. Dumont put it in his 'Preface' to the French edition of *The Nuer*:

> I am a member of a group A in a situation which opposes it to group B, but in another situation in which two first-order segments of A are opposed, say A1 and A2, I am a member not of A but of A1, and so on for the lower-order segments. The groupings at different levels coexist all the time, but they are manifest only alternately, according to the circumstances. The permanent reality is the tendency towards fission and fusion. In particular, there is no unilineal group which could properly be called 'corporate', through existing permanently as a *persona moralis* holding goods in common.[49]

Fortes, on the other hand, insisted strongly on the corporate nature of unilineal descent groups. The shift from Evans-Pritchard's analysis is striking. Where Evans-Pritchard emphasised unilineal descent as the basis of an idiom used to conceptualise shifting relationships or alliances often based on other things, Fortes saw it as the basis of solid, collective corporate entities. As he explained:

> The most important feature of unilineal descent groups in Africa brought into focus by recent field research is their corporate organization.
> ... In societies of this type the lineage is not only a corporate unit in the legal or jural sense but is also the primary political association. Thus the individual has no legal or political status except as a member of a lineage; or to put it in another way, all legal and political relations in the society take place in the context of the lineage system.[50]

The influence of this 'discovery' of the importance of unilineal descent has been profound; as one writer has noted (and complained):

> For thirty years the idea that stateless societies needed unilineal descent as the basis for ordered social life led a generation of investigators to search, above all else, for evidence regarding the significance and workings of patrilineages and matrilineages, and phenomena related to these.[51]

Moreover, for some time it was in Fortes's corporate understanding that the significance of unilineal descent was conceived.

Even in Fortes's version, however, one can talk more easily of the interests of various corporate components of a society rather than of an overarching public interest. For in contemporary, centralised states, the 'public interest' is usually treated as society-wide — or polity-wide; the interest shared by 'the people of Australia' rather than, say, the residents of Bondi. In segmentary societies, however, often composed of a congeries of clans, lineages and within them lineage segments, conceptions of common society-wide interests are likely to be weak, and may not exist at all. Generally, there is an inverse correlation between the corporateness of a group and the depth of ancestral connection of its members. As Roger Keesing explains:

> There is an important axis of variation in segmentary patrilineal systems ... In most such systems, it is only the lowest lineage level (minimal lineages) or lowest two levels that occupy single or contiguous territories and are thus localised. And usually it is only such localised segments ... that are strongly corporate ... The higher-

level, dispersed lineage segments ... are usually less strongly corporate (i.e. there are fewer contexts in which people act as a corporate unit, relative to fewer or less important things). At the highest level, descent units ... are not likely to be groups at all, but rather social categories that serve to define the outer limits of exogamy or minimal kinship obligation.[52]

Of course, in terms of actual daily interaction, the situation in a modern state is not altogether dissimilar to that which Keesing describes. But there are two related respects in which it is more plausible to talk of society-wide public interests in contemporary nation states than in stateless societies. First, the existence of an officialdom concerned to impose national boundaries and oversee and regulate traffic across them makes more explicit and clear-cut — to insiders and outsiders — where at least the national 'public' stops. Secondly, the same officialdom seeks to ensure that, while lower level loyalties may be more intense and important for many people than their sense of sharing in a wider public interest, these loyalties are not expressed through conflict among low-level corporate groupings. In plural societies this attempt often fails, but in relatively homogeneous ones, it has some success, if we disregard team sports. Thus, the existence of a unified legal system, enforced by officials professing to be embodiments and bearers of the public interest, is not altogether without significance.

On the other hand, as individualists and pluralists, not to mention Marxists, argue, the idea of a society-wide interest might be an ideological mystification of the truth that in no society is there *a* public interest, though it might still be useful to speak of public as distinct from private interests. In every society, not merely 'stateless' ones, individuals coalesce into groups in competition with other groups; in every society, then, there are many 'publics', if no single public. [See above Ch. 2, p. 36, and Ch. 8, §IV, for discussions of 'publics', pluralism, and corporatism in western liberal cultures. — Eds.]

This point forms the basis of an attempt by the anthropologist M.G. Smith to refine corporate analysis and extend it to the structure of all societies, not merely those which he considers misleadingly characterised as 'stateless'. Smith's ideas are particularly relevant to our discussion, for he explicitly ties the notion of corporateness to that of a 'public'. As Smith defines it, not every aggregate of people constitutes a 'public'. Instead:

> As I use the term, *public* does not include mobs, crowds, casual assemblies, or mass-communication audiences. It does not refer to

such categories as resident aliens, the ill, aged, or unwed, or to those social segments which lack common affairs and organised procedures to regulate them ... Such categories are part of one or more publics; they are not separate publics of their own.[53]

For Smith, a *public* is a corporate group, that is,

an enduring, presumably perpetual group with determinate boundaries and membership, having an internal organisation and a unitary set of external relations, an exclusive body of common affairs, and autonomy and procedures adequate to regulate them.[54]

For comparative structural analysis, Smith believes, it is as important to grasp what 'publics' in different types of society have in common as it is to point to differences in the particular ways in which certain public functions are institutionalised. Whether they have differentiated public agencies, all societies, or at least (for Smith is occasionally ambiguous here) all 'publics', have 'government', that is, processes for the regulation of public affairs:

The critical element in government is its public character. Without a public, there can be neither public affairs nor processes to regulate them. Moreover, while all governments presuppose publics, all publics have governments for the management of their affairs. The nature of these publics is therefore the first object of study.[55]

Moreover, most societies will have many such publics; understanding their structure and activities is crucial for an understanding of the society.

In all of this, the central notion is that of corporateness. In groups that are 'publics' in Smith's sense, one can talk sensibly of public interests, of individuals as members of specific publics, and so on. And though different societies may cash out the notion in different ways, it does appear at least plausible that societies in which corporate ideology is strong will have concepts which overlap with some of the corporate senses of 'publicness'. However, despite the ambiguity of Smith's discussion — sometimes he speaks only of 'publics', sometimes of 'all societies' — this does not account for all societies.

First of all, as Smith appears aware, it has become increasingly clear that many more societies than earlier anthropologists believed have existed without conceptions of relationship on the basis of unilineal descent, and therefore without the neat pattern of their 'society', which Fortes considered so important. Keesing observes, for example:

> [T]ribal societies without unilineal descent systems were long relegated to a kind of negative leftovers bag.
> When a careful sorting out of the contents of the leftover bag was finally undertaken, it turned out that at least one third of all known tribal societies should have been in it. But in sorting them out, anthropologists discovered that it was a very mixed bag.[56]

In the bag are societies with elements that do, according to circumstance, form corporate groups (if not in the prescribed manner) as well as societies with no conception of descent groups and of which it seems to be rather odd to speak of publics or public interests. Among many hunters and gatherers, such as Shoshoni Indians and Eskimos, the primary social groups are nuclear families; among tribal agriculturalists in Southeast Asia, social organisation rests on nuclear families and personal relations (kindred). 'These modes of organisation can, in the absence of corporate descent groupings, assume a much heavier "functional load".'[57] It is stretching terminology rather far to attempt here to maintain sharp distinctions between public and domestic domains.

Moreover, in the past 15-20 years there has been a markedly increased individualism in anthropological accounts of the life of small societies. In part this appears to be a product of changing post-structural-functionalist fashion. Durkheim's stock has fallen; that of Simmel and Malinowski has risen. In part also, however, it is a response to the study of different, more apparently individualistic, societies, especially in the New Guinea Highlands. Thus, much research after Fortes's work, and initially seeking to apply it, especially in the New Guinea Highlands but also in Africa, has revealed the existence of societies which it seems highly artificial to analyse in Fortes's terms. In New Guinea, anthropologists in the 1950s sought to apply his ideas to recently contacted societies in the Highlands. Many of them concluded, following J.A. Barnes's much discussed article, that there is, at least for a large number of New Guinea's many societies, a sharp contrast 'between African group solidarity and New Guinea network cohesion', 'between group solidarity and individual enterprise'.[58] Indeed, on the basis of comparison between the Konso of Ethiopia and the Tauade of Papua, one anthropologist makes a perhaps overdrawn but highly suggestive contrast between two sorts of cognitive orientation, the Aristotelean and the Heraclitean.[59] The former, he believes, characterises Konso ways of conceptualising the social world and Konso modes of social interaction; the latter is characteristic of the Tauade. The former have what Benn and Gaus would call an 'organic' conception of social life (Ch. 2, §III); they 'treat groups and categories as fundamental, and regard behaviour both actual and normative as deriving from the groups and categories of which the agent is a member'.[60] The latter see society individualistically, atomistically; 'the opposite type of society ... will be one which regards relationships between individuals as basic, and any existing groups and categories as the precipitate of these relationships'.[61]

> We may ... summarize the concerns of Konso society as 'the social order' in general, and in particular as boundaries both spatial and social ... For the Tauade the individual, the particular, is significant; the general, the categorical, elicits no attention or interest. Thus we find a great indifference to boundaries, social, spatial, and conceptual.[62]

In societies closer to the 'Heraclitean' pole, it is likely, for the reasons suggested by Benn and Gaus, that conceptions which we could recognise as similar to that of the public interest will be weak or non-existent. In Africa, too, several students of processes of disputing and dispute settlement found groupings which became involved in disputes, such as age mates, kin, neighbours, which are in no sense corporate in character. Thus Gulliver explains of the Arusha of Tanzania that:

> It should be clear that this Arusha patrilineal system differs from the segmentary lineage systems which have been described for a number of African societies. In those cases, lineage segments of whatever order act as specifically corporate groups in opposition to like segments of the encompassing whole ... Among the Arusha, where there exist only structural categories of relationships, the first consideration is given to the individual support of a person involved in a dispute. Each party of supporters is, therefore, orientated to a particular person; it is only a collectivity of people which that person musters and engages on his behalf for the specific purpose at that time ... That is to say, a pair of patrilineal segments cannot act in opposition to each other *qua* segments; groups brought into opposition are entirely of an *ad hoc* constitution.[63]

Similarly, the Ndendeuli of East Africa 'had no corporate groups, or enduring units definable in terms of actual interaction, based on kinship, lineal or otherwise'.[64]

Quite apart from the number of societies which do not profess the importance of unilineal descent, there is a separate question as to what role such conceptions — where they exist — actually play in social life. Since in our own society it is not obvious either that conceptions of the public interest are irrelevant to social action or that they determine it, anthropological discussion of this question deserves to be more widely known and appreciated than it appears to be. In the past 15 years or so, anthropologists have argued that many earlier corporate theorists exaggerated or misinterpreted the significance of corporate ideology in actual social interaction. Even where such ideology exists, it often has a far more limited range of relevance and importance than Fortes, for example, suggested. Where Fortes argued that conceptions of unilineal descent are the rules for and the basis of groups allegiance and division, the situation on the ground has come to appear far more complicated. Many studies of social interaction in small societies have revealed groupings, alliances, conflicts that cut across ideologies of descent and involve other sources of connection or division based on non-corporate relationships, such as family ties, age-sets and locality. E.L. Peters has observed, for example, that:

> When a Bedouin kills another in Cyrenaica, one of a number of consequences ensues. According to the Bedouin, the particular consequence is determined by the genealogical positions of the persons or groups concerned . . . [in fact] the lineage model neither covers several important areas of social relationships nor enables an accurate prediction of events to be made . . . The argument advanced [by Peters] is that the lineage model is not a sociological one, but that it is a frame of reference used by a particular people to give them a common-sense kind of understanding of their social relationships. For sociological purposes this means that the lineage model, with its supporting theoretical presuppositions, must perforce be abandoned.[65]

Such examples make the point, perhaps not earthshaking but important for students of the public/private distinction *in social life*, that one should be careful to distinguish at least between use of conceptions of corporate connection, as means of conveying what people *say* they do and as means of describing what they *actually* do. The existence of discrepancies does not, of course, necessarily imply that corporate ideology is unimportant, nor, of course, that such discrepancies are found only in pre-literate societies; similar sorts of discrepancies also arise in relation to talk and action in western societies.

However, merely to distinguish between what people say they do and what they actually do is inadequate to capture the role of ideology in social life, both in small and large societies. S.F. Moore distinguishes usefully between three levels of analysis: the 'ideological', the 'jural', and the 'statistical-behavioural'. Descent ideology occupies the first level and it

> is an *ideology of identities*, a model of relationships in the sense of *homologies*, not of behavior. As such, it is an idea that can be used in many different ways, and it is enormously adaptable and manipulable. It may be used literally to define the membership of social categories or units. It may be used symbolically to represent identities of interest or category that, in fact, are not genealogical descent relationships at all.[66]

Distinct from, but influenced in complex and varying ways by, such an ideology of identities are 'those practical binding rules that actually regulate the "on the ground" operations of a particular society'.[67] It is not merely a question of discrepancy between ideology and practice, but between ideology, authoritative legal norms and social practice. Just as one cannot read off complex jural realities from ideology, which 'sometimes has descent and its elaborations as the be-all and end-all',[68] so, too, as a wealth of contemporary legal anthropology has demonstrated, and a second's thought about the relations of law and life in our own society would suggest, the law-affected behaviour of ordinary people cannot simply be deduced from the laws they profess to obey. Thus a doctrine of unilineal connection may exist and be an important element in people's conception of their societies and themselves, while at the same time neither necessarily prescribing what they should do nor describing what they actually do. Conversely, to discover discrepancies between conceptions such as the public interest, legal rules and actual practice is merely the beginning of insight. By themselves such discrepancies in no way show that the conceptions are untrue, unimportant or impotent.

On the one hand, then, where corporate ideology, whether based on lineage or public interest, does exist, legal anthropology is a useful corrective against either resting with it as an explanation of or prescription for action or rejecting it as 'merely' a mystification of the flux of everyday life.

On the other hand, very many small-scale aggregations exist which cannot be said to be or to belong to 'publics' in Smith's sense. Smith does talk of 'quasi-corporations' and 'corporate categories' (almost but not quite corporate groups), but one might object to such formulations on much the same grounds as Smith objects to contrasts between states and stateless societies. They prejudge the question of whether corporateness (or its partial absence) is the best starting-point for analysing social life. Moreover, in terms of the public/private distinction, what are we to say of these aggregations: if some are quasi-corporations, are they quasi-publics? Do they have quasi-public affairs? If so, we will mean something very different from what someone would mean who talked about 'quasi-public' and 'quasi-private' officers within a state, in QANGOs, for instance, working *for* it but not unambiguously of it (see Ch. 2, §II.C, above). Yet it would, as we have seen, put a considerable strain on language to call such aggregations, or the lives, pursuits, disputes of people within them, private.

V. 'Primitive Law': Public, Private, Neither, Both?

The preceding discussion of the importance and complexity of the ties which bind members of small societies can help us to re-examine some of the contrasts, with which we began, between contemporary western and primitive law. Whether or not such systemic public/private contrasts caricature the legal systems of complex societies, they certainly serve to obscure some of the most distinctive characteristics of the law of small societies.

A number of authors, it will be remembered, have suggested that law has developed from private self-help in stateless societies to public law enforcement in states. The most anthropologically sophisticated among them, E.A. Hoebel, was aware, however, that even the most 'private' form of legitimate retribution or redress has a necessary 'public' aspect, for its legitimacy rests on public approval, or at least tolerance. Thus he writes:

> In any primitive society the so-called 'private prosecutor' of a private injury is implicitly a public official pro tempore, *pro eo solo delicto*. He is not and cannot be acting solely on his own, his family's, or his clan's behalf and yet enjoy the approval or tacit support of the 'disinterested' remainder of his society.[69]

But in making this quasi-Durkheimian concession, Hoebel simply lurches from one false extreme to the other, for he insists that 'the private prosecutor remains the representative of the general social interest as well as that which is specifically his own'.[70] But quite apart from the difficulty of specifying the 'general social interest' in, for example, segmentary societies, few disputes in small societies can satisfactorily be portrayed *either* as clearly private *or* public in any of the senses suggested above, and few of the matters which lead to disputes or grievance can be, at least in prospect, classified as being of their nature either public or private. Certainly, the fact that in the first instance an aggrieved individual instigates action is not of great moment.

I mentioned earlier, and it is an anthropological commonplace, that in small societies, not mere *acts* but *relationships* count for a great deal. This is true both of disputes which do not, and those which do, follow corporate lines. In small societies of both sorts, first of all the relationship between the *disputants* is crucial, for it affects the way the dispute develops, who else will become involved, and what pressures they will bring to bear. Moreover, disputants, unless they are very closely related, will seek to muster supporters, and their success in doing so, in raising their dispute to one of more *public* concern, will depend not primarily on the nature of the act which has caused grievance – and not simply on the relationships between the original disputants – but also on the relationships between disputants and those from whom they seek support, between supporters of one disputant and those of another and between disputants and their allies and parties with links to both sides. According to who is, who can be induced to be, and in whose interest it is, for whatever reason, to become involved, disputes over the same *acts* can have quite different ramifications and consequences.

This is why attempts to categorise the law of small societies as either private or public on the grounds either of the nature of the offending act or of who instigates legal action are so unsatisfying. Lawrence illustrates the problem well for the Papua New Guinea context. Criticising Radcliffe-Brown's distinction between public and private delicts in terms of whether the community takes action or not, Lawrence argues:

> Such an approach to Papua New Guinea society – which differs, in fact, little from the uncritical use of the terms crime and tort – can be criticised cogently on the ground that nothing is truly 'public' or 'private'. Thus offences such as adultery, homicide and pig-killing may lead to a violent reaction from any number of people. Yet they are not public in the sense that Radcliffe-Brown intended.

They do not affect the society at large nor does the society at large inflict punishment. At most they affect a tribe, a phratry, a clan, or a lineage (each of which is only a *part* of a Papua New Guinea society) according to the range of the dispute, but people outside that range (although of the same society) do not get involved ... By the same token, it is impossible to define a purely 'private delict'. *Ceteris paribus*, some offences such as pig-killing could be so regarded ... Retaliatory action is determined by the social range of the relationship between the parties concerned and also by the state of relations between the groups to which they belong. If the two groups are at peace, the plaintiff's reaction is likely to be individual and mild. Yet it generally happens that they are in a state of mutual enmity or feud, in which case the plaintiff's personal reaction is overshadowed by that of the group to which he belongs and which thinks that its interests have been threatened.[71]

Moreover, anyone seeking more than vindication by definition of the claim that in stateless societies there can be no public law should appreciate one of the most important features of disputes and law in small societies: what Moore terms the 'expandability of disputes'. Given the multiplexity of relationships and the many structural bases of potential alliance and opposition in small societies, contrasts between systems of 'self-help', allegedly characteristic of primitive societies, and 'impartial official justice', allegedly the norm in developed societies, are quite unrealistic. Moore is one of the few anthropologists to have examined such contrasts closely and critically. She dissents strongly from Hoebel's view that 'private law predominates on the primitive scene'; disputes between individuals in pre-industrial societies can have a far wider structural impact than analogous disputes in complex societies. 'Self-help', as used to characterise a type of dispute settlement, must be taken to include the possible mobilisation, in appropriate circumstances, of a number of supporters on each side. These supporters' *own* interests, relationships and antagonisms will all be relevant in determining the range of people who ultimately become involved. Consequently, disputes over similar matters of substance can sometimes expand, and at others can be held to disputes between the contending individuals. It all depends on the kinds of networks, groups and administrative structures that are or choose to be implicated.

When a man invokes the help of others, he is likely to avail himself of relationships and structures already existing in terms of other contexts of action. He may mobilize his lineage or his village. He may mobilize local political or religious leaders. His cause then also serves the purposes of others and will reinforce pre-existing groupings, relationships and political positions.[72]

Though Moore rejects system-wide contrasts between legal systems in terms of their essentially 'public' or 'private' character, she does not abandon the distinction. Rather she finds it useful to follow Smith in defining a 'public' as a corporate group, as a consequence of which one will be able to talk of public law wherever there are corporate groups, in pre-industrial and industrial settings. One will not be reduced to facile contrasts between whole social and legal systems.

Although it deviates considerably from lawyers' notions of public law, Moore's extension of Smith is particularly useful for comparative analysis. It avoids the common and misleading tendency to portray as *conceptually* necessary what are merely contingent features of a writer's world. But, as Moore recognises, many groups exist which fall outside this definition, since they are not corporate. Here, too, in relations within and between such groups, much goes on *in* public that is not the doing of *a* public.

VI. Conclusions

Some years ago there was a long and ultimately rather fruitless controversy among legal anthropologists about what concepts were proper to use when writing about the norms and social processes of other societies.[73] On one side some, notably Max Gluckman, drew explicitly and unashamedly on concepts from western law and jurisprudence in order both to illumine the processes of the people they studied and to enable comparisons between what they saw in the field and what occurred in their own and other societies. On the other side, such anthropologists as Paul Bohannan insisted that Gluckman's methods were inherently ethnocentric, for the following reason. Each society works with what Bohannan called 'folk' concepts, concepts used within a society by its members 'for the purposes of action'. Blithely to talk of 'law', 'rights', 'torts', 'contracts' when describing the activities of societies quite unlike our own is to run the risk of imposing one's own 'folk' concepts on those of the society one is observing, and thus of distorting them. Bohannan distinguished a folk system, 'a systematization of ethnographic fact for purposes of social action', from an 'analytic' system, 'a systematization of ethnographic fact for purposes of analysis'; and he warned that 'the anthropologist's chief danger is that he will change one of the folk systems of his own society into an analytic system, and try to give it wider application than its merit and usefulness allow'.[74]

In Bohannan's terms, the public/private distinction is clearly part of the folk system of many in the developed West. Moreover, as I have sought to indicate, presupposed in our use of the distinction are matters not merely of 'ideology' as opposed to logic, but of political and social structures and relationships, housing and settlement patterns, technological development, even architecture. Of what importance is it to know that many societies differ greatly from ours in all or some of these respects?

The answer to this question depends on the context within which the distinction is used. Three such contexts seem to me important. In 'folk' discussions of our own law, such data should make us aware of the contingency of much that is familiar and that might otherwise appear necessary or at least natural. Thus one writer likens the intellectual profit to be gained from anthropology to the pleasures of travel:

> Differences of physical environment, modes of social intercourse, or patterns of culture awaken us to phenomena which at home are so mundane as to be almost invisible. When we resume our mundane round, the residue of such impressions compels us to recognize the contingency of our own ways, and leads us to look for explanations.[75]

Such knowledge might make our use of folk conceptions more enlightened, and our explanations of the familiar better informed. More important, it might direct those interested in understanding law toward reflection on those areas of law-affected life in industrial societies where public institutions are not customarily invoked and one or other form of 'private ordering', such as bargaining, threatening, compromising, resigning, is relied upon. *Most* law-affected life, after all, is of this sort: it is affected but frequently neither determined by nor transacted before public institutions. Recognition of this, and of its implications for our understanding of the social significance of such institutions, would redress the simplistic over-emphasis on public institutions which often occurs both in liberal ideology and legal theory.[76]

Not knowing the language of any small society, I have no way of knowing, but also no reason to believe, that such languages contain concepts akin to our public/private distinction. There are and have been many societies, and, as cognitive anthropologists have been at pains to remind us, it is no small matter to glean, unravel and reveal the concepts used in any *one* society, however small and apparently simple. In our own language, the public/private distinction does not merely operate along the three dimensions discussed by Benn and Gaus but it links all three dimensions in a concept that we often use imprecisely but readily understand. Moreover, it does so in a highly abstract, decontextualised manner. But there is no obvious reason why distinctions along these three dimensions *need* to be made in terms of one common, or even linked, set of conceptual categories. Moreover, it has been strongly argued, if not conclusively established, that in literate cultures more abstract concepts become available than in oral cultures, that

> writing establishes a different kind of relationship between the word and its referent, a relationship that is more general and more abstract, and less closely connected with the particularities of person, place and time, than obtains in oral communication.[77]

I know of no discussion focusing specifically on the public/private distinction, but I find suggestive Jack Goody's discussion of the influence of literacy on modes of thought generally, and a much-discussed and in some ways analogous distinction — that between 'nature' and 'culture' — in particular:

> This opposition has penetrated so deeply into cultural analyses that we regard it as 'natural', inevitable. However, the division between nature and culture is in some ways rather artificial. For example, many foods fall into an intermediate category, being uncooked yet cultivated, or only collected by human hand.
> If the dichtomy is not all that obvious in our own society . . . in many other cultures we find no corresponding pair of concepts . . . I would claim that there is no such pair in either of the two African languages known personally to me (LoDagaa and Gonja). Though there is certain 'opposition' of 'bush' and 'house', 'cultivated' and 'uncultivated', there is nothing that would correspond to the highly abstract and rather eighteenth-century dichotomy that is current in Western intellectual circles — though less evident in popular usage.[78]

If there is any weight in Goody's argument, I would for analogous reasons consider it highly unlikely that the public/private distinction is a cultural universal.

If, however, we seek to use the distinction for cross-cultural analytic purposes, we are in principle not tied either to our own folk concepts nor those of others. On the one hand, since so much of our use of concepts is impregnated with unexamined assumptions, it is important to be wary when calling on them to travel. This is especially the case when, like some of the authors discussed here, one gives little thought to the complexity of the processes one is seeking to encapsulate with this ambiguous and well-worn (not to say shop-soiled) distinction. On the other hand, it is not obvious to me that we should disqualify familiar and important concepts from use in any but narrowly 'internal' contexts. In any event that would not be easy to do successfully, given the pervasiveness of conceptions such as publicness and privateness in our language, thought and moral life. Nor is it clear that mental hygiene requires it. It does require precise definition and deliberate effort to counteract conceptual imperialism, a common disease among philosophers, and equally to avoid conceptual parochialism, which, like malaria, often afflicts anthropologists who have spent time in the field. Finally, however, as the sociologist Vilhelm Aubert concluded in another context:

'It may well be that a good way of understanding what goes on in the other people's minds is to use the schemes which are available in one's own mind. They may, or may not, fit, but this method seems to be one of those we always have to use. Some do it well, others do it less well. Some read into others what they find in themselves, but some also fail to see parallels which are actually there. The one fallacy is as dangerous as the other one. But I do not think this is a point which can profitably be pursued in abstract debates without simultaneously having a chance to inspect the data.'[79]

Notes

I am grateful to Dr Owen Jessep of the University of New South Wales, Professor Sally Falk Moore of Harvard University and the editors for their generous and useful advice on an earlier draft of this chapter.

1. Bronislaw Malinowski, 'A New Instrument for the Interpretation of Law — Especially Primitive', *Yale Law Journal*, 51 (1942), p. 1238.

2. S.I. Benn and G.F. Gaus, Ch. 1, §III, p. 6, above.
3. Emile Durkheim, *The Division of Labor in Society*, George Simpson (trans.) (The Free Press of Glencoe, New York, 1964), p. 68.
4. Ibid., p. 113.
5. Ibid., p. 68.
6. Ibid., p. 102.
7. Ibid., p. 115.
8. Cf. Sally Falk Moore, 'Legal Liability and Evolutionary Interpretation: Some Aspects of Strict Liability, Self-help, and Collective Responsibility', reprinted in her *Law as Process* (Routledge and Kegan Paul, London, 1978), pp. 87-89.
9. A.R. Radcliffe-Brown, 'Primitive Law', reprinted in his *Structure and Function in Primitive Society* (Cohen and West, London, 1952), pp. 212-13.
10. L.T. Hobhouse, *Morals in Evolution* (Chapman and Hall, London, 1951) (first published in 1906), p. 354.
11. R.R. Marett, *Anthropology* (Thornton Butterworth, London, 1914), p. 193.
12. E. Adamson Hoebel, *The Law of Primitive Man* (Harvard University Press, Cambridge, Mass., 1954), pp. 327, 329.
13. Richard A. Posner, 'The Economic Theory of Primitive Law', in his *The Economics of Justice* (Harvard University Press, Cambridge, Mass., 1981), p. 192.
14. Roberto Mangabeira Unger, *Law in Modern Society: Toward a Criticism of Social Theory* (The Free Press, New York, 1976), p. 58.
15. See my 'Anthropological Approaches' in Eugene Kamenka and Alice Erh-Soon Tay (eds.), *Law and Social Control* (Edward Arnold, London, 1980).
16. Benn and Gaus, Ch. 1, §VI.B, p. 17, above.
17. Ibid., §IV.B, p. 9. See also Finn, Ch. 4, above.
18. Kenneth Maddock, *The Australian Aborigines: A Portrait of Their Society* (Penguin, Harmondsworth, 1975), p. 44.
19. A.L. Epstein (ed.), his 'Introduction' to *Contention and Dispute* (Australian National University Press, Canberra, 1974), p. 28.
20. Marshall D. Sahlins, 'Poor Man, Rich Man, Big Man, Chief: Political Types in Melanesia and Polynesia' in Ian Hogbin and L.R. Hiatt (eds.), *Readings in Australian and Pacific Anthropology* (Melbourne University Press, Melbourne, 1966), pp. 163, 165.
21. Hoebel, *Law of Primitive Man*, p. 133.
22. Cf. Peter Lawrence, 'Papua New Guineans and the Rule of Law', paper presented to the World Congress on Philosophy of Law and Social Philosophy, Sydney/Canberra, 14-21 August 1977, pp. 16-17.
23. Fredrik Barth, *Ritual and Knowledge among the Baktaman of New Guinea* (Yale University Press, New Haven, Conn., 1975), p. 24.
24. Ibid., p. 26.
25. John M. Roberts and Thomas Gregor, 'Privacy: A Cultural View' in J. Roland Pennock and John W. Chapman (eds.), *NOMOS XIII: Privacy* (Atherton Press, New York, 1971), pp. 199-225, at p. 204.
26. Thomas Gregor, 'Exposure and Seclusion: A Study of Institutionalized Isolation Among the Mehinacu Indians of Brazil', *Ethnology*, 9 (1970), pp. 234-50, at p. 238.
27. Roberts and Gregor, 'Privacy: A Cultural View', p. 201.
28. Thomas Gregor, *Mehinaku: The Drama of Daily Life in a Brazilian Indian Village* (University of Chicago Press, Chicago, 1977), p. 361.
29. Posner, 'A Broader View of Privacy', in *Economics of Justice*, pp. 268-69.
30. See Kurt H. Wolff (ed. and trans.), *The Sociology of Georg Simmel* (The Free Press of Glencoe, New York, 1950), esp. Pt. Four, 'The Secret and the Secret Society', pp. 307-76; and Robert F. Murphy, 'Social Distance and the Veil', *American Anthropologist*, 66 (1964), pp. 1257-74.

31. Barth, *Ritual and Knowledge among the Baktaman*, p. 26.
32. Gregor, *Mehinaku*, pp. 1-2.
33. Murphy, 'Social Distance and the Veil', *passim*.
34. Alan F. Westin, *Privacy and Freedom* (Association of the Bar of the City of New York, New York, 1967), pp. 15, 18.
35. Elizabeth Colson, *Tradition and Contract: The Problem of Order* (Aldine, Chicago, 1974), p. 58.
36. Posner, 'A Broader View of Privacy', p. 288.
37. Richard Sennett, *The Fall of Public Man* (Cambridge University Press, Cambridge, 1974), p. 23.
38. Lorna Marshall, 'Sharing, Talking, and Giving: Relief of Social Tensions among !Kung Bushmen', *Africa*, 31 (1961), pp. 231-49, at p. 232.
39. Gregor, *Mehinaku*, pp. 220-21.
40. H. Ian Hogbin, 'A Study of Social Conformity in a New Guinea Village', *Oceania*, vol. 17 (1947), p. 273.
41. Michael W. Young, *Fighting with Food* (Cambridge University Press, Cambridge, 1971), pp. 261-62.
42. Posner, 'A Broader View of Privacy', pp. 277-78.
43. Maddock, *Australian Aborigines*, p. 43.
44. Max Gluckman, *The Judicial Process Among the Barotse of Northern Rhodesia [Zambia]*, 2nd edn (Manchester University Press, Manchester, 1955), pp. 80-81.
45. M. Fortes and E.E. Evans-Pritchard (eds.), their 'Introduction' to *African Political Systems* (Oxford University Press, London, 1940) pp. 1-23.
46. Ibid., p. 5.
47. Ibid., p. 6.
48. E.E. Evans-Pritchard, *The Nuer* (Oxford University Press, Oxford, 1940), p. 264.
49. L. Dumont, 'Preface to the French Edition of E.E. Evans-Pritchard's *The Nuer*', M. Douglas and J. Douglas (trans.) in J.H.M. Beattie and R.G. Lienhardt (eds.), *Studies in Social Anthropology* (Clarendon Press, Oxford, 1975), p. 335.
50. M. Fortes, 'The Structure of Unilineal Descent Groups', *American Anthropologist*, 55 (1953), pp. 25, 26.
51. Herbert S. Lewis, 'Neighbors, Friends, and Kinsmen: Principles of Social Organization Among the Cushitic-Speaking Peoples of Ethiopia', *Ethnology*, 13 (1974), p. 145.
52. Roger M. Keesing, *Kin Groups and Social Structure* (Holt, Rinehart and Winston, New York, 1975), p. 32.
53. M.G. Smith, 'A Structural Approach to Comparative Politics' in his *Corporations and Society* (Duckworth, London, 1974), p. 93.
54. Ibid., p. 94.
55. Ibid., p. 93.
56. Keesing, *Kin Groups and Social Structure*, p. 91.
57. Ibid., p. 97.
58. J.A. Barnes, 'Africian Models in the New Guinea Highlands', *Man*, 62 (1962), pp. 8, 9. For recent discussions of this literature see Ivan Karp, 'New Guinea Models in the African Savannah', *Africa*, 48 (1978), pp. 1-16, and Michel Verdon, 'Descent: An Operational View', *Man* (N.S.), 15 (1980), pp. 129-50.
59. C.R. Hallpike, *Bloodshed and Vengeance in the Papuan Mountains: The Generation of Conflict in Tauade Society* (Clarendon Press, Oxford, 1977), pp. 77-79 and *passim*.
60. Ibid., p. v.
61. Ibid.

62. Ibid., pp. 79, 81.

63. P.H. Gulliver, *Social Control in an African Society* (Routledge and Kegan Paul, London, 1963), pp. 126-27.

64. P.H. Gulliver, *Neighbours and Networks* (University of California Press, London, 1971), p. 5.

65. E.L. Peters, 'Some Structural Aspects of the Feud Among the Camel-herding Bedouin of Cyrenaica', *Africa*, 37 (1967), p. 261.

66. Moore, 'Descent and Legal Position' in *Law as Process*, p. 156.

67. Ibid., p. 158.

68. Ibid., p. 175.

69. Hoebel, *Law of Primitive Man*, p. 27.

70. Ibid.

71. Lawrence, 'Papua New Guineans and the Rule of Law', p. 16.

72. Moore, 'Legal Liability and Evolutionary Interpretation', p. 106.

73. The controversy was carried on for some time in a number of fora. See, for example, Max Gluckman, 'Concepts in the Comparative Study of Tribal Law', in Laura Nader (ed.), *Law in Culture and Society* (Aldine, Chicago, 1969), pp. 337-73, and Paul Bohannan, 'Ethnography and Comparison in Legal Anthropology' in ibid., pp. 401-18.

74. Paul Bohannan, *Justice and Judgment among the Tiv* (Oxford University Press, Oxford, 1957), p. 5.

75. Richard L. Abel, 'A Comparative Theory of Dispute Institutions in Society', *Law and Society Review*, 8 (1973), p. 219.

76. For suggestions of some obvious parallels between the 'law' of small societies and many forms of 'private ordering' in law-affected life in our own society, see my 'Anthropological Approaches', pp. 55-59, and Simon Roberts, 'Law and the Study of Social Control in Small-scale Societies', *Modern Law Review*, 39 (1976), pp. 663-79, at pp. 676-79. For a particularly thorough critique of what he calls the 'legal centralist model' of /western legal systems, see Marc Galanter, 'Justice in Many Rooms: Courts, Private Ordering, and Indigenous Law', *Journal of Legal Pluralism*, 19 (1981), pp. 1-47.

77. Jack Goody and Ian Watt, 'The Consequences of Literacy', *Comparative Studies in Society and History* (1963), p. 44.

78. Jack Goody, *The Domestication of the Savage Mind* (Cambridge University Press, Cambridge, 1977), p. 64.

79. Vilhelm Aubert, as quoted in Laura Nader, 'Introduction' to *Law in Culture and Society*, p. 3.

14 PRIVACY IN A MEXICAN INDIAN VILLAGE

Leslie K. Haviland and John B. Haviland

The guarded privacy of peasant life has long been a commonplace of European folk wisdom. One portrait of the peasant shows him to be narrow-minded, distrustful, mean and quarrelsome, having only slightly more use for his neighbour than he has for a stranger, a thorough unbeliever in the concept of the public good, an 'amoral familist' whose social ethics stop at his own front door. Peasant privacy in this picture is but another face of selfish ignorance. Competing with this unappealing fellow is the sturdy, self-reliant, open-hearted salt of the earth, the unhurried husbander of nature's forces, whose elemental skills protect him from the vagaries of modern civilisation. Peasant privacy in this view is the natural outcome of thoroughgoing independence.

In our work in a Mexican Indian village, we too have been struck by the extreme privacy of peasant social life. Zinacantecos have a well-developed respect for self-reliance and the security it brings, a deep distrust of relations with outsiders. One can, in the village of Nabenchauk, and, indeed, in many small farming communities around the world, track a constellation of behaviours that monitor interaction between people, that limit cooperation, and that otherwise isolate social units, of varying dimensions, from one another. We have sought in our research first to characterise this constellation of behaviours in Zinacantan. Second, we have tried to discover, in the social structure of the village, in its economic and political history, and in the beliefs and understandings of its inhabitants, the sources and concomitants of this constellation of behaviours. In seeking to understand Zinacanteco social life, we do not begin with an ideology of privacy — with a 'peasant world view', tracing the shoots of this root idea out into the social relations among people; rather, we begin with the complex relations between the social institutions of peasant life and the material conditions which people interpret in terms of an ideology of privacy and atomism. Finally, from this work, we have aimed to portray peasant social life more generally and to understand its determinants. In this chapter we explore privacy in one Mexican Indian village — the spatial and social boundedness of households, the delineation of property and resources, the careful control of information and the cautious nature of social interaction.

I. Zinacantan

Nabenchauk is one of a cluster of Indian villages known collectively as the township of Zinacantan, nestled in the high valleys of the mountains of Chiapas, in southern Mexico. The villages of Zinacantan share an ethnic identity signalled by their style of dress and by their dialect of Tzotzil, one of four Mayan languages in the region. Zinacanteco ethnic identity is also codified and institutionalised by a long-governing tradition of colonial and republican Mexico, which organised the Indian communities into civic entities with a formal political structure for purposes of intercourse with the wider legal and political framework.

The Spanish conquest reached Zinacantan within five years of the fall of the Aztec empire, and, by the sixteenth century, Zinacantecos were paying tribute and organising forced labour gangs for their new Spanish overlords. In the later years of the colony, and throughout the pre-revolutionary republican era, Zinacantecos progressively lost control of most of their lands. Some became debtor peons on hacienda estates; others exchanged their day labour for rights to farm the marginal lands of the ranches carved from formerly Zinacanteco lands. The return of freed peons to their ancestral villages in the twentieth century and the tide of demographic increase completely outstripped the gains made through the redistribution of land to Indian communities. Zinacantecos today are growers of maize, beans and squash, producers of almost all their material needs, trading in a small way for specialised commodities, and providing a surplus for the metropolitan centres. If they are to feed themselves from their own produce, however, let alone produce a surplus to exchange for cash in the marketplace, modern Zinacanteco farmers must rent land.

The social result of the skimming of surplus production by members of the urban-based society is double. Through it the peasant is socially linked by ties of dependency, whether jural or economic, to the urban society, ties which may proliferate in a market economy. And, by this outflow of surplus production, the peasant is reduced to a subsistence economy at home, in which all hands available in a household are turned to a broad range of productive activities of self-sustenance.

We may surmise — and in part this description grows out of an anthropological myth about traditional Middle American societies — that the ancestors of modern Zinacantecos once inhabited a society of thoroughgoing communality. Land, the principal resource, was held communally by the group; production was organised through corporate groups of kin (lineages). Moreover, ritual practices were aimed at securing the welfare of the entire group: each individual soul was to be in harmony with itself and with souls of other members of the domestic group; each house participated in common ritual with others who shared the same waterhole; the well-being of the whole community was the joint responsibility of ritual practitioners, whose activities were subsidised by the entire population.

But Zinacanteco life, under the management of the colony, the republic, the revolutionary state and its present descendant, derives from changed conditions which all conspire to render social relations somewhat more individualistic, somewhat more commutable today than yesterday. In numerous ways the social relations among villagers today and the customary exchanges which surround and express them show the ongoing effects of the transformation of Zinacanteco Indians into market-oriented peasants. Social obligations and expectations once satisfiable only through specific goods and services have become market relationships, relationships that can accept a generalised medium of exchange, such as money, in the place of specific, socially imbedded goods and services.

For one example, weaving labour appears once to have been a matter solely of social obligation, the labour given under certain circumstances and to certain people without direct or immediate reciprocation – sister to sister, mother to daughter, aunt to niece. As such, it remained undefined by any specified value equivalencies for the purpose of sale or exchange. Today, as woven garments find a market in the tourist shops of the cities, women are struggling to determine a cash value for their labour input. Very young women and widows today weave for cash the garments needed in the households of their kinsmen to whom only two generations ago they would have given them freely.

Today, the capacity of the agriculturalist to maintain the family by the efforts of the family alone, unimpeded by social ties of kinship and cooperative ownership which characterise tribal horticulturalists, makes of the smallholder a potential social anarchist. In Zinacantan, the scarcity of land and the decreased productivity occasioned by land rent as a condition of production, have prised the individual producing household out of its social imbeddedness, leaving Zinacantecos to define and carry out their life choices individually, within the parameters of the market economy, and with a position in it as illiterate, unskilled producers with an inadequate command of the national language.

Language and dress still set Zinacantecos apart from other Chiapas peasants, and there are still religious ceremonies that engage all members of the municipality and distinguish them from their neighbours, both Indian and non-Indian. But for a Zinacanteco, ethnic identity is not enough to sustain commonality of interest, not enough to inspire cooperation or to ensure loyalty. It is more like a fence by which an individual Zinacanteco can shield himself from the outside, thus limiting the social universe with which he must deal.

II. 'Public' and 'Private': Problems of Translation in Ethnography

When we come as anthropologists to a village like Nabenchauk, we do not confront a place, a society, a way of life which we already command. We cannot rely, as we look at what is happening around us, on our ordinary presumptions, as competent members of the society. Our need is not only to untangle the conceptual underpinnings of our language in order to describe phenomena; we must discover as well what the phenomena are. Our problem is not a matter of classification or assignment at all ('Is this act public or private?'), but something rather more primitive. At this first stage of understanding, we must discover what counts as an act; we must locate behaviour, belief, institutions; we must learn how to attach meaning to action or to work out functions and purposes. (For the ethnographer in the field, there is often a further, pressing problem: how to behave oneself. And though we may not be completely at a loss, living as we do among other human beings, our blunders will be constant and often disastrous.)

Within this low-level anthropological task, we may make three different sorts of appeal to the public/private dichotomy. We may encounter native notions (as evidenced, for example, through forms of speech) about how social life is conceived by native actors themselves – notions that, for one reason or another, we may gloss by words like 'private' or 'public'. For example, when an event is described in Nabenchauk as taking place *ta jamaltik*, we may feel justified, given a certain context, in glossing the phrase which means literally 'in the open', as 'in public'. Second, it may be that a distinction between public and private domains – places, property, behaviour, information – can enhance our ethnographic analysis, whether or not natives can be seen to employ such notions in their own social discourse. So, for example, we may say, felicitously, that certain behaviour – say, a Zinacanteco girl's running away from a visitor – evinces a 'desire for privacy', even when the most the girl herself can say is *tol chk'elvan*, literally 'people look too much'. Finally, we make more contentious, rhetorical, motivated use of notions of privacy and publicness (appealing to a 'public good' or sneering at 'private interests') as we evaluate native life. Such appeals frequently figure in the discourse of agents of manipulative social and political change — advocates of 'development' — in Zinacantan, a community of habitual victims.

Zinacantecos are, speaking in ordinary terms, extraordinarily private people. This description confounds a common image of small-scale, 'face-to-face' communities, where people are supposed to live in one another's pockets: to have access to everyone else, to have some reason to be interested in them (by virtue of, say, corporate, family-based ties to them), perhaps even to have some say in what everyone else does. According to this common picture, such matters are taken both to be given by physical (brute) facts — proximity, limited resources both material and social — and to have normative force: there is a supposed ideology of communality.

III. Space, Publicity and Privacy

But in Zinacantan, privacy must be seen, first, in relation to geography. The valley of Nabenchauk is rimmed by three intersecting ridges, which form a roughly equilateral triangle. The village houses hug the slopes of these ridges and cluster on the higher portion of the valley floor. At the three points of intersection of the ridges are the passes through which foot trails wind down into the valley from other Zinacanteco settlements. Through the northwest corner a rock-paved truck road enters the valley, straight down to the plaza in front of the church. Here in the centre of the village is the town hall, a government grocery store, four cantinas, and the church, all spaced around the recently terraced and paved plaza area that is a product of the public works projects run by the state government development agency, *PRODESCH*. The plaza is the scene of public dispute settlement, whose focal point is the veranda of the town hall. Except during the Saturday morning market when it is abustle with men, women and children of all ages, the plaza is a rather empty place, too open, too formal for people to sit or even to pass through comfortably. It is, of course, the most 'public' part of town. Next to it, the broad roadway that runs through the middle of the valley, the trails that lead out of the valley, and the footpaths that run along fences and through cornfields connecting the houses to each other are public areas, of free access, and of public, constrained behaviour. Last, there is the lake bed and its flood plain, owned but not tilled, and anyone who wishes may walk there, graze sheep or horses there, and use the wells and the washing stones beside them. For the rest, all the land — whether valley floor, rocky slope or wooded mountain top — is privately owned.

Almost all the tilled land is fenced in Nabenchauk, no single piece of it larger than three-quarters of an acre. The fields are fenced against straying sheep and turkeys and against the hungry dogs that run down young corn plants and will eat the corn raw in the ear. The house sites are also fenced, both against animals and against the trespass of other villagers. Where a footpath passes close by a house, the fencing is often built up by long pieces of split oak firewood stood on one end and stacked close together to obscure the view to a height of five or six feet.

Almost all of the houses in Nabenchauk are constructed of unplastered adobe brick and roofed with red clay tiles supported on timber beams. Most houses are rectangular, four to five metres by three to four metres, and contain a single room. The cooking fire is built on the packed earth floor, and the smoke escapes upward, unobstructed by any ceiling, through the roof tiles and under the open eaves. No window penetrates the thick brown walls of these houses; the only light which enters comes through the open doorway.

There is no place in the village where a person can be certain to be hidden from the gaze of other people. Years of living with other people in close quarters undivided by interior walls have provided Zinacantecos with many ways of preserving personal modesty, chief among which is the trick of remaining fully clothed at all times, even in sleep. Privacy within the household is also guaranteed by a sense of responsibility for the modesty of others — when intruding unintentionally on someone, one simply averts the eyes. Within the household one is as careful of another's privacy as one is of one's own. Beyond the household, however, such constraint is quite lacking.

The space outside the house itself, within the fence or yard boundaries, is the workplace of the home. On an ordinary day, several activities are going on at once in the yard — the children are playing, someone is weaving, someone else repairing a chair. The yard is a space shared with chickens, turkeys and dogs, which continually wander through in their forages and which must be guarded against lest they soil the weaving or steal a bit of food. In most cases, it is also a space open to prying eyes, often, in this mountainous place, prying from a considerable distance. This lends a certain ambivalence to attitudes toward this area. One assumes that anything done there can be observed, that anything said there above a whisper will be overheard. Even in a well-sheltered patio a woman's weaving can be heard in the resounding thump of the beater, or seen as the shaking branches of the tree to which her loom is tied.

This is seen in part as a good thing: if one has nothing particular to hide at the moment, one is exhibiting this fact to those who are interested while keeping in good position to see and hear the doings of others on the paths or in their patios. Much of the conversation that goes on between people working in the yard is speculation on the immediate affairs and destinations of the people visible from this vantage point. Similarly, staying indoors or, even more unheard of, closing the house door is a gross and open admission of being up to no good. Prying, with the eyes and ears tuned to all goings on around one, is an ordinary behaviour in Nabenchauk. One expects that all one's business that is carried on where it *could* be seen or overheard is, in fact, seen and overheard. Similarly, one presumes that ignoring any aspect of others that can be perceived is simply foolish.

There are, however, strict canons of privacy which pertain to the physical intrusion by others into private space. A Zinacanteco house is a private area; it is 'set apart'. A new house is dedicated by completing a ritual circuit around it to protect it from the outside. One cannot sleep in a new house until its sides are secure, its orifices sealed. It is spoken of as a sick person (whose soul is not well fastened to his body). Moreover, with illness, during a period of seclusion (and after childbirth), a patient can leave the house only if guarded, and no visitor may enter the house.

The isolation of the house is more than just conceptual: it is material as well. Zinacanteco houses, as we observed earlier, do not have windows. (And when the government development agency built houses for Indians with large, unshuttered windows, their owners carefully papered the windows over or bricked them in. Windows are for *ladinos*, non-Indians, who can sit by the windows where everyone can watch them eat.) Fences surround the yard, and the common phrase to describe one's private place, where members of a household can relax in their own company, is *ta yut mok* 'inside the fence'. There one hopes to be relatively safe from prying eyes, though people watch for spies (there is a monolexemic Tzotzil verb which means 'to observe in secret, from a hiding place') and complain bitterly about new roads near to their yards that allow passers-by to 'look at you'.

E.Z. Vogt writes of the Zinacanteco house compound that 'the patio is of social significance because often guests are entertained there rather than inside the house'.[1] But this remark overlooks the fact that the choice between inside and outside the house is not just random (a matter, perhaps, of the weather) but significant. There is a scale of admission to the house compound, when visitors arrive, as follows: On the path/just outside the gate/in the patio/on the porch/inside the house in the 'visitors' area' (far from the fire)/by the fire. For a non-member of the household (even an intimate kinsman) entry to each new stage is by invitation only, and most people do not get beyond the first few stages, on most occasions.

All space in Zinacantan is carefully divided by categories of access. You can step up to my gate uninvited, but you can't come in. My brother can draw water from my well, but my cousin can't. Anyone from Nabenchauk can walk into the church, but others will have to ask the sacristan. Anybody can graze his sheep near the lake, but only I can chop wood on my plot of forest land. What we have called 'public behaviour' above means, in this context, what one does in public places — places of unrestricted access. In Zinacantan, in fact, public places constitute a socially *restricted* arena, where one monitors one's behaviour all the more severely for being in the public eye.

IV. Publicity and Privacy in Conversation

The tension between what is private (often, even, secret) and what is public (or allowed to leak out) is most obvious in interpersonal interaction, especially in conversation. Ordinary talk between Zinactecos is, in fact, almost the canonical case of social intercourse, and the properties of conversation give instructive examples of the tenor of Zinacanteco social life.

Consider how ordinary polite talk in their language, Tzotzil, differs from English conversation. On Grice's well-known analysis,[2] co-operative principles which operate in all well-formed conversation (at least, in the circles Grice frequented) enable a range of interpretations and inferences not available from, for example, the literal meanings of utterances or from discursive conversational organisation alone. These principles constrain participants in conversation to make their remarks relevant, to speak the whole truth (as much as they know within a given context), and so on. Two Gricean examples illustrate these maxims of relevance and quantity:

A: I am out of petrol.
B: There is a garage around the corner.
 (Allowed inference: you can get petrol there.)

* * * * *

A: Where does C live?
B: Somewhere in the south of France.
(Allowed inference: I don't know anything more exact than that.)

These maxims are disobeyed from time to time for particular purposes: to be deliberately perverse, to snub, to mislead, and so on.

Elinor Ochs Keenan has suggested, however, that these principles do not obtain (or, at least, not as stated for English conversation) for Malagasy-speaking peasants in Madagascar.[3] There, she argues, information is treated as a scarce good; what's more, Malagasy peasants espouse an ideology of the collective responsibility for action which causes people to avoid any action that draws attention to individual ability or that commits people to individual responsibility. Malagasy conversation, according to Keenan, is non-committal, indirect, guarded, and often, for the Western ethnographer, deliberately stripped of both relevance and quantity.

In a similar way, ordinary polite conversation in Zinacantan is marked by formulaic inanity. On the path one asks another: 'Where are you going?' and receives the ordinary polite reply: 'I am going nowhere.' One asks another about the purpose of his errand: 'What have you to say?' The answer, belied by the occasion, is commonly: 'I have nothing to say.' In many Tzotzil conversations, one party seems to be trying his best to pump information from his interlocutor, while the interlocutor uses every ploy he can to evade and deflect the other's purpose. The formulas of polite conversation set a tone in which Gricean cooperative principles are turned off.

A striking example of the metaphor of ordinary conversation can be seen by comparing standard greetings (for example, when people meet on a path) with 'full conversations' in English and Tzotzil. In both cases, a conversation typically has an opening ('Hello, how are you?'); a body (during which some matter is discussed); and a closing (which in turn has an opening gambit and an ending: 'Well, I've got to be going', 'OK, see you.') In English (or, at least, American), a reduced greeting exchange is lifted from an opening sequence:

Hi, how're you doing?

But the standard greeting in Tzotzil is taken clearly from a closing sequence:

Chibat che'e. (I'm going.)
Batan! (Go then!)

A Tzotzil greeting constitutes a metaphorical shutting down of interaction and communication. A greeting is, formally, a farewell and not a hello. (In either language, of course, a greeting is essentially empty, a hollow interaction at best.)

Looking at ordinary talk in Nabenchauk leads to the conclusions that all information is taken as inherently dangerous; that people's interests are thought to be inevitably opposed; that access to one another's business invites not shared confidences but breaches of confidence. Living in Nabenchauk involves, as we shall see, constant circumspect hiding. Tzotzil conversation is kinesically well contained. As novices in the village, and as potential inadvertent blurters of household secrets, we were constantly tutored in conversational conventions, often instructed in precisely how to talk about (or to avoid talking about) private affairs.

Here a brief semantic detour may be in order. There are, so far as we know, no Tzotzil words for 'public' or 'private' (despite elaborate syntactic mechanisms for marking possession obligatorily). But consider the sorts of verbs that appear frequently to describe what happens to information:

Tzotzil	English
-vinaj	appear, become perceivable
-lok'	emerge, become public
-lik	arise, begin to circulate
-'il-e	be seen, be obvious
-'a'y-at	be heard, be perceived
-lam	be eased, grow less severe
-paj	cease
-mak	be covered up
-nak'	be hidden
-muk	be buried, be kept secret or private
-laj	finish
-ch'ab	disappear, cease to exist
'ep-bat	increase
-muk'ib	enlarge
-ch'amuj	spread
-batz'ij	become more severe
-kechi	remain, be left over, persist

These verbs, applied to gossip stories, evidence a Tzotzil theory of information and reputation which clearly involves notions of privacy and publicness.

In Nabenchauk, what is private is a matter of gradually (and, one might say, grudgingly) widening concentric social circles to which villagers may belong. What is private, what is one's own, pertains to what is inside the circle; what is public, open (and usually, potentially dangerous), is what remains on the outside. (In fact, for Zinacantan, 'private' seems logically the primitive term; 'public' is defined by opposition to the well-bounded, closed private domains, with no independent motivation, no notion of 'public good' or 'general public'.) But the smallest such circle may not be as small an object as a single, psychologically self-aware individual – socially, there may be no such creature. (Equally, we can imagine societies in which the smallest social unit is less than a single person: a manifestation of an aspect of one person's personality, perhaps, or a spirit – who knows what remains private in an asylum?) In Zinacantan, one starts life as an adjunct to one's parents or grandparents – one's name is usually even a possessed form: *y-Antun li mol Petul-e* 'Old Peter's Anthony'. Full social identity ordinarily comes only when a person establishes his or her own household.

V. Households and Privacy

Every person in Nabenchauk has one and only one *-na* 'house' which can be claimed as his or her own. Statistically, and ideally, households in Nabenchauk are small, usually containing only a nuclear family, although the period of postmarital patrilocal residence, which may last from between one and five years, creates periodic extended family households. Sharing a household can be defined as eating together. Zinacantecos do not indiscriminately lump together the fruits of their individual labours and share them out willy-nilly. If two men eat together every day tortillas made over a single fire, then they have worked together on a single patch of land to produce the corn that is in the tortillas (or pooled their cash resources in an explicitly agreed way to purchase it). Put another way, two Zinacanteco men who farm separate pieces of land keep their harvests separate and eat separately; only people who share the ownership of the staple food resources eat together around the same fire.

Take the case of, say, an old woman who sleeps alone in her own house. If she eats in the house of her married son or daughter, then she shares in the ownership of the corn supply in the same manner as a child in that household does. If, however, she cooks for herself at her own fire in her own house, even though she eats mostly corn supplied to her by her children, producing little income for herself, she does not share in the total corn supply of her children at all. Rather, explicit gifts, or loans, of corn (or cash) are made to her by her children, and the ownership of that food, the right to dispose of it as she will, is transferred to her. No fraction of the harvest automatically accrues to her, nor can she simply consider her children's resources to be her own. Bag by bag, she must acquire her corn in gifts, formally and explicitly made by them, or formally requested by her. Lest this be interpreted as a mere formal nicety, it ought to be pointed out that many old women with prosperous offspring go about in rags for lack of the wherewithal to buy new clothes.

When sufficient land is available, young married sons prefer to build their houses on land contiguous to their father's land. This may result in a compound of two or possibly three related households, each with its own house and courtyard within the same fence.

With regard to matters of crowding and of personal space — personal body privacy, work space, the noise of children — there is little difference between a single dwelling or several around a central courtyard. What does change significantly when a second household is set up is the question of ownership and the privacy of one's financial affairs attendant upon private ownership. A second household requires a separate supply of corn, separate cooking equipment, and sooner or later separate work tools for farming, weaving and regular maintenance work. Ownership of any item is never ambiguous between Zinacanteco households, although the freedom to borrow back and forth can be extensive when relations are good.

The existence of more than one household as defined here implies the existence of two or more economic units which are at least partially distinct. Where farm land is involved, it will have been divided, as will the household goods. Articles will be bought and sold separately, with separate purses carefully maintained, right down to the cost of the grinding of a bucket of corn which may amount to only 10 *centavos*. This means that in time, and no doubt in a very short time, both real differences as well as perceived potential differences in the interests of the two households can arise.

The coming and going of visitors will be noted between households, but the actual transactions can go on behind the walls of a house, and at night behind closed doors. Visitors to one household in a compound not infrequently time their visits to occur after everyone has closed his doors, and they will enter the yard as silently as they can, whispering at the door of the house they wish to visit. At the very least, such occurrences of events involving one household — a sudden visitor, a shout in the night, whatever — put the other household in the position of knowing that something has happened without knowing what. They then must wait to be told about it spontaneously or be bold enough to ask about it themselves, which amounts more or less to a constant test of the extent of mutuality and trust between them. This is a situation of structural ambiguity — separate units with close historical ties, physically close enough to know *of* one another's business without knowing, as a matter of course, *about* it. Both inquiring and not inquiring, telling and not telling, are active responses in a situation of this sort, and tension and curiosity are the inevitable result. The existence of more than one household in a compound by the very nature of the Zinacanteco household raises ambiguities about space and property that may be at the root of the empirical finding that Nabenchauk residents consistently choose to live either in larger single households or smaller single households and appear to avoid extended family compound living arrangements.

VI. Social Life and Publicness

The domain of the private in Zinacantan, then, is the individual household, what goes on *ta yut jmok* 'inside my fence'. Publicness means *outside* the fence, and its dangers are not unlike the dangers, at another level, of the surrounding *te'tik* 'forest', or of the non-Zinacanteco world of the local Mexican towns where different social rules are in force. However, much ordinary social life *must* take place outside the fence: sociability and publicness are linked conceptually, and danger is involved. Social life requires display of self, invites others to -*k'elvan* 'look at you', and exposes one to the possibilities of *k'exlal* 'shame' or -*ak' ?elav* 'making a spectacle of oneself'. The defining conditions of Zinacanteco life, the circumstances of productive life, provide for a certain necessary interaction between social units, and all involve potential breaches of confidentiality. They do not, however, promote a higher level of publicness. We shall consider ordinary sociability, features of Zinacanteco marriage, and cooperative labour as telling examples.

A. Women in Public Places

The realities of domestic tasks in Nabenchauk require that a good deal of the household routine has to be carried out beyond the confines of the household fence. Corn, which has for generations been ground by hand on a stone *metate* by the hearth, is today taken to electric corn mills dotted about the village. These are places fraught with social dangers, and in them constrained behaviour is at its extreme. Women carry their buckets of corn in the crooks of their arm, covered by the lower edges of their shawls; buckets which are carried hanging from the hand by the handle most of the way from home will be shifted to this covered position as the mill is approached.

As soon as women or children come within a few metres of the mill, they lower their voices to a whisper and most conversation ceases. Shawls are raised to cover the mouth, and each person takes her place in line silently, raising her eyes only to scan newcomers in a wary fashion. Once inside the mill people rarely greet each other openly, although some adolescent girls, taking what may be their only opportunity in a day to see one another, often allow friends into the line ahead of them. Most mills have a bench or table on which waiting customers may rest their buckets. Women carefully keep their buckets of corn in order in the line, their rims just touching. If a newcomer is allowed into the middle of the line, each woman in adjusting her own bucket is very cautious not even to touch the bucket of another. To do so is regarded as taking a very great liberty.

Another ceaseless daily labour of women is carrying water. Girls and young women, unable freely to visit one another's houses, time their regular trips for water to coincide with the trips of their friends; in this way they can exchange gossip in low whispers as they walk together on the path. But in Nabenchauk these social moments do not in the least resemble the very garrulous and convivial tones we have witnessed at wells in the water-scarce western villages of Zinacantan, where houses are clearly clustered in patrilineal groups, each group with its special hour for water collection at the community well. In Nabenchauk one may meet *anyone* at the standpipe, and the eyes of any of fifty houses may be watching. It is a moment for very guarded behaviour indeed and, as at the mill, women do not gather at the watertap itself but may cluster in small groups of two or three some five or ten metres away where they cannot be approached except by friends joining the conversation.

Waterholes have two related social aspects: they are both sociable and public. Washing at the waterhole can provide a woman with a good occasion for a prolonged chat with women of other households, an opportunity unequalled by any other task. Since no Zinacanteco drops in on another without good reason, people, and particularly women, can find themselves talking to members of only their own households for days at a time. Even though life is generally unhurried, women do not stop long by the path or at the shop to talk with others lest someone observing take note and make something of it. But washing clothes is a very long business, and who can think ill of anyone for spending an hour or two at the chore chatting the while? For all their anxieties, Zinacantecos love a good joke, and women washing clothes are rarely sober faced and are even, on occasion, boisterous.

On the other hand, these waterholes are undoubtedly public places. Groups of women at a waterhole may laugh and joke continuously, even obscenely, but never freely. They remain ever ready to parry a remark aimed to catch them off guard; questions like 'Where were you going up past the cemetery yesterday?' must never be answered directly but cleverly sidestepped with an implied denial or a vague reply, or outright lie.

On any Saturday morning the women of Nabenchauk will take produce to sell at the village market. Indians of other ethnic groups as well as lowland *ladino* peasants and potters come to this market to exchange their vegetables for fleece, corn and flowers. These foreigners spread their wares in wide circles around them and settle themselves on chairs or tarpaulins in a very comfortable manner, often buying soft drinks from the nearby *cantinas*, lounging back, legs akimbo, to snack on fruit or peanuts, shouting amiably to one another, laughing and verbally accosting the Zinacanteco shoppers as they pass by.

To this rather common market behaviour the demeanour of the women sellers from Nabenchauk could not present a greater contrast. Each woman or girl sits with her belongings closely gathered around her, occupying in this large plaza the smallest space she possibly can. Her legs are tucked under her in the usual manner of sitting, her shawl drawn up over her mouth, her eyes cast downward or at least carefully avoiding meeting the gaze of others. Everything about her seems to say, 'I am not really here.' This is quite normal public behaviour for most Zinacanteco women, in particular for adolescent girls and young women. But on Saturday morning they are there to sell something; whatever it is, it will most likely be well out of sight, wrapped in one of the white cotton flour sacks ubiquitous in the highlands as luggage containers, or in a layer or two of red and white woven bags. Perhaps in front of them will be displayed one or two samples of the goods they are offering; perhaps the passerby will have to inquire what it is they have for sale. Many women will avoid looking at their interlocutor at all as inquiries are made or goods and money exchanged.

At one level this reflects propriety of manner and a nervousness about encounters with strangers. It also, however, reflects the extreme discomfort these women feel at making known their intentions and their goods in this place which is not merely public, and filled with strangers, but, even worse, filled with villagers and relatives who will thus learn the nature and extent of their business.

B. Marriage and the Privacy of the Household

In Nabenchauk there are only two legitimate occasions for social intercourse with members of another household: business and ritual. Apart from these kinds of events, social interaction between members of different households rarely will amount to more than remarks made in passing, or otherwise brief, guarded and purposeful interchanges. Informal, prolonged, or intimate contact is relatively rare, but when it occurs, it is sure to be between kinsmen or between the pseudo-kin created through the institution of *compadrazgo*.[4]

Virtually all social intercourse is guarded and purposeful, but insofar as deeper intimacy is ever achieved, it is possible only between kin. Conversely, kinship does not carry with it the obligation of intimacy, only the potential for it. Propriety dictates that the impetus in a marriage proposal come from the young man. Most opportunities for young people to observe one another are limited to public moments − to passing on the path, standing nearby while observing a fiesta, while attending a market, or while riding a truck. Moments such as these are precisely those in which Zinacanteco behaviour, particularly female behaviour, is most restrained. At such times even to hear clearly the voice of a possible mate, let alone overhear her conversation, is practically impossible.

The children of one's mother's sister or brother, however, may well be people one has seen on a regular basis since childhood, at weddings and religious ceremonies, while hanging around the washing well or on a wood gathering trip. Similarly young people living in the same part of the village will have many more opportunities to observe one another, albeit at some distance and perhaps clandestinely, than have people separated by such distances and whom they do not cross paths with often. This simple issue of opportunity and intimacy of knowledge determines more than any other the frequency with which matches are sought between neighbours and collateral kinsmen.

During a courtship, and following the marriage, the natal households of the marriage partners come into what, for Zinacantan, is an intense contact; this is particularly true during the years which the new bride will spend in the home of her husband's parents. During this time the newly expanded household lives in the intolerable situation of having in its midst a person who, regardless of her personality, will serve inevitably as a conduit of information about it back to her own natal household. People soon grow anxious and exhausted from the effort of behaving around their own hearth with as much cautious circumspection as they customarily do 'in public'.

These tensions often lead to the failure of the marriage and are a major reason why Zinacantecos prefer to arrange marriages between members of households which are linked already by a marriage in the same or previous generation. Further, marriages between people so linked — especially cousins — provides a network of kin linking the bride to her mother-in-law with whom she has the most intense contact in the new situation.

Once children are born to a new couple, the issue of the ultimate disposition of the fruits of productive labour, especially male productive labour, must arise. The new child represents the beginning of a new generation, whose patrimony must ultimately be separable from that of other potential lines of inheritance. The joint labour of a man and his unmarried brothers can no longer be equally divided, nor do the brothers stand to inherit any longer from the new young father, whose property now ultimately belongs to his offspring.

Land and goods are always passed from parent to child. Siblings never inherit directly from one another, but they do stand to benefit or to be disadvantaged by each other's actions, as wealth amassed by one can be reclaimed by the father and redistributed among his children in times of ill will. Fathers retain the bulk of their property in their own hands until near death, distributing it according to their own preferences at that time.

Siblings, then, remain in competition with one another for parental favour throughout the life of the parent, and tensions between them over responsibility for the aging parent grow over the years. The issue of the ultimate division of property can pit the interests of one household against those of its closest kinsmen; the more closely related the households, the greater the interest in each other's affairs, for the more each one stands to lose or gain by that interest. In this way, households related by kinship have far more potential for acrimony and feud than do those not so related, and the social resource which family ties represent in Nabenchauk is easily turned to liability.

C. *Production and the Division of Labour*

The division of labour by sex, which remains the most significant division of labour internal to this society, while strengthening the male-female co-operative tie also renders the conjugal or nuclear family – in technological terms, at any rate – self-sufficient in production (self-sufficient in relation to other Zinacanteco households, although not in relation to the wider society and its markets).

In Nabenchauk most work tasks are structured in ways that allow them to be carried out from beginning to end by a person working alone. Men can and do farm alone, for no aspect of the work so rewards co-operation that men are forced to maintain social groups for its sake alone or fail. The weaving, gardening, cooking and washing that women perform are also arranged for the solitary worker, although the pressures on a woman's time created by the birth of children will inundate a single woman's capacities. The solution to this in Nabenchauk is not the maintenance of extended family residential arrangements nor the creation of social obligations between kinsmen but the establishment of paid services for weaving and cooking between households. This is an example of a primary characteristic of the social relations of work in the village: all labour is paid labour.

The only point in the corn cycle in which the labour of more than one man is absolutely essential is weeding time, when a single man working more land than he can weed quickly risks losing his corn to encroaching weeds. At other points in the corn cycle, a man *can* choose to exploit his own labour to the maximum and simply begin sooner and end later any one task than he would with help. The essential point is that additional labour in the swidden cultivation of corn on the rocky sloping land which Zinacanteco renters farm – land which is not suitable for plow technology – is a matter of aggregating like units of labour and not of complex co-operation. Each man works alone, even if side by side and in timing with fellow workers, moving up the hillside together. They work together for company and motivation, stopping to chat and laugh together, to have a drink and a moment's rest. But aggregating all these equal units of labour does not increase productivity. It is the difference between one man working six days or six men working one day. Except for weeding time it makes little difference to the yield of the field. Thus the actual tasks of the corn cycle do not materially require co-operation, nor do they reward it with higher productivity.

Because landlords prefer to rent land in large blocks, Zinacantecos often form renting groups to acquire land and then parcel it out among themselves. Such an association of men for renting in the lowlands is likely to be formed on the basis of kinship because kinship is the primary social link which exists between households in Zinacantan.

But this link does not amount to a necessary association; neither ritual nor economic forces require the maintenance of social bonds between households. The concentration of productive resources and of consumption in the household unit is so strong that it precludes the formation of social units larger than the household.

Zinacantecos actively avoid being obligated to anyone, and they actively reject responsibilities for others; they are equally ambivalent about being debtors and being creditors. Life in Zinacantan is primarily about the acquisition of property – land, cash or corn – and the business of life is the work necessary to this acquisition. To the producer belong all rights in the product, and Zinacantecos appear to like to keep accounts straight right from the start. The distinction between mine and thine is fundamental in this village. The virtue in the work is the virtue inherent in the property – the independence, and freedom from being controlled, which it is hoped it will bring.

Many households do not contain the necessary personnel to maintain the full cycle of male and female production; these incomplete units do not undergo incorporation into larger family groups but maintain themselves through the sale of their labour to other households. No social obligations exist between adults in Nabenchauk which compel a person to care for another in time of need: between brother and brother, sister and sister, father and son, money is lent, not shared; work is paid for, not pooled. It is perfectly possible to starve to death, alone in one's house, in Nabenchauk. Scarce resources pit households against one another through the market economy, which has eroded the obligations and interdependencies of kinship by directing ties outward to the wider economy, and which has transformed socially embedded goods and services into wage labour.

In Zinacantan there seems to be no sense of corporateness, no feeling for an 'all-embracing public good'. True, there is an obvious ethnic and linguistic unity about the place, and there is a religious hierarchy, recruited from all parts of the municipality, which assumes responsibility, year by year, for the rituals which maintain the patron saints of Zinacantan. However, the political and ceremonial cohesiveness of Zinacantan barely impinges on everyday social life in a village like Nabenchauk. Zinacanteco ethnic identity simply defines, for most purposes, the outer limits of the social universe. Within Zinacantan what is good for me (and my household) is construed in opposition to, rather than as part of, what is good for everyone else. In the face of calls for cooperative efforts, spawned by local development agencies and usually phrased in Spanish rhetoric (*la mayoriá, el beneficio de la comunidad*, etc.), members of our household, at least, express suspicions about the motives of the people concerned: What do they get out of it? What does it cost us? The form of social organisation sets limits to the levels and applications of 'publicness.'

Conclusion

As Benn and Gaus suggest in Chapter 1, above, questions of access, interest and agency are, perhaps, unavoidable in all human social life, requiring different solutions from one culture to the next or in varying circumstances. Distinctions such as those which we draw in our own culture between public and private can also be discovered in other cultures. Nevertheless, the resources, practices and social units which underlie and take shape through these distinctions confound an easy application of these notions cross-culturally. Zinacantecos have a conscious concern with issue of access, for example, but these issues intersect with notions of agency and interest — what there is to be interested *in*, what 'having an interest' means — in culturally specific ways.

The anthropologist quickly learns, in another society, that — whatever the conceptual confusions — the details of what is private and what public may be very different from what he or she is used to at home. Circumstances are different, and appropriate behaviour may be hard to master. There is, as well, a final paradox. For the outsider, at least in a village like Nabenchauk where people are social atoms and where villagers seem to be obsessed with privacy, one ultimately comes to feel oppressed, hemmed in by the constantly prying eyes and heavy expectations of others. Whereas, at the other extreme, in, say, an Australian Aboriginal community where there are no walls and there is no private property, where people barge in, stare unabashedly and comment unreservedly on what they see — the lack of secrecy produces just the feeling of freedom to do what one likes that is so often associated, in western liberal thought, with privacy and restricted access.

Notes

A different version of this paper (under the title, 'Inside the Fence: The Social Basis of Privacy in Nabenchauk') will appear in the journal *Estudios de Cultura Maya*, published by El Centro de Estudios Mayas of the Universidad Nacional Autónoma de México.

1. E.Z. Vogt, *Zinacantan* (Belknap Press of Harvard University Press, Cambridge, Mass., 1969).
2. H.P. Grice, 'Logic and Conversation', in P. Cole and J. Morgan (eds.), *Syntax and Semantics 3: Speech Acts* (Academic Press, New York, 1975), pp. 41-58.
3. E. Ochs Keenan, 'On the Universality of Conversational Implicatures', *Language and Society*, 5 (1976), pp. 67-80.
4. *Compadrazgo* refers to the Meso-American institution of ritual co-parenthood in which the parents of a child form important social ties with other people through the life-cycle rituals their child undergoes in the Roman Catholic Church.

15 CLASSICAL GREEK CONCEPTIONS OF PUBLIC AND PRIVATE

Arlene W. Saxonhouse

The Greek *polis* was a unique historical configuration. The translation so often ascribed to the word '*polis*', 'city-state', does little justice to the social, political and religious relationships entailed in the term. 'City' suggests small size and 'state' suggests sovereignty, but neither reveals the unity implicit in the term, a unity approaching the perfect historical example of the organic model elaborated in Chapter 2 of this volume. The *polis* was not an aggregate of individuals or citizens who had a self-conscious awareness of themselves in opposition to an entity that was public. There was no 'Athens' for the Greeks as there is for us moderns describing the ancient world. There were only Athenians. One could not describe Athens without reference to those who comprised the city. In the vision of the perfect *polis*, there was no opposition between the self and the political entity of which one was a part.

This is not to suggest that the Greeks were exclusively duty-bound individuals who cared only for the welfare of the community. Altruism was not part of the Greek moral code. Rather, the Greeks understood that their own well-being depended on the well-being of the group of which they were a part.[1] Thus, the hero for the Greeks was one whose stature came from an ability to preserve the public unit in war and the courage to exercise that ability. His stature came not because he cared for the public unity above all else but because he had the requisite talents to protect it. The community would respond by giving to the warrior the sought-after fame (*kleos*) which was accorded only to the best of the warriors. *Kleos* was a reward possible only as the result of one's role in fighting for the community. Private life could offer no greatness for a Greek, no *kleos*. Among the Romans, private morality such as chastity and piety were as much the basis for renown as courage.

The concept *res publica*, as opposed to *res privata*, was an invention of the Romans. Contemporary understanding of Plato's famous work on justice is hindered by the latinate title *Republic*. The Greek title is *Politeia*, suggesting not an abstract object of veneration but a way of life shared by the members of the same *polis*. The *politeia* or what we might call constitution or regime was not a set of laws elaborated by succeeding generations of judges and legislators. It was a regime that defined the patterns of behaviour for all in the *polis*, that put each individual squarely into a set of relationships with other members of the same society. It was this *politeia*, what was shared by all citizens through their equal participation in it, that united the members of the *polis*. The symbol of this unity was the acropolis, a public space in which the members of the city could find protection and a divine space in which the gods of the city lived and were worshipped.

The conception of self apart from *polis*, as not governed by the *politeia* of one's city, as not tied by religion to the city and one's dead ancestors, was a foreign import, brought to the Greek peninsula during the latter part of the fifth century B.C. by the radical Sophists coming largely from the East and from Sicily two centuries after the rise of the *polis*. These itinerant teachers taught that the human being — not the city and not the gods — was the measure of all things; they encouraged individual self-sufficiency rather than dependence on others and trained young men in the art of rhetoric to enable them to pursue a virtue based on the domination of others and the independence from the laws of the city. The Athenian authors of this period and the next century — the playwrights, the historians, the philosophers, those we associate with the acme of Greek civilisation — all reacted against the alien affirmation of self-conscious independence for the individual, and stressed in a variety of ways the impossibility of isolating oneself from the unity which was the *polis*. One's existence, one's values, one's fulfilment as a member of the human species was dependent on being a member of the *polis*. Exile — self-imposed or otherwise — from the *polis* amounted to separation from humanity, to animality (for animals did not live in *poleis*), or perhaps to divinity (a state of perfect self-sufficiency inaccessible to the ordinary mortal).

The private realm for the Greeks of this period does not centre on the individual. Rather, we must understand by the term 'private', the family. The family, though, is a community in its own right — with its own deities who require constant tendance. It is a community which demanded the devotion of its members to honour the ancestors and to create future generations who in their turn would continue the care for the ancestral gods. It is this unit or community which stands in opposition to the public community of the city.[2]

The Greek words which are most commonly translated public and private are *to koinon* and *to idion*. The nuances, though, must be understood: *koinon* has within its meaning a sense of sharing, a commonality. The family (*oikos*) is a *koinōnia* in that it shares ancestors, space, religion, meals and so forth.³ The *polis* is also a *koinōnia*. Aristotle, in Book II of the *Politics*, states that a *polis* must share something, must be a *koinōnia*, or not be a *polis* at all. It must at least share land. The question for him is how much is to be shared. (1260b37-1261a1)⁴ The *idion* in contrast refers to that which is distinctive, which separates one from another. For example, the characteristic of reason, *phronēsis*, is *idion* to the human being in that other species of animals do not share in reasoned thought. It is what separates them from others. Thus the family *within* the context of the city is *idion*, though in its own structure it is a community. While in the modern family we may often talk about the interests of the individuals in opposition to the interests of the family, and the conflicts which arise from treating the members of the family in an egalitarian fashion, in the hierarchically structured Greek family there were no interests which could separate one individual out from it. [Cf. the discussion of modern liberal conceptions in Ch. 2, p. 38 and pp. 54-55 — Eds.] The unit needed to remain over time, not the individuals who were part of it. Within the political context, the use of the word *idion* was largely derogatory, for it referred to that which separates one out from the unity of the community, the humanity of the *polis*. The modern derivative 'idiot' gives some sense of this.⁵

While the ancient Greek *polis* offers us this model of organic unity, the authors throughout the history of Greek literature also suggest for us the tensions implicit in the model by revealing the dependence of the organic unit on the smaller communities out of which it is built. The confrontation which we find in classical Greek thought is not between the competing rights of an individual and the needs and the demands of the community, but rather between the competing demands of different communities — one larger, one smaller, each with its own set of relationships and each with its own divinities which require care and nurture. Specifically, they are in opposition because the city demands that the citizen be a warrior and that the warrior be willing to die for the city. The city accords *kleos* for this willingness. And yet the family demands that the husband, father, male head of the household continue to live to carry on the worship of the family gods and produce more male heirs who will carry forth this religion. One man cannot do both.

What emerges from a consideration of ancient Greek thought on public and private is a sense of the tragic interdependence of the realm of the city and the family. It is a tragic relationship because each realm demands full, and not partial, devotion; one cannot die for the city and yet live for the family. Each realm cannot get that complete devotion it demands without leading to the destruction of the other. It is Aristotle, as we shall see, who tries to overcome this tragedy by making the *polis* the highest and most worthy association, i.e. by transforming what was a parallel set of relationships into an hierarchical set. He, however, can do this only because he removes from Greek politics its focus on war and thus its inherent tension with the community of the family. Others before him see war as the primary characteristic of the *polis*, which thus demands the ultimate sacrifice for the community of the family.[6]

I. Homer

The Homeric epics were written well before the political landscape of Greece was dominated by the *polis*, but they presented to Greek society of the classical age its heroic models and their gods. The poems appeared sometime at the end of the so-called dark ages, probably during the eighth century B.C., though they reflected the social structure of a more distant age. One finds, particularly in the *Iliad*, a clash between two value systems.[7] On the one hand there is the hero, the warrior, whose pursuit of *kleos* dominates all other values; on the other hand there is the hero who fights for something more than himself, who lives as part of what has been called the pre-*polis*, whose valour is displayed not only for his own glory and *kleos*, but to protect his family, the *kleos* of his family and the city within which his family exists.

We thus find Achilles, the demigod, who does try to exist by and for himself, free from the domination of a universal public, a freedom allowed him by the loose political structure of the Achaean army. He is nevertheless dependent on the whole for his glory and reputation. He must fight well to receive the fame he desires. When his success in battle is not accorded the proper respect by the leader of the Achaeans, he withdraws from the army and the story begins. Achilles exists in opposition to the hero Hector who lives within a set of relationships that tie him to the private world of his family and the public world of the city. He must live within both. His glory and renown come not only from savagery on the battlefield but also from the ability to protect those individuals who live within the city with whom he has special relationships of son, husband and father. However, Hector's failure to protect the city and family he had fought for denied him the stature of his opponent Achilles. When a collective was to be protected, good intentions were not sufficient.

As the army of the Achaeans surges around the walls of Troy, Achilles, the demigod, sulks by his ships, his pride wounded and his anger roused by the way he has been treated by the leader of the Achaean forces. There is no way to bring him back into battle save persuasion, but this fails. The common purpose of the Achaean army does not move him. The pleas coming from Odysseus that Achilles 'rescue the afflicted sons of the Achaeans from the Trojan onslaught' (*Iliad*, 9.248) go unheeded. 'Fate is the same for the man who holds back, the same if he fights hard. We are all held in a single honour, the brave with the weaklings.' (9.318-319) Achilles exists as the individual who can choose to fight or not to fight with the rest of the Achaeans. When his own dignity is threatened, when he sees no personal gain in the battle for himself, when past treatment and past disrespect suggest that honour shall not be his, he withdraws — with no loss of stature for the generations of Greeks who will see in his courage and success on the battlefield their model of the hero. It is later in the *Iliad* that Achilles' willingness to live a brief life for the sake of glory, his love of his friend and his savage hatred of his enemy establish him as the military hero.

Meanwhile, in Troy, behind the walls which unify the city of Troy spatially and psychologically, in the palace, the focal point of this city's unity, Hector searches for his wife. He finds her, though, on the battlements, looking out over the plain below the city, and it is here that he bids her farewell. It is a tender scene which vividly captures the tensions, as well as the interdependence, between the family and the city. Andromache says to him:

> Your strength will destroy you, nor do you pity your son or unfortunate me, who will soon be your widow . . . Hector you are to me a father and honored mother, a brother and vigorous husband . . . Come now, pity me and remain on the wall, do not make your child an orphan and your wife a widow. (6.407-408 . . . 429-432)

Andromache recognises the death which awaits Hector, should he venture beyond the wall, and with his death the destruction of the family of which they with their son are a part. But he is also a part of the unity of the city and devoted to the lofty towers of Ilium. He cannot stay with her as she bids him: 'All these things are in my mind also, lady, yet I would feel deep shame before the Trojans.' (6.441-442) He is not only a father; he is also a warrior and protector.[8] The community of the Trojans demands that Hector fight for the city; it distributes honours to those who fight and shame to those who do not. His brother

Paris, a coward on the battlefield, is shameful to his city and to his family. His lack of concern with his *kleos* among the multitude, and his preference for the sweet bed of Helen, illustrate his failure to sense the tension between the conflicting demands of the realm within the city and the demands of the city for protection. He has none of the heroic stature accorded Hector or Achilles.

Hector's dual roles and the tensions between them is dramatised most vividly in his farewell scene as he reaches out to kiss his young son. The child shrinks back from him, 'frightened at the aspect of his own father, terrified as he saw the bronze and the crest with its horse hair, nodding dreadfully . . . from the peak of his helmet'. (6.467-470) The identity of the human relationship, of the specific attachment between father and son, is obliterated behind the gear for the city's battle. By becoming a public person through being a warrior, he obscures his existence as a private person. Hector must sacrifice, as this scene clearly shows, what is dear to him – his family – what is private, peculiar to him in order to protect it. And he can only protect it by becoming part of the collectivity which is the city.

This city in its turn will give him glory, but this is not enough for Hector, pricked by the foreboding image of his wife led off by some Achaean to work at the loom of another and to carry water from a foreign spring. (6.455-58) 'May I be dead and the piled earth hide me under before I hear you crying and know by this that they drag you captive.' (6.464-65) Glory is all that Achilles in his conflict with Agamemnon wants; but Hector, caught in the web of relationships of the family and the collectivity of the city, fights for more.[9] However, whereas the death which awaits Achilles will not diminish his glory, the death awaiting Hector destroys the family; so that the collectivity may at least grasp at continuity not promised by the fates, Hector himself must die.

It is, of course, Achilles, the independent hero, who will kill Hector, the father, the son, the citizen. Achilles had not been drawn back into battle by any concern for the Achaeans. He returns in anger, angry at the death of his beloved Patroclus, who himself had been moved by Nestor's pleas with regard to health and safety of the whole. Achilles' glory comes as he avenges one who had died – not as he tries to preserve those who live. However, it is in the emotionally charged final book of the *Iliad* that Hector's values come to dominate. As Priam comes to ask for the body of his son, the anger of Achilles yields; the memory of his own father and of his beloved friend softens him, and the two – the aged Priam and the glorious Achilles – weep together at the sorrowful lot of man. As he weeps, Achilles rises from the simple hero in battle who can savagely cut down the opposing host to one who has learned through his wrath and his isolation the dependence of one on others and his ties to something greater than himself. Both Priam and Achilles weep in Achilles' tent; they weep for their private losses, but each loss was endured for the sake of the whole. In a sense, here in Book 24 of the *Iliad* we find the preparation for the devotion to family and subsequently the *polis*, rather than to the self, which is at the base of Greek political life. Hector recognises the conflicting demands of both realms; Achilles' growth in the poem is to learn the pain which comes from these irreconcilable demands.[10]

II. Drama

War is a constant theme in Greek literature, as it was indeed in Greek life. War was the natural condition of Greek cities, war among themselves and against foreign invaders.[11] The acropolis, that symbol of unity, was the point of defence at a time of war and reflected the warlike origins of that unity. The community was thus constantly demanding, as Troy demanded of Hector, the death of its male members. In most cities the general had the highest political office. To participate in a war was to participate in a public activity.[12] To try to disassociate oneself from the city's participation in war was something fit for the comic stage, as one sees in the story of Dikaiopolis in Aristophanes' *Archarnians*.

As in all societies, modern as well as ancient, fighting for one's city can mean the obliteration through death of all that is private for the sake of the public community. The death in battle of young heroes stands in sharp contrast to the private realm of the family, a realm emphasising life through its focus on procreation and preservation. The opposition between private and public becomes thus an opposition between life and death. For the Greeks, though, the procreative role of the family was not simply a means of extending oneself into the future through one's child; the religious dimensions of procreation could not be ignored. The child born today would carry on the religion of the family and the worship of the ancestors. Thus, the conflict between death for the city and life for the family reflected also a conflict between the public gods of the city and the private gods of the family.[13] Each realm had its own divinities. The conflict inherent in these contradictory demands provided the background for some of the great tragedies of the fifth century – tragedies which can only be understood if we discard the modern liberal vision of the secularised individual and state and see the Greeks as caught between two divine forces – making demands as opposed as life and death. What has been too little acknowledged in our readings of these plays is the sensitivity of the Greek authors to the anguish of the private realm, often symbolised by the female, who must suffer from the male's necessary attention to that public good, the city, which is to be protected by his glorious, if death-dealing, defence of it. Often this association of glory with the protection of the whole leads the warriors to forget what Hector understood so well – the family which stood behind the walls of the city which was to be protected. The zealousness of the warrior must be moderated by a sense of why he seeks that glory. The tragedy often expressed in Greek drama comes from a failure to understand the conflicting demands. The men give themselves to one realm only to be taught, through suffering, what they have chosen to ignore.

Agamemnon has set out, in Aeschylus' grand trilogy, the *Oresteia*, to wreak havoc on the Trojans who have stolen the wife of his brother. War is here a male adventure carried on by those who love it, those who desire revenge for pricked vanity and those who seek to make whole again the family destroyed by the rape of Helen. The war is thus initially pursued to preserve the family, but as it progresses that goal is forgotten, and victory and the glory associated with it become the end. The family unit initially meant to be preserved is destroyed as Agamemnon himself kills his own daughter in sacrifice to the goddess Artemis. Meanwhile, Agamemnon's wife, left at home, longing for the absent male becomes herself a male, ruling the city of Argos, bringing her sexual partner into her house and ultimately delivering death blows to her husband. In the first play of the *Oresteia*, *Agamemnon*, we are not led to sympathise with the murderous queen, but we are given a sense of how the military endeavours of the city can in their turn distort and disrupt the private realm which they seek to preserve. Agamemnon hesitates before he kills his daughter. But then he reflects: 'Disband the fleet, sail home, and earn/ The deserter's badge – abandon my command,/ Betray the alliance – now? The wind must turn,/ There must be sacrifice, a maid must bleed –/ Their chafing rage demands it.' (211-215)[14]

In another play by Aeschylus, *The Seven Against Thebes*, the female Chorus stand as a counterpoint to the male warriors sent out to defend the gates of the city. Six heroes have come with Polyneices, the son of

Oedipus and Jocasta, to the seven gates of Thebes to take over the city. Eteocles, the other son of the incestuous marriage, defends the city, which he transforms through his language into a mother. For the sake of a public mother he forgets his real mother who bore both himself and his brother. Six Theban heroes go first to each of the six gates in the wall protecting Thebes. There, each one meets in battle the hero stationed there from Polyneices' forces. At the seventh gate Polyneices stands. Without hesitation, without thought of the implications of going to face his brother in a battle which will mean the death of at least one of them, Eteocles heads off — indeed, to his own and his brother's death. Concern for the preservation of the public political unit transcends the awareness of the impiety implicit in killing his own brother. It is the Chorus of females treated by Eteocles with such contempt who try to restrain him, but they fail. It is they, the women, who question whether a city, the public unity, can be saved by the destruction of what is private, the family, whether a brother can be the same as the enemy. It is they who reveal that Eteocles' 'noble dedication to the city is the obverse of his fatal indifference to the family'.[15] And yet it is they who must also realise that without that devotion to the city their own survival, the private survival of the family, cannot persist. Eteocles is unaware of this conflict. His failing is an unreflective dismissal and arrogant refusal to hear the demands of the private as expressed by the female Chorus.

Sophocles' tragedy told in the *Antigone* contains both the story and the themes of Aeschylus' *Seven*. Antigone, emphasising her ties to the family and devotion to its gods, insists on burying the brother who died as a traitor to the city. Unlike Eteocles, she is not willing to ignore the ties for the sake of an abstract public. Her resolve and ultimately her deed is in opposition to the necessities of Creon's political world, for he has denied Polyneices a burial in trying to preserve the city against future traitors. Antigone thus fights against the edicts and necessities of Creon's political realm in order to preserve the religion and the divine law of the family of her parents. However, Ismene, her sister, stands in contradiction to Antigone's attempts. She illustrates that the private sphere traditionally associated with the female is particular and weak (*Antigone*, 59-67), it is dependent upon the protection which the polity dominated by the males can provide through its attention to warfare. Antigone, by trying to preserve the family of her parents, threatens the political stability of a community suffering from a recent war and precludes a family of her own. Death, not Creon's son, is her mate. Creon in turn suffers the death of his wife and his son by refusing to recognise Antigone's and society's need to preserve the religious unit of the family, and by pretending that only that which is public is worth protecting.[16]

By the end of the fifth century there is, at least in the plays of Euripides, no longer the tragic opposition between a war fought for some necessary political unity and the family which must suffer for that war. Rather, under the influence of the demoralising and degrading Peloponnesian War, which ravaged Greece in the last third of the fifth century, the glory of war is debased before the suffering, now vividly apparent, inflicted on the private realm of the family. The war of the Greeks against Troy appears in Euripides' *Trojan Women* as an ill-conceived, vicious adventure carried out by despicable, arrogant men who fight not for a common purpose but for individual greed and lust. Hecuba stands in the centre throughout the play enduring one grief after another — her daughter Cassandra carried off to be a slave to an Argive wife, her daughter-in-law to be the concubine to the son of Hector's murderer, her grandson thrown to his death from the battlements of her city. It is a play which elicits our sympathy for those women who suffer from the excesses of men who find fulfilment through the acquisition of glory attained on the battlefield. And yet, so ingrained is the unity of glory and the masculine world of war, that the women who suffer so deeply in this play continue to accept the male values. Hecuba notes, as she buries her grandson, 'if god did not from above, seize and overturn the earth (Troy), unknown we would be unsung and not give songs to the muses of coming mortals'. (*Trojan Women*, 1242-1245) Hecuba hints that the fame of her city and its men may make up for all the pain she experiences. There is an irony in this ending. Euripides, for sure, wishes to demonstrate to his audience the calamity of war, and yet Hecuba, who suffers the most, still seems willing to accept those calamities for the sake of a noble warrior's death on the battlefield.

As the examples above suggest, the opposition between public and private was often expressed in sexual images of the male warrior and the female householder. The imagery had a complementary spatial component as well. That which was public (war and politics) was a male adventure carried on outdoors, while that which was female was familial and existed behind the doors of the home. But we must not overemphasise the sexual division; while the male was usually associated with what was public, he was also involved in the affairs of the household just as we also find women outdoors in the public arena participating in the religious festivals of the city.

III. Thucydides

It is Thucydides, the historian of the Peloponnesian War from which Greek society never fully recovered, who chronicles the final attempt of Greeks, especially the Athenians, to preserve an impossible balance between public and private. He portrays the *polis*, under the stress and degradation of war, as struggling to preserve itself against the centrifugal force of individualism, a concern with the self of the sort promoted by the Sophists. Pericles, in his renowned funeral oration for those who died in the first year of the war, offers a panegyric for the Athenian way of life, the *politeia*, which emphasises the community and one's participation in that community. The Athenians, Pericles claims, live as free men, but his understanding of freedom here is not that of the rights of the individual; rather, it is both the absence of a foreign power controlling them and participation in the governance of their own city. That participation, though, is not a matter of choice; it is the definition of citizenship and the criterion of manhood. 'We alone think of one who does not participate in these affairs not as a quiet man, but as a useless one.' (*Histories*, II.40.2) Failure to participate goes far beyond our contemporary notions of poor citizenship (cf. II.60.3-4). The final expression of this participation is fighting in the war against Sparta. Such a concern with public life, Pericles claims, is ultimately more important than the individual's life as a private man. 'For it is just to set manly virtues in war on behalf of one's fatherland before evil in other affairs; for they hid the bad with the good and gave more service publicly than they did harm as individuals.' (II.42.3) In dying for the sake of the community, these men became truly Athenians. The highest glory, as Pericles suggests here, is to be united with the *polis* through self-sacrifice. With this exaltation of the subordination of the individual to the city there is the concomitant belittling of the family with its competing claims on the individual. The funeral oration ends with what seem to us heartless words to the relatives of the dead soldiers: sons and brothers, imitate your fathers and older brothers so that you too may find fulfilment through death for the city; and parents, if still of an age to do so, have more sons to serve as security to the city. (II.44.3) The public realm completely overshadows the values of family.

The devotion to that which is public in Athens during the Peloponnesian War does not last long beyond the famous speech by Pericles. By his final speech in Thucydides' history, Pericles must exhort the Athenians to sacrifice the exclusive attention to their private woes

(II.61.2-4). The whole, the public, is greater than the sum of its individual parts. The language which Pericles must now use reflects the growing individualism which led to the decay of the city state. His rhetoric is that of the Sophists and closer to modern liberalism than to the *polis* he had praised in the funeral oration.

Pericles' pleas are unheeded and the history of the war for Thucydides is the history of the increased importance of the individual as a private being with private interests, as one concerned with the *idion* rather than the *koinon*. This is manifest first in the discussion of the plague — a certain symbol of the war itself — where human nature, released from the fear of gods and men, gives full expression to its individualistic orientation, particularly the pursuits of private pleasures. It is manifest again in Thucydides' assessment of the leadership in Athens after the death of Pericles. These were leaders who no longer cared about the public realm, but allowed a jealous love of honour (*idias philotimias*) and private profit outside the war to dominate their decisions. (II.65.7)

The full expression of this concern for one's self appears in the extreme self-centredness of Alcibiades, who can, in total opposition to the values expressed by Pericles, claim that his acts as an individual — victories at Olympia, for example — bring glory to the city and not the city glory to him. When the city no longer serves his private needs and interests, when he as an individual no longer feels secure in the city, he leaves and helps the Spartans defeat the Athenians at Sicily. Achilles, the heroic warrior, depended on the community for respect and demands that from the community, but he needed also the moderation finally shown in his shared grief with Priam at the end of the *Iliad*. Alcibiades shows none of this moderation and none of this grief. He stands as the isolated individual unaware of or insensitive to the ties to the city and to family that give meaning to the deaths of the truly Homeric heroes.

Thucydides thus depicts the decay of the organic model of political society so vividly and poetically expressed by Pericles in his funeral oration. Thucydides sees the war as bringing to the forefront of political activity a concern with one's own private welfare. The needs of the city are lost in the self-serving individualism of the Athenian leaders. The war indeed tolls the end of the Homeric ideal.

IV. Plato

In considering ever so briefly Plato's contribution to the ways of thinking about public and private, we must note two aspects of his thought.

On the one hand, Plato is concerned with the place of philosophy in the public community, a problem which for him became the relation of private to public. This is a theme which runs through all his writings but is especially evident in such works as the *Apology* and the *Crito*. On the other hand, in his discussion of the 'best city' in the *Republic*, he appears to suggest the priority of the public over the private, rather than the inherent tension which he recognises elsewhere.

At the base of Plato's consideration of political life in general is of course the personage of Socrates. As philosopher, Socrates must stand apart from the city; that is, Socrates must withdraw from the dominant opinions and values of the city, from the *koinon* of the city. He is, as he describes himself in the *Apology*, a foreigner to the public life of the city, as one who speaks almost a foreign language. He is, though, also withdrawn from the community of his family, which he neglects, making the shrewish Xanthippe justified in her complaints. The community of the family is not what draws him away from the city, what makes him a private rather than a public individual. Rather, the activity of philosophy, the constant questioning of young and old make him withdraw from the active pursuit of political power in the city. It is philosophy that makes him *apragmōn* (uninvolved) — in Pericles' vision, a useless one for the city. The private for him now means a new family, which comes from philosophic discourse engaged in by his companions and followers. Within the new family Socrates often takes the woman's role and that which is traditionally most private (birth) comes to dominate (in the form of birth of ideas) over the male role of warrior and citizen in the public realm. While this private realm stands in opposition to the city, it is no more individualised than the Greek family. The philosophic endeavour is a common one among those engaged in the pursuit of knowledge. It cannot be carried on in isolation. Platonic dialectic entails discourse. Furthermore, the philosophic endeavour is directed to a common world which transcends the city.

Thus we find in Plato's works two understandings of the nature of the public. On one level there is the particularised city from which the philosopher withdraws; on the other, there are the forms which we all have (potentially) in common. The objects of philosophic speculation replace the city as the source of values and the source of knowledge. The consequence of this transformation of public and private in the Platonic corpus is to undermine the status of the city and of the citizen. That is, whereas the city had definitional powers, defining what is good and what is bad, and most importantly who is friend and who is foe, the forms or ideas which Socrates proposes introduce new values and reject the arbitrary definitions of the city. The philosopher's friends are not defined by the boundaries of the city walls. As Socrates often says, he will philosophise with anyone, citizen or freeman or slave, Athenian or foreigner. The non-political activity in which he engages with others does not recognise the community of the *polis* as the definer of its boundaries or of its *koinon*.

However, as the philosophic activity of a Socrates removes him from the city, as the family removes the female involved in reproduction from the city, Socrates recognises his own dependence on the city. Thus, we find at the end of the *Apology* and in the *Crito* the same tension between public and private which we noted in the dramatic works of the fifth century. While intellectually Socrates may transcend the limiting definitions of the city, his body cannot, and the human being comprised of both body and intellect cannot escape the ties to others which come from the body. It is his body that makes him part of the city — that makes him fight for Athens when he is called to, that makes him most significantly refuse to escape from the jail cell in the *Crito*. His body, that which is most private, is what ultimately ties him to that which is public. The philosopher, the idiot, the private being, needs the city in order to continue his own existence. While not participating actively in its communal life, the philosopher, like the female, is dependent on it. Neither can afford to destroy it. Whether Socrates is as essential for Athens as the female is for the city or the city is for both of them is more open to question. He claims his importance to the city in the famous gadfly image of the *Apology*, but that very image itself raises questions. Does the steed or beast, Athens, need to be constantly stirred up by the gadfly's bites? Could not the community sleep happily on? It is only Socrates' questioning of the values of the city based on his perceptions of a good common to more than just the city that makes movement necessary — a movement or striving that so far from aiding the city may actually destroy it.

In his consideration of the relationship of the philosopher to the city there is no question that Plato revels in Socrates' existence — his privateness that lets him stand apart from what was traditionally the public realm and introduce a new sense of community among his disciples. However, when Plato writes with a view to the needs and interests of the political community, he suggests precisely the need to eliminate the private for the sake of the stability of the whole. This is done most dramatically and powerfully in his proposal for the community (*koinōnia*) of wives, children and property in his *Republic*. The city he proposes is one free from discord and one in which devotion to the whole is not limited by devotion to a part, that which is private. To destroy the private as a potentially divisive force Socrates makes everything public, belonging to all, not one. He acknowledges here not only the threat of the family but also the threat of the private realm of the philosopher to the stability of the public realm. All share, by the time Socrates finishes this publicisation of the private realm, not only wives, children and property but also pains and happiness, opinions and knowledge. The idiot does not exist here.

While many have taken Socrates' proposals here as serious, as a vision of an ideal polity, it seems to me that Plato is rather suggesting the ludicrous extremes to which politics must go in order to transcend the eternal conflict between public and private, the extreme distortions of nature which politics must perpetrate in order to secure its existence. The extremes so transform the human being that he or she is no longer distinguishable from the animals in a barnyard. Eliminating all that is private — the family, children, wealth — is simply ludicrous in the life of the city. For the philosophical life, however, it is a necessary surrender for the sake of what is truly common, truly public, namely the forms. While in the life which he actually leads Socrates is constantly torn between that which is public — both the forms and the city — and that which is private, in his vision of the 'perfect city' and perhaps the 'perfect philosopher' he suggests the total elimination of the private. Neither political being nor philosophic being can be limited or undercut by what is private. The consequence, though, of eliminating the tension is to transform the human into the animal in the city of Socrates' *politeia*, or into the god that the philosopher becomes when he sheds all that is private, including his body, and ascends to the eternal vision of truth and beauty.[17]

V. Aristotle

Aristotle introduces his major work on politics:

> Since every *polis* is some sort of *koinōnia* and every *koinōnia* has been established for the sake of some sort of good (for all do everything for the sake of what seems to be good), it is clear that all communities aim at some good, especially at that which is highest of all and that which is highest of all encompasses all the rest. (*Politics*, 1252a1-7)

With this Aristotle establishes a hierarchical relationship which attempts to overcome the tensions with which previous Greek authors had fought. Politics is the highest association: it is the one with the greatest authority and the one that encompasses all the others within it. The characteristic aspect of political life is choice, particularly the choice to live the good life, which is possible only in so far as one is member of the city. The family, by contrast, is directed towards the process of procreation and comes from inclination, not choice, and thus it is similar to the animal world. The hierarchy places the citizen over the householder (the economist) in terms of his aim towards the highest good. But while the tension is in some way transcended — or one might say ignored — through the hierarchy, the interdependence is not.

Book I of the *Politics*, devoted to the study of the household, reveals many of the difficulties in understanding even this most basic of *koinōniai*. For, as with the *polis*, it is directed towards some good, but what that good is, whose it is and indeed even how it is to be attained is open to discussion. The questions are not easily answered. The slave is not easily defined; the conquest of nature on which the family is dependent for its survival is not so easily accomplished. The questions surrounding the nature of the private realm detain Aristotle; they halt his consideration of the highest association because the highest association builds on the lesser ones. Indeed what one learns in the second book of the *Politics* is that the study of the city must not only begin from the study of what is private as opposed to what is public, but must also be concerned with how the private and the public are interrelated. The *polis* is a *koinōnia*, that is the starting point. But the question is, how much is encompassed in the *koinōnia*? How much is to be shared by the city and how much not?

The answer first proposed and later developed is that, in opposition to Socrates, there must be a private realm which retains respect and support if there is to be a viable public realm. The first way of suggesting this interdependence comes in Aristotle's critique of Socrates' proposals for the community of wives, children and property. Socrates' proposals will not work, Aristotle claims, for they transform the city from a realm of diversity that comes from the multiplicity of private households and private individuals into an individual, which is the city. It is no longer a *polis* which holds some things in common but an individual which has everything in common within itself. More serious, Socrates takes away a love for one's own, an intense feeling of affection, attachment and care that can only be nurtured in a private realm where individuals are drawn together in the common process of survival and procreation. Love, or friendly feeling, is crucial for the *polis*, but 'just as a little bit of sugar mixed in a great deal of water is not tasted' so, in Socrates' city, affection, or seeing others as closely related to oneself, is watered down. (1262b17-22) Or in another often-quoted phrase: 'A private (*idion*) cousin is worth more than a son shared by all.' (1262a13) Some things can be shared and others cannot. For Aristotle, love and virtue can be transferred to the public realm only after they are moulded in the crucible of family.

Implicit in this attack on Socrates is also an attack against the Pericles of Thucydides, who had asked his Athenians to become lovers of a city while demanding they disregard their own private loves. That love of the city, Aristotle suggests, cannot be nurtured without a sense of how it relates to one's private existence and attachments to specific others — be they objects or other human beings. The sense of one's own and the affection directed towards that which is one's own is both the source and the consequence of human creativity. We are creative beings in the private realm; we create children and we create artefacts. That creativity cannot be replicated for Aristotle on the public level (except in the unique case of the lawgiver), for what one creates there is never entirely one's own; it is implemented, distorted, appropriated, dismissed by the many.

What can and must be common for the city to survive is the education which comes from the *politeia*. The family cannot educate freely; it does not have the strength to enforce the rules of behaviour on those who are not persuaded. That power to enforce certain patterns of behaviour on the city's young must be used to create a unity, a community which, though natural to humans, does not exist by nature. The highest form of human association comes from force originally, while the lower forms — the private — come from love. The private realm thus introduces into the public realm moderation or a tempering element.

When Aristotle finally, in Book III of the *Politics*, turns to a consideration of the *polis*, we find him grappling with the questions that seem to exclude considerations of the private realm. We find the individual disassociated from his family ties, from productive labour and physical creativity. Whereas in Book II Aristotle had talked about the citizen as shoemaker or carpenter, by Book III these artisans are no longer admitted to the ranks of citizenship. The public individual has transcended the private realm to claim his place as a part of the higher association. Behind this, however, lies the demand that political life acknowledge its dependence not only on the physical concerns of the family but also on its emotional ties without which the love of the city would not develop.

Strikingly absent from Aristotle's discussion thus far is war. The tragic tension between the two realms which had dominated the other thinkers in ancient Greece is avoided. The life in one realm is not dependent on death in the other; in fact, the life in one depends on life in the other. The abstract citizen which the city demands in its search for a higher level of community is just that: abstracted, drawn away from his roots firmly planted in the private realm of *to idion*, that which is particular to him.

I have emphasised the interdependence of private and public in Aristotle despite the initial hierarchy at the beginning of Book I of the *Politics* because an important and often referred to interpretation of Greek life, seemingly derived from Aristotle, appears in the work of Hannah Arendt.[18] Arendt, in the process of idealising the political, denigrates the private and suggests that her model of political life could be found in the thought and practice of the Greek *polis*. I believe that we should accept her models of Aristotle and of the Greek *polis* only with great caution. Her analysis can be simply summarised with reference to a neat model that portrays portions of reality in dichotomous opposition:

public	private
polis	household
freedom	necessity
male	female
equality	inequality
immortality	mortality (birth and death)
open	closed

This seems to come from *Politics* I, but Aristotle later modifies his stand. He makes clear that the *polis* is not a realm only of freedom. While it is indeed a realm of moral choice, where men are trained to select the good rather than the bad, the *polis* is also limited — by bodies which must be organised, which must be punished by the city, by human passions which focus the individual on self-interest, by climate, by geography and so forth. The choices with regard to public life are freer than those determined by instinct, but these choices are in turn limited by the physical demands made on the city. The sexual dichotomy also is too simple, for, as we noted at the end of section II, just as the male must participate in the money making of the family, in the procreation of the children, so the female must participate in the religious festivals of the city and the raising of future citizens. The immortality of the city is dependent on the life and death of its citizens; the family likewise enjoys its own immortality through its devotion to the ancestors and the honours anticipated from ancestor worship by future generations.

The equality of the *polis* is an arbitrary one, working against a natural inequality among humans. Aristotle clarifies in Book V of the *Politics* that who is judged equal is always subject to debate and therefore the source of revolutions within cities. The criteria for equality are ambiguous, especially those which relate to virtue. Since we have difficulty recognising who is the virtuous man, such an individual may or may not be one of those who rules within the city. The city, in its orientation towards equality on the public level, will often distort a natural inequality of worth for the sake of equality of wealth or free birth. The political is inferior in this point because it will treat as equals those who are not; it will turn humans who are better and therefore should rule into subjects for the sake of the city. The inequality which Aristotle finds in the family comes, according to Aristotle, from nature; the male by nature has authority over the female, the master over the slave. It is not artificial and it does not distort natural human relations. Though we may reject this family hierarchy, we should not see in it Aristotle's attempt to belittle the family or the private realm, but rather his respect for a natural order which men, in creating cities based on human choice and limited knowledge, can never hope to attain.

Arendt's idealised vision of the ancient city is impossible precisely because she ignores what the ancient Greeks understood so well: the interdependence of *polis* and *oikos*, of public and private, an interdependence demanded by the ever-present threat of war. When Aristotle chose to eliminate the focus on war, he could raise the *polis* to the highest level of human achievement since it would no longer require the destruction of what was private. But he could not ignore the private realm, nor does he undervalue the ties of the family for the sake of an abstract polity. Rather he recognises that the city survives only as long as the private particular world of the family does.

VI. Conclusion

We could not expect to find in ancient Greece over several hundred years a unified conception of the public and the private. In summary,

I may suggest that we see at least seven different orientations towards public and private offered in the varied literature of ancient Greece:
1. *Achilles*: The glorious warrior whose heroic stature comes from his success and ability to protect the community. He himself exists for the fame accorded him by the community; should he withdraw from the fighting, he would lose that most desirable fame. In the course of the *Iliad*, he comes to recognise the value of specific relationships with others, the model offered by Hector.
2. *Hector*: The hero who is caught in the tragic conflict between existence within the family and death on the battlefield for the sake of protecting the city and the family within.
3. *Attic tragedies*: The characters here, from Agamemnon to Antigone, become tragic as they devote themselves exclusively to one realm or the other. It is only through suffering that they learn the interdependence of the two.
4. *Sophists*: Individualism and the priority of the individual over the public sphere is introduced here. The political community is justified only by the degree to which it protects private interests. Alcibiades is the incarnation of this view.
5. *Pericles*: He responds first to the individualism of the Sophists in the Funeral Oration by asserting the total priority of the city over the individual. Later in the war he has to yield in his rhetoric to their self-interested visions.
6. *Socrates*: The philosopher who *vis-à-vis* the city remains a private individual, withdrawn from its activity, though he recognises his necessary dependence on the city for the needs of his body. He also introduces a new understanding of what is public, common to all men, namely the forms which are not linked to any specific city or individuals.
7. *Aristotle*: The solution to the tragic opposition found by focusing on the city not as a realm of war but of moral choice, and by asserting the hierarchical priority of the city at the same time that he asserts the importance of an attachment to the private realm if the city is to exist.

We find throughout Greek thought a sensitivity to the conflicting demands made on the individual by his or her commitments and attachments. The all-encompassing character of the *polis* sharpened the conflicts in a way that is seldom so vital today, except perhaps under the pressures of war. Comparably, the religious character of the family made a concern with the private appear to come not from self-interest but from familial piety, which in its turn was countered by the religions of the cities. The finely drawn distinctions which could be made spatially between what was within and what was outside the household did not help to resolve the conflict between what one owed to each. No one among the Greeks could escape freely the implications of that conflict.

Notes

1. A.W.H. Adkins, *Moral Values and Political Behavior in Ancient Greece: From Homer to the End of the Fifth Century* (W.W. Norton, New York, 1972), Ch. 2.

2. One needs here to compare the works of Gustave Glotz, *The Greek City and its Institutions*, N. Mallinson (trans.) (Alfred A. Knopf, New York, 1930), and Numa Denis Fustel de Coulanges, *The Ancient City* (Johns Hopkins University Press, Baltimore, 1980). Both authors discuss the rise of the *polis*, but Glotz puts a far greater emphasis on the individual as needing to break out of the family in order to become a member of the *polis*, while Fustel de Coulanges emphasises the dependence of the city on the family and their parallel development.

3. As an example, at the very beginning of Sophocles' *Antigone*, Antigone is talking to her sister about their dead and unburied brother. She refers to him as *koinon autadelphon*, 'our own brother whom we share in common'.

4. All references to works by the Greek authors will be included in the text and noted, according to the standard divisions used in the Oxford Classical ·ts (*Scriptorum Classicorum Bibliotheca Oxoniensis*).

5. The word *idion* also means prose, that is, the language which is spoken in private. Public speech, that of the stage, was in metre.

6. Significantly, the use of mercenaries only becomes an issue when the unity of the *polis* begins to deteriorate at the end of the fifth century. The attitude towards mercenaries is expressed perhaps most vividly in Thucydides' description of Thracian mercenaries who, having been sent back unused and unpaid, attacked a defenceless village, killing women and children indiscriminately, and slaughtering all those in the local schoolhouse. (*Histories*, VII.30) See also I.32.

7. The following section depends heavily on the insights of James M. Redfield, *Nature and Culture in the 'Iliad': The Tragedy of Hector* (University of Chicago Press, Chicago, 1975), and Marilyn B. Arthur, 'Early Greece: The Origin of the Western Attitude Toward Women', *Arethusa*, 6, no. 1 (1973), pp. 7-58.

8. Cf. Gregory Nagy, *The Best of the Achaeans: Concepts of the Hero in Archaic Greek Poetry* (Johns Hopkins University Press, Baltimore, 1979), p. 146, for a discussion of the etymological origins of Hector's name in the word for 'protector'.

9. Hector is similarly impervious to the pleas of his father and mother, who, recalling their parental ties to him, urge him not to face Achilles in battle. (*Iliad*, 22.28-93).

10. Though space does not permit for the *Odyssey* even the kind of summary treatment given above to the *Iliad*, we should note that the themes are similar. That work begins with Odysseus on the enchanted island of the goddess Calypso. Though he has the affections of a goddess far more beautiful than his mortal wife, he sits in loneliness, isolated from human contacts, longing for his home, Penelope, his son, and his city. He chooses to return to them rather than enjoy the immortality and divine beauty offered him by Calypso. The longing, the human desire to be set into a series of human relationships is what leads to his

mortality as well as his humanity. It is the choice which Achilles makes when he gives up long life to avenge the death of Patroclus and which Hector makes when he dies to protect those who live within the city and his family.

11. J.-P. Vernant, *Mythe et société en Grèce ancienne* (Maspero, Paris, 1974), p. 31.

12. Ibid., p. 41: 'L'armée c'est l'assemblée populaire sous les armes, la cité en campagne, comme inversement la cité est une communauté des guerrières, les droits politiques n'appartiennent pleinement qu'à ceux qui peuvent à leur frais s'équipper en hoplites.'

13. Fustel de Coulanges, *The Ancient City*, Book Third, is particularly helpful on this topic.

14. I have used the translation by Phillip Vellacott in Aeschylus, *The Oresteian Trilogy* (Penguin Books, Harmondsworth, 1959).

15. Clifford Orwin, 'Feminine Justice: The End of the *Seven Against Thebes*', *Classical Philology*, 75 (1980), pp. 187-96, at p. 191.

16. In Creon's case there were clear signals from the gods that the realm of the private world needed to be preserved. See further, Sarah B. Pomeroy, *Goddesses, Whores, Wives, and Slaves: Women in Classical Antiquity* (Schocken Books, New York, 1975), p. 20.

17. See esp. Diotima's speech in Plato's *Symposium*.

18. Especially in Hannah Arendt, *The Human Condition* (University of Chicago Press, Chicago, 1958), Ch. 2.

CONTRIBUTORS

Stanley I. Benn is Professorial Fellow in Philosophy in the Research School of Social Sciences of the Australian National University. He is co-author, with R.S. Peters, of *Social Principles and the Democratic State* (1959) and co-editor of *Rationality and the Social Sciences* (1976) and co-author of *Political Participation* (1978). His numerous contributions to volumes of essays and periodicals on basic principles and ideals in moral and political theory include 13 entries in the *Encyclopedia of Philosophy*. He is currently working on a book on moral and social philosophy, provisionally entitled *Persons and Values*.

Paul D. Finn is a Reader in Law in the Law Faculty of the Australian National University. He is the author of articles on public officials, public authorities and electoral law, and of a book entitled *Fiduciary Obligations* (1977).

Gerald F. Gaus was formerly a Research Fellow in the Research School of Social Sciences of the Australian National University and is at present Assistant Professor of Politics at Wake Forest University in the United States. He is the author of *The Modern Liberal Theory of Man* (1983) and of articles on moral philosophy.

Ruth Gavison is Senior Lecturer in the Faculty of Law of the Hebrew University of Jerusalem. She is the author of articles on jurisprudence and ethics, in legal journals and anthologies, with a particular interest in privacy, which was the subject of her doctoral thesis.

John B. Haviland is Senior Research Fellow in Anthropology in the Research School of Pacific Studies of the Australian National University. He is the author of *Gossip, Reputation and Knowledge in Zinacantan* (1977), *Sk'op Sotz'leb; El Tzotzil de San Lorenzo Zinacantan* (1981), and has contributed to the *Handbook of Australian Languages*.

Leslie K. Haviland is Senior Tutor in the Department of Prehistory and Anthropology, Faculty of Arts, of the Australian National University. Since 1967 she has lived for more than four years for stays of varying lengths in Zinacantan. Her research there has been concerned with socio-economic organisation, and, in particular, with women's labour. Since 1975 she has also been engaged in research at an Australian Aboriginal mission.

Eugene Kamenka is Professor of the History of Ideas in the Research School of Social Sciences of the Australian National University. His books, which include *The Ethical Foundations of Marxism* (1972),

Marxism and Ethics (1972), and *The Philosophy of Ludwig Feuerbach* (1970), have been translated into French, Hebrew, Japanese and Spanish. He has edited and co-edited some 20 volumes of studies in social thought and the history of ideas, the most recent including *Law and Social Control* (1980), *Law-making in Australia* (1980), *Community as a Social Ideal* (1982), and *The Portable Karl Marx* (1980).

Martin Krygier is Senior Lecturer in Law in the University of New South Wales. He is co-editor (with Eugene Kamenka) of *Bureaucracy: The Career of a Concept* (1979) and has written articles on jurisprudence, political and social theory, and law and anthropology.

Carole Pateman is Reader in Government in the University of Sydney. She is the author of *Participation and Democratic Theory* (1970) and *The Problem of Political Obligation* (1979). She has contributed numerous articles to political science and philosophy journals on political theory and on the status of women.

Alan Ryan is Reader in Politics in the University of Oxford, and Fellow of New College, Oxford. He is the author of *The Philosophy of John Stuart Mill* (1970), *The Philosophy of the Social Sciences* (1970), and *J.S. Mill* (1975), and the editor of *Social Explanation* (1973) and *The Idea of Freedom* (1979). He is currently completing *The Political Theory of Property* and *Bertrand Russell's Politics*.

Arlene Saxonhouse is Associate Professor of Political Science in the University of Michigan. She has written articles on Greek political thought, particularly on Plato, and is currently working on a book, *Women in the History of Political Thought: Ancient Greece to the Reformation*.

Alice Erh-Soon Tay is Professor of Jurisprudence in the University of Sydney. She is the author of numerous articles on common law, jurisprudence, comparative law, Soviet law and Chinese law, and of several contributions to the *Encyclopedia of Soviet Law*, besides being co-author, with her husband, Eugene Kamenka, of two forthcoming books, *Marxism and the Theory of Law* and *Sowjetische Rechtstheorie*. She has co-edited and contributed to *Law and Society*, *Human Rights* (both 1978) and *Justice* (1979), and co-contributed to *Bureaucracy* (1979); she is also co-editor (with E. Kamenka) of *Law-making in Australia* and *Law and Social Control* (both 1980).

Anthony S. Walton is Lecturer in the Philosophy of the Social Sciences in the Open University, Milton Keynes, England. He is currently preparing a book on Hegel's social and political theory.

INDEX OF PERSONS

Achilles, 366, 367, 368, 369, 374, 382, 383, 384
Adkins, A.W.H., 383
Aeschylus, 370, 371
Agamemnon, 167, 370, 382
Alcibiades, 374, 382
Alfonso X, 72
Andromache, 367
Anthony, S.B., 56
Antigone, 137, 371, 372, 382, 383
Aquinas, Thomas, St, 81
Arendt, H., 18, 27, 64, 380, 384
Aristophanes, 369
Aristotle, 81, 141, 142, 144, 153, 365, 366, 377-81, 382
Arthur, M.B., 383
Astell, M., 302
Aubert, V., 337, 340
Augustine, St, 19
Austin, J.L., 285
Austin, John, 215
Auxter, T., 180, 181
Avineri, S., 266
Azcarate, M., 278, 279

Bacon, F., 73, 92, 111
Bahr, O., 76
Banfield, E.C., 62
Banton, M., 153
Barker, D.L., 303
Barker, E., 51, 64, 65
Barnes, J.A., 327
Barnet, R.J., 63
Barron, J., 134
Barry, B., 31, 32, 45, 61, 63
Barth, F., 315, 338
Beaumanoir, 72
Benn, S.I., 10, 27, 65, 87, 93, 100, 114, 134, 249, 250, 252, 255, 263, 264, 265, 282, 283, 285, 286, 294, 301, 307, 312-13, 317, 318, 321, 322, 328, 336, 338, 360, Chs. 1, 2, 7
Bentham, J., 32, 33, 35, 41, 44, 47, 48, 59, 61, 62, 63, 158, 190, 194, 203, 215, 216, 217, 224, 225, 226, 228, 243, 244, 252, 259
Bentley, A.F., 220
Bergson, A., 221

Berlin, I., 134, 264
Beveridge, W., 196, 218, 219, 220
Blau, P.M., 62
Bodin, J., 73
Bohannan, P., 334, 335
Bosanquet, B., 49, 52, 56, 63, 64, 65, 181, 221, 301
Bourgiba, Habib, 27
Box, S., 154
Bracton, Henry de, 72
Bramwell, B., 111
Brandeis, L., 133
Brandt, R.B., 161, 162
Brennan, T., 301
Bronte, Charlotte, 218
Brutus, L. Junius, 141
Burckhardt, W., 82, 92
Burdick, C.K., 111
Burke, E., 52

Calvin, J., 19
Camus, A., 142, 153, 161
Carritt, E.F., 64
Carter, J., President, 165
Cassandra, 372
Cecil, H., 162, 181
Chabod, F., 181
Chanina, Rabbi, 21
Chapman, J.W., 219, 221
Clarke, P., 217, 219
Connolly, W.E., 264
Coulson, N.J., 27
Cranston, M., 64, 243
Creon, 371, 384
Croce, B., 160
Crosland, C.A.R., 243, 244
Cross, Lord, 62

Dahl, R., 206, 220
Davidson, D., 154
Deng Xiao-ping, 80
Denning, Lord, 117
Devlin, Lord, 155, 175, 176, 180, 181
Dewey, J., 51, 56, 64, 65, 183, 197, 200, 203, 209, 214, 218, 219, 220
Diderot, D., 153
Dikaiopolis, 369

Index of Persons

Diotima, 384
Donagan, A., 161-62, 181
Donne, J., 179
Donzelot, J., 297, 303
DuBois, E., 292, 302
Duguit, L., 83, 92
Dumont, L., 323
Durkheim, E., 83, 92, 137, 138, 142, 143-44, 146, 153, 154, 309, 310, 327, 332
Dworkin, R., 45, 63, 164, 219

Eisenstein, Z., 301, 303
Elshtain, J.B., 291, 292, 302
Engels, F., 273, 278
Epstein, A.L., 338
Eteocles, 371
Euripides, 167, 372
Evans, P., 220
Evans-Pritchard, E.E., 322, 323

Feuerbach, L., 272
Filmer, 283, 284
Finer, H., 220
Finn, P., 9, 13, 17, 79
Firestone, S., 289, 302
Fleta, 72
Fortes, M., 322, 323, 324, 327, 329
Freeden, M.,217, 218
Freud, S., 140, 141, 149, 153
Fried, C., 124, 129, 134
Friedman, M., 205, 208
Friedman, M. and R., 183, 189, 207, 212, 214, 215, 220, 221
Fustel de Coulanges, N.D., 383, 384

Galanter, M., 340
Galbraith, J.K., 53, 208, 209, 210, 211, 212, 221
Gardet, L., 27
Gaus, G.F., 5, 87, 93, 100, 114, 249, 250, 252, 255, 263, 264, 265, 282, 283, 285, 286, 294, 301, 307, 312-13, 317, 318, 321, 322, 328, 336, 338, 360, Chs. 1, 2, 8
Gavison, R., 8, 11, 12, 133, 134
Gelasius, 19
George, V., 219
Gerstein, R., 134
Ginsburg, L.Ya., 92
Gladstone, W.E., 165
Glanvill, 72
Glotz, G., 383
Gluckman, M., 316, 321, 334

Goffman, E., 27, 136, 144, 146, 150, 153, 154, 245
Goldberg, S., 303
Gombay, A., 61
Goody, J., 336, 337, 340
Gotbaum, V., 220
Gough, J.W., 63
Gould, C., 303
Graham, O., 206, 218, 219, 220
Gratian, 72
Green, P., 303
Green, T.H., 49, 50, 59, 63, 65
Gregor, T., 316, 317
Grice, H.P., 348, 349, 361
Gross, H., 133
Gulliver, P.H., 328
Gutmann, A., 212, 216, 221, 265

Habermas, J., 286, 298, 301, 303
Hale, Sir Matthew, 93, 97-98, 99, 111
Halevy, E., 215
Hamilton, R., 302
Hampshire, S., 155, 162, 180, 181
Haraway, D., 302
Hare, R.M., 158, 161, 162
Hargreaves, K., 303
Harré, R., 154, 243, 245
Harris, J., 243
Harrison, R.J., 221
Hart, H.L.A., 174, 176
Hartmann, H., 302
Haviland, L. and J., 24
Hayek, F.A., 53, 64, 205, 215
Heckscher, E.F., 216
Hector, 366, 367, 368, 369, 370, 372, 382, 383, 384
Hecuba, 372
Hegel, G.W.F., 17, 48, 49, 50, 51, 56, 63, 64, 65, 137, 153, 164, 211, 231, 234-37, 240, 244, 249-64, 265, 266, 271, 272, 278, 300, 301
Helen, 368
Henry II, 70
Hobbes, T., 39-40, 43, 48, 62, 65, 73, 142, 143, 190, 225, 243, 258, 260, 289, 312, 314, 315, 320, 322
Hobhouse, L.T., 50, 63, 65, 197, 200, 203, 210, 218, 219, 220, 221, 264, 310, 338
Hobson, J.A., 196, 197, 199, 200, 201, 202, 217, 218, 219, 220, 221

Index of Persons

Hoebel, E.A., 311, 331, 332, 333, 338
Hoederer, 159
Hollis, M., 148, 154
Holt, Lord, 97, 99
Homer, 167, 366
Honoré, A.M., 243, 244
Hume, D., 139, 153, 230

Iglitzin, L.B., 303
Ihering, R. von, 83
Ilting, K.-H., 265, 266
Ismene, 371

Jackson, P., 134
Jaquette, J., 303
Jocasta, 371
Johnson, A.G., 303
Jourard, S.M., 123, 134
Jouvenel, B. de, 198, 219
Justinian, 67, 72

Kafka, F., 123
Kamenka, E., 17, 92, 239, 279
Kant, I., 145, 154, 157, 158, 165, 171, 180, 181, 226, 231, 243
Keenan, E.O., 349, 361
Keesing, R., 324, 325, 327
Kelsen, H., 82, 83, 92
Keynes, J.M., 188, 196, 197, 199, 200, 203, 204, 205, 211, 214, 216, 217, 218, 219, 220
Kline, G., 276, 279
Krushchev, N., 80, 277
Krygier, M., 24

Lawrence, P., 338
Lawson, F.H., 244
Leach, E., 153
Lenin, V., 273, 274, 275, 276
Lessnoff, M., 153
Lévi-Strauss, C., 138, 153
Lewis, Sir George Cornewall, 31, 32, 33, 41, 61
Lindblom, C.E., 53, 64, 209, 210, 211, 212, 221
Locke, J., 48, 74, 225, 234, 244, 283, 284, 285, 286, 295, 297, 301, 302
Loomis, C.P., 278
Lukes, S., 264
Luther, M., 157
Lyons, D., 243

MacCallum, G.C., 170-71, 181

McCulloch, J.R., 184, 185, 187, 189, 192-93, 215, 216, 217, 218, 219
Machiavelli, N., 155, 159, 160, 161, 162, 166, 167, 180, 243
MacIver, R.M., 220
Mackenzie, W.J.M., 62
Macpherson, C.B., 211-12, 220, 221, 264
McWilliams, N., 303
Maddock, K., 320, 338
Maitland, 111
Makarenko, A.N., 275
Malinowski, B., 307, 314, 322, 327, 337
Malthus, T.R., 185, 188, 189, 195, 201, 202, 215, 216, 217, 219
Mao Tse-tung, 80, 275, 276
Marcuse, H., 154
Marett, R.R., 311, 338
Marsilius of Padua, 19
Marx, K., 17, 233, 237-40, 244, 267-74, 276, 278, 296, 299, 300
Mazzini, G., 51, 64
Mead, G.H., 143, 145-46, 154
Meade, J.E., 219
Meiklejohn, A., 134
Mill, J.S., 26, 36, 47-48, 51, 52, 53, 58, 62, 63, 64, 114, 135, 174, 175, 176, 188, 191, 192, 194, 196, 197, 199, 202, 213, 215, 216, 217, 218, 219, 221, 226, 230, 243, 244, 265, 287, 290, 292-93, 294, 295, 301, 302, 303
Mill, James, 188, 215, 216, 228, 243
Miller, D., 64
Millett, K., 297, 303
Mills, P., 301
Milne, A.J.M., 65
Mishan, E.J., 219
Montesquieu, 73, 154
Moore, S.F., 330, 333, 334, 338
Morris, Lord, 37-38
Morrison, H., 233
Mortimore, G.W., 265
Müller, R.E., 63
Mummery, A.F., 196, 217
Mussolini, B., 220

Nader, L., 340
Nagy, G., 383
Nestor, 368
Nicholas, B., 244
Niebuhr, R., 162, 166, 181
Nietzsche, F., 141, 276
Nimmer, M.B., 133

Index of Persons

Nixon, R., President, 166, 218
Nozick, R., 164, 217, 243, 244, 261, 265

Oakeshott, M., 27, 40, 62
Oakley, A., 302
O'Brien, D.P., 215, 216, 217, 218
Odysseus, 137, 367, 383
Oedipus, 371
Okun, A.M., 219
Ollman, B., 264
Orestes, 167
Ortner, S.B., 288, 302
Orwin, C., 384

Panitch, L., 208, 221
Paris, 368
Parsons, T., 145, 154
Pashukanis, E.B., 80, 84, 85-86, 88, 92, 275
Pateman, C., 17-18, 57, Ch. 12
Patroclus, 368, 384
Penelope, 383
Pericles, 373, 374, 375, 379, 382
Petchesky, R.P., 303
Peters, E.L., 329
Pettit, P., 264
Plamenatz, J., 244, 265
Plato, 257, 363, 374-77, 384
Polyneices, 370, 371
Pomeroy, S.B., 384
Popper, K., 146
Posner, R., 133, 134, 311, 317, 319, 320, 338
Pound, R., 83, 84, 86, 92
Priam, 368, 369, 374
Prosser, W., 118, 133

Quesalid, 138

Radbruch, G., 82, 92
Radcliffe-Brown, A.R., 310, 332, 338
Rawls, J., 51, 59, 64, 65, 164, 197, 199, 214, 218, 219, 243, 244, 301
Redfield, J.M., 383
Reiman, J., 134, 301
Ricardo, D., 185, 188, 215, 216, 217
Ritchie, D.G., 49, 51, 52, 63, 64, 197, 202, 219
Robbins, Lord, 186-87, 204, 214, 215, 216, 217, 219, 220
Roberts, J.M., 316, 338

Robinson, J., 199, 219
Robson, J.M., 64
Roosevelt, F.D., President, 196, 200, 218, 219
Rosaldo, M.Z., 288-89, 290, 302
Rousseau, J.-J., 48, 49, 51, 54, 56, 63, 64, 74, 143, 154, 187, 210-11, 267, 270, 278, 300, 302
Rubel, M., 268, 278
Ruskin, J., 291, 302
Ryan, A., 8, 11, 27, 58, 123, 243, 265, 269

Sahlins, M., 314, 338
Sartre, J.-P., 141, 153, 159-60, 180
Saxonhouse, A., 20, 55, Ch. 15
Say, J.-B., 184, 185, 190, 191, 193, 199, 215, 216, 217
Schmitt, C., 71
Schmitter, P., 207, 208, 209, 210, 220, 221
Schwartz, P., 215, 216
Sen, A.K., 265
Senior, N.W., 184, 194, 215, 216, 217
Sennett, R., 35, 62, 64, 245, 318, 319
Shah, A.S., 37-38
Shils, E., 61
Simmel, G., 317, 327
Simon, Lord, 37
Simpson, A.W.B., 111
Singer, I.B., 27
Singer, P., 243, 245
Smart, J.J.C., 181, 265
Smith, A., 92, 183, 185, 186, 189, 191, 193, 194, 202, 214, 215, 216, 217, 219, 232, 244
Smith, M.G., 325, 326, 331, 334
Socrates, 375, 376, 377, 378, 379, 382
Sophocles, 371, 383
Spencer, H., 63
Stalin, J., 168, 277
Steinberg, J., 302
Stephen, J.F., 175
Stone, L., 302
Szladits, C., 74-75, 76, 77, 92

Tay, A.E-S., 92, Ch. 3
Taylor, C., 245
Thomas, J.A.C., 68, 92
Thompson, D.F., 65
Thucydides, 373-74, 379, 383

Thurow, L., 220
Tocqueville, A. de, 36, 62
Tolstoy, N., 181
Tonnies, F., 273, 278
Torrens, R., 194, 215, 217
Trilling, L., 142, 153
Trotsky, L., 275
Truman, D.B., 205, 220
Tufts, J.H., 64, 219
Tussman, J., 65

Ulpian, 67, 68, 71, 72, 83
Unger, R.M., 303, 311, 338

Vellacott, P., 384
Vernant, J.-P., 384
Vogt, E.Z., 347, 361

Wallace, I., 116, 133
Walton, A., 17
Walzer, M., 160, 161-62, 168, 169, 181
Warren, S., 133
Wartofsky, M., 303
Watt, I., 340
Weber, M., 161, 162, 168, 169, 181
Weir, A., 92
West, J., 303
Westin, A.F., 134, 318, 339
Wilberforce, Lord, 107
Wilding, P., 219
Wiles, P.J.D., 221
Williams, B., 162, 167, 168, 169, 181, 259, 264, 265
Wilson, E., 303
Wilson, E.O., 303
Winkler, J.T., 207, 208, 209, 210, 220, 221
Wittgenstein, L., 4, 27, 156
Wolfe, T., 242
Wolff, R.P., 298, 299, 303
Wolin, S.S., 264, 265, 285, 286, 298, 301
Wollstonecraft, M., 287
Wrong, D., 143, 144-45, 146, 154
Wyclif, J., 19

Xanthippe, 375

Young, M.W. 319

Zeigler, H., 220

INDEX OF SUBJECTS

aborigines, Australian 313, 314, 360
access 7-9, 15, 23-24, 307
    to activities and intercourse 7-8, 9
    to the media 125, 134n.21
    physical 7
    privileged, to personal experience 33-34
    public and private, in stateless societies 314-21
accessibility
    as dimension of privateness and publicness 114
    of information, and free availability of 120
    see also information, access to; information, availability
accountability 127
    as dimension of publicness and privateness 114
Achaeans 366-69
acquired rights
    in 18th-century Germany 74
Acropolis 364, 369
Act of Supremacy (1534) 19
Act of Uniformity (1559) 19
Adams v. *State of Alaska* (1976) 111n.38
administrative law 74
    in England 71
    see also droit administratif; public law; public officials
admissibility of evidence
    in litigation in small societies 320-21
agency 7, 9-10, 16, 23, 24, 307, 312-14
agents
    public/private, distinguished 9-10, 312-13
aggregations, social 35-38, 49, 50
alienation
    in Marx's social theory 17, 239, 267-71
    in Rousseau 269-70
altruism
    and Greek morals 363
American Revolution 74

ancestors
    in Greece 364
Anns v. *Merton London Borough* (1978) 107, 111n.35
anomie 143
anonymity and privacy 35, 318
Ansell v. *Waterhouse* (1817) 111n.7
Antigone of Sophocles 371-72
anti-individualism 250-51
anti-social impulses, Freud on 140
apathy, political 47
Apology of Plato 375, 376
appropriation 238
Archanians of Aristophanes 369
art 16-17
Arusha of Tanzania
    individualist conception of society 328
Ashby v. *White* (1703) 106, 111n.34
Athens 363, 364, 373-74, 376
Atkinson v. *Newcastle & Gateshead Waterworks Co.* (1877) 111n.13
atomic bomb 168
authenticity and social roles 142.
    See also self; self/role relationship
autonomous ego
    in Freudian theory 149-50
autonomy
    of politics, Croce on 160
    see also moral autonomy; personal autonomy
Aztecs 342

Baden
    administrative courts in 76
Baktaman of New Guinea
    whether privacy among 315, 317
Barber v. *Time Inc.* (1942) 134n.31
Bedouins of Cyrenaica 329
beliefs
    and values 146-48
    intentionality of 147
benevolence. *See* paternalism
Bennet & Fisher v. *Electricity Trust (S.A.)* (1962) 111n.16
Beth Din 21
big-men, Melanesian 313-14

Index of Subjects 393

biology, and status of women. *See* women
bi-polarity. *See* distinctions, bi-polar
Bologna, University of 72
boundary conditions of public. *See* public, definition of boundary of
bourgeois legalism
   rejected in Maoist China and U.S.S.R. 80
Briscoe v. *Reader's Digest Association* (1971) 133n.10
British Steel Corporation v. *Granada Television* (1980) 117, 133n.5
Busama of New Guinea
   and *maya* 319

canon law 19, 72
capital goods
   ownership of in Marx 238
capitalism
   as alienating, according to Marx 239, 270
   as inefficient, according to Marx 239
   J.M. Keynes on 204
Carolingian kings 72
cash nexus
   in *Gesellschaft* 274
categorical imperative 158
Chamberlaine v. *The Chester & Birkenhead Railway Co.* (1848) 111n.20
Charter's Case. *See Race Relations Board* v. *Charter and Others* (1973)
children, paternalist concern for 178. *See also* paternalism
China. *See* communes; law and society, in Communist China
Christianity 19, 21, 253
Church 17, 19
Church of England 19
civil law 19, 94
civil liability in English law
   of common callings 96
civil society 17, 25, 41, 42, 43, 50-52, 56, 255-58
   as common political life of community 298
   Hegel on 255-58
   as private 51, 53, 313
   and private interests, in Hegel 256, 265n.17, 272
   as public, in feminist analysis 284-86

civil society (cont'd)
   and state, in Marx's political theory 272
   see also classical political economy; market; Hegel, G.W.F.; Locke, J.; Marx, K.
class interests
   government interference as vehicle for 186
classical economists 10, 215n.4. *See also* classical political economy; McCulloch, J.R.; Malthus, T.R.; Mill, James; Ricardo, D.; Say, J.-B.; Senior, N.W.; Smith, A.
classical liberalism 53. *See also* individualism; liberalism
classical political economy 183, 184-95
   individualism of 184
   and 'spontaneous order' 186-87
   theory of the state 193
   see also classical economists
Code Napoléon 73
Codex 72. *See also Digest*
codification of law 77, 79
   in Communist China and U.S.S.R. 80
collective farms in U.S.S.R. 277
collectivism
   and individualism, in Marxist-Leninist regimes 276-78
   see also public property
Comanche Indians 314
Committee of Public Safety 74
Committee on Privacy. *See* Younger Committee Report (1972)
common callings
   in English law 96, 98, 100, 109
common carrier. *See* common callings
common good 48, 99. *See also* public interest
common law 17, 73, 78, 79, Ch. 4 *passim*
   courts of 73, Ch. 4 *passim*
common morality 161-62, 173
   Alan Donagan on 161
   see also private morality; public morality
Common Prayer, The Book of 19
common will 260-62
Commonwealth 39

Index of Subjects

communal landholding 342
communality, ideology of 345
communes 8, 275, 276, 277
communism 17, 27, 270-71
    and human freedom, in Marx 267-68, 270-71
    Lenin's theory and practice of 273
    see also property; public property
communist educational theory 275
community
    Greek family as 364-65
    individualist account of 41, 44, 48
    in Plato, criticised by Aristotle 378-79
    in Plato's *Republic* 376-77
compadrazgo 356, 361n.4
competition
    failure of 201, 261
complex-structured concepts 3-5, 7, 31, 158. *See also* publicness and privateness
confidentiality 126-27
conflict
    of nature and duty 141-42
    of roles 141-42, 158-59
conflicts, moral
    of public and private roles 158-59
    rational solution of 162
    of role commitments and private morality 163
conscience 20, 156-57, 169-72
    priority over law, questioned by MacCallum 170
conscientious objection 159, 169-72
Conseil d'Etat 74
consumer sovereignty
    critics of theory of 212
consumers
    in classical political economy 185, 188
continuous distinctions. *See* distinctions, continuous
contract
    and *Gesellschaft* 87ff, 274
contract theory 41-42, 43, 283
conversation
    Grice's analysis of principles of 348-49
co-ordination, social 42, 256, 258-59
    Hobbes's theory of 260
copyright 134n.29
corporate analysis
    of stateless societies 322ff
corporate ideology
    anthropological discussions of 329-30

corporations, business 43, 53-54, 200-1, 207-11
    and social responsibility 54
corporations, multi-national 62-63n.15
corporatism 205-11
    in fascist ideology 220n.118
    two types of 208
    see also corporate analysis; corporate ideology
Corpus Juris Civilis 72
Cox Broadcasting Corporation v. *Cohn* (1975) 133n.13
creativity in private realm 379
criminal law 25, 78, 94, 172-76, 192
criminal liability
    of common callings in English law 96
Crito of Plato 375, 376
cross-cultural comparisons 23-25, 339, 344, 360
Crown, the
    in English law 71, 93
cults 20
Cutler v. *Wandsworth Stadium* (1949) 111n.27

Daily Times Democrat v. *Graham* (1964) 120, 133n.13
damages action
    against public officials 104ff
dangerous drugs
    control over sale of 176
data banks 8, 9
democracy
    and government by the people 202
    and information control 124-27
    and private law 90
    and public control of economy 211ff
democratic state
    as public state 202
descent ideology. *See* lineage
Dharma
    Weber's account of, as specialised ethic 162
dialectic
    in Hegel 251-52
dichotomies
    Arendt's account of Aristotle's 380
dichotomous distinctions. *See* distinctions, dichotomous
Dickson v. *Reuter's Telegram Co.* (1877) 111n.11
Digest (of Justinian) 67, 72

Index of Subjects 395

dimensions. *See* publicness and privateness, dimensions of; multi-dimensionality
Dionysus 20
dirty hands, moral problem of 159-69
   Donagan on 161
   Niebuhr on 166
   Walzer on 160-61
   Weber on 161-62
Dirty Hands, J.-P. Sartre's 159-60
distinctions
   bi-polar 14ff, 17. *See also* liberalism
   continuous 13ff
   dichotomous 13ff
   multi-polar 14ff
division of labour
   Marx on 268, 270
   in Nabenchauk 357-60
   Say on benefits and drawbacks of 191
   sexual division of. *See* women; family; domestic
domain 70
domestic
   as irrelevant to liberal social theory 286
   as private 283-87, 288, 289, 291, 293, 294, 351-53. *See also* family
   as women's appropriate sphere Ch. 12 *passim*
domestic life
   equal sharing of sexes in 299
droit administratif 71, 82. *See also* administrative law; public law
due process 126

East Ham South Conservative Club 37-38, 62n.9
economic anarchy
   new liberals and 202-3
economic growth. *See* wealth, growth of
economic man 147
economy
   antithesis of state, in classical liberalism 194-95, 204-5
   collective management of 202-3
   see also civil society; market economy
education
   for citizenship, J.S. Mill on 47-48, 293-94. *See also* J.S. Mill

education (cont'd)
   part of public sphere, for Aristotle 379
   religious 19
elders, tribal 314
Elizabeth I, of England 19
English Civil War 73
entails 236
Epicureanism 20
equality
   in Aristotle's *Politics* 381
   in new liberalism 197, 262. *See also* wealth, redistribution of
   Hegel on 261, 262
equilibrium. *See* market
equity
   conflict with efficiency, in new liberalism 198
Erastianism 19
Eskimos 314, 327
ethical life
   norms of, in Hegel 259
   and reflective capacity 254, 260
   as universality, in Hegel 260
ethics
   of responsibility, Weber on 161
   of ultimate ends, Weber on 161
ethnocentrism 23, 334
ethnography
   problems of translation in 344-45
   see also cross-cultural comparisons; folk concepts
Eurocommunism
   coexistence of public and private sectors in 278
evidence
   duty to give 116, 126
exchange
   as model for *Gesellschaft* law 87
exchange theorists 43, 62n.14
existentialist notion of moral freedom as private 157
externalities 192

face-to-face relations
   in stateless societies 315, 317
   in Zinacanteco life 345
fame. *See kleos*
family
   as community in classical Greece 364-65
   as education in liberal ideals, J.S. Mill on 47-48, 293-94
   Hegel on 301n.3
   as organic whole 54-55

Index of Subjects

family (cont'd)
    as political 295-98
    political regulation of 297
    as private 15-16, 18, 20, 21, 35, 37-38, 51, 54-55, 151-52, 282
    as private sphere in classical Greece Ch. 15 *passim*
    and religion in classical Greece 364-65, 369, 371-72, 382
    as a public 15-16, 151
    as threat to public, in Plato 377
    in Zinacantan 351-53, 356-57
    see also domestic; *Race Relations Board* v. *Charter and Others* (1973)
family name 62n.10
family resemblances 4
feminism 18, 62n.10, Ch. 12 *passim*
    seen as completion of bourgeois revolution, 281
ferryman. *See* common callings
feudal law, king in 70
feudalism 69
First Amendment rights 125, 134n.21
fisc (*Fiskus*) 76
folk concepts
    in anthropology 334-37
forms
    as public, for Socrates 375-76, 382
fornication
    in Islamic law 23
Frankfurt School 152
freedom
    of individual, as supreme value, in Hegel 235-36
    Marx on 267, 268, 270-71
    from paternalist interference 177-79
    Pericles view of 373
    see also privacy
freedom of information legislation 127
freehold ownership 232
French Revolution (1789-99) 70, 73, 74
friendship 35, 38, 124, 241, 379
Fueros 72
Funeral Oration of Pericles 373-74, 382

Garnet v. *Ferrand* (1827) 111n.33
Gemeinrecht 71
Gemeinschaft 69, 70, 73, 87ff, 273-74

general will 271
Geneva 19, 21
German law 69, 71, 72
German princes (eighteenth century) 74
Germanic custom
    European law and 69, 71
Germany
    imperial courts in 75
Gesellschaft 73, 87ff, 273-74
    and individualism 87ff
    see also Gemeinschaft
Gildea v. *Ellershaw* (1973) 111n.32
Glossop v. *Heston & Isleworth Local Board* (1879) 111n.12
government
    incompetence of, in liberal political economy 194
    of publics 326
Granada Television 117
Greece, classical 20, 21, 55, Ch. 15 *passim*
Greek drama 369-74, 382
Greek gods 364, 366, 369, 383n.10, 384n.16
Greek society
    Hegel on 255, 257
    see also war
Gregoire v. *Biddle* (1949) 111n.39
Griswold v. *Connecticut* (1965) 54, 64n.52, 127, 134n.28, 181n.29
groups
    as corporate agents 39
    political life based on, in pluralist theory 205
    see also publics; social groups
growth. *See* wealth, growth of
guilt model of society 319-20

Halachah 21
harm
    and the criminal law 172f
    and morality 172-73, 178
harmony
    of public and private advantage 192, 196, 201, 256. *See also* classical political economy
health service, organisation of 233
hero in Greek culture 363, 366-69, 382
High Commission, Court of 73
Hindu ethics. *See* Dharma
Hiroshima 168
Hobbesian war of all against all 190

Holy Roman Empire 72
Homeric epics 366-69
Homosexual Offences and Prostitution, Committee on (UK). *See* Wolfenden Committee, Report of
homosexuality 172f
household
   in Aristotle's *Politics* 378ff
   see also domestic; family
human dependence, Marx on 268-69, 270
human nature
   Aristotelian view of, as pre-adapted to social roles 141
   and choice 141
   endowed by society, according to Rousseau 143
   existence of, denied by Nietzscheans and Sartreans 141
   Freudian theories of 140-41, 149
   Goffman's view of, as role-playing 150ff
   according to Hobbes 142
   materialist accounts of 152-53
   Mead's account of, and socialisation 143, 145-46
   according to Parsons 145
   as raw material for social processes, according to Durkheim 143-44
   teleological account of 142
   Wrong's critique of oversocialised picture of 143, 144-45, 149
   see also man, models of
human rights
   and *Gesellschaft* ideology 92
   President Carter and 165
   see also natural rights; property rights; rights
human values
   incommensurability of, Berlin on 264n.1

ideology
   role of, in social life 330
   see also corporate ideology; public/private distinction; publicness and privateness
idion, to
   as 'private' 364, 365, 374, 380, 383n.5
Iliad of Homer 366-69, 374, 382
imperium 72
independence
   in Sophist teaching 364

independence (cont'd)
   see also moral autonomy; personal autonomy
individual
   and family in classical Greece 364, 365, 367-78
   logical priority of, in liberal individualism 34, 57, 250-51
   rights of 92, 257, 260
   in Sophist teaching 364, 374, 382
   status of, denied to women 284-85, 292
   subordinated to collective struggle, in War Communism 275
   as ultimate source of moral judgement 157
individual interests
   and public interest 44, 251, 363. *See also* public interest
   see also private interest; private interests
individual/social distinction
   in Marx 272
individualism 17
   account of corporative action in 39
   in anthropology of small societies 327
   and the decline of the Greek *polis* 373-74, 382
   Durkheim's account of, as duty-fulfilment 143-44
   and *Gesellschaft* 87ff
   Hegel on Ch. 10 *passim*
   limits of, in Hegel 258-60
   logical primacy of individual person in 250
   methodological 34, 41, 44, 321
   of Zinacantecan peasants 343ff
   see also Gesellschaft; liberal individualism; social contract
information 15, Ch. 5 *passim*
   access to 8, 9
   accessibility 120
   availability 115ff, 120
   availability and personal autonomy and development 123, 129
   availability, limits of legal controls on 129-30
   availability subject to natural regulators 130-31
   and the democratic ideal 122-33
   and democratic participation 125
   freedom of 60, 132
   intimate 116, 120

information (cont'd)
    paternalist refusals of medical 123, 132
    scarce good among Malagasy peasants 349
    suppression of, in defence of democracy 125
information control Ch. 5, 318
    diverse interests in 120-21
    guidelines 131-33
    and privacy Ch. 5 *passim*, 151f, 317-18
ingratitude 173
inner and outer experience
    Freud's account of 140-41
Inner Light, the
    conscience and the duty to follow 172
    reason and 157
    see also conscience
innkeeper in English law 96
Institutes of Justinian 67, 72, 81
integrity, moral
    and dirty hands 167-69, 170
integrity, personal 173
    MacCallum on 170-71
interest 7, 10-11, 17, 23, 24, 307
interest groups 36
interest in privacy 117
interest in publicity 117
interests
    balancing of, in information availability cases 117-18
    balancing of, in liability rules for public officials 105ff, 109
    conflicts of, in information availability cases 121
    of consumers, in classical political economy 185
    evaluative character of 264n.13, 265n.36
    jurisprudence of, Ihering on 83
    sectional, liberal account of 58
    shared 44-45, 63n.18
    as subjective preferences 257-58
    universal and particular, in Hegel 251ff, 256
    vested and legitimate, in liberalism 46-47, 58-59
interference
    liberal challenge to 178
    limits of, in liberal individualism 174
international relations
    rhetoric of 165

interventionist state
    in new liberal political economy 183
intimacy
    as dimension of publicness and privateness 114
    not appropriately regulated by legal duties 130
    and privacy of information 119, 120, 122, 129, 181n.29
    see also marriage; privacy, and marital relations; sexual relations
'invisible hand' 183, 201
Iran 22
Islam 21-23
Isis 20
Israel, State of 21
ius eminens
    as interest of public good 75
ius politiae. See police power
ius privatum. See private law, Roman

Jacobins 74
Jews 21-22, 27n.11
jihād 27n.14
Jim and Pedro, parable of 167, 168
John Fairfax Ltd v. *Australian Postal Commission* (1977) 111n.17
Johnson v. *Midland Railway Co.* (1849) 111n.10
Judaism 21-22
jus ad personam 226
jus ad rem 226
justice
    Aristotle on 81
    Institutes on 81
    as an intellectual activity 89
    and public court proceedings 126
    and public interest in classical political economy 186
    socialist views of 81

King, the
    in English law 93. *See also* Crown, the
kinship 316, 356, 357, 358
    and law-enforcement 310, 311, 323
    erosion of obligations of, in Nabenchauk 359
kinship roles 138
kleos
    in classical Greece 363, 365, 366, 382
koinon, to
    as 'public' 364, 374, 375, 376

koinonia 364, 376, 377, 378
Konso of Ethiopia
   organic conception of society 327-28
Kronstadt (1921) 276
!Kung bushmen 319

labour
   alienated 269
   free, according to Marx 270-71
   organised 200-1
   and ownership 228-29, 231
   see also trade unions
labouring class
   in classical political economy 185, 191, 196
labour relations
   and corporatism, Panitch on 208
laissez-faire 183, 219n.80
   a general rule admitting of exceptions 194
   refutation of, by Keynes 196
   see also classical economists; classical political economy; 'nightwatchman state'
land tenure
   and incentive arguments 244n.31
Lane v. *Cotton* (1701) 97, 111n.8
language
   Wittgenstein on publicness of 156
Lares 20
law
   bureaucratic-administrative paradigm of 87, 88, 90
   as commercial phenomenon, Pashukanis on 84
   function of 86
   Gemeinschaft paradigm of 88ff. *See also Gemeinschaft*
   Gesellschaft paradigm of 87ff. *See also Gesellschaft*
   imperative theory of, and property 224
   liberal view of, as public institution 308, 312-13
   Pound on stages of 84
   primitive Ch. 13 *passim*
   primitive and modern, distinguished by Durkheim 309
   primitive and modern, distinguished by Posner 311
   primitive and modern, distinguished by Unger 311
   private. *See* private law; public and private law distinction

law (cont'd)
   public. *See* public law; public and private law distinction
   and society, in Communist China 80-81, 275-76
   and society, in U.S.S.R. 80-81, 274-77. *See also* Pashukanis
   viewed in U.S.S.R. and China as having basically administrative function 80, 277-78
legal immunity
   of judicial officials 106, 110
   of public officials from civil action 104-5, 106
   see also public law; public officials
legal moralism 159, 172-76
legal officials
   as agents of public interests, in liberal view 308
Leges Henrici Primi 72
Leviathan 258, 260
liberal feminism 281-82, 301n.1, 302n.12
   radical implications of 281
liberal individualism
   excludes women Ch. 12 *passim*
   Hegel's view of 249
   and legal moralism 172-76
   and respect for persons 178-79
   see also individualism; liberalism; publicness and privateness, individualist model in liberalism
liberal morality
   public and private aspects of 155-57
liberal organicism
   Hegel's view of 249
   see also organicism; publicness and privateness, organic model in liberalism
liberal political economy Ch. 8 *passim*
   and wages 193
liberal rhetoric 45, 46-47, 59-61
liberalism 17
   ambiguities of 59
   attitudes to wickedness 172
   and feminism Ch. 12 *passim*
   feminist critique of 18. *See also* patriarchalism
   Kantian strain in 158
   and 'nightwatchman state' 193
   and patriarchalism. *See* patriarchalism
   utilitarian strain in 158

liberalism (cont'd)
    see also individualism; new
        liberalism
liberty. See freedom
life and death
    in Greek view of world Ch. 15
        passim
lineage 322, 329-30, 334, 342
listening devices 9
logic of the situation
    explanations by 146-48
love. See friendship; intimacy
Lozi of N. Rhodesia 321

Machiavellian problem 155, 159-69.
    See also dirty hands, moral
        problem of
Madagascar 349
man as universal being, Marx on 271
man, models of 148-53
    autonomous model 149-50
    plastic model 149
    theatrical model 150-53
    see also human nature
Manes 20
market
    influence of, on Zinacantecan
        peasant life 343, 358, 359
    and the public interest, in classical
        political economy 189-92
    self-equilibrating in classical
        economics 188, 192, 194
    as self-equilibrating, new liberal
        critique of 199-200, 201
market economy 41, 42, 53, Ch. 8
    passim
    competency of, to public interest
        195
    competency questioned by
        Malthus 195, 202
    in need of regulation, in liberal
        political economy 194, 199,
        202-4
    underconsumption in 195
    see also civil society; private sector
markets, law of. See Say's Law
marriage
    as a career, J.S. Mill on 293-94
    and privacy of Zinacanteco
        household 356-57
    as private 54, 181n.29
    see also domestic; family; intimacy
martyrdom
    and injustice 171

Marxism 80, 84, Ch. 11 passim
    Nietzschean strain in 276
    recent developments in 277-78
    see also Marx, K.
Marxist practice 274-78. See also
    China; U.S.S.R.
Massachusetts 19
Massengill v. Yuma County (1969)
    111n.36
maya. See shame
Mayor of Lyme Regis v. Henley
    (1834) 111n.18, n.23
Maẓālim 22
medieval law 69, 70, 72
    in England 70
medieval society
    and feudal compact 69
Mehinaku of Brazil
    whether privacy among 316,
        318, 319
Melanesia 313
Melvin v. Reid (1931) 133n.10
mercenaries in classical Greece
    383n.6
Merovingian kings 72
Mexico Ch. 14 passim
Middle Ages 19, 20, 72. See also
    medieval law; medieval society
military service, conscientious
    objection to 169-72
Miller v. Horton (1891) 111n.31
Mithras 20
modesty. See privacy
money, Marx on 268-70
monopolies 97-99
moral autonomy 157. See also
    personal autonomy
moral conflicts. See conflicts, moral
moral consensus
    James Fitzjames Stephens on need
        for 175
    seen by Devlin as logically necessary
        to society 175-76
moral failure 173
moral fallibilism 156
moral freedom 157
moral judgement, individual as
    ultimate source of 157
moral law
    as public rationality 157
moral pluralism 156
moral reasons, types of 163-64
    expediency 163-67
    principles 163

Index of Subjects   401

moral values
   as intuitions 156
   as non-demonstrable 156
   as preferences 156
moralisation of politics 165, 166
morality
   common 161-62, 173
   and the criminal law 173-76
   liberal view of 155-56. *See also* liberalism
   and patriotism, Machiavelli on 160
   and politics 159-69
   public and private Ch. 7 *passim*. *See also* public morality and private morality
   public and private realms of 159
   relations between states 164ff
   in use 157-58
morality/power
   and private/public, in feminist critique 287, 290-95, 297-98, 302n.22, n.23
Mühlhaüser Rechtsbuch 72
multi-dimensionality
   of concepts 10-11, 14
   of criteria 14
   of 'state' 40
multiplex relations
   in small societies 316, 317, 320, 321, 333
multi-polarity. *See* distinctions, multi-polar
Munn v. *Illinois* (1876) 111n.15

NAACP v. *Alabama* (1958) 134n.22
Nabenchauk Ch. 14 *passim*. *See also* Zinacantecos
nation
   and state 51
national interest 164, 165. *See also* public interest
nationalisation
   of industry, new liberal attitudes to 203
   Morrisonian pattern of 233
   and public ownership 232. *See also* public ownership
natural inequality
   in Aristotle's *Politics* 381
natural justice 126, 134n.25
natural law
   Hobbes and Locke on 225
natural liberty
   Adam Smith on 232
natural rights 224, 225, 230, 255

natural rights (cont'd)
   Bentham on 224ff
   as social 255
   see also human rights; ownership; property rights; rights
nature/culture
   anthropological discussions of 288, 336
   and feminist analysis of private/public 287-90, 302n.13, n.23
   radical feminist discussion of 289-90
nature, state of
   and Lockean theory of property 234
Nazis
   and German law 71
nazism 27n.11
negligence
   and liability of public officials 106ff, 110
nepotism
   ambivalence of 314
new liberal pluralism 205-6
New Economic Policy
   and private rights, in U.S.S.R. 275
new liberal political economy 195-204
   shift in emphasis from utility to justice 198
   and wealth 197
new liberalism 183, 195-204
   and corporatism 207
   organicism in 201, 209-10
   and state socialism 209
'nightwatchman state'
   not state of classical liberalism 193
'nominal defendant'
   in English law 71
non-feasance 101
Nuer, Evans-Pritchard's account of 323
nuisance 174, 175

obscenity 174, 175
offensive behaviour 173-74
oikos
   as private 364, 381
order, maintenance of, in stateless societies 314, 318-21
Oresteia of Aeschylus 370
organic conception of society
   and *Gemeinschaft* 87

organic conception of society (cont'd)
see also publicness and privateness, organic model in liberalism
organic conception of state
Greek *polis* and 363ff, 374
and national interest 164, 201
organicism
of Devlin and Stephen 175
in liberalism 48-58, 175, 181n.30, 201, 209-10
and personhood, in Hegel 255
Ostgötalag 72
outsider, the 142
ownership
as assertion of human will 231, 233-36
as a bundle of rights 232
dramaturgical account of 223, 224, 240-43
extent of rights of 231-33
Hegel on 234-37
instrumental theories of 223, 224-33
natural rights of, denied by instrumentalists 224, 227
natural rights theories of 223
in Roman law and common law, contrasted 236
self-developmental theories of 223, 233-40
as sovereignty over matter 234-35
see also private ownership; private property; property; property rights; public ownership

Pakistan 22
Papua New Guinea
small societies in 332
participation, political 47-48, 52-53, 59, 373
participation, social
as primary phenomenological fact in organicism 57
particularity
as external determination, in Marx 271
and universality, in Marx 271
particulars
and universals, dialectics of, in Hegel 251-55, 260
patents 134n.29, 231
pater familias 20, 38, 68-69
paternal power
Locke's theory of 283-85

paternalism 123, 132, 159, 176-79
organicist view of 179
public right to interfere 177
patria potestas 69
patriarchalism
liberalism and 282-87
Locke on Filmer's 283-84
in Marx 300
Peace of Westphalia (1648) 75
peasant privacy 341, Ch. 14 *passim*
Peloponnesian War 372, 373-74
Penates 20
people, a 51
perpetual peace
Kant on 165
personal autonomy 149-50, 168, 173, 180
and information availability 122, 123, 127
and role-behaviour 149
see also moral autonomy
personal/political 295-98
and private/public, in feminist critique 287
personality
liberal idea of 58, 178-79
and possessions 241-43
see also individual; personal autonomy; self
persons
respect for, and paternalism 178-79
as self-aware project-makers 33-34, 57, 253, 264n.15
philosophical anthropology of Hegel 252
philosophy
Plato and place of, in public community 375-77, 382
as private non-individual activity, for Socrates 375-77, 382
phronesis 365
planning, economic
and liberalism 203-4
pluralism 205-7, 257
and repudiation of public interest 205
police power (*ius politiae*) 75, 92n.4
policy, economic 54
polis, Ch. 15 *passim*
Arendt's model of, criticised 380-81
Aristotle's view of 377-81, 382

Index of Subjects 403

polis (cont'd)
    dependent on family, in Aristotle 379-80
    and family, conflict of duties to Ch. 15 *passim*
    and individualism 373-74, 382
    priority of, over family, in Aristotle 378
    as realm of choice, in Aristotle 378, 380
Politeia 363-64, 373. *See also Republic* of Plato
political
    as area of shared values 298
    feminist interpretations of 295-98
    identified with power 297-98
political authority
    and private law in Middle Ages 69
    Hegel on 261
    Hobbesian view of 257, 258, 261
    in individualist tradition 257
political economy Ch. 8 *passim*
    classical. *See* classical political economy
    Lord Robbins's usage of 214n.1
political life 17
political morality 166. *See also* public morality; public morality and private morality
political organisation 17
political power 165-67
    and consent, in Locke 283-85
politics
    and conscience, Niebuhr on 166
    moralisation of 165, 166
    morality and 159-69
Politics of Aristotle 365, 377-81
polity 17, 42-43, 48, 92n.4, 93
Polizeistaat 75
polyarchy 53
Polynesia 313
population increase
    in classical political economy 188
pornography 172f
positivism, legal 86
possession 230-31. *See also* ownership
poverty
    J.B. Say on 190
praetor peregrinus 69
pressure groups 205, 262-63
privacy 6, 7, 8, 9, 11, 34, 54, 60, Ch. 5 *passim*, 175, 241-42

privacy (cont'd)
    absence of, among Baktaman 315-16
    absence of, in small societies 315ff, 360
    as bourgeois, in War Communism 274-75
    and control of information about self Ch. 5 *passim*, 151f
    cross-cultural study of 316-17
    within family 15-16, 151, 152, 241, 356-57
    and home ownership 241
    individual interest in 117
    and interpersonal relations 124, 241
    and liberty (freedoms) 119, 121, 125-26, 129, 134n.23, 360
    and marital relations 127-28, 356-57. *See also* sexual relations; intimacy; marriage
    in a Mexican Indian village Ch. 14 *passim*
    and modesty, in Nabenchauk household 346
    and personal autonomy 123, 124
    and personal development 124, 129
    and personal non-accountability 127
    and publicity Ch. 5 *passim*
    and publicity in conversation in Nabenchauk 348-51
    restricted to individuals in U.S. law 133n.14
    and sanity, Jourard on 123
    and self-presentation by individual 123, 150-53, 241-43
    universally necessary, in Simmel's view 317
    see also secrecy; tact
Privacy, Report of the Committee on. *See* Younger Committee Report (1972)
private access. *See* access
private Acts of Parliament
    as contracts with statutory corporations 102
private agency 16. *See also* agency; agents
private citizens 9, 10, 52
private corporations 39. *See also* corporations, business; corporations, multi-national

404 *Index of Subjects*

private duty
  in common law 94
private enterprise 12, 41
  regulation of 97
  see also private sector
private grouping
  family as paradigmatic 37-38
private individual
  as male, in liberal patriarchalism 285
private information 118-19
private interest 10-11, 17, 39, 95, 109, 257
  in privacy 175, 241
  and state 51-52
private interests
  co-ordination of 256, 258-59
  in market order 183
  and public interest, Adam Smith on 189, 193
  and public interests, Hegel on Ch. 10 *passim*
  purpose of *polis* to protect, in Sophists' view 382
  see also private rights; public interest, and private interests
private law Ch. 3
  and democracy 90
  existence of, denied by Duguit 83
  existence of, denied by Durkheim 83
  Jewish 21
  Roman 67ff, 88ff
  and state regulation 90-91
  in western legal tradition 89
  see also public law and private law distinction
private letters 11, 12, 13
private life 20, 33, 52-56, 57, 174, 175
private lives of animals 33, 153
private morality
  as 'common morality', in Donagan 161-62
  conscience and, in liberalism 157
  as personal positive morality 157-58
  reasons of principle normally uppermost in 163
  as sphere immune from criminal law 172-76
  see also public morality and private morality
private offences
  Bentham on 32

private ownership Ch. 9 *passim*
  of industry, new liberal attitudes to 203
  and public control, in corporatism 207
  see also private property; property; property rights
private persons 13, 16, 51, 257
private property 10-11, Ch. 9 *passim*
  Augustinian argument for 187-88
  as an aid to privacy 224
  in classical economics 186
  and community participation in Hegel 236-37
  considered as natural in classical political economy 187
  as enemy of self-development, in Marx 237-40
  as internally contradictory, in Marx 237-38
  Marx on 237-40, 268, 269, 270
  as normative concept 115
  as structuring market economy 192
  see also ownership; private ownership; property; property rights
private prosecutors in stateless societies 331-34
private realm
  elimination of, in Plato's *Republic* 375-77
  in Aristotle's *Politics* 378
  family as, in classical Greece Ch. 15 *passim*
  symbolised by female in Greek tragedy 370-72
private rights 179, 257
  Adam Smith on 186
  Hegel's account of 252-53
  vested (*wohlerworbene Privatrechte*) 76
  see also rights
private sector 41, 42, 203-4. *See also* civil society; economy; market economy; private enterprise
private self 22. *See also* self
private space 8, 318, 347-48, 352
privateness
  of aggregations in organic model 49-50
  of 'assignable individual' in individualist model 32-35
  in communist regimes, recent concessions to 277

privateness (cont'd)
    of groups, in individualist model
        35-38
    of law, Pashukanis on 84
    Marxists' rejection of 274
    see also public/private distinction;
        publicness and privateness
privileged relations 128
privilegium de non appellando 76
PRODESCH 345
production
    household, in Zinacantan 358-59
profit
    rate of, in classical economics 191
progressive state. *See* stationary state
Prohibition of Defamation Act
    (1965) (Israel) 116
promising 225. *See also* rights;
    property rights; natural rights
property Ch. 9 *passim*
    personal, under communism 277
    positivist approach to 224
    public 10-11
    socially important, as public 91
    as stage set 242-43
    testamentary disposition of,
        Hegel's view of 236
    in Zinacantan 342-43, 346,
        351-53, 357, 359
    see also ownership; private
        ownership; private property;
        property rights; public ownership
property rights
    acquisition of title 230-31
    as freedoms 225, 359
    Hegel on 235-36, 252-53
    and incentives to production
        228-29, 231
    J.S. Mill on 226, 230
    as legal 223
    and natural rights, three views of
        227
    and promising 225ff
    and security 228-29
prostitution 172f
Protection of Privacy Act (1981)
    (Israel) 116, 133n.14
Prussia
    administrative courts in 76
prying 347, 360. *See also*
    information control; privacy
psychological theory of role
    behaviour 139. *See also* role;
    Goffman, E.

public
    definition of boundary of 36,
        40-43, 51, 325
    distinguished from domestic in
        stateless societies 322, 323,
        327
public, the 16, 44
    as community at large 93
    as the mass 35-36, 186
    sections of 36-38, 46, 52-56,
        62n.9, 210
    see also publics
public access. *See* access
public agency
    absence of, in stateless societies
        314-15
    central to modern western idea of
        law and state 312, 314
public and private agency
    in small stateless societies 312-14
    see also agency; agents
public authorities as representatives
    of community 202
public authority 42
public corporations 40
public debt 93
public duty 169-72
    in common law 94, 96
public duty rule
    in English law 101-2, 106
    in U.S. law 107-8
public enterprise 10. *See also*
    collectivism; public ownership;
    public property; public sector
public function in common law 94,
    95, 103
public good 97
    no corresponding term in Tzotzil
        351, 359
    and pursuit of wealth, in new
        liberal view 197
    see also common good; public
        interest
public goods 5, 62n.7, 192
public housing 241
public information 118
public interest 10-11, 17, 39, 40
    absence of society-wide, in
        stateless societies 325
    ambiguity of normative/descriptive
        status 115
    business corporations and 54
    as condition for co-ordination of
        private interests 256-57

public interest (cont'd)
  in consumer protection legislation 176-77
  as consumers' interest 185, 196
  as criterion for information availability 116-18
  in English common law 79, Ch. 4 *passim*
  as increase in community's aggregate wealth 184, 186, 189, 190
  independent moral claims of, in Hegel 262
  as interest of any individual member of community 97, 99, 100, 109, 164
  as interest of community 82, 95, 96, 99, 109, 110, 163, 164
  as interest of everyone *qua* member of public 45-46, 96, 97
  as interest of representative citizen 46-47
  as interest of state 79, 163ff
  in Islam 22
  and justice, in classical political economy 186
  and justice, in new liberal political economy 198, 201
  in law and order 156, 175
  and liabilities of privately owned statutory corporations 98
  in liberal individualist model 44-47, 163-64, 184ff, 189-92, 249, 258
  maximised by maximising private 189f
  and monopoly, in Australian law 100
  and monopoly, in English law 97-98
  and monopoly, in U.S. law 99
  as moral reason in politics 44-47, 59-61, 164
  as negative in common law 95-96
  as net interest of everyone 44, 185
  not aggregate of individual interests, according to Mummery and Hobson 196
  not conclusive in conflict resolution 117-18, 164
  not sacrificed by courts in formulating liability rule 110
  only sometimes overriding, in *Gesellschaft* 87, 117

public interest (cont'd)
  organic model of 57, 196, 262, 322
  organic strain in new liberal conception of 196
  pluralist repudiation of 205
  and political participation 48
  and pollution controls 44
  priority over individual interests 118
  and private interests 192, 196, 213. *See also* private interests; private rights; public interest, and private rights
  and private interests, harmony of 192, 196, 201
  and private interests, Hegel on Ch. 10 *passim*
  and private interests in small societies 321-31
  and private rights 59-61, 79, 163ff
  and private rights, in Adam Smith 186
  public law and 90
  regulation of service enterprises, in English law 97ff
  as resultant of private pressure groups 206, 257-58
  role analysis of 45-46, 96, 97, 185, 196
  as shared interest of everyone 44-45, 63
  and special interests 46-47, 205-6
public interests, conflicts of 117
public international law 68
public law Ch. 3 *passim*
  as administration. *See* Pashukanis
  public interest and 90
  Roman 67-69, 72
  see also administrative law; *droit administratif*; public officials
public law and private law distinction Ch. 3 *passim*
  conceptual, not institutional 82
  denied by Durkheim 83, 309
  denied in English legal doctrine 73, 78, 79
  according to enforcing agencies 310-11
  in French law 77, 79, 82
  in German law 78, 79, 82
  according to interest served 83
  as penal/restitutive in Radcliffe-Brown 309-10

public law and private law distinction (cont'd)
    in Soviet theory 275
    see also Bacon, F.; Burkhardt, W.; Duguit, L.; Kelsen, H.; Montesquieu; Pashukanis, E.B.; Radbruch, G.; Ulpian
public life 17, 20, 33, 48, 52-56
    as civic 53
    Pericles' view of 373-74
    reasons for salience of expediency in 163-67. *See also* public morality and private morality
public morality
    and conscientious objection 169-72
    and political power 165-67
    as 'the public's (positive) morality' 157-58
public morality and private morality Ch. 7 *passim*
    Lord Devlin on distinction between 155
    Wolfenden Committee on distinction between 155
public nuisance 175
public offences, Bentham on 32
public officers. *See* public officials
public officials 9, 10, 13, 16, 52, 71, 103-8
    accountability of 71, 74, 103-8
    accountability of, and information availability 120, 127
    civil liability of, in English law 101
    criminal prosecutions of, in English law 101
    defined 103-4
    in English law 71, Ch. 4 *passim*
    as guardians of public interest 74, 308
    liability of, and the 'neighbourhood' principle 107, 109
    liability of, in English law 71, 100, 103-8, 110
    liability of, in U.S. law 107-8, 110
    see also administrative law; agency; agents; public agency; public law
public opinion 36
public ownership Ch. 9 *passim*
    instrumentalist view of, in Marx 238, 239

public places, Zinacanteco women in 353-56
public policy in Islam 22
public/private, boundary between 286. *See also* publicness and privateness
public/private distinction
    as cross-cultural analytical tool 23ff, 339, 344, 360
    in ethnography 344-45. *See also* cross-cultural comparisons
    in feminist writings Ch. 12 *passim*
    as folk concept. *See* folk concepts
    as ideological, in feminists' view 282-83, 295
    as ideology, for Galbraith and Lindblom 209-10
    in Locke's *Second Treatise* 283
    made within civil society 285, 291
    in Marx 272
    as outdated, for Schmitter and Winkler 209-10
    in Plato 374-77
    rejected, as bourgeois ideology, by Marxists 273
    symbolised by sexual images in Greek drama 369-72
    undermined by radical liberal democrats 212
    whether a cultural universal 23ff, 334-39
public property 10-11, Ch. 9 *passim*
public realm
    in Greek drama 370-72
    in Thucydides 373
public record cases 133n.13
public sector 42-43, 203-4
public services
    in English law 95, 97
public space 8
public spirit 53, 199, 294
public state, Galbraith on 209
public utilities
    in Australian law 100
    in English law 98, 99
    and the 'public duty rule' 101-2
    in U.S. law 99
public welfare
    in classical political economy 184
public works
    classical economists on 195, 217n.43, n.58
public world 20ff

publicity 6, Ch. 5 *passim*
   and enforcement of order in stateless societies 315
   individual interest in 117
   and the rule of law 126
   and zones of privacy in small societies 318
publick
   in eighteenth century English law 93, 97
publicness
   of 'anyone', in individualist model 33-35, 177
   of 'everyone', in the individualist model 35-38
   as institutional realisation of abstract whole 51
publicness and privateness
   accessibility as dimension of 114
   accountability as dimension of 114
   Auxter, on Kant's view of 180n.6, n.30
   'being known' as dimension of 114
   as complex-structured concepts. *See* complex-structured concepts
   as continuum 13ff
   control as dimension of 114
   descriptive 11-12, 13, 114, 115
   as dichotomy 13ff
   dimensions of 7-11, 23, 25, 114, 336
   domain of the distinction 33
   in English law 70-71
   in feudal law 70
   as generality and particularity 50, 54
   as ideological distinction 5, 16, 17, 25, 32, 34, 85
   individualised realisation of, in organic model 56-57
   individualist model in liberalism 31-48, 249ff
   of information 113ff
   institutionalisation of, in individualist model 39-41
   integrally related spheres, in feminism 293, 296-97
   integration of, in corporatism 207-11
   internal semantic relations of 5, 336
   intimacy as dimension of 114
   in Islam 22-23
   levels of, in individualist model 32

publicness and privateness (cont'd)
   liberal conception of 3, 25, Ch.2 *passim*, 87, 307-9
   liberal division of society into 281-82, 292-95, 296
   normative 11-13, 34, 114
   not distinguished in *Gemeinschaft* social paradigm 87
   organic model in liberalism 48-58
   ownership as dimension of 114
   practical realisation of 52
   prescriptive 12, 13
   semantic theory of 5, 25, 312
   two model account of liberal conception of 31, 58-61, 249ff
   as universal distinction in liberalism 17ff
   verbal correspondences in Tzotzil 350
publicness of social wholes
   in liberal organicism 49-50
publics 36, 325-26
   corporate analysis of 325-31, 333-34
   see also corporatism; groups; social groups

qāḍī 22
QUAGO 40
QUANGO 40, 331

R. v. *Bembridge* (1783) 111n.1, n.21, n.29
R. v. *Dr Burnell* (1698) 111n.28
Race Relations Act (1968) 37
Race Relations Board v. *Charter and Others* (1973) 36-38, 62n.9
radical democracy 211-13
radical egalitarianism
   in Communist China 275-76
radical feminism 289, 302n.12
radical liberal democrats
   concerned with public control of economy 212-13
Ramadan 22, 27n.14
rational choice theory 259
rational will 157, 253-54
rationality
   in Hegel 253, 254
Reformation 19, 157
Regierung 75
regulative agencies in modern state 206, 208

Reichskammergericht. See Germany, Imperial Courts in
religion 19-23
    in classical Greece 20, 364, 369, 371-72, 381
remorse 161
representation, functional 264n.3
representative institutions 262. *See also* democracy; participation, political
Republic of Plato 363-64, 375, 376
reputation
    in small societies 319
res publica 39, 40, 41, 54, 363
resources, access to 9
Respublica v. *Sparhawk* (1788) 111n.5, n.30
restraint of trade
    non-enforceability of contracts in 95
rights
    Bentham on 224ff
    as claim rights 225-26
    as immunities 225
    J.S. Mill on 226
    liberalism and 59
    political 59
    private, and public interests 59-61
    and social recognition, according to Hegel 234, 235
    see also human rights; individual, rights of; natural rights; private rights; property rights
roads
    duty to repair, in English law 100, 101, 102
role
    fulfilment of duties of 137ff
role conflict 141-42
role distance 150
    Goffman on 144
role performance 24, 25, 135, 136
roles 8
    public and private 158-59
    as supplying reasons for action 147
Roman law 67ff, 88-89
    family in 38
    and individual 72
    and the Roman state 67-69
Roman world
    Hegel's view of 266n.50
Rome, classical 20, 21, 38, 363

rule of law
    and information availability 126, 127
rules of recognition 86
Russell v. *Men of Devon* (1788) 101, 111n.24

Sachsenspiegel 72
safety helmets 176-77. *See also* paternalism
safety standards 176-77
savings
    in classical economics 184, 188
    and investment, Keynes on 199
    and production 188
Say's Law 188, 199
Schuster v. *City of New York* (1958) 111n.37
Schwabenspiegel 72
seat belt legislation 176-77. *See also* paternalism
seclusion practices in small societies 318
secrecy 8, 11, 12, 119, 124-25
    and the public interest 95
segmentary lineage and political order 322
self 135
    G.H. Mead's view of 145
    and Homeric hero 366-69
    Hume on 139
    and moral consistency 168
    and *polis* 363, 364, 368-69, 374
    presentation of, in public 150ff
    problem of 139ff
    as substratum 139-40, 145
    see also personality; persons
self/role relationship Ch. 6 *passim*, 223
    in modern world 186ff
self-consciousness
    and privacy 153
    see also persons
self-determination 271. *See also* personal autonomy
self-help in law of stateless societies 331-34
self-incrimination 119, 126, 134n.26
self-sufficiency in Sophist teaching 364, 373
'separate but equal'
    and male domination over women 283, 290-91

separate spheres of men and women 290-95. *See also* domestic; family; Greece, classical; Ruskin, J.
separation of powers 74
Seven Against Thebes, The, of Aeschylus 370-71
sexual politics
  Millet on 297
sexual relations
  privacy of 315, 316
  see also intimacy; privacy
shaman
  Quesalid and role of 138
shame
  in classical Greece 367-68
  and publicity, in Zinacantan 353
shame model of society 319-20
shame, public
  and conformity 319
Sharī'ā 22
Shoshoni Indians 327
Siete Partidas 72
silence, right of witness to maintain 119
sincerity and social roles 142. *See also* self; self/role relationship
Sittlichkeit. See ethical life
siyāsa shar'iyya 22
Skanske Lov 72
slavery 227-28, 378
social, the 18, 297, 303n.34
social contract 63n.16, 85, 208, 220n.122. *See also* contract theory; Hobbes, T.; Locke, J.; Rousseau, J.-J.
social groups
  logical priority of, in liberal organicist model 50
  as threats to the public good 210
social justice
  and public interest sometimes divergent, in new liberalism 198
social mind
  ethical life of society as, in Hegel 253-54
social practices
  individual volitions and, in Hegel 253
social relations and individuals 252. *See also* individual; individual/social distinction; social whole; social world; society
social roles 135

social science, explanation of action in 146-48
social whole 17, 50, 253, 322
  ontological priority of, in organic model 57
social work 297
social world
  ontology of, in Hegel 250-55
socialisation 252. *See also* human nature
socialism 240
  J.S. Mill on 199
  as liberating, for Marx 270
  and private law 85. *See also* Pashukanis
socialist economy
  and the new liberals 203
society
  viewed by Devlin as community of ideas 175-76
sociobiology 153, 296, 303n.32
sociological theory of role behaviour 139
Sophists 364, 373, 374, 382
sovereign's immunity from suit 71, 73, 76, 104
sovereignty 68, 73
  of state, invaded by private groups 206
Soviet state
  as granting rights to individuals 275
  see also U.S.S.R.
Spanish in Mexico 342
Sparta 373
special interests
  pluralism and 205
Star Chamber, Court of 73
state 39
  and business corporations, Galbraith on 208-9
  and business corporations, Lindblom on 209, 211
  and civil society, in Hegel 258
  as co-ordinator of private interests 257
  dissolution of, in pluralist critique of new liberalism 207
  and economy, in classical liberalism 194-95, 204-5
  and ethical life, in Hegel 259ff
  as extra-legal domination (Pashukanis) 85
  Hegelian theory of 250, 258-64, 272

state (cont'd)
  input-output model, Hegel on 257-58
  as institutional expression of common will 259, 260
  as institutionalisation of the public 39-41, 202
  liberal conception of 39-41, 50-52, 193-95, 201-3, 250
  libertarian conception of 261
  and the market, Winkler on 209
  Marx's view of 268, 272-3
  minimal role of, in liberal theory 250
  and private interests, in corporatism 208
  as promoter of private interests 257
  as public power, Marx's critique of 272-73
  publicness of 39-41, 50-52, 202
  as reactive to pressure groups 205
  regulative role for, in new liberalism 204
  as supreme organ of community 202, 259
  and the 'technostructure', Galbraith on 208
  unselfishness inappropriate to actions of (Cecil) 162
  withering away of, in Marxist theory 273
  welfare functions of, in Hegel 261
  see also sovereignty; Soviet state
state agencies 14, 43
state, corporatist
  and control of privately-owned business 207
state, democratic. *See* democratic state
state provision of public goods 192
stateless societies 24, 307, 313ff, 322
statesman
  moral tension in role of, in liberal theory 168
  responsibilities of 164f
  as trustee for public, in liberal theory 167
stationary state in classical economics 191-92
statutory corporations
  liabilities of, in English law 98, 99, 102

Stoicism 20, 67
subjectivity in Hegel 253-54. *See also* self
suffragists. *See* women, enfranchisement of
suicide
  altruistic, Durkheim on 137-38
  and moral failure 173
supply and demand 188. *See also* classical economists; classical political economy
Sutton v. Johnstone (1786) 101, 111n.22

tact 150ff
Tauade of Papua
  individualist conception of society 327-28
temporal/spiritual duality 19
toleration 19, 125, 127
  and moral fallibilism 156
  moral scepticism as basis for 156
trade boards 210
trade unions 43, 208. *See also* labour; labour relations
transplant surgery
  rights of donors 228
tripartite conception of society 18
Trojan Women of Euripides 372
Troy 366-69, 370
Tuareg of North Africa, seclusion practices of 318
Tzotzil 342, 349-51

U.S.S.R. 80-81, 274-77
ummat al-nabi 21
underconsumptionist theories 189, 195, 199-200. *See also* Hobson, J.A.; Keynes, J.M.; Malthus, T.R.
unemployment 195, 200
unilineal descent groups
  and corporate organisation 323-25
universals
  and particulars, dialectics of, in Hegel 251-55, 256
utilitarianism
  of classical political economy 198
  and paternalism 177
  and property rights 224ff, 227-33
  and the problem of co-ordination of interests 259
  in public/affairs Ch. 7 §II *passim*, 168

value scepticism 156
values and beliefs 146-48
Västgötalagen 72
Vaughan v. *Taff Vale Railway Co* (1860) 111n.14
voting. *See* participation, political; women, enfranchisement of; Mill, J.S.

wages
   in classical political economy 186, 188, 193, 215n.12, n.13
   and growth, in new liberalism 197
war
   in Greek society 363, 365, 366-74, 380, 381, 382
War Communism (1918-1921) 274-75
Warne v. *Varley* (1795) 111n.31
wealth, growth of
   in classical political economy 184, 186, 189, 190, 196, 216n.29
   J.S. Mill and new liberals on 197, 201, 204
wealth, redistribution of
   in new liberalism 197, 199, 201, 204, 218n.71
   Robert Dahl advocating 206
welfare economics 259
welfare services, socialisation of 43
Willkür
   as arbitrary will, in Hegel 259
Wolfenden Committee, Report of 155, 175
   Lord Devlin's attack on 175
women
   education of 290, 296
   enfranchisement of 290-94. *See also* Anthony, S.B.; Mill, J.S.
   excluded from liberal universalism 283, 286
   as guardians of morality 292
   paid employment of 296
   privateness and 56-57, 283-87. *See also* domestic; family
   reproductive capacity and status of 287-89
   subordination of Ch. 12 *passim*. *See also* nature/culture; morality/power; personal/political
   subordination of, as natural, in Locke 284ff

women (cont'd)
   subordination of, J.S. Mill on 287, 292-95
   suffragists 290-94
work, alienated 269-70
worker control 211
workers
   as commodities, in Marx 269
working class. *See* labouring class
World War I
   and collective management of economy 203

Younger Committee Report (1972) 134n.30
Yugoslav market socialism
   Lindblom and 211

Zinacantecos 24, Ch. 14 *passim*. *See also* Nabenchauk